The Java™ Application Programming Interface, Volume 1

The Java™ Series

Lisa Friendly, Series Editor
Bill Joy, Technical Advisor

The Java™ Programming Language
Ken Arnold and James Gosling

The Java™ Application Programming Interface, Volume 1
Core Packages
James Gosling, Frank Yellin, and the Java Team

The Java™ Application Programming Interface, Volume 2
Window Toolkit and Applets
James Gosling, Frank Yellin, and the Java Team

The Java™ Language Specification
James Gosling, Bill Joy, and Guy Steele

The Java™ Virtual Machine Specification
Tim Lindholm and Frank Yellin

The Java™ Tutorial
Object-Oriented Programming for the Internet
Mary Campione and Kathy Walrath

The Java™ Class Libraries
An Annotated Reference
Patrick Chan and Rosanna Lee

The Java™ FAQ
Frequently Asked Questions
Jonni Kanerva

The Java™ Application Programming Interface, Volume 1

Core Packages

James Gosling
Frank Yellin
The Java Team

Addison-Wesley Publishing Company
Reading, Massachusetts • Menlo Park, California • New York
Don Mills, Ontario • Harlow, England • Amsterdam • Bonn
Sydney • Singapore • Tokyo • Madrid • San Juan
Seoul • Milan • Mexico City • Tiapei

THE PUBLISHER OFFERS DISCOUNTS ON THIS BOOK WHEN ORDERED IN QUANTITY FOR SPECIAL SALES. FOR MORE INFORMATION, PLEASE CONTACT:
CORPORATE AND PROFESSIONAL PUBLISHING GROUP
ADDISON-WESLEY PUBLISHING COMPANY
ONE JACOB WAY
READING, MASSACHUSETTS 01867

ISBN: 0-201-63453-8
Text printed on recycled and acid-free paper.
12345678910 - MA -99989796
First Printing, May 1996

In memory of FirstPerson, Inc.
To the Java Team, past and present

Volume I

Contents

Contents for Volume II. xi

Preface xv
    A Bit of History. xv
    About the Java Series xvi
    Contributors to the API xvii
    About the Java Packages xvii
    References xxi

Class Hierarchy Diagrams xxiii

Package java.lang 1
  Classes
    1.1   Class Boolean 2
    1.2   Class Character 5
    1.3   Class Class. 16
    1.4   Class ClassLoader 19
    1.5   Class Compiler. 23
    1.6   Class Double 25
    1.7   Class Float 32
    1.8   Class Integer 39
    1.9   Class Long 48
    1.10 Class Math 57
    1.11 Class Number. 66
    1.12 Class Object. 67
    1.13 Class Process 74
    1.14 Class Runtime 76
    1.15 Class SecurityManager 83
    1.16 Class String 96
    1.17 Class StringBuffer 112
    1.18 Class System 125
    1.19 Class Thread 134
    1.20 Class ThreadGroup 147
    1.21 Class Throwable 154
  Interfaces
    1.22 Interface Cloneable 156
    1.23 Interface Runnable. 156

Exceptions

1.24 Class ArithmeticException.................................157
1.25 Class ArrayIndexOutOfBoundsException......................158
1.26 Class ArrayStoreException.................................159
1.27 Class ClassCastException..................................159
1.28 Class ClassNotFoundException..............................160
1.29 Class CloneNotSupportedException..........................161
1.30 Class Exception...162
1.31 Class IllegalAccessException..............................162
1.32 Class IllegalArgumentException............................163
1.33 Class IllegalMonitorStateException........................164
1.34 Class IllegalThreadStateException.........................165
1.35 Class IndexOutOfBoundsException...........................165
1.36 Class InstantiationException..............................166
1.37 Class InterruptedException................................167
1.38 Class NegativeArraySizeException..........................167
1.39 Class NoSuchMethodException...............................168
1.40 Class NullPointerException................................169
1.41 Class NumberFormatException...............................170
1.42 Class RuntimeException....................................170
1.43 Class SecurityException...................................171
1.44 Class StringIndexOutOfBoundsException.....................172

Errors

1.45 Class AbstractMethodError.................................173
1.46 Class ClassCircularityError...............................173
1.47 Class ClassFormatError....................................174
1.48 Class Error...175
1.49 Class IllegalAccessError..................................175
1.50 Class IncompatibleClassChangeError........................176
1.51 Class InstantiationError..................................177
1.52 Class InternalError.......................................178
1.53 Class LinkageError..178
1.54 Class NoClassDefFoundError................................179
1.55 Class NoSuchFieldError....................................180
1.56 Class NoSuchMethodError...................................180
1.57 Class OutOfMemoryError....................................181
1.58 Class StackOverflowError..................................182
1.59 Class ThreadDeath...182
1.60 Class UnknownError..183
1.61 Class UnsatisfiedLinkError................................184
1.62 Class VerifyError...184
1.63 Class VirtualMachineError.................................185

Package java.io **187**

Classes

2.1 Class BufferedInputStream..................................189
2.2 Class BufferedOutputStream.................................194
2.3 Class ByteArrayInputStream.................................197
2.4 Class ByteArrayOutputStream................................200
2.5 Class DataInputStream......................................204
2.6 Class DataOutputStream.....................................217
2.7 Class File...224
2.8 Class FileDescriptor.......................................233

2.9   Class FileInputStream 234
2.10   Class FileOutputStream. 239
2.11   Class FilterInputStream 243
2.12   Class FilterOutputStream. 249
2.13   Class InputStream 253
2.14   Class LineNumberInputStream 257
2.15   Class OutputStream 262
2.16   Class PipedInputStream. 264
2.17   Class PipedOutputStream 267
2.18   Class PrintStream. 270
2.19   Class PushbackInputStream. 277
2.20   Class RandomAccessFile. 281
2.21   Class SequenceInputStream. 299
2.22   Class StreamTokenizer 302
2.23   Class StringBufferInputStream 309

Interfaces
2.24   Interface DataInput 312
2.25   Interface DataOutput 318
2.26   Interface FilenameFilter. 322

Exceptions
2.27   Class EOFException 323
2.28   Class FileNotFoundException. 324
2.29   Class IOException 324
2.30   Class InterruptedIOException 325
2.31   Class UTFDataFormatException. 326

Package java.util. 327

Classes
3.1   Class BitSet 328
3.2   Class Date 332
3.3   Class Dictionary. 341
3.4   Class Hashtable 344
3.5   Class Observable 349
3.6   Class Properties 351
3.7   Class Random 354
3.8   Class Stack. 356
3.9   Class StringTokenizer 358
3.10   Class Vector. 362

Interfaces
3.11   Interface Enumeration 369
3.12   Interface Observer 370

Exceptions
3.13   Class EmptyStackException 371
3.14   Class NoSuchElementException 371

Package java.net 373

Classes
4.1   Class ContentHandler 374
4.2   Class DatagramPacket. 375
4.3   Class DatagramSocket. 377

4.4 Class InetAddress 380
4.5 Class ServerSocket 383
4.6 Class Socket 387
4.7 Class SocketImpl 392
4.8 Class URL 397
4.9 Class URLConnection 406
4.10 Class URLEncoder 420
4.11 Class URLStreamHandler 421

Interfaces
4.12 Interface ContentHandlerFactory 423
4.13 Interface SocketImplFactory 424
4.14 Interface URLStreamHandlerFactory 424

Exceptions
4.15 Class MalformedURLException 425
4.16 Class ProtocolException 426
4.17 Class SocketException 426
4.18 Class UnknownHostException 427
4.19 Class UnknownServiceException 428

Index **429**

Volume II

Contents

Contents for Volume I vii

Preface xv
    A Bit of History xv
    About the Java Series xvi
    Contributors to the API xvii
    About the Java Packages xvii
    References xxi

Class Hierarchy Diagrams xxiii

Package java.awt 1
  Classes
    1.1   Class BorderLayout 3
    1.2   Class Button 7
    1.3   Class Canvas 9
    1.4   Class CardLayout 11
    1.5   Class Checkbox 15
    1.6   Class CheckboxGroup 19
    1.7   Class CheckboxMenuItem 21
    1.8   Class Choice 23
    1.9   Class Color 27
    1.10 Class Component 35
    1.11 Class Container 63
    1.12 Class Dialog 71
    1.13 Class Dimension 74
    1.14 Class Event 76
    1.15 Class FileDialog 87
    1.16 Class FlowLayout 90
    1.17 Class Font 95
    1.18 Class FontMetrics 100
    1.19 Class Frame 106
    1.20 Class Graphics 112
    1.21 Class GridBagConstraints 131
    1.22 Class GridBagLayout 137
    1.23 Class GridLayout 143
    1.24 Class Image 148
    1.25 Class Insets 151

1.26 Class Label 153
1.27 Class List 157
1.28 Class MediaTracker 167
1.29 Class Menu 177
1.30 Class MenuBar 180
1.31 Class MenuComponent 183
1.32 Class MenuItem 185
1.33 Class Panel 188
1.34 Class Point 189
1.35 Class Polygon 191
1.36 Class Rectangle 194
1.37 Class Scrollbar 200
1.38 Class TextArea 207
1.39 Class TextComponent 213
1.40 Class TextField 215
1.41 Class Toolkit 221
1.42 Class Window 230

Interfaces
1.43 Interface LayoutManager 232
1.44 Interface MenuContainer 234

Exceptions
1.45 Class AWTException 235

Errors
1.46 Class AWTError 236

Package java.awt.image **237**

Classes
2.1   Class ColorModel 238
2.2   Class CropImageFilter 241
2.3   Class DirectColorModel 245
2.4   Class FilteredImageSource 249
2.5   Class ImageFilter 252
2.6   Class IndexColorModel 257
2.7   Class MemoryImageSource 264
2.8   Class PixelGrabber 270
2.9   Class RGBImageFilter 277

Interfaces
2.10 Interface ImageConsumer 284
2.11 Interface ImageObserver 290
2.12 Interface ImageProducer 294

Package java.awt.peer **297**

Interfaces
3.1   Interface ButtonPeer 297
3.2   Interface CanvasPeer 298
3.3   Interface CheckboxMenuItemPeer 298
3.4   Interface CheckboxPeer 299
3.5   Interface ChoicePeer 300
3.6   Interface ComponentPeer 301
3.7   Interface ContainerPeer 307
3.8   Interface DialogPeer 308

3.9   Interface FileDialogPeer 308
3.10 Interface FramePeer. 309
3.11 Interface LabelPeer 311
3.12 Interface ListPeer. 312
3.13 Interface MenuBarPeer 313
3.14 Interface MenuComponentPeer. 315
3.15 Interface MenuItemPeer 316
3.16 Interface MenuPeer 316
3.17 Interface PanelPeer 317
3.18 Interface ScrollbarPeer 317
3.19 Interface TextAreaPeer 319
3.20 Interface TextComponentPeer. 320
3.21 Interface TextFieldPeer 321
3.22 Interface WindowPeer. 323

Package java.applet **325**

Classes
4.1   Class Applet. 326

Interfaces
4.2   Interface AppletContext. 334
4.3   Interface AppletStub 336
4.4   Interface AudioClip. 338

Index. **341**

Preface

A Bit of History

JAVA is a general-purpose object-oriented programming language. Its syntax is similar to C and C++, but it omits semantic features that make C and C++ complex, confusing, and insecure. Java was initially developed to address the problems of building software for small distributed systems to embed in consumer devices. As such it was designed for heterogeneous networks, multiple host architectures, and secure delivery. To meet these requirements, compiled Java code had to survive transport across networks, operate on any client, and assure the client that it was safe to run.

The popularization of the World Wide Web helped catapult these attributes of Java into the limelight. The Internet demonstrated how interesting, media-rich content could be made accessible in simple ways. Web browsers like Mosaic enabled millions of people to roam the Net and made Web surfing part of popular culture. At last there was a medium where what you saw and heard was essentially the same whether you were using a Mac, PC, or UNIX machine, connected to a high-speed network or a modem.

With popularity comes scrutiny, however, and soon Web enthusiasts felt that the content supported by the Web's HTML document format was too limited. HTML extensions, such as forms, only highlighted those limitations while making it clear that no browser could include all the features users wanted. Extensibility was the answer. At just this time the Java programming language found itself looking for another application.

Sun's HotJava browser was developed to showcase Java's interesting properties by making it possible to embed Java programs inside Web pages. These Java programs, known as *applets*, are transparently downloaded into the HotJava browser along with the HTML pages in which they appear. Before being accepted by the browser, applets are carefully checked to make sure they are safe. Like HTML pages, compiled Java programs are network- and platform-independent. Applets behave the same regardless of where they come from or what kind of machine they are being loaded into.

The Web community quickly noticed that Java was something new and important. With Java as the extension language, a Web browser could have limitless capabilities. Programmers could write an applet once and it would then run on any machine, anywhere. Visitors to Java-powered Web pages could use the content found there with confidence that nothing would damage their machine.

With applets as the initial focus, Java has demonstrated a new way to make use of the Internet to distribute software. This new paradigm goes beyond browsers. We believe it is an innovation with the potential to change the course of computing.

Tim Lindholm
Senior Staff Engineer
JavaSoft
April 1996

About the Java Series

THE Java Series provides definitive reference documentation for Java programmers and end users. These books are written by members of the Java Team and published under the auspices of JavaSoft, a Sun Microsystems business. The World Wide Web allows Java documentation to be made available over the Internet, either by downloading or as hypertext. Nevertheless, the world wide interest in Java led us to write these books.

To learn the latest about Java or to download the latest Java release, visit our World Wide Web site at `http://java.sun.com`. For updated information about the Java Series, including sample code, errata, and previews of forthcoming books, visit `http://java.sun.com/books/Series`.

We would like to thank the Corporate and Professional Publishing Group at Addison-Wesley for their partnership in putting together the Series. Our editor, Mike Hendrickson, and his team have done a superb job of navigating us through the world of publishing. The support of James Gosling, Ruth Hennigar, and Bill Joy of Sun Microsystems ensured that this series would have the resources it needed to be successful. A personal note of thanks to my children, Christopher and James, for putting a positive spin on the many trips to my office during the development of the Series.

Lisa Friendly
Series Editor

Contributors to the API

Designers of Classes and Interfaces

Tom Ball
Lee Boynton
Patrick Chan
David Connelly
Pavani Diwanji
Amy Fowler
James Gosling
Jim Graham
Herb Jellinek

Bill Joy
Tim Lindholm
Jonathan Payne
Sami Shaio
Doug Stein
Arthur van Hoff
Chris Warth
Frank Yellin

Testers

Carla Schroer
Kevin Smith

Vijay Srinivasan
Headley Williamson

Layout and Supplemental Documentation

Lisa Friendly
James Gosling
Jonni Kanerva
Guy Steele

Annette Wagner
Kathy Walrath
Frank Yellin

About the Java Packages

These two volumes describe the Java Application Programming Interface (API), a standard set of libraries for writing Java programs. The libraries evolved over several years of writing Java code to implement a variety of systems, ranging from consumer device networks to animated user interfaces to operating systems to compilers. In 1995, the libraries were reorganized to support Internet programming, and thus the Java API was created. Many people, both from inside and outside Sun, have been involved in the design of the API.

Although the API has not reached perfection yet, we believe it is useful and hope to make it a ubiquitous layer, available to all Internet applications.

Have fun.

Arthur van Hoff

Introduction

These books are reference manuals for Java application and applet programmers. To make full use of them you should be familiar with the Java programming language and its core concepts such as object orientation, garbage collection, and multithreading.

The extent of the API and the choice of functionality have been driven by several factors. First and foremost, the API should be simple and easy to use. Parts of the API, such as the support for multithreading, might introduce functionality that is new to you, but we think you will find these new concepts simpler and easier to use than in most other programming environments.

The libraries in these books are the first generation of an API for writing Internet programs. A simple form of an Internet program is an *applet*—a small Java program that can be embedded in an HTML page.

The API has been designed with the Java language in mind. Important Java features such as object orientation, garbage collection, and multithreading played an important role in the API design. Instead of taking existing libraries and simply rewriting them in Java, we designed and implemented the API with full use of the Java language.

For Java 1.0, we have tried to stay away from certain complex functionality, such as video and 3D, so that library implementations can be ported easily. We can include only functionality that is not proprietary and that is easily implemented on many platforms.

We expect to add to the API, but not to subtract from it or change its behavior. The API documented in this book will remain available to all Java programs through future releases.

If you have ideas about how the API could be improved or how to implement some of the missing functionality, we would like to hear from you. Please send your ideas and implementations to java@java.sun.com.

Using These API Books

Do not get overwhelmed by the multitude of classes documented in these two books. The structure of the Java language encourages the programmer to break up libraries into many classes, each describing a small part of the functionality. The class diagrams in the following section are a good starting point for getting an impression of the relationships among classes.

As you design and implement Java programs, you should write short test programs to verify your understanding of the classes. When in doubt, try it out!

The Java web site, `http://java.sun.com/`, contains many excellent and sometimes interactive explanations that can help you along. Another good source of information is the newsgroup `comp.lang.java`.

Package Overview

This overview describes each package in the Java API, starting with the most general-purpose package (`java.lang`) and ending with one of the most specialized packages (`java.applet`). Each package groups classes and interfaces that have similar functionality. The API contains the following packages:

- ◆ Volume I: Core Packages
  - ◆ java.lang: The Java Language Package
  - ◆ java.io: The Java I/O Package
  - ◆ java.util: The Java Utility Package
  - ◆ java.net: The Java Networking Package
- ◆ Volume II: Window Toolkit and Applets
  - ◆ java.awt: The Abstract Window Toolkit (AWT) Package
  - ◆ java.awt.image: The AWT Image Package
  - ◆ java.awt.peer: The AWT Peer Package
  - ◆ java.applet: The Java Applet Package

`java.lang`: THE JAVA LANGUAGE PACKAGE

The `java.lang` package provides the classes and interfaces that form the core of the Java language and the Java Virtual Machine. For example, the classes `Object`, `String`, and `Thread` are used by almost every program and are closely intertwined with the Java language definition. Other `java.lang` classes define the exceptions and errors that the Java Virtual Machine can throw.

Another set of `java.lang` classes provide wrappers for primitive types. For example, the `Integer` class provides objects to contain `int` values.

Still other classes, such as `ClassLoader`, `Process`, `Runtime`, `Security-Manager`, and `System`, provide access to system resources. For other generally useful classes, see the `java.util` package.

The `java.lang` package is imported automatically into every Java program.

`java.io`: THE JAVA I/O PACKAGE

The `java.io` package provides a set of input and output (I/O) streams used to read and write data to files or other I/O sources. Java streams are byte oriented and the classes defined here can be chained to implement more sophisticated stream functionality.

`java.util`: THE JAVA UTILITY PACKAGE

The `java.util` package contains a collection of utility classes and related interfaces. It includes classes that provide generic data structures (`Dictionary`, `Hashtable`, `Stack`, `Vector`), string manipulation (`StringTokenizer`), and calendar and date utilities (`Date`).

The `java.util` package also contains the `Observer` interface and `Observable` class, which allow objects to notify one another when they change.

`java.net`: THE JAVA NETWORKING PACKAGE

The `java.net` package contains networking classes and interfaces, including classes that represent a URL and a URL connection, classes that implement a socket connection, and a class that represents an Internet address.

`java.awt`: THE ABSTRACT WINDOW TOOLKIT (AWT) PACKAGE

The `java.awt` package provides the standard graphical user interface (GUI) elements such as buttons, lists, menus, and text areas. It also includes containers (such as windows and menu bars) and higher-level components (such as dialogs for opening and saving files). The AWT contains two more packages: `java.awt.image` and `java.awt.peer`.

`java.awt.image`: THE AWT IMAGE PACKAGE

The `java.awt.image` package contains classes and interfaces for performing sophisticated image processing. These classes and interfaces can be used by applications that need to create or manipulate images and colors.

`java.awt.peer`: THE AWT PEER PACKAGE

The `java.awt.peer` package contains interfaces used to connect AWT components to their window system–specific implementations (such as Motif widgets).

Unless you are creating a window system–specific implementation of the AWT, you should not need to use the interfaces in the `java.awt.peer` package.

`java.applet`: THE APPLET PACKAGE

The `java.applet` package contains classes and interfaces for creating applets.

References

IEEE Standard for Binary Floating-Point Arithmetic, ANSI/IEEE Std. 754-1985. Available from Global Engineering Documents, 15 Inverness Way East, Englewood, Colorado 80112-5704 USA, 303-792-2181 or 800-854-7179.

The Unicode Standard: Worldwide Character Encoding, Version 1.0, Volume 1 ISBN 0-201-56788-1 and Volume 2 ISBN 0-201-60845-6. Additional information about Unicode 1.1 may be found at `ftp://unicode.org`.

Class Hierarchy Diagrams

Key

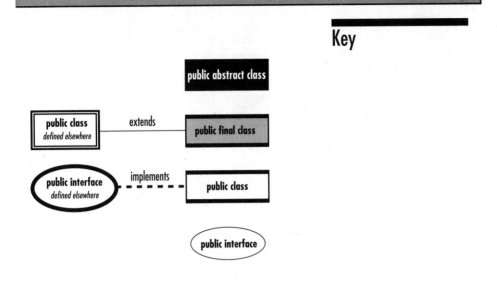

Hierarchy Diagrams redrawn with permission of Charles Perkins. Original diagrams are found at http://rendezvous.com/Java/hierarchy

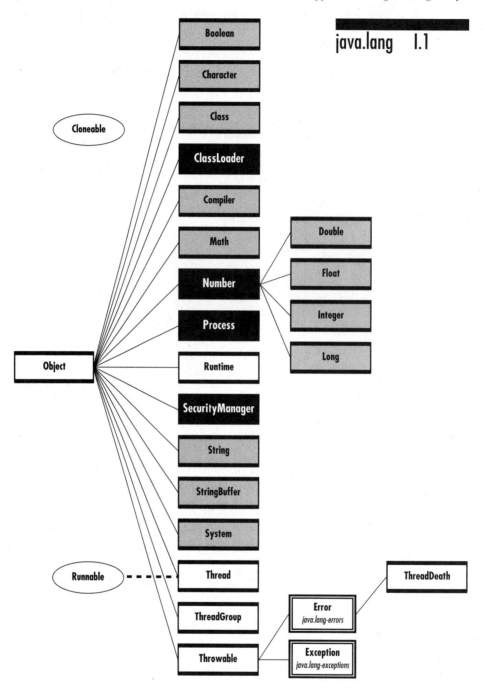

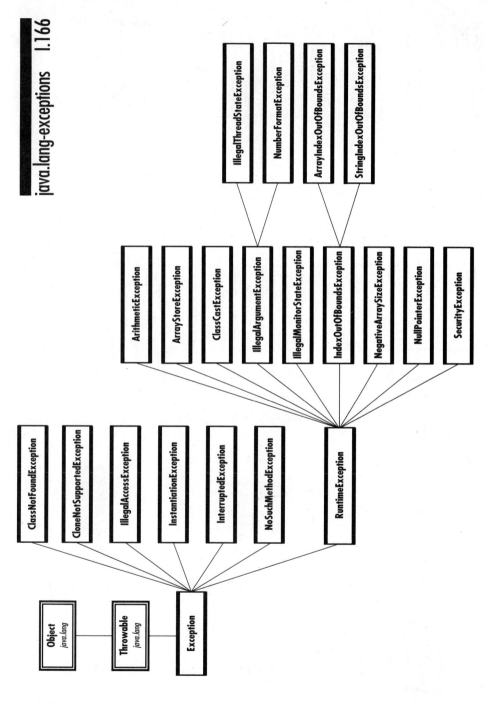

java.lang-exceptions 1.166

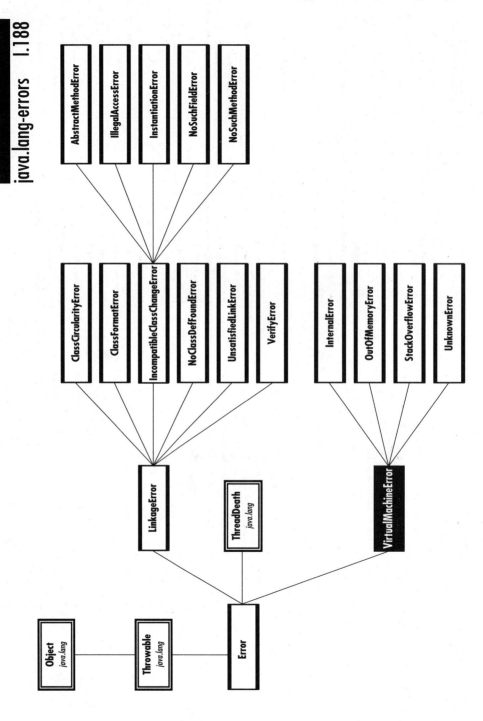

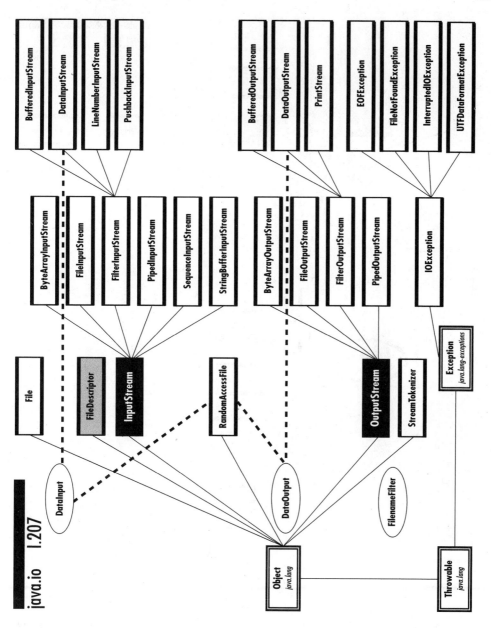

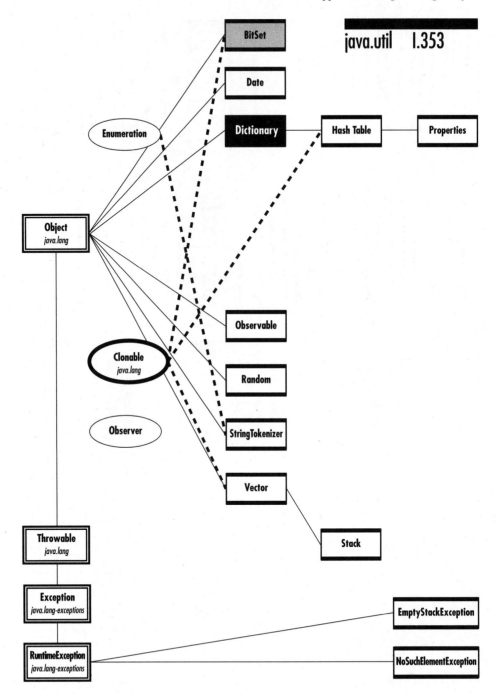

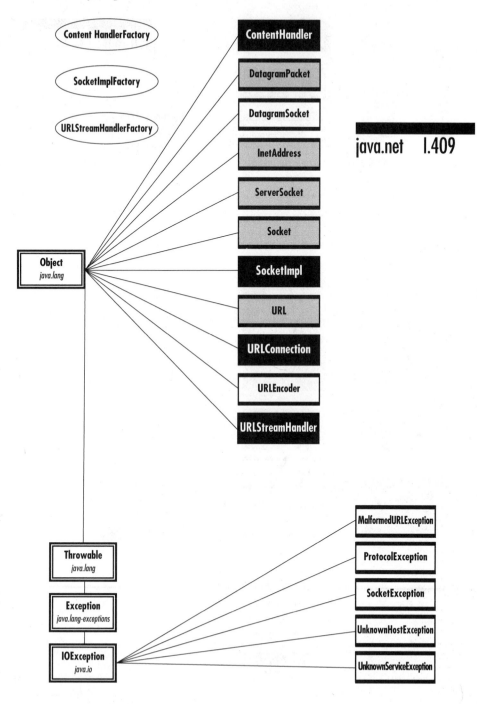

ContentHandlerFactory

SocketImplFactory

URLStreamHandlerFactory

ContentHandler

DatagramPacket

DatagramSocket

InetAddress

ServerSocket

Socket

SocketImpl

URL

URLConnection

URLEncoder

URLStreamHandler

java.net   l.409

Object
java.lang

Throwable
java.lang

Exception
java.lang-exceptions

IOException
java.io

MalformedURLException

ProtocolException

SocketException

UnknownHostException

UnknownServiceException

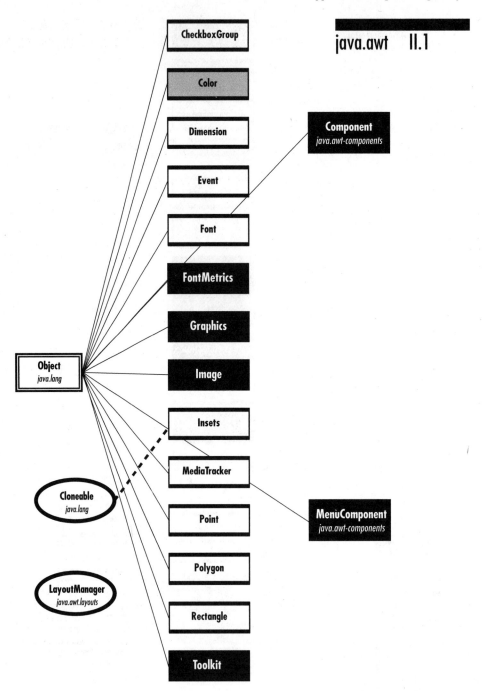

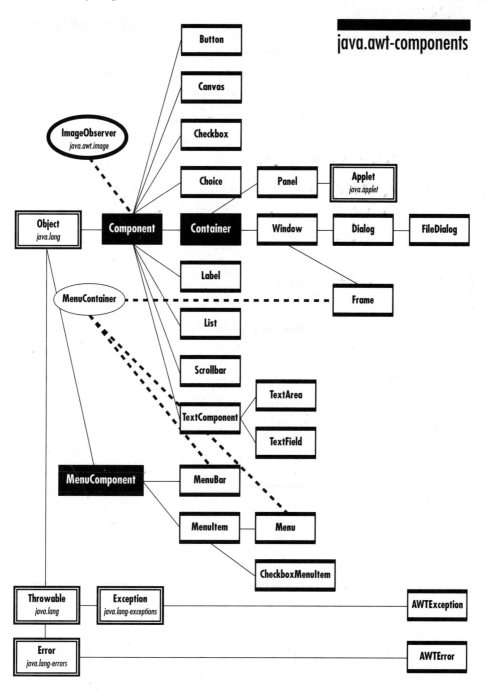

java.awt-layouts

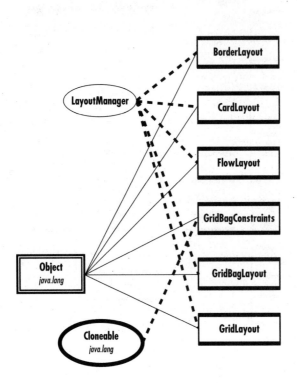

java.awt.image **II.249**

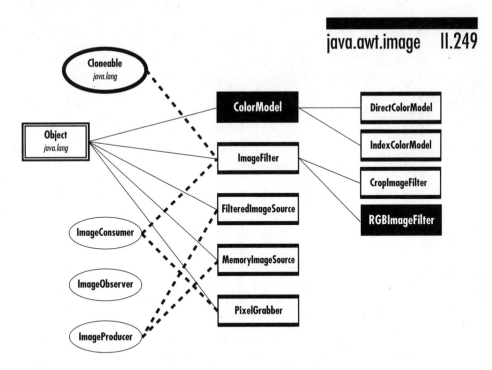

java.awt.peer   II.311

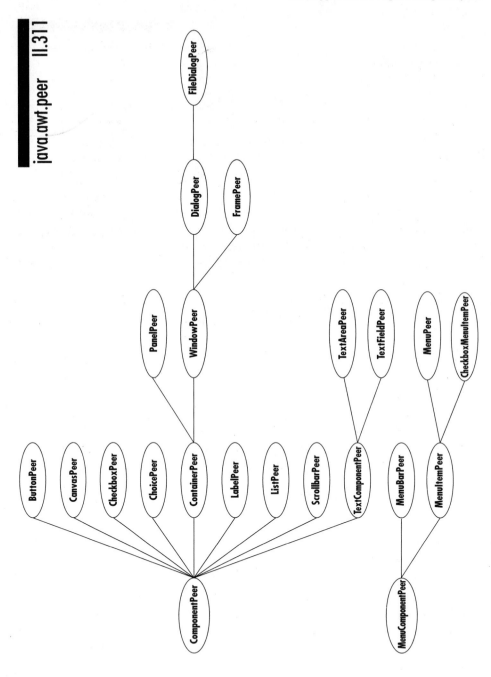

java.applet   II.339

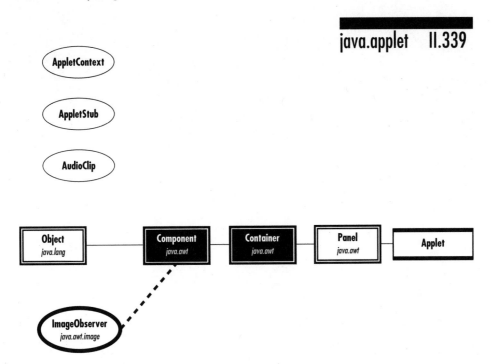

CHAPTER 1

Package java.lang

THE java.lang package provides the classes and interfaces that are the core of the Java language.

The classes and interfaces in java.lang can be divided into several groups:

♦ **Basic Classes:** The classes Object (I-§1.12), Class (I-§1.3), String (I-§1.16), and StringBuffer (I-§1.17) are used by almost every program. They are closely intertwined with the Java language definition.

♦ **Thread Classes:** The classes Thread (I-§1.19) and ThreadGroup (I-§1.20) are primitives used by the Java Virtual Machine to implement Java's multithreading, and to allow the user to create new threads. The interface Runnable (I-§1.23) allows the user to create threads from classes that are not subclasses of Thread.

♦ **Container Classes:** These classes, which include Boolean (I-§1.1), Character (I-§1.2), Double (I-§1.6), Float (I-§1.7), Integer (I-§1.8), Long (I-§1.9), and Number (I-§1.11), are used to provide wrappers for primitive types. For example, the Integer class provides an object that contains an integer value.

♦ **System Resources:** The classes ClassLoader (I-§1.4), Math (I-§1.10), Process (I-§1.13), Runtime (I-§1.14), SecurityManager (I-§1.15), and System (I-§1.18) provide access to system functions and resources.

♦ **Compiler:** The class Compiler (I-§1.5) is provided as a hook to outside vendors so that they can provide users with tools to improve the performance of the Java Virtual Machine.

♦ **Errors and Exceptions:** All errors and exceptions in the Java language are subclasses of the class Throwable (I-§1.21). The java.lang package includes all exceptions and errors than can be thrown by the Java Virtual Machine.

1.1 Class Boolean

```
public final class java.lang.Boolean
    extends java.lang.Object  (I-§1.12)
{
    // Fields
    public final static Boolean FALSE;                  §1.1.1
    public final static Boolean TRUE;                   §1.1.2

    // Constructors
    public Boolean(boolean value);                      §1.1.3
    public Boolean(String s);                           §1.1.4

    // Methods
    public boolean booleanValue();                      §1.1.5
    public boolean equals(Object obj);                  §1.1.6
    public static boolean getBoolean(String name);      §1.1.7
    public int hashCode();                              §1.1.8
    public String toString();                           §1.1.9
    public static Boolean valueOf(String s);            §1.1.10
}
```

This class wraps a value of the primitive type `boolean` in an object. An object of type `Boolean` contains a single field whose type is `boolean`.

In addition, this class provides a number of methods for converting a `boolean` to a `String` and a `String` to a `boolean`, as well as other constants and methods useful when dealing with a `boolean`.

Fields

FALSE   §1.1.1

```
public final static Boolean FALSE = new Boolean(false)
```
The `Boolean` object corresponding to the primitive value `false`.

TRUE   §1.1.2

```
public final static Boolean TRUE = new Boolean(true)
```
The `Boolean` object corresponding to the primitive value `true`.

Constructors

Boolean   §1.1.3

    public Boolean(boolean value)

   Allocates a `Boolean` object representing the `value` argument.

PARAMETERS:
`value`: the value of the `Boolean`.

Boolean   §1.1.4

    public Boolean(String s)

   Allocates a `Boolean` object representing the value `true` if the string argument is not `null` and is equal, ignoring case, to the string `"true"`. Otherwise, allocate a `Boolean` object representing the value `false`.

PARAMETERS:
`s`: the string to be converted to a `Boolean`.

Methods

booleanValue   §1.1.5

    public boolean booleanValue()

RETURNS:
the primitive `boolean` value of this object.

equals   §1.1.6

    public boolean equals(Object obj)

   The result is `true` if and only if the argument is not `null` and is a `Boolean` object that contains the same `boolean` value as this object.

PARAMETERS:
`obj`: the object to compare with.

RETURNS:
`true` if the objects are the same; `false` otherwise.

OVERRIDES:
`equals` in class `Object` (**I-§1.12.3**).

getBoolean   §1.1.7

```
public static boolean getBoolean(String name)
```

The result is `true` if and only if the system property **(I-§1.18.9)** named by the argument exists and is equal, ignoring case,[1] to the string `"true"`.

PARAMETERS:

`name`: the system property name.

RETURNS:

the `boolean` value of the system property.

hashCode   §1.1.8

```
public int hashCode()
```

RETURNS:

a hash code value for this object.

OVERRIDES:

`hashCode` in class `Object` **(I-§1.12.6)**.

toString   §1.1.9

```
public String toString()
```

If this object contains the value `true`, a string equal to `"true"` is returned. Otherwise, a string equal to `"false"` is returned.

RETURNS:

a string representation of this object.

OVERRIDES:

`toString` in class `Object` **(I-§1.12.9)**.

valueOf   §1.1.10

```
public static Boolean valueOf(String s)
```

A new `Boolean` object is constructed. This `Boolean` contains the value `true` if the string argument is not `null` and is equal, ignoring case, to the string `"true"`.

PARAMETERS:

`s`: a string.

RETURNS:

the `Boolean` value represented by the string.

---

[1] In Java 1.0, the string had to be equal to the string `"true"`, where the comparison was case sensitive. Beginning with Java 1.1, the test is case insensitive.

1.2 Class Character

```
public final class java.lang.Character
    extends java.lang.Object (I-§1.12)
{
    // Fields
    public final static int MAX_RADIX;              §1.2.1
    public final static char MAX_VALUE;             §1.2.2
    public final static int MIN_RADIX;              §1.2.3
    public final static char MIN_VALUE;             §1.2.4

    // Constructors
    public Character(char value);                   §1.2.5

    // Methods
    public char charValue();                        §1.2.6
    public static int digit(char ch, int radix);    §1.2.7
    public boolean equals(Object obj);              §1.2.8
    public static char forDigit(int digit, int radix);  §1.2.9
    public int hashCode();                          §1.2.10
    public static boolean isDefined(char ch);       §1.2.11
    public static boolean isDigit(char ch);         §1.2.12
    public static boolean isJavaLetter(char ch);    §1.2.13
    public static boolean isJavaLetterOrDigit(char ch);  §1.2.14
    public static boolean isLetter(char ch);        §1.2.15
    public static boolean isLetterOrDigit(char ch); §1.2.16
    public static boolean isLowerCase(char ch);     §1.2.17
    public static boolean isSpace(char ch);         §1.2.18
    public static boolean isTitleCase(char ch);     §1.2.19
    public static boolean isUpperCase(char ch);     §1.2.20
    public static char toLowerCase(char ch);        §1.2.21
    public String toString();                       §1.2.22
    public static char toTitleCase(char ch);        §1.2.23
    public static char toUpperCase(char ch);        §1.2.24
}
```

This class wraps a value of the primitive type char in an object. An object of type Character contains a single field whose type is char.

In addition, this class provides several methods for determining the type of a character and converting characters from uppercase to lowercase and vice versa.

Many of the methods of class Character are defined in terms of a "Unicode attribute table" that specifies a name for every defined Unicode code point. The table also includes other attributes, such as a decimal value, an uppercase equivalent, a lowercase equivalent, and/or a titlecase equivalent. The Unicode attribute table is available on the World Wide Web as the file

```
ftp://unicode.org/pub/MappingTables/UnicodeData1.1.5.txt
```

Fields

MAX_RADIX   §1.2.1

```
public final static int MAX_RADIX = 36
```

The constant value of this field is the largest value permitted for the radix argument in radix-conversion methods such as the `digit` (**I-§1.2.7**) method, the `forDigit` (**I-§1.2.9**) method, and the `toString` (**I-§1.8.21**) method of class `Integer`.

MAX_VALUE[2]   §1.2.2

```
public final static char MAX_VALUE = '\uffff'
```

The constant value of this field is the largest value of type char.

MIN_RADIX   §1.2.3

```
public final static int MIN_RADIX = 2
```

The constant value of this field is the smallest value permitted for the radix argument in radix-conversion methods such as the `digit` (**I-§1.2.7**) method, the `forDigit` (**I-§1.2.9**) method, and the `toString` (**I-§1.8.21**) method of class `Integer`.

MIN_VALUE[3]   §1.2.4

```
public final static char MIN_VALUE = '\u0000'
```

The constant value of this field is the smallest value of type char.

Constructors

Character   §1.2.5

```
public Character(char value)
```

Constructs a `Character` object and initializes it so that it represents the primitive `value` argument.

PARAMETERS:

`value`: value for the new `Character` object.

[2.] This field is new in Java 1.1.
[3.] This field is new in Java 1.1.

Methods

charValue §1.2.6

```
public char charValue()
```
RETURNS:

the primitive char value represented by this object.

digit §1.2.7

```
public static int digit(char ch, int radix)
```

Returns the numeric value of the character ch in the specified radix.

If the radix is not in the range MIN_RADIX ≤ radix ≤ MAX_RADIX or if the ch is not a valid digit in the specified radix, -1 is returned. A character is a valid digit if at least one of the following is true:

♦ The method isDigit (**I-§1.2.12**) is true of the character and the Unicode decimal digit value of the character (or its single-character decomposition) is less than the specified radix. In this case the decimal digit value is returned.

♦ The character is one of the uppercase Latin letters 'A' through 'Z' and its code is less than radix + 'A' -10. In this case, ch – 'A' + 10 is returned.

♦ The character is one of the lowercase Latin letters 'a' through 'z' and its code is less than radix + 'a' -10. In this case, ch – 'a' + 10 is returned.

PARAMETERS:

ch: the character to be converted.
radix: the radix.

RETURNS:

the numeric value represented by the character in the specified radix.

SEE ALSO:

forDigit (**I-§1.2.9**).

equals §1.2.8

```
public boolean equals(Object obj)
```

The result is true if and only if the argument is not null and is a Character object that represents the same char value as this object.

PARAMETERS:

obj: the object to compare with.

RETURNS:

true if the objects are the same; false otherwise.

OVERRIDES:

equals in class Object (**I-§1.12.3**).

forDigit   §1.2.9

```
public static char forDigit(int digit, int radix)
```

Determines the character representation for a specific digit in the specified radix. If the value of radix is not a valid radix, or the value of digit is not a valid digit in the specified radix, the null character ('\u0000') is returned.

The radix argument is valid if it is greater than or equal to MIN_RADIX (I-§1.2.3) and less than or equal to MAX_RADIX (I-§1.2.1). The digit argument is valid if $0 \le$ digit $<$ radix.

If the digit is less than 10, then '0' + digit is returned. Otherwise, the value 'a' + digit – 10 is returned.

PARAMETERS:

digit: the number to convert to a character.
radix: the radix.

RETURNS:

the char representation of the specified digit in the specified radix.

SEE ALSO:

digit (I-§1.2.7).

hashCode   §1.2.10

```
public int hashCode()
```

RETURNS:

a hash code value for this object.

OVERRIDES:

hashCode in class Object (I-§1.12.6).

isDefined[4] §1.2.11

```
public static boolean isDefined(char ch)
```

Determines if a character has a defined meaning in Unicode. A character is defined if at least one of the following is true:

◆ It has an entry in the Unicode attribute table.

◆ Its value is in the range '\u3040' ≤ ch ≤ '\u9FA5'

◆ Its value is in the range '\uF900' ≤ ch ≤ '\uFA2D'

PARAMETERS:
ch: the character to be tested

RETURNS:
true if the character has a defined meaning in Unicode; false otherwise.

isDigit[5] §1.2.12

```
public static boolean isDigit(char ch)
```

Determines whether the specified character is a digit. A character is considered to be a digit if it is not in the range '\u2000' through '\u2FFF' and its Unicode name contains the word "DIGIT".

PARAMETERS:
ch: the character to be tested.

RETURNS:
true if the character is a digit; false otherwise.

[4.] This method is new in Java 1.1.
[5.] In Java 1.0, this version returns true only for the 10 ASCII digits '0' through '9'.

isJavaLetter[6]   §1.2.13

```
public static boolean isJavaLetter(char ch)
```

Determines whether the specified character is a "Java" letter, that is, the character is permissible as the first character in an identifier in the Java language.

A character is considered to be a Java letter if and only if it is a letter, the ASCII dollar sign character '$', or the underscore character '_'.

PARAMETERS:

ch: the character to be tested.

RETURNS:

true if the character is a Java letter; false otherwise.

SEE ALSO:

isLetter (I-§1.2.15).
isLetterOrDigit (I-§1.2.16).
isJavaLetterOrDigit (I-§1.2.14).

isJavaLetterOrDigit[7]   §1.2.14

```
public static boolean isJavaLetterOrDigit(char ch)
```

Determines whether the specified character is a "Java" letter or digit, that is, the character is permissible as a non-initial character in an identifier in the Java language.

A character is considered to be a Java letter or digit if and only if it is a letter, a digit, the ASCII dollar sign character '$', or the underscore character '_'.

PARAMETERS:

ch: the character to be tested.

RETURNS:

true if the character is a Java letter or digit; false otherwise.

SEE ALSO:

isLetter (I-§1.2.15).
isLetterOrDigit (I-§1.2.16).
isJavaLetter (I-§1.2.13).

[6.] This method is new in Java 1.1.
[7.] This method is new in Java 1.1.

isLetter §1.2.15

```
public static boolean isLetter(char ch)
```
   Determines whether the specified character is a letter.

PARAMETERS:

ch: the character to be tested.

RETURNS:

true if the character is a letter; false otherwise.

SEE ALSO:

isJavaLetter (I-§1.2.13).
isJavaLetterOrDigit (I-§1.2.14).

isLetterOrDigit[8] §1.2.16

```
public static boolean isLetterOrDigit(char ch)
```
PARAMETERS:

ch: the character to be tested.

RETURNS:

true if the character is a letter or digit; false otherwise.

SEE ALSO:

isDigit (I-§1.2.12).
isLetter (I-§1.2.15).
isJavaLetter (I-§1.2.13).
isJavaLetterOrDigit (I-§1.2.14).

isLowerCase[9] §1.2.17

```
public static boolean isLowerCase(char ch)
```
   Determines whether the specified character is a lowercase character.
   A character is lowercase if it is not in the range '\u2000' through '\u2FFF', the Unicode attribute table does not specify a mapping to lowercase for the character, and at least one of the following is true:

♦ The attribute table specifies a mapping to uppercase for the character.

♦ The name for the character contains the words "SMALL LETTER".

♦ the name for the character contains the words "SMALL LIGATURE".

---

8. This method is new in Java 1.1.
9. In Java 1.0, this version returns true only for lowercase characters in the range '\u0000' to '\u00FF'.

PARAMETERS:

ch: the character to be tested.

RETURNS:

true if the character is lowercase; false otherwise.

SEE ALSO:

isUpperCase (I-§1.2.20).
isTitleCase (I-§1.2.19).
toLowerCase (I-§1.2.21).

isSpace   §1.2.18

```
public static boolean isSpace(char ch)
```

Determines if a character is white space.

This method returns true for the following five characters only:

```
'\t'    \u0009    HORIZONTAL TABULATION
'\n'    \u000A    NEW LINE
'\f'    \u000C    FORM FEED
'\r'    \u000D    CARRIAGE RETURN
' '     \u0020    SPACE
```

PARAMETERS:

ch: the character to be tested.

RETURNS:

true if the character is ISO-LATIN-1 white space; false otherwise.

isTitleCase[10]   §1.2.19

```
public static boolean isTitleCase(char ch)
```

Determines if the character is a titlecase character.

The printed representations of four Unicode characters look like pairs of Latin letters. For example, there is an uppercase letter that looks like "LJ" and has a corresponding lowercase letter that looks like "lj". A third form, which looks like "Lj", is the appropriate form to use when rendering a word in lowercase with initial capitals, as for a book title.

These are the Unicode characters for which this method returns true:

♦ LATIN CAPITAL LETTER D WITH SMALL LETTER Z WITH CARON

♦ LATIN CAPITAL LETTER L WITH SMALL LETTER J

♦ LATIN CAPITAL LETTER N WITH SMALL LETTER J

♦ LATIN CAPITAL LETTER D WITH SMALL LETTER Z

---

[10] This method is new in Java 1.1.

PARAMETERS:

ch: the character to be tested.

RETURNS:

true if the character is titlecase; false otherwise.

SEE ALSO:

isUpperCase **(I-§1.2.20).**
isLowerCase **(I-§1.2.17).**
toTitleCase **(I-§1.2.23).**

isUpperCase[11]   §1.2.20

```
public static boolean isUpperCase(char ch)
```

Determines whether the specified character is an uppercase character.

A character is uppercase if it is not in the range '\u2000' through '\u2FFF', the Unicode attribute table does not specify a mapping to uppercase for the character, and at least one of the following is true:

♦ The attribute table specifies a mapping to lowercase for the character.

♦ The name for the character contains the words "CAPITAL LETTER".

♦ The name for the character contains the words "CAPITAL LIGATURE".

PARAMETERS:

ch: the character to be tested.

RETURNS:

true if the character is uppercase; false otherwise.

SEE ALSO:

isLowerCase **(I-§1.2.17).**
isTitleCase **(I-§1.2.19).**
toUpperCase **(I-§1.2.24).**

[11.] In Java 1.0, this method returns true only for uppercase characters in the range '\u0000' to '\u00FF'.

toLowerCase[12]   §**1.2.21**

```
public static char toLowerCase(char ch)
```

The given character is mapped to its lowercase equivalent; if the character has no lowercase equivalent, the character itself is returned.

A character has a lowercase equivalent if and only if a lowercase mapping is specified for the character in the Unicode attribute table.

Note that some Unicode characters in the range `'\u2000'` to `'\u2FFF'` have lowercase mappings; this method does map such characters to their lowercase equivalents even though the method `isUpperCase` (**I-**§**1.2.20**) does not return `true` for such characters.

PARAMETERS:

`ch`: the character to be converted.

RETURNS:

the lowercase equivalent of the character, if any; otherwise the character itself.

SEE ALSO:

`isLowerCase` (**I-**§**1.2.17**).

toString   §**1.2.22**

```
public String toString()
```

Converts this `Character` object to a string. The result is a string whose length is 1. The string's sole component is the primitive `char` value represented by this object.

RETURNS:

a string representation of this object.

OVERRIDES:

`toString` in class `Object` (**I-**§**1.12.9**).

---

12. In Java 1.0, this method only works on characters in the range `'\u0000'` to `'\u00FF'`. For characters outside this range, the method returns its argument unchanged.

toTitleCase[13]   §1.2.23

```
public static char toTitleCase(char ch)
```

Converts the character argument to titlecase. A character has a titlecase equivalent if and only if a titlecase mapping is specified for the character in the Unicode attribute table.

Note that some Unicode characters in the range `'\u2000'` through `'\u2FFF'` have titlecase mappings; this method does map such characters to their titlecase equivalents even though the method `isTitleCase` (I-§1.2.19) does not return `true` for such characters.

PARAMETERS:

`ch`: the character to be converted.

RETURNS:

the titlecase equivalent of the character, if any; otherwise the character itself.

SEE ALSO:

`isTitleCase` (I-§1.2.19).

toUpperCase[14]   §1.2.24

```
public static char toUpperCase(char ch)
```

Converts the character argument to uppercase. A character has an uppercase equivalent if and only if a titlecase mapping is specified for the character in the Unicode attribute table.

Note that some Unicode characters in the range `'\u2000'` to `'\u2000FFF'` have uppercase mappings; this method does map such characters to their titlecase equivalents even though the method `isLowerCase` (I-§1.2.17) does not return `true` for such characters.

PARAMETERS:

`ch`: the character to be converted.

RETURNS:

the uppercase equivalent of the character, if any; otherwise the character itself.

SEE ALSO:

`isUpperCase` (I-§1.2.20).

[13.] This method is new in Java 1.1.

[14.] In Java 1.0, this method only works on characters in the range `'\u0000'` to `'\u00FF'`. For characters outside this range, the method returns its argument unchanged.

1.3 Class Class

```
public final class java.lang.Class
    extends java.lang.Object (I-§1.12)
{
    // Methods
    public static Class forName(String className);        §1.3.1
    public ClassLoader getClassLoader();                  §1.3.2
    public Class[] getInterfaces();                       §1.3.3
    public String getName();                              §1.3.4
    public Class getSuperclass();                         §1.3.5
    public boolean isInterface();                         §1.3.6
    public Object newInstance();                          §1.3.7
    public String toString();                             §1.3.8
}
```

Instances of the class Class represent classes and interfaces in a running Java application.

There is no public constructor for the class Class. Class objects are constructed automatically by the Java Virtual Machine as classes are loaded and by calls to the defineClass method (I-§1.4.2) in the class loader.

Methods

forName   §1.3.1

```
public static Class forName(String className)
throws ClassNotFoundException
```

Returns the Class object associated with the class with the given string name.

For example, the following code fragment returns the runtime Class descriptor for the class named java.lang.Thread:

```
Class t = Class.forName("java.lang.Thread")
```

PARAMETERS:

className: the fully qualified name of the desired class.

RETURNS:

the Class descriptor for the class with the specified name.

THROWS:

ClassNotFoundException (I-§1.28)
if the class could not be found.

getClassLoader §1.3.2

    `public ClassLoader getClassLoader()`

  Determines the class loader (**I-§1.4**) for the class.

RETURNS:

  the class loader that created the class or interface represented by this object,
    or `null` if the class was not created by a class loader.

getInterfaces §1.3.3

    `public Class[] getInterfaces()`

  Determines the interfaces implemented by the class or interface represented by this object.

  If this object represents a class, the return value is an array containing objects representing all interfaces implemented by the class. The order of the interface objects in the array corresponds to the order of the interface names in the `implements` clause of the declaration of the class represented by this object.

  If this object represents an interface, the array contains objects representing all interfaces extended by the interface. The order of the interface objects in the array corresponds to the order of the interface names in the `extends` clause of the declaration of the interface represented by this object.

  If the class or interface implements no interfaces, the method returns an array of length 0.

RETURNS:

  an array of interfaces implemented by this class.

getName §1.3.4

    `public String getName()`

RETURNS:

  the fully qualified name of the class or interface represented by this object.

getSuperclass §1.3.5

    `public Class getSuperclass()`

  If this object represents any class other than the class `Object`, then the object that represents the superclass of that class is returned.

  If this object is the one that represents the class `Object` or this object represents an interface, `null` is returned.

RETURNS:

  the superclass of the class represented by this object.

isInterface   §1.3.6
```
public boolean isInterface()
```
RETURNS:

true if this object represents an interface; false otherwise.

newInstance   §1.3.7
```
public Object newInstance()
throws InstantiationException, IllegalAccessException
```
   Creates a new instance of a class.

RETURNS:

a newly allocated instance of the class represented by this object. This is
   done exactly as if by a new expression with an empty argument list.

THROWS:

InstantiationException (I-§1.36)

if an application tries to instantiate an abstract class or an interface, or if the
   instantiation fails for some other reason.

THROWS:

IllegalAccessException (I-§1.31)

if the class or initializer is not accessible.

toString   §1.3.8
```
public String toString()
```
   Converts the object to a string. The string representation is the string
"class" or "interface" followed by a space and then the fully qualified
name of the class.

RETURNS:

a string representation of this class object.

OVERRIDES:

toString in class Object (I-§1.12.9).

1.4 Class ClassLoader

```
public abstract class java.lang.ClassLoader
    extends java.lang.Object (I-§1.12)
{
    // Constructors
    protected ClassLoader();                                    §1.4.1

    // Methods
    protected final Class                                       §1.4.2
        defineClass(byte data[], int offset,
                    int length);
    protected final Class findSystemClass(String name);         §1.4.3
    protected abstract Class                                    §1.4.4
        loadClass(String name, boolean resolve);
    protected final void resolveClass(Class c);                 §1.4.5
}
```

The class ClassLoader is an abstract class. Applications implement sub-classes of ClassLoader in order to extend the manner in which the Java Virtual Machine dynamically loads classes.

Normally, the Java Virtual Machine loads classes from the local file system in a platform-dependent manner. For example, on UNIX systems, the Virtual Machine loads classes from the directory defined by the CLASSPATH environment variable.

However, some classes may not originate from a file; they may originate from other sources, such as the network, or they could be constructed by an application. The method defineClass (I-§1.4.2) converts an array of bytes into an instance of class Class (I-§1.3). Instances of this newly defined class can be created using the newInstance method in class Class (I-§1.3.7).

The methods and constructors of objects created by a class loader may reference other classes. To determine the class(es) referred to, the Java Virtual Machine calls the loadClass method (I-§1.4.4) of the class loader that originally created the class. If the Java Virtual Machine only needs to determine if the class exists and if it does exist to know its superclass, the resolve flag is set to false. However, if an instance of the class is being created or any of its methods are being called, the class must also be resolved. In this case the resolve flag is set to true, and the resolveClass method (I-§1.4.5) should be called.

For example, an application could create a network class loader to download class files from a server. Sample code might look like:

```
ClassLoader loader = new NetworkClassLoader(host, port);
Object main = loader.loadClass("Main", true).newInstance();
    ....
```

The network class loader subclass must define the method `loadClass` to load a class from the network. Once it has downloaded the bytes that make up the class, it should use the method `defineClass` to create a class instance. A sample implementation is:

```
class NetworkClassLoader {
    String host;
    int port;
    Hashtable cache = new Hashtable();
    private byte loadClassData(String name)[] {
    // load the class data from the connection
    ...
    }

    public synchronized Class loadClass(String name,
                                        boolean resolve) {
        Class c = cache.get(name);
        if (c == null) {
            byte data[] = loadClassData(name);
            c = defineClass(data, 0, data.length);
            cache.put(name, c);
        }
        if (resolve)
            resolveClass(c);
        return c;

    }
}
```

Constructors

ClassLoader   §1.4.1

```
protected ClassLoader()
```

Constructs a new class loader and initializes it.

If there is a security manager, its `checkCreateClassLoader` method (I-§1.15.8) is called. This may result in a security exception (I-§1.43).

THROWS:

`SecurityException` (I-§1.43)

if the current thread does not have permission to create a new class loader.

Methods

---

defineClass §1.4.2

```
protected final Class
defineClass(byte data[], int offset, int length)
```

Converts an array of bytes into an instance of class `Class`.

PARAMETERS:

`data`: the bytes that make up the `Class`.
`offset`: the start offset of the `Class` data.
`length`: the length of the `Class` data.

RETURNS:

the `Class` object that was created from the data.

THROWS:

`ClassFormatError` **(I-§1.47)**
if the data does not contain a valid Class.

findSystemClass §1.4.3

```
protected final Class findSystemClass(String name)
throws ClassNotFoundException
```

Finds the system class with the specified name, loading it in if necessary.

A system class is a class loaded from the local file system in a platform-dependent way. It has no class loader.

PARAMETERS:

`name`: the name of the system `class`.

RETURNS:

a system class with the given name.

THROWS:

`NoClassDefFoundError` **(I-§1.54)**
if the class is not found.

THROWS:

`ClassNotFoundException` **(I-§1.28)**
if it could not find a definition for the class.

loadClass   §1.4.4

```
protected abstract Class
loadClass(String name, boolean resolve)
throws ClassNotFoundException
```

Requests the class loader to load a class with the specified name. The loadClass method is called by the Java Virtual Machine when a class loaded by a class loader first references another class. Every subclass of class ClassLoader must define this method.

If the resolve flag is true, the method should call the resolveClass method on the resulting class object.

Class loaders should use a hashtable or other cache to avoid defining classes with the same name multiple times.

PARAMETERS:

name: the name of the desired Class.
resolve: true if the Class must be resolved.

RETURNS:

the resulting Class, or null if it was not found.

THROWS:

ClassNotFoundException (I-§1.28)
if the class loader cannot find a definition for the class.

resolveClass   §1.4.5

```
protected final void resolveClass(Class c)
```

Resolves the class so that an instance of the class can be created, or so that one of its methods can be called. This method should be called by loadClass if the resolve flag is true.

PARAMETERS:

c: the Class instance to be resolved.

1.5 Class Compiler

```
public final class java.lang.Compiler
    extends java.lang.Object (I-§1.12)
{
    // Methods
    public static Object command(Object any);          §1.5.1
    public static boolean compileClass(Class clazz);    §1.5.2
    public static boolean compileClasses(String string); §1.5.3
    public static void disable();                       §1.5.4
    public static void enable();                        §1.5.5
}
```

The Compiler class is provided in support of Java-to-native-code compilers and related services.

When the Java Virtual Machine first starts, it determines if the system property (**I-§1.18.9**) java.compiler exists. If so, it is assumed to be the name of a library (with a platform-dependent exact location and type); the loadLibrary method (**I-§1.18.13**) in class System is called to load that library. If this loading succeeds, the function named java_lang_Compiler_start() in that library is called.

If no compiler is available, these methods do nothing.

Methods

command   §1.5.1

```
public static Object command(Object any)
```

The Compiler should examine the argument type and its fields and perform some documented operation. No specific operations are required.

PARAMETERS:

any: an argument.

RETURNS:

a compiler-specific value, or null if no compiler is available.

compileClass   §1.5.2

```
public static boolean compileClass(Class clazz)
```

The indicated class is compiled.

PARAMETERS:

`clazz`: a class.

RETURNS:

`true` if the compilation succeeded; `false` if the compilation failed or no compiler is available.

compileClasses   §1.5.3

```
public static boolean compileClasses(String string)
```

Indicates that the application would like the third-party software to compile all classes whose name matches the indicated string.

PARAMETERS:

`string`: the name of the classes to compile.

RETURNS:

`true` if the compilation succeeded; `false` if the compilation failed or no compiler is available.

disable   §1.5.4

```
public static void disable()
```

Cause the `Compiler` to cease operation.

enable   §1.5.5

```
public static void enable()
```

Cause the `Compiler` to resume operation.

1.6 Class Double

```
public final class java.lang.Double
    extends java.lang.Number (I-§1.11)
{
    // Fields
    public final static double MAX_VALUE;                §1.6.1
    public final static double MIN_VALUE;                §1.6.2
    public final static double NaN;                      §1.6.3
    public final static double NEGATIVE_INFINITY;        §1.6.4
    public final static double POSITIVE_INFINITY;        §1.6.5

    // Constructors
    public Double(double value);                         §1.6.6
    public Double(String s);                             §1.6.7

    // Methods
    public static long doubleToLongBits(double value);   §1.6.8
    public double doubleValue();                         §1.6.9
    public boolean equals(Object obj);                   §1.6.10
    public float floatValue();                           §1.6.11
    public int hashCode();                               §1.6.12
    public int intValue();                               §1.6.13
    public boolean isInfinite();                         §1.6.14
    public static boolean isInfinite(double v);          §1.6.15
    public boolean isNaN();                              §1.6.16
    public static boolean isNaN(double v);               §1.6.17
    public static double longBitsToDouble(long bits);    §1.6.18
    public long longValue();                             §1.6.19
    public String toString();                            §1.6.20
    public static String toString(double d);             §1.6.21
    public static Double valueOf(String s);              §1.6.22
}
```

This class wraps a value of the primitive type double in an object. An object of type Double contains a single field whose type is double.

In addition, this class provides several methods for converting a double to a String and a String to a double, as well as other constants and methods useful when dealing with a double.

Fields

MAX_VALUE   §1.6.1

    public final static double
        MAX_VALUE = 1.79769313486231570e+308d
    The largest positive value of type double.

MIN_VALUE   §1.6.2

    public final static double
        MIN_VALUE = 4.94065645841246544e-324
    The smallest positive value of type double.

NaN   §1.6.3

    public final static double NaN = 0.0 / 0.0
    A NaN value of type double.

NEGATIVE_INFINITY   §1.6.4

    public final static double
        NEGATIVE_INFINITY = -1.0 / 0.0
    The negative infinity of type double.

POSITIVE_INFINITY   §1.6.5

    public final static double
        POSITIVE_INFINITY = 1.0 / 0.0
    The positive infinity of type double.

Constructors

Double   §1.6.6

    public Double(double value)
    Constructs a newly allocated Double object that represents the primitive
    double argument.
    PARAMETERS:
    value: the value to be represented by the Double.

Double §1.6.7

```
public Double(String s)
throws NumberFormatException
```

Constructs a newly allocated `Double` object that represents the floating-point value of type `double` represented by the string. The string is converted to a double value as if by the `valueOf` method (**I-§1.6.22**).

PARAMETERS:

`s`: a string to be converted to a `Double`.

THROWS:

`NumberFormatException` (**I-§1.41**)
if the string does not contain a parsable number.

Methods

doubleToLongBits §1.6.8

```
public static long doubleToLongBits(double value)
```

The result is a representation of the floating-point argument according to the IEEE 754 floating-point "double format" bit layout.

Bit 63 represents the sign of the floating-point number. Bits 62–52 represent the exponent. Bits 51–0 represent the significand (sometimes called the mantissa) of the floating-point number.

If the argument is positive infinity, the result is `0x7ff0000000000000L`.
If the argument is negative infinity, the result is `0xfff0000000000000L`.
If the argument is NaN, the result is `0x7ff8000000000000L`.

PARAMETERS:

`value`: a double precision floating-point number.

RETURNS:

the bits that represent the floating-point number.

doubleValue §1.6.9

```
public double doubleValue()
```

RETURNS:

the double value represented by this object.

OVERRIDES:

`doubleValue` in class `Number` (**I-§1.11.1**).

equals   **§1.6.10**

```
public boolean equals(Object obj)
```

The result is true if and only if the argument is not null and is a Double object that represents a double that has the identical bit pattern to the bit pattern of the double represented by this object.

Note that in most cases, for two instances of class Double, d1 and d2, the value of d1.equals(d2) is true if and only if

```
d1.doubleValue() == d2.longValue()
```

also has the value true. However, there are two exceptions:

♦ If d1 and d2 both represent Double.NaN, then the equals method returns true, even though Double.NaN==Double.NaN has the value false.

♦ If d1 represents +0.0 while d2 represents -0.0, or vice versa, the equal test has the value false, even though +0.0==-0.0 has the value true.

PARAMETERS:

obj: the object to compare with.

RETURNS:

true if the objects are the same; false otherwise.

OVERRIDES:

equals in class Object **(I-§1.12.3)**.

floatValue   **§1.6.11**

```
public float floatValue()
```

RETURNS:

the double value represented by this object is converted to type float and the result of the conversion is returned.

OVERRIDES:

floatValue in class Number **(I-§1.11.2)**.

hashCode   **§1.6.12**

```
public int hashCode()
```

RETURNS:

a hash code value for this object.

OVERRIDES:

hashCode in class Object **(I-§1.12.6)**.

intValue §1.6.13

```
public int intValue()
```

RETURNS:

the double value represented by this object is converted to type int and the
result of the conversion is returned.

OVERRIDES:

intValue in class Number (I-§1.11.3).

isInfinite §1.6.14

```
public boolean isInfinite()
```

RETURNS:

true if the value represented by this object is positive infinity (I-§1.6.5) or
negative infinity (I-§1.6.4); false otherwise.

isInfinite §1.6.15

```
public static boolean isInfinite(double v)
```

PARAMETERS:

v: the value to be tested.

RETURNS:

true if the value of the argument is positive infinity (I-§1.6.5) or negative
infinity (I-§1.6.4); false otherwise.

isNaN §1.6.16

```
public boolean isNaN()
```

RETURNS:

true if the value represented by this object is NaN (I-§1.6.3); false otherwise.

isNaN §1.6.17

```
public static boolean isNaN(double v)
```

PARAMETERS:

v: the value to be tested.

RETURNS:

true if the value of the argument is NaN (I-§1.6.3); false otherwise.

longBitsToDouble §1.6.18

```
public static double longBitsToDouble(long bits)
```

The argument is considered to be a representation of a floating-point value according to the IEEE 754 floating-point "double precision" bit layout. That floating-point value is returned as the result.

If the argument is `0x7f80000000000000L`, the result is positive infinity.

If the argument is `0xff80000000000000L`, the result is negative infinity.

If the argument is any value in the range `0x7ff0000000000001L` through `0x7fffffffffffffffL` or in the range `0xfff0000000000001L` through `0xffffffffffffffffL`, the result is NaN. All IEEE 754 NaN values are, in effect, lumped together by the Java language into a single value.

PARAMETERS:

`bits`: any `long` integer.

RETURNS:

the `double` floating-point value with the same bit pattern.

longValue §1.6.19

```
public long longValue()
```

RETURNS:

the `double` value represented by this object is converted to type `long` and the result of the conversion is returned.

OVERRIDES:

`longValue` in class `Number` (I-§1.11.4).

toString §1.6.20

```
public String toString()
```

The primitive `double` value represented by this object is converted to a string exactly as if by the method `toString` of one argument (I-§1.6.21).

RETURNS:

a `String` representation of this object.

OVERRIDES:

`toString` in class `Object` (I-§1.12.9).

toString §1.6.21

```
public static String toString(double d)
```

Creates a string representation of the `double` argument.

The values `NaN`, `NEGATIVE_INFINITY`, `POSITIVE_INFINITY`, `-0.0`, and `+0.0` are represented by the strings `"NaN"`, `"-Infinity"`, `"Infinity"`, `"-0.0"`, and `"0.0"`, respectively.

If `d` is in the range $10^{-3} \le |d| \le 10^{7}$, then it is converted to a string in the style `[-]ddd.ddd`. Otherwise, it is converted to a string in the style `[-]m.ddddE±xx`.

There is always a minimum of one digit after the decimal point. The number of digits is the minimum needed to uniquely distinguish the argument value from adjacent values of type `double`.

PARAMETERS:

`d`: the double to be converted.

RETURNS:

a string representation of the argument.

valueOf §1.6.22

```
public static Double valueOf(String s)
throws NumberFormatException
```

Parses a string into a `Double`.

PARAMETERS:

`s`: the string to be parsed.

RETURNS:

a newly constructed `Double` initialized to the value represented by the string argument.

THROWS:

`NumberFormatException` (I-§1.41)
if the string does not contain a parsable number.

1.7 Class Float

```
public final class java.lang.Float
    extends java.lang.Number (I-§1.11)
{
    // Fields
    public final static float MAX_VALUE;                    §1.7.1
    public final static float MIN_VALUE;                    §1.7.2
    public final static float NaN;                          §1.7.3
    public final static float NEGATIVE_INFINITY;            §1.7.4
    public final static float POSITIVE_INFINITY;            §1.7.5

    // Constructors
    public Float(double value);                             §1.7.6
    public Float(float value);                              §1.7.7
    public Float(String s);                                 §1.7.8

    // Methods
    public double doubleValue();                            §1.7.9
    public boolean equals(Object obj);                      §1.7.10
    public static int floatToIntBits(float value);         §1.7.11
    public float floatValue();                              §1.7.12
    public int hashCode();                                  §1.7.13
    public static float intBitsToFloat(int bits);          §1.7.14
    public int intValue();                                  §1.7.15
    public boolean isInfinite();                            §1.7.16
    public static boolean isInfinite(float v);             §1.7.17
    public boolean isNaN();                                 §1.7.18
    public static boolean isNaN(float v);                  §1.7.19
    public long longValue();                                §1.7.20
    public String toString();                               §1.7.21
    public static String toString(float f);                §1.7.22
    public static Float valueOf(String s);                 §1.7.23
}
```

This class wraps a value of primitive type float in an object. An object of type Float contains a single field whose type is float.

In addition, this class provides several methods for converting a float to a String and a String to a float, as well as other constants and methods useful when dealing with a float.

Fields

MAX_VALUE §1.7.1

```
public final static float MAX_VALUE
    = 3.40282346638528860e+38.
```
The largest positive value of type float.

MIN_VALUE §1.7.2

```
public final static float MIN_VALUE
    = 1.40129846432481707e-45
```
The smallest positive value of type float.

NaN §1.7.3

```
public final static float NaN = 0.0f/0.0f
```
The NaN value of type float.

NEGATIVE_INFINITY §1.7.4

```
public final static float NEGATIVE_INFINITY
    = -1.0f/0.0f
```
The negative infinity of type float.

POSITIVE_INFINITY §1.7.5

```
public final static float POSITIVE_INFINITY
    = 1.0f/0.0f
```
The positive infinity of type float.

Constructors

Float §1.7.6

```
public Float(double value)
```
Constructs a newly allocated Float object that represents the argument converted to type float.

PARAMETERS:

value: the value to be represented by the Float.

Float   §1.7.7

```
public Float(float value)
```

Constructs a newly allocated `Float` object that represents the primitive `float` argument.

PARAMETERS:

`value`: the value to be represented by the `Float`.

Float   §1.7.8

```
public Float(String s)
throws NumberFormatException
```

Constructs a newly allocated `Float` object that represents the floating-point value of type `float` represented by the string. The string is converted to a `float` value as if by the `valueOf` method **(I-§1.7.23)**.

PARAMETERS:

`s`: a string to be converted to a `Float`.

THROWS:

`NumberFormatException` **(I-§1.41)**
if the string does not contain a parsable number.

Methods

doubleValue   §1.7.9

```
public double doubleValue()
```

The `float` value represented by this object is converted to type `double` and the result of the conversion is returned.

OVERRIDES:

`doubleValue` in class Number **(I-§1.11.1)**.

equals   §1.7.10

```
public boolean equals(Object obj)
```

The result is `true` if and only if the argument is not `null` and is a `Float` object that represents a `float` that has the identical bit pattern to the bit pattern of the `float` represented by this object.

Note that in most cases, for two instances of class `Float`, f1 and f2, the value of `f1.equals(f2)` is `true` if and only if

```
f1.floatValue() == f2.floatValue()
```

also has the value `true`. However, there are two exceptions:

♦ If f1 and f2 both represent Float.NaN, then the equals method returns true, even though Float.NaN==Float.NaN has the value false.

♦ If f1 represents +0.0f while f2 represents -0.0f, or vice versa, the equal test has the value false, even though 0.0f==-0.0f has the value true.

RETURNS:

true if the objects are the same; false otherwise.

SEE ALSO:

floatToIntBits (**I-§1.7.11**).

OVERRIDES:

equals in class Object (**I-§1.12.3**).

floatToIntBits §1.7.11

```
public static int floatToIntBits(float value)
```

The result is a representation of the floating-point argument according to the IEEE 754 floating-point "single precision" bit layout.

Bit 31 represents the sign of the floating-point number. Bits 30–23 represent the exponent. Bits 22–0 represent the significand (sometimes called the mantissa) of the floating-point number.

If the argument is positive infinity, the result is 0x7f800000.

If the argument is negative infinity, the result is 0xff800000.

If the argument is NaN, the result is 0x7fc00000.

PARAMETERS:

value: a floating-point number.

RETURNS:

the bits that represent the floating-point number.

floatValue §1.7.12

```
public float floatValue()
```

RETURNS:

the float value represented by this object.

OVERRIDES:

floatValue in class Number (**I-§1.11.2**).

hashCode §1.7.13

```
public int hashCode()
```

RETURNS:

a hash code value for this object.

OVERRIDES:

hashCode in class Object (**I-§1.12.6**).

intBitsToFloat §1.7.14

```
public static float intBitsToFloat(int bits)
```

The argument is considered to be a representation of a floating-point value according to the IEEE 754 floating-point "single precision" bit layout. That floating-point value is returned as the result.

If the argument is `0x7f800000`, the result is positive infinity.

If the argument is `0xff800000`, the result is negative infinity.

If the argument is any value in the range `0x7f800001` through `0x7f8fffff` or in the range `0xff800001` through `0xff8fffff`, the result is NaN. All IEEE 754 NaN values are, in effect, lumped together by the Java language into a single value.

PARAMETERS:

`bits`: an integer.

RETURNS:

the single-format floating-point value with the same bit pattern.

intValue §1.7.15

```
public int intValue()
```

RETURNS:

the `float` value represented by this object converted to type `int` and the result of the conversion is returned.

OVERRIDES:

`intValue` in class Number (**I-§1.11.3**).

isInfinite §1.7.16

```
public boolean isInfinite()
```

RETURNS:

`true` if the value represented by this object is positive infinity (**I-§1.7.5**) or negative infinity (**I-§1.7.4**); `false` otherwise.

isInfinite §1.7.17

```
public static boolean isInfinite(float v)
```

PARAMETERS:

`v`: the value to be tested.

RETURNS:

`true` if the argument is positive infinity (**I-§1.7.5**) or negative infinity (**I-§1.7.4**); `false` otherwise.

isNaN   §1.7.18

    `public boolean isNaN()`

    RETURNS:

    true if the value represented by this object is NaN (**I-§1.7.3**); `false` other-
        wise.

isNaN   §1.7.19

    `public static boolean isNaN(float v)`

    RETURNS:

    true if the argument is NaN (**I-§1.7.3**); `false` otherwise.

    PARAMETERS:

    `v`: the value to be tested.

longValue   §1.7.20

    `public long longValue()`

    RETURNS:

    the `float` value represented by this object is converted to type `long` and the
        result of the conversion is returned.

    OVERRIDES:

    `longValue` in class `Number` (**I-§1.11.4**).

toString   §1.7.21

    `public String toString()`

    The primitive `float` value represented by this object is converted to a
    `String` exactly as if by the method `toString` of one argument (**I-§1.7.22**).

    RETURNS:

    a `String` representation of this object.

    OVERRIDES:

    `toString` in class `Object` (**I-§1.12.9**).

toString   §1.7.22

```
public static String toString(float f)
```

Creates a string representation of the `float` argument.

The values NaN, NEGATIVE_INFINITY, POSITIVE_INFINITY, -0.0, and +0.0 are represented by the strings "NaN", "-Infinity", "Infinity", "-0.0", and "0.0", respectively.

If d is in the range $10^{-3} \le |d| \le 10^{7}$, then it is converted to a String in the style [-]ddd.ddd. Otherwise, it is converted to a string in the style [-]m.ddddE±xx.

There is always a minimum of 1 digit after the decimal point. The number of digits is the minimum needed to uniquely distinguish the argument value from adjacent values of type `float`.

PARAMETERS:

d: the float to be converted.

RETURNS:

a string representation of the argument.

valueOf   §1.7.23

```
public static Float valueOf(String s)
throws NumberFormatException
```

Parses a string into a `Float`.

PARAMETERS:

s: the string to be parsed.

RETURNS:

a newly constructed `Float` initialized to the value represented by the `String` argument.

THROWS:

NumberFormatException (I-§1.41)
if the string does not contain a parsable number.

1.8 Class Integer

```
public final class java.lang.Integer
    extends java.lang.Number (I-§1.11)
{
    // Fields
    public final static int MAX_VALUE;                      §1.8.1
    public final static int MIN_VALUE;                      §1.8.2

    // Constructors
    public Integer(int value);                              §1.8.3
    public Integer(String s);                               §1.8.4

    // Methods
    public double doubleValue();                            §1.8.5
    public boolean equals(Object obj);                      §1.8.6
    public float floatValue();                              §1.8.7
    public static Integer getInteger(String nm);            §1.8.8
    public static Integer getInteger(String nm, int val);   §1.8.9
    public static Integer getInteger(String nm,
                                     Integer val);          §1.8.10
    public int hashCode();                                  §1.8.11
    public int intValue();                                  §1.8.12
    public long longValue();                                §1.8.13
    public static int parseInt(String s);                   §1.8.14
    public static int parseInt(String s, int radix);        §1.8.15
    public static String toBinaryString(int i);             §1.8.16
    public static String toHexString(int i);                §1.8.17
    public static String toOctalString(int i);             §1.8.18
    public String toString();                               §1.8.19
    public static String toString(int i);                   §1.8.20
    public static String toString(int i, int radix);        §1.8.21
    public static Integer valueOf(String s);                §1.8.22
    public static Integer valueOf(String s, int radix);     §1.8.23
}
```

This class wraps a value of the primitive type int in an object. An object of type Integer contains a single field whose type is int.

In addition, this class provides several methods for converting an int to a String and a String to an int, as well as other constants and methods useful when dealing with an int.

Fields

MAX_VALUE   §1.8.1

```
public final static int MAX_VALUE = 2147483647
```

The largest value of type int.

MIN_VALUE   §1.8.2

```
public final static int MIN_VALUE = -2147483648
```
The smallest value of type `int`.

Constructors

Integer   §1.8.3

```
public Integer(int value)
```
Constructs a newly allocated `Integer` object that represents the primitive `int` argument.

PARAMETERS:

`value`: the value to be represented by the `Integer`.

Integer   §1.8.4

```
public Integer(String s)
throws NumberFormatException
```
Constructs a newly allocated `Integer` object that represents the value represented by the string. The string is converted to an `int` value as if by the `valueOf` method (**I-§1.8.22**).

PARAMETERS:

`s`: the `String` to be converted to an `Integer`.

THROWS:

`NumberFormatException` (**I-§1.41**)
if the `String` does not contain a parsable integer.

Methods

doubleValue   §1.8.5

```
public double doubleValue()
```
RETURNS:

the `int` value represented by this object is converted to type `double` and the result of the conversion is returned.

OVERRIDES:

`doubleValue` in class Number (**I-§1.11.1**).

equals

```
public boolean equals(Object obj)
```

The result is `true` if and only if the argument is not `null` and is an `Integer` object that contains the same `int` value as this object.

PARAMETERS:

`obj`: the object to compare with.

RETURNS:

`true` if the objects are the same; `false` otherwise.

OVERRIDES:

`equals` in class `Object` **(I-§1.12.3)**.

floatValue

```
public float floatValue()
```

RETURNS:

the `int` value represented by this object is converted to type `float` and the result of the conversion is returned.

OVERRIDES:

`floatValue` in class `Number` **(I-§1.11.2)**.

getInteger

```
public static Integer getInteger(String nm)
```

Determines the integer value of the system property with the specified name.

The first argument is treated as the name of a system property to be obtained as if by the method `System.getProperty` **(I-§1.18.10)**. The string value of this property is then interpreted as an integer value and an `Integer` object representing this value is returned. The full details of the possible numeric formats are given in **I-§1.8.10**.

If there is no property with the specified name, or if the property does not have the correct numeric format, then `null` is returned.

PARAMETERS:

`nm`: property name.

RETURNS:

the `Integer` value of the property.

getInteger

```
public static Integer getInteger(String nm, int val)
```

Determines the integer value of the system property with the specified name.

The first argument is treated as the name of a system property to be obtained as if by the method `System.getProperty` (**I-§1.18.10**). The string value of this property is then interpreted as an integer value and an `Integer` object representing this value is returned. The full details of the possible numeric formats are given in **I-§1.8.10**.

If there is no property with the specified name, or if the property does not have the correct numeric format, then an `Integer` object that represents the value of the second argument is returned.

PARAMETERS:

`nm`: property name.
`val`: default value.

RETURNS:

the `Integer` value of the property.

getInteger

```
public static Integer getInteger(String nm, Integer val)
```

Determines the integer value of the system property with the specified name.

The first argument is treated as the name of a system property to be obtained as if by the method `System.getProperty` (**I-§1.18.10**). The string value of this property is then interpreted as an integer value and an `Integer` object representing this value is returned.

If the property value begins with "0x" or "#", not followed by a minus sign, the rest of it is parsed as a hexadecimal integer exactly as for the method `Integer.valueOf` (**I-§1.8.23**) with radix 16.

If the property value begins with "0" then it is parsed as an octal integer exactly as for the method `Integer.valueOf` (**I-§1.8.23**) with radix 8.

Otherwise the property value is parsed as a decimal integer exactly as for the method `Integer.valueOf` (**I-§1.8.23**) with radix 10.

The second argument is the default value. If there is no property of the specified name, or if the property does not have the correct numeric format, then the second argument is returned.

PARAMETERS:

`nm`: property name.
`val`: default value.

RETURNS:

the `Integer` value of the property.

hashCode   §1.8.11

    public int hashCode()

RETURNS:

a hash code value for this object.

OVERRIDES:

hashCode in class Object (**I-§1.12.6**).

intValue   §1.8.12

    public int intValue()

RETURNS:

the int value represented by this object.

OVERRIDES:

intValue in class Number (**I-§1.11.3**).

longValue   §1.8.13

    public long longValue()

RETURNS:

the int value represented by this object that is converted to type long and
the result of the conversion is returned.

OVERRIDES:

longValue in class Number (**I-§1.11.4**).

parseInt   §1.8.14

    public static int parseInt(String s)
    throws NumberFormatException

Parses the string argument as a signed decimal integer. The characters in
the string must all be decimal digits, except that the first character may be an
ASCII minus sign '-' to indicate a negative value.

PARAMETERS:

s: a string.

RETURNS:

the integer represented by the argument in decimal.

THROWS:

NumberFormatException (**I-§1.41**)
if the string does not contain a parsable integer.

parseInt   §1.8.15

```
public static int parseInt(String s, int radix)
throws NumberFormatException
```

Parses the string argument as a signed integer in the radix specified by the second argument. The characters in the string must all be digits of the specified radix (as determined by whether `Character.digit` [**I-§1.2.7**] returns a nonnegative value), except that the first character may be an ASCII minus sign '-' to indicate a negative value. The resulting integer value is returned.

PARAMETERS:

`s:` the `String` containing the integer.
`radix:` the radix to be used.

RETURNS:

the integer represented by the string argument in the specified radix.

THROWS:

`NumberFormatException` (**I-§1.41**)
if the string does not contain a parsable integer.

toBinaryString[15]   §1.8.16

```
public static String toBinaryString(int i)
```

Creates a string representation of the integer argument as an unsigned integer in base 2.

The unsigned integer value is the argument plus 2^{32} if the argument is negative; otherwise it is equal to the argument. This value is converted to a string of ASCII digits in binary (base 2) with no extra leading 0s.

PARAMETERS:

`i :` an integer.

RETURNS:

the string representation of the unsigned integer value represented by the argument in binary (base 2).

[15.] This method is new in Java 1.1.

toHexString[16] §1.8.17

```
public static String toHexString(int i)
```

Creates a string representation of the integer argument as an unsigned integer in base 16.

The unsigned integer value is the argument plus 2^{32} if the argument is negative; otherwise, it is equal to the argument. This value is converted to a string of ASCII digits in hexadecimal (base 16) with no extra leading 0s.

PARAMETERS:

i : an integer.

RETURNS:

the string representation of the unsigned integer value represented by the argument in hexadecimal (base 16).

toOctalString[17] §1.8.18

```
public static String toOctalString(int i)
```

Creates a string representation of the integer argument as an unsigned integer in base 8.

The unsigned integer value is the argument plus 2^{32} if the argument is negative; otherwise, it is equal to the argument. This value is converted to a string of ASCII digits in octal (base 8) with no extra leading 0s.

PARAMETERS:

i : an integer

RETURNS:

the string representation of the unsigned integer value represented by the argument in octal (base 8).

toString §1.8.19

```
public String toString()
```

RETURNS:

a string representation of the value of this object in base 10.

OVERRIDES:

toString in class Object (**I-§1.12.9**).

[16.] This method is new in Java 1.1.
[17.] This method is new in Java 1.1.

toString   §1.8.20

```
public static String toString(int i)
```
PARAMETERS:

i : an integer to be converted.

RETURNS:

a string representation of the argument in base 10.

toString   §1.8.21

```
public static String toString(int i, int radix)
```
Creates a string representation of the first argument in the radix specified by the second argument.

If the radix is smaller than `Character.MIN_RADIX` (**I-§1.2.3**) or larger than `Character.MAX_RADIX` (**I-§1.2.1**), then the radix 10 is used instead.

If the first argument is negative, the first element of the result is the ASCII minus character '-'. If the first argument is not negative, no sign character appears in the result. The following ASCII characters are used as digits:

```
0123456789abcdefghijklmnopqrstuvwxyz
```

PARAMETERS:

i : an integer.
radix : the radix.

RETURNS:

a string representation of the argument in the specified radix.

valueOf   §1.8.22

```
public static Integer valueOf(String s)
throws NumberFormatException
```
PARAMETERS:

s : the string to be parsed.

RETURNS:

a newly constructed `Integer` initialized to the value represented by the string argument.

THROWS:

`NumberFormatException` (**I-§1.41**)
if the string does not contain a parsable integer.

valueOf §1.8.23

```
public static Integer valueOf(String s, int radix)
throws NumberFormatException
```

PARAMETERS:

s: the string to be parsed.

RETURNS:

a newly constructed Integer initialized to the value represented by the string argument in the specified radix.

THROWS:

NumberFormatException (I-§1.41)

if the String does not contain a parsable integer.

1.9 Class Long

```
public final class java.lang.Long
    extends java.lang.Number (I-§1.11)
{
    // Fields
    public final static long MAX_VALUE;                      §1.9.1
    public final static long MIN_VALUE;                      §1.9.2

    // Constructors
    public Long(long value);                                 §1.9.3
    public Long(String s);                                   §1.9.4

    // Methods
    public double doubleValue();                             §1.9.5
    public boolean equals(Object obj);                       §1.9.6
    public float floatValue();                               §1.9.7
    public static Long getLong(String nm);                   §1.9.8
    public static Long getLong(String nm, long val);         §1.9.9
    public static Long getLong(String nm, Long val);         §1.9.10
    public int hashCode();                                   §1.9.11
    public int intValue();                                   §1.9.12
    public long longValue();                                 §1.9.13
    public static long parseLong(String s);                  §1.9.14
    public static long parseLong(String s, int radix);       §1.9.15
    public static String toBinaryString(long i);             §1.9.16
    public static String toHexString(long i);                §1.9.17
    public static String toOctalString(long i);              §1.9.18
    public String toString();                                §1.9.19
    public static String toString(long i);                   §1.9.20
    public static String toString(long i, int radix);        §1.9.21
    public static Long valueOf(String s);                    §1.9.22
    public static Long valueOf(String s, int radix);         §1.9.23
}
```

This class wraps a value of the primitive type long in an object. An object of type Long contains a single field whose type is long.

In addition, this class provides several methods for converting a long to a String and a String to a long, as well as other constants and methods useful when dealing with a long.

Fields

MAX_VALUE   §1.9.1

```
public final static long MAX_VALUE = 9223372036854775807L
```
The largest value of type long.

MIN_VALUE §1.9.2

```
public final static long MIN_VALUE = -9223372036854775808L
```
The smallest value of type long.

Constructors

Long §1.9.3

```
public Long(long value)
```
Constructs a newly allocated Long object that represents the primitive long argument.

PARAMETERS:

value: the value to be represented by the Long.

Long §1.9.4

```
public Long(String s)
throws NumberFormatException
```
Constructs a newly allocated Long object that represents the value represented by the string. The string is converted to a long value as if by the valueOf method (I-§1.9.22).

PARAMETERS:

s: the string to be converted to a Long.

THROWS:

NumberFormatException (I-§1.41)
if the String does not contain a parsable long integer.

Methods

doubleValue §1.9.5

```
public double doubleValue()
```
RETURNS:

the long value represented by this object that is converted to type double and the result of the conversion is returned.

OVERRIDES:

doubleValue in class Number (I-§1.11.1).

equals   §1.9.6

```
public boolean equals(Object obj)
```

The result is `true` if and only if the argument is not `null` and is a `Long` object that contains the same `long` value as this object.

PARAMETERS:

`obj`: the object to compare with.

RETURNS:

`true` if the objects are the same; `false` otherwise.

OVERRIDES:

`equals` in class `Object` (I-§1.12.3).

floatValue   §1.9.7

```
public float floatValue()
```

RETURNS:

the `long` value represented by this object is converted to type `float` and the result of the conversion is returned.

OVERRIDES:

`floatValue` in class `Number` (I-§1.11.2).

getLong   §1.9.8

```
public static Long getLong(String nm)
```

Determines the `long` value of the system property with the specified name.

The first argument is treated as the name of a system property to be obtained as if by the method `System.getProperty` (I-§1.18.10). The string value of this property is then interpreted as a `long` value and a `Long` object representing this value is returned. The full details of the possible numeric formats are given in **I-§1.9.10**.

If there is no property with the specified name, or if the property does not have the correct numeric format, then `null` is returned.

PARAMETERS:

`nm`: property name.

RETURNS:

the `Long` value of the property.

getLong

```
public static Long getLong(String nm, long val)
```

Determines the `long` value of the system property with the specified name.

The first argument is treated as the name of a system property to be obtained as if by the method `System.getProperty` (**I-§1.18.10**). The string value of this property is then interpreted as a `long` value and a `Long` object representing this value is returned. The full details of the possible numeric formats is given in **I-§1.9.10**.

If there is no property with the specified name, or if the property does not have the correct numeric format, then a `Long` object that represents the value of the second argument is returned.

PARAMETERS:

`nm`: property name.
`val`: default value.

RETURNS:

the `Long` value of the property.

getLong §1.9.10

```
public static Long getLong(String nm, Long val)
```

Determines the long value of the system property with the specified name.

The first argument is treated as the name of a system property to be obtained as if by the method `System.getProperty` (**I-§1.18.10**). The string value of this property is then interpreted as a long value and a `Long` object representing this value is returned.

If the property value begins with "0x" or "#", not followed by a minus sign, the rest of it is parsed as a hexadecimal integer exactly as for the method `Long.valueOf` (**I-§1.9.23**) with radix 16.

If the property value begins with "0", then it is parsed as an octal integer exactly as for the method `Long.valueOf` (**I-§1.9.23**) with radix 8.

Otherwise the property value is parsed as a decimal integer exactly as for the method `Long.valueOf` (**I-§1.9.23**) with radix 10.

Note that, in every case, neither L nor l is permitted to appear at the end of the string.

The second argument is the default value. If there is no property of the specified name, or if the property does not have the correct numeric format, then the second argument is returned.

PARAMETERS:

nm: the property name.
val: the default `Long` value.

RETURNS:

the long value of the property.

hashCode §1.9.11

```
public int hashCode()
```

RETURNS:

a hash code value for this object.

OVERRIDES:

hashCode in class `Object` (**I-§1.12.6**).

intValue §1.9.12

```
public int intValue()
```

RETURNS:

the long value represented by this object is converted to type `int` and the result of the conversion is returned.

OVERRIDES:

intValue in class `Number` (**I-§1.11.3**).

longValue §1.9.13

```
public long longValue()
```
RETURNS:

the long value represented by this object.

OVERRIDES:

longValue in class Number (**I-§1.11.4**).

parseLong §1.9.14

```
public static long parseLong(String s)
throws NumberFormatException
```
Parses the string argument as a signed decimal long. The characters in the string must all be decimal digits, except that the first character may be an ASCII minus sign '-' to indicate a negative value.

PARAMETERS:

s: a string.

RETURNS:

the long represented by the argument in decimal.

THROWS:

NumberFormatException (**I-§1.41**)

if the string does not contain a parsable long.

parseLong §1.9.15

```
public static long parseLong(String s, int radix)
throws NumberFormatException
```
Parses the string argument as a signed long in the radix specified by the second argument. The characters in the string must all be digits of the specified radix (as determined by whether Character.digit [**I-§1.2.7**] returns a nonnegative value), except that the first character may be an ASCII minus sign '-' to indicate a negative value. The resulting long value is returned.

PARAMETERS:

s: the String containing the long.
radix: the radix to be used.

RETURNS:

the long represented by the string argument in the specified radix.

THROWS:

NumberFormatException (**I-§1.41**)

if the string does not contain a parsable integer.

toBinaryString[18]   §1.9.16

```
public static String toBinaryString(long i)
```

Creates a string representation of the long argument as an unsigned integer in base 2.

The unsigned long value is the argument plus 2^{64} if the argument is negative; otherwise, it is equal to the argument. This value is converted to a string of ASCII digits in binary (base 2) with no extra leading 0s.

PARAMETERS:

i : a long.

RETURNS:

the string representation of the unsigned long value represented by the argument in binary (base 2).

toHexString[19]   §1.9.17

```
public static String toHexString(long i)
```

Creates a string representation of the long argument as an unsigned integer in base 16.

The unsigned long value is the argument plus 2^{64} if the argument is negative; otherwise, it is equal to the argument. This value is converted to a string of ASCII digits in hexadecimal (base 16) with no extra leading 0s.

PARAMETERS:

i : a long.

RETURNS:

the string representation of the unsigned long value represented by the argument in hexadecimal (base 16).

[18.] This method is new in Java 1.1.

[19.] This method is new in Java 1.1.

toOctalString[20] §1.9.18

```
public static String toOctalString(long i)
```

Creates a string representation of the long argument as an unsigned integer in base 8.

The unsigned long value is the argument plus 2^{64} if the argument is negative; otherwise, it is equal to the argument. This value is converted to a string of ASCII digits in octal (base 8) with no extra leading 0s.

PARAMETERS:

i : a long.

RETURNS:

the string representation of the unsigned long value represented by the argument in octal (base 8).

toString §1.9.19

```
public String toString()
```

RETURNS:

a string representation of this object in base 10.

OVERRIDES:

toString in class Object (I-§1.12.9).

toString §1.9.20

```
public static String toString(long i)
```

PARAMETERS:

i : a long to be converted.

RETURNS:

a string representation of the argument in base 10.

toString §1.9.21

```
public static String toString(long i, int radix)
```

Creates a string representation of the first argument in the radix specified by the second argument.

If the radix is smaller than Character.MIN_RADIX (I-§1.2.3) or larger than Character.MAX_RADIX (I-§1.2.1), then the radix 10 is used instead.

If the first argument is negative, the first element of the result is the ASCII minus sign '-'. If the first argument is not negative, no sign character appears in the result. The following ASCII characters are used as digits:

```
0123456789abcdefghijklmnopqrstuvwxyz
```

---

[20] This method is new in Java 1.1.

PARAMETERS:

`i`: a long.
`radix`: the radix.

RETURNS:

a string representation of the argument in the specified radix.

valueOf   §1.9.22

```
public static Long valueOf(String s)
throws NumberFormatException
```

PARAMETERS:

`s`: the string to be parsed.

RETURNS:

a newly constructed Long initialized to the value represented by the string argument.

THROWS:

`NumberFormatException` (I-§1.41)
If the `String` does not contain a parsable `long`.

valueOf   §1.9.23

```
public static Long valueOf(String s, int radix)
throws NumberFormatException
```

PARAMETERS:

`s`: the `String` containing the `long`.
`radix`: the radix to be used.

RETURNS:

a newly constructed Long initialized to the value represented by the string argument in the specified radix.

THROWS:

`NumberFormatException` (I-§1.41)
If the `String` does not contain a parsable `long`.

1.10 Class Math

```
public final class java.lang.Math
    extends java.lang.Object (I-§1.12)
{
    // Fields
    public final static double E;                              §1.10.1
    public final static double PI;                             §1.10.2

    // Methods
    public static double abs(double a);                        §1.10.3
    public static float abs(float a);                          §1.10.4
    public static int abs(int a);                              §1.10.5
    public static long abs(long a);                            §1.10.6
    public static double acos(double a);                       §1.10.7
    public static double asin(double a);                       §1.10.8
    public static double atan(double a);                       §1.10.9
    public static double atan2(double a, double b);            §1.10.10
    public static double ceil(double a);                       §1.10.11
    public static double cos(double a);                        §1.10.12
    public static double exp(double a);                        §1.10.13
    public static double floor(double a);                      §1.10.14
    public static double                                       §1.10.15
        IEEEremainder(double f1, double f2);
    public static double log(double a);                        §1.10.16
    public static double max(double a, double b);              §1.10.17
    public static float max(float a, float b);                 §1.10.18
    public static int max(int a, int b);                       §1.10.19
    public static long max(long a, long b);                    §1.10.20
    public static double min(double a, double b);              §1.10.21
    public static float min(float a, float b);                 §1.10.22
    public static int min(int a, int b);                       §1.10.23
    public static long min(long a, long b);                    §1.10.24
    public static double pow(double a, double b);              §1.10.25
    public static double random();                             §1.10.26
    public static double rint(double a);                       §1.10.27
    public static long round(double a);                        §1.10.28
    public static int round(float a);                          §1.10.29
    public static double sin(double a);                        §1.10.30
    public static double sqrt(double a);                       §1.10.31
    public static double tan(double a);                        §1.10.32
}
```

The class Math contains methods for performing basic numeric operations such as the elementary exponential, logarithm, square root, and trigonometric functions.

To help ensure portability of Java programs, the definitions of many of the numeric functions in this package require that they produce the same results as certain published algorithms. These algorithms are available from the well-known network library `netlib` as the package "Freely Distributable Math Library" (`fdlibm`). These algorithms, which are written in the C programming language, are then to be understood as executed with all floating-point operations following the rules of Java floating-point arithmetic.

The network library may be found on the World Wide Web at

    http://netlib.att.com

then perform a keyword search for `fdlibm`.

The Java math library is defined with respect to the version of `fdlibm` dated January 4, 1995. Where `fdlibm` provides more than one definition for a function (such as `acos`), use the "IEEE 754 core function" version (residing in a file whose name begins with the letter e).

Fields

E   §1.10.1

    public final static double E = 2.7182818284590452354

The `double` value that is closer than any other to e, the base of the natural logarithms.

PI   §1.10.2

    public final static double PI = 3.14159265358979323846

The `double` value that is closer than any other to π, the ratio of the circumference of a circle to its diameter.

Methods

abs   §1.10.3

    public static double abs(double a)

Calculates the absolute value of the argument.

PARAMETERS:
a: a `double` value.

RETURNS:
the absolute value of the argument.[21]

---

[21] In Java 1.0, abs(-0.0) returns -0.0. This bug is fixed in Java 1.1.

abs §1.10.4

```
public static float abs(float a)
```
Calculates the absolute value of the argument.

PARAMETERS:

a: a float **value.**

RETURNS:

the absolute value of the argument.[22]

abs §1.10.5

```
public static int abs(int a)
```
Calculates the absolute value of the argument. If the argument is not negative, the argument is returned. If the argument is negative, the negation of the argument is returned.

Note that if the argument is equal to the value of Integer.MIN_VALUE (I-§1.8.2), the most negative representable int value, the result is that same value, which is negative.

PARAMETERS:

a: **an** int **value.**

RETURNS:

the absolute value of the argument.

abs §1.10.6

```
public static long abs(long a)
```
Calculates the absolute value of the argument. If the argument is not negative, the argument is returned. If the argument is negative, the negation of the argument is returned.

Note that if the argument is equal to the value of Long.MIN_VALUE (I-§1.9.2), the most negative representable long value, the result is that same value, which is negative.

PARAMETERS:

a: a long value.

RETURNS:

the absolute value of the argument.

---

[22] In Java 1.0, abs(-0.0f) returns -0.0f. This bug is fixed in Java 1.1.

acos   §1.10.7

```
public static double acos(double a)
```
PARAMETERS:
a: a double value.
RETURNS:
the arc cosine of the argument.

asin   §1.10.8

```
public static double asin(double a)
```
PARAMETERS:
a: a double value.
RETURNS:
the arc sine of the argument.

atan   §1.10.9

```
public static double atan(double a)
```
PARAMETERS:
a: a double value.
RETURNS:
the arc tangent of the argument.

atan2   §1.10.10

```
public static double atan2(double a, double b)
```
PARAMETERS:
a: a double value.
b: a double value.
RETURNS:
the θ component of the polar coordinate $\langle r, \theta \rangle$ that corresponds to the Cartesian coordinate $\langle a, b \rangle$.

ceil   §1.10.11

```
public static double ceil(double a)
```
Returns the smallest (closest to negative infinity) double value that is not less than the argument and is equal to a mathematical integer.
PARAMETERS:
a: a double value.
RETURNS:
the value $\lceil a \rceil$.

cos §1.10.12

```
public static double cos(double a)
```
PARAMETERS:

a: an angle, in radians.

RETURNS:

the cosine of the argument.

exp §1.10.13

```
public static double exp(double a)
```
PARAMETERS:

a: a double value.

RETURNS:

the value e^a, where where e (I-§1.10.1) is the base of the natural logarithms.

floor §1.10.14

```
public static double floor(double a)
```
Returns the largest (closest to positive infinity) double value that is not greater than the argument and is equal to a mathematical integer.

PARAMETERS:

a: a double value.

PARAMETERS:

a: an assigned value.

RETURNS:

the value $\lfloor a \rfloor$.

IEEEremainder §1.10.15

```
public static double IEEEremainder(double f1, double f2)
```
Computes the remainder operation on two arguments as prescribed by the IEEE 754 standard: the remainder value is mathematically equal to $f1 - f2 \times n$ where n is the mathematical integer closest to the exact mathematical value of the quotient $f1/f2$, and if two mathematical integers are equally close to $f1/f2$, then n is the integer that is even. If the remainder is zero, its sign is the same as the sign of the first argument.

PARAMETERS:

f1: the dividend.
f2: the divisor.

RETURNS:

the remainder when f1 is divided by f2.

log   §1.10.16

```
public static double log(double a)²³
```
PARAMETERS:

a: a number greater than 0.0.

RETURNS:

the value ln a , the natural logarithm of a.

max   §1.10.17

```
public static double max(double a, double b)
```
PARAMETERS:

a: a double value.
b: a double value.

RETURNS:

the larger of a and b.²⁴

max   §1.10.18

```
public static float max(float a, float b)
```
PARAMETERS:

a: a float value.
b: a float value.

RETURNS:

the larger of a and b.²⁵

max   §1.10.19

```
public static int max(int a, int b)
```
PARAMETERS:

a: an int value.
b: an int value.

RETURNS:

the larger of a and b.

---

[23]. In Java 1.0, the method log was declared as follows
```
public static log sqrt(double a)
throws ArithmeticException
```
even though the ArithmeticException was never thrown. This bug is fixed in Java 1.1.

[24]. In Java 1.0, max(-0.0, 0.0) returns -0.0. This bug is fixed in Java 1.1.

[25]. In Java 1.0, max(-0.0f, 0.0f) returns -0.0f. This bug is fixed in Java 1.1.

max §1.10.20

    `public static long max(long a, long b)`

    PARAMETERS:

    a: a long value.

    b: a long value.

    RETURNS:

    the larger of a and b.

min §1.10.21

    `public static double min(double a, double b)`

    PARAMETERS:

    a: a double value.

    b: a double value.

    RETURNS:

    the smaller of a and b.[26]

min §1.10.22

    `public static float min(float a, float b)`

    PARAMETERS:

    a: a float value.

    b: a float value.

    RETURNS:

    the smaller of a and b.[27]

min §1.10.23

    `public static int min(int a, int b)`

    PARAMETERS:

    a: an int value.

    b: an int value.

    RETURNS:

    the smaller of a and b.

min §1.10.24

    `public static long min(long a, long b)`

    PARAMETERS:

    a: a long value.

    b: a long value.

    RETURNS:

    the smaller of a and b.

---

[26] In Java 1.0, `min(0.0, -0.0)` returns `0.0`. This bug is fixed in Java 1.1.

[27] In Java 1.0, `min(0.0f, -0.0f)` returns `0.0f`. This bug is fixed in Java 1.1.

pow   §1.10.25

    `public static double pow(double a, double b)`[28]

PARAMETERS:

a: a double value.
b: a double value.

RETURNS:

the value a^b.

random   §1.10.26

    `public static double random()`

RETURNS:

a pseudorandom double between `0.0` and `1.0`.

SEE ALSO:

nextDouble in class Random (**I-§3.7.3**).

rint   §1.10.27

    `public static double rint(double a)`

      Calculates the closest integer to the argument.

PARAMETERS:

a: a double value.

RETURNS:

the closest `double` value to a that is equal to a mathematical integer. If two
    `double` values that are mathematical integers are equally close to the
    value of the argument, the result is the integer value that is even.

[28.] In Java 1.0, the method pow was declared as follows:
    `public static double sqrt(double a, double b)`
    `throws ArithmeticException`
even though the `ArithmeticException` was never thrown. This bug is fixed in Java 1.1.

round §1.10.28

```
public static long round(double a)
```

Calculates the closest long to the argument.

If the argument is negative infinity or any value less than or equal to the value of Long.MIN_VALUE (I-§1.9.2), the result is equal to the value of Long.MIN_VALUE.

If the argument is positive infinity or any value greater than or equal to the value of Long.MAX_VALUE (I-§1.9.1), the result is equal to the value of Long.MAX_VALUE.

PARAMETERS:

a: a double value.

RETURNS:

the value of the argument rounded to the nearest long value.

round §1.10.29

```
public static int round(float a)
```

Calculates the closest int to the argument.

If the argument is negative infinity or any value less than or equal to the value of Integer.MIN_VALUE (I-§1.8.2), the result is equal to the value of Integer.MIN_VALUE.

If the argument is positive infinity or any value greater than or equal to the value of Integer.MAX_VALUE (I-§1.8.1), the result is equal to the value of Integer.MAX_VALUE.

PARAMETERS:

a: a float value.

RETURNS:

the value of the argument rounded to the nearest int value.

sin §1.10.30

```
public static double sin(double a)
```

PARAMETERS:

a: a double value.

RETURNS:

the sine of the argument.

sqrt   §1.10.31

`public static double sqrt(double a)`[29]

PARAMETERS:

a: a double value.

RETURNS:

the value of $\sqrt{a}$. If the argument is NaN or less than zero, the result is NaN.

tan   §1.10.32

`public static double tan(double a)`

PARAMETERS:

a: a double value.

RETURNS:

the tangent of the argument.

1.11 Class Number

```
public abstract class java.lang.Number
    extends java.lang.Object (I-§1.12)
{
    // Methods
    public abstract double doubleValue();          §1.11.1
    public abstract float floatValue();            §1.11.2
    public abstract int intValue();                §1.11.3
    public abstract long longValue();              §1.11.4
}
```

The abstract class Number is the superclass of classes Float (I-§1.7), Double (I-§1.6), Integer (I-§1.8), and Long (I-§1.9).

Subclasses of Number must provide methods to convert the represented numeric value to int, long, float, and double.

---

[29] In Java 1.0, the method sqrt was declared as follows:

```
public static double sqrt(double a)
throws ArithmeticException
```

even though the ArithmeticException was never thrown. This bug is fixed in Java 1.1.

Methods

doubleValue §1.11.1

    `public abstract double doubleValue()`

    RETURNS:

    the numeric value represented by this object after conversion to type `double`.

floatValue §1.11.2

    `public abstract float floatValue()`

    RETURNS:

    the numeric value represented by this object after conversion to type `float`.

intValue §1.11.3

    `public abstract int intValue()`

    RETURNS:

    the numeric value represented by this object after conversion to type `int`.

longValue §1.11.4

    `public abstract long longValue()`

    RETURNS:

    the numeric value represented by this object after conversion to type `long`.

1.12 Class Object

```
public class java.lang.Object
{
    // Constructors
    public Object();                                    §1.12.1

    // Methods
    protected Object clone();                           §1.12.2
    public boolean equals(Object obj);                  §1.12.3
    protected void finalize();                          §1.12.4
    public final Class getClass();                      §1.12.5
    public int hashCode();                              §1.12.6
    public final void notify();                         §1.12.7
    public final void notifyAll();                      §1.12.8
    public String toString();                           §1.12.9
    public final void wait();                           §1.12.10
    public final void wait(long timeout);               §1.12.11
    public final void wait(long timeout, int nanos);    §1.12.12
}
```

Class Object is the root of the class hierarchy. Every class has Object as a superclass. All objects, including arrays, implement the methods of this class.

Constructors

Object   §1.12.1

    public Object()

    Allocates a new instance of class Object.

Methods

clone   §1.12.2

    protected Object clone()
    throws CloneNotSupportedException

    The clone method of class Object creates a new object of the same class as this object. It then initializes each of the new object's fields by assigning it the same value as the corresponding field in this object. No constructor is called.

    The clone method of class Object will only clone an object whose class indicates that it is willing for its instances to be cloned. A class indicates that its instances can be cloned by declaring that it implements the Cloneable (**I-§1.22**) interface.

RETURNS:

a clone of this instance.

THROWS:

OutOfMemoryError (**I-§1.57**)
if there is not enough memory.

THROWS:

CloneNotSupportedException (**I-§1.29**).

The object's class does not support the Cloneable interface. Subclasses that override the clone method can also throw this exception to indicate that an instance cannot be cloned.

equals §1.12.3

```
public boolean equals(Object obj)
```

Indicates whether some other object is "equal to" this one.
The equals method implements an equivalence relation:

♦ It is *reflexive*: for any reference value x, x.equals(x) should return true.

♦ It is *symmetric*: for any reference values x and y, x.equals(y) should return true if and only if y.equals(x) returns true.

♦ It is *transitive*: for any reference values x, y, and z, if x.equals(y) returns true and y.equals(z) returns true, then x.equals(z) should return true.

♦ It is *consistent*: for any reference values x and y, multiple invocations of x.equals(y) consistently return true or consistently return false.

♦ For any reference value x, x.equals(null) should return false.

The equals method for class Object implements the most discriminating possible equivalence relation on objects; that is, for any reference values x and y, this method returns true if and only if x and y refer to the same object (x==y has the value true).

PARAMETERS:

obj: the reference object with which to compare.

RETURNS:

true if this object is the same as the obj argument; false otherwise.

SEE ALSO:

Hashtable (**I-§3.4**).
hashCode (**I-§1.12.6**).

finalize §1.12.4

```
protected void finalize()
throws Throwable
```

The finalize method is called by the garbage collector on an object when garbage collection determines that there are no more references to the object. A subclass overrides the finalize method in order to dispose of system resources or to perform other cleanup.

Any exception thrown by the finalize method causes the finalization of this object to be halted, but is otherwise ignored.

The finalize method in Object does nothing.

getClass   §1.12.5

`public final Class getClass()`

Determines the runtime class of an object.

RETURNS:

the object of type `Class` (**I-§1.3**) that represents the runtime class of the object.

hashCode   §1.12.6

`public int hashCode()`

Calculates a hash code value for the object. This method is supported for the benefit of hashtables such as those provided by `java.util.Hashtable` (**I-§3.4**).

The general contract of `hashCode` is:

♦ Whenever it is invoked on the same object more than once during an execution of a Java application, the `hashCode` method must consistently return the same integer. This integer need not remain consistent from one execution of an application to another execution of the same application.

♦ If two objects are equal according to the `equals` method (**I-§1.12.3**), then calling the `hashCode` method on each of the two objects must produce the same integer result.

RETURNS:

a hash code value for this object.

notify   §1.12.7

`public final void notify()`

Wakes up a single thread that is waiting on this object's monitor. A thread waits on an object's monitor by calling one of the `wait` methods (**I-§1.12.10– §1.12.12**).

This method should only be called by a thread that is the owner of this object's monitor. A thread becomes the owner of the object's monitor in one of three ways:

♦ By executing a synchronized instance method of that object.

♦ By executing the body of a `synchronized` statement that synchronizes on the object.

♦ For objects of type `Class`, by executing a synchronized static method of that class.

Only one thread at a time can own an object's monitor.

THROWS:

`IllegalMonitorStateException` (I-§1.33)
if the current thread is not the owner of this object's monitor.

SEE ALSO:

`notifyAll` (I-§1.12.8).

notifyAll §1.12.8

`public final void notifyAll()`

Wakes up all threads that are waiting on this object's monitor. A thread waits on an object's monitor by calling one of the `wait` methods (I-§1.12.10–§1.12.12).

This method should only be called by a thread that is the owner of this object's monitor. See the `notify` method (I-§1.12.7) for a description of the ways in which a thread can become the owner of a monitor.

THROWS:

`IllegalMonitorStateException` (I-§1.33)
if the current thread is not the owner of this object's monitor.

toString §1.12.9

`public String toString()`

Creates a string representation of the object. In general, the `toString` method returns a string that "textually represents" this object. The result should be a concise but informative representation that is easy for a person to read.

The `toString` method for class `Object` returns a string consisting of the name of the class of which the object is an instance, the at-sign character '@', and the unsigned hexadecimal representation of the hash code of the object.[30]

RETURNS:

a string representation of the object.

---

[30] In Java 1.0, the hexadecimal string printed after the '@' is based on the hash code value, but may not be the actual hash code value.

wait   **§1.12.10**

```
public final void wait()
throws InterruptedException
```

Waits to be notified by another thread of a change in this object.

The current thread must own this object's monitor. The thread releases ownership of this monitor and waits until another thread notifies threads waiting on this object's monitor to wake up either through a call to the `notify` method (**I-§1.12.7**) or the `notifyAll` method (**I-§1.12.8**). The thread then waits until it can re-obtain ownership of the monitor and resumes execution.

This method should only be called by a thread that is the owner of this object's monitor. See the `notify` method (**I-§1.12.7**) for a description of the ways in which a thread can become the owner of a monitor.

THROWS:

`IllegalMonitorStateException` (**I-§1.33**)
If the current thread is not the owner of the object's monitor.

THROWS:

`InterruptedException` (**I-§1.37**)
if another thread has interrupted this thread.

wait   **§1.12.11**

```
public final void wait(long timeout)
throws InterruptedException
```

Waits to be notified by another thread of a change in this object.

The current thread must own this object's monitor. The thread releases ownership of this monitor and waits until either of the following two conditions has occurred:

◆ Another thread notifies threads waiting on this object's monitor to wake up either through a call to the `notify` method (**I-§1.12.7**) or the `notifyAll` method (**I-§1.12.8**).

◆ The timeout period, specified by the `timeout` argument in milliseconds, has elapsed.

The thread then waits until it can re-obtain ownership of the monitor and resumes execution

This method should only be called by a thread that is the owner of this object's monitor. See the `notify` method (**I-§1.12.7**) for a description of the ways in which a thread can become the owner of a monitor.

PARAMETERS:

`timeout`: the maximum time to wait in milliseconds.

THROWS:

`IllegalMonitorStateException` (**I-§1.33**)
if the current thread is not the owner of the object's monitor.

THROWS:

`InterruptedException` (**I-§1.37**)
if another thread has interrupted this thread.

`wait`   **§1.12.12**

```
public final void wait(long timeout, int nanos)
throws InterruptedException
```

Waits to be notified by another thread of a change in this object.

This method is similar to the `wait` method (**I-§1.12.11**) of one argument, but it allows finer control over the amount of time to wait for a notification before giving up.

The current thread must own this object's monitor. The thread releases ownership of this monitor and waits until either of the following two conditions has occurred:

♦ Another thread notifies threads waiting on this object's monitor to wake up either through a call to the `notify` method (**I-§1.12.7**) or the `notifyAll` method (**I-§1.12.8**).

♦ The timeout period, specified by `timeout` milliseconds plus `nanos` nanoseconds arguments, has elapsed.

The thread then waits until it can re-obtain ownership of the monitor and resumes execution

This method should only be called by a thread that is the owner of this object's monitor. See the `notify` method (I-§1.12.7) for a description of the ways in which a thread can become the owner of a monitor.

PARAMETERS:

`timeout`: the maximum time to wait in milliseconds.
`nano`: additional time, in nanoseconds range 0–999999.

THROWS:

`IllegalMonitorStateException` (I-§1.33)
if the current thread is not the owner of this object's monitor.

THROWS:

`InterruptedException` (I-§1.37)
if another thread has interrupted this thread.

1.13 Class Process

```
public abstract class java.lang.Process
    extends java.lang.Object (I-§1.12)
{
    // Constructors
    public Process();                                       §1.13.1

    // Methods
    public abstract void destroy();                         §1.13.2
    public abstract int exitValue();                        §1.13.3
    public abstract InputStream getErrorStream();           §1.13.4
    public abstract InputStream getInputStream();           §1.13.5
    public abstract OutputStream getOutputStream();         §1.13.6
    public abstract int waitFor();                          §1.13.7
}
```

The exec methods (I-§1.14.1–§1.14.4) return an instance of a subclass of Process that can be used to control the process and obtain information about it.

The subprocess is not killed when there are no more references to the Process object, but rather the subprocess continues executing asynchronously.

Constructors

Process   §1.13.1

```
public Process()
```

    The default constructor.

Methods

destroy	§1.13.2

```
public abstract void destroy()
```
Kills the subprocess.

exitValue	§1.13.3

```
public abstract int exitValue()
```
RETURNS:

the exit value of the subprocess.

getErrorStream	§1.13.4

```
public abstract InputStream getErrorStream()
```
Gets the error stream of the subprocess.

RETURNS:

the input stream connected to the error stream of the subprocess. This stream is usually unbuffered.

getInputStream	§1.13.5

```
public abstract InputStream getInputStream()
```
Gets the input stream of the subprocess.

RETURNS:

the input stream connected to the normal output of the subprocess. This stream is usually buffered.

getOutputStream	§1.13.6

```
public abstract OutputStream getOutputStream()
```
Gets the output stream of the subprocess.

RETURNS:

the output stream connected to the normal input of the subprocess. This stream is usually buffered.

waitFor   §1.13.7

```
public abstract int waitFor()
throws InterruptedException
```

   Waits for the subprocess to complete. This method returns immediately if
the subprocess has already terminated.

RETURNS:

the exit value of the process.

THROWS:

```
InterruptedException (I-§1.37)
if the waitFor was interrupted.
```

1.14 Class Runtime

```
public class java.lang.Runtime
    extends java.lang.Object (I-§1.12)
{
    // Methods
    public Process exec(String command);                    §1.14.1
    public Process exec(String command, String envp[]);     §1.14.2
    public Process exec(String cmdarray[]);                 §1.14.3
    public Process exec(String cmdarray[], String envp[]);  §1.14.4
    public void exit(int status);                           §1.14.5
    public long freeMemory();                               §1.14.6
    public void gc();                                       §1.14.7
    public InputStream                                      §1.14.8
        getLocalizedInputStream(InputStream in);
    public OutputStream                                     §1.14.9
        getLocalizedOutputStream(OutputStream out);
    public static Runtime getRuntime();                     §1.14.10
    public void load(String filename);                      §1.14.11
    public void loadLibrary(String libname);                §1.14.12
    public void runFinalization();                          §1.14.13
    public long totalMemory();                              §1.14.14
    public void traceInstructions(boolean on);              §1.14.15
    public void traceMethodCalls(boolean on);               §1.14.16
}
```

   Every Java application has a single instance of class Runtime that allows the
application to interface with the environment in which the application is running.
The current runtime can be obtained from the getRuntime method (**I-§1.14.10**).

   An application cannot create its own instance of this class.

Methods

exec §1.14.1

```
public Process exec(String command)
throws IOException
```

Executes the string command in a separate process.

The command argument is parsed into tokens and then executed as a command in a separate process. This method has exactly the same effect as exec(command, null) (**I-§1.14.2**).

PARAMETERS:

command: a specified system command.

RETURNS:

a Process (**I-§1.13**) object for managing the subprocess.

THROWS:

SecurityException (**I-§1.43**)
if the current thread cannot create a subprocess.

exec §1.14.2

```
public Process exec(String command, String envp[])
throws IOException
```

Executes the string command in a separate process with the specified environment.

This method breaks the command string into tokens and creates a new array cmdarray containing the tokens; it then performs the call exec(cmdarray, envp) (**I-§1.14.4**).

PARAMETERS:

command: a specified system command.
envp: array containing environment in format *name=value*

RETURNS:

a Process (**I-§1.13**) object for managing the subprocess.

THROWS:

SecurityException (**I-§1.43**)
if the current thread cannot create a subprocess.

exec   §1.14.3

```
public Process exec(String cmdarray[])
throws IOException
```

Executes the command in a separate process with the specified arguments.

The command specified by the tokens in cmdarray is executed as a command in a separate process. This has exactly the same effect as exec(cmdarray, null) (I-§1.14.4).

PARAMETERS:

cmdarray: array containing the command to call and its arguments.

RETURNS:

a Process (I-§1.13) object for managing the subprocess.

THROWS:

SecurityException (I-§1.43)
if the current thread cannot create a subprocess.

exec   §1.14.4

```
public Process exec(String cmdarray[], String envp[])
throws IOException
```

Executes the command in a separate process with the specified arguments and the specified environment.

If there is a security manager, its checkExec method (I-§1.15.10) is called with the first component of the array cmdarray as its argument. This may result in a security exception (I-§1.43).

Given an array of strings cmdarray, representing the tokens of a command line, and an array of strings envp, representing an "environment" that defines system properties, this method creates a new process in which to execute the specified command.

PARAMETERS:

cmdarray: array containing the command to call and its arguments.
envp: array containing environment in format *name=value*.

RETURNS:

a Process (I-§1.13) object for managing the subprocess.

THROWS:

SecurityException (I-§1.43)
if the current thread cannot create a subprocess.

exit §1.14.5

```
public void exit(int status)
```

Terminates the currently running Java Virtual Machine. This method never returns normally.

If there is a security manager, its `checkExit` method (**I-§1.15.11**) is called with the status as its argument. This may result in a security exception (**I-§1.43**).

The argument serves as a status code; by convention, a nonzero status code indicates abnormal termination.

PARAMETERS:

`status`: exit status.

THROWS:

`SecurityException` (**I-§1.43**)

If the current thread cannot exit with the specified status.

freeMemory §1.14.6

```
public long freeMemory()
```

Determines the amount of free memory in the system. The value returned by this method is always less than the value returned by the `totalMemory` method (**I-§1.14.14**). Calling the `gc` method (**I-§1.14.7**) may result in increasing the value returned by `freeMemory`.

RETURNS:

an approximation to the total amount of memory currently available for future allocated objects, measured in bytes, is returned.

gc §1.14.7

```
public void gc()
```

Calling this method suggests that the Java Virtual Machine expend effort toward recycling unused objects in order to make the memory they currently occupy available for quick reuse. When control returns from the method call, the Java Virtual Machine has made its best effort to recycle all unused objects.

The name `gc` stands for "garbage collector." The Java Virtual Machine performs this recycling process automatically as needed even if the `gc` method is not invoked explicitly.

getLocalizedInputStream   §1.14.8

`public InputStream getLocalizedInputStream(InputStream in)`

Creates a localized version of an input stream. This method takes an InputStream (I-§2.13) and returns an InputStream equivalent to the argument in all respects except that it is localized: as characters in the local character set are read from the stream, they are automatically converted from the local character set to Unicode.

If the argument is already a localized stream, it may be returned as the result.

RETURNS:

a localized input stream.

getLocalizedOutputStream   §1.14.9

`public OutputStream getLocalizedOutputStream(OutputStream out)`

Creates a localized version of an output stream. This method takes an OutputStream (I-§2.15) and returns an OutputStream equivalent to the argument in all respects except that it is localized: as Unicode characters are written to the stream, they are automatically converted to the local character set.

If the argument is already a localized stream, it may be returned as the result.

RETURNS:

a localized output stream.

getRuntime   §1.14.10

`public static Runtime getRuntime()`

RETURNS:

the Runtime object associated with the current Java application.

load   §1.14.11

```
public void load(String filename)
```

Loads the given filename as a dynamic library. The filename argument must be a complete pathname.

If there is a security manager, its `checkLink` method **(I-§1.15.12)** is called with the `filename` as its argument. This may result in a security exception **(I-§1.43)**.

PARAMETERS:

`filename`: the file to load.

THROWS:

`UnsatisfiedLinkError` **(I-§1.61)**
if the file does not exist.

THROWS:

`SecurityException` **(I-§1.43)**
if the current thread cannot load the specified dynamic library.

loadLibrary   §1.14.12

```
public void loadLibrary(String libname)
```

Loads the dynamic library with the specified library name. The mapping from a library name to a specific filename is done in a system-specific manner.

First, if there is a security manager, its `checkLink` method **(I-§1.15.12)** is called with the `filename` as its argument. This may result in a security exception **(I-§1.43)**.

If this method is called more than once with the same library name, the second and subsequent calls are ignored.

PARAMETERS:

`libname`: the name of the library.

THROWS:

`UnsatisfiedLinkError` **(I-§1.61)**
if the library does not exist.

THROWS:

`SecurityException` **(I-§1.43)**
if the current thread cannot load the specified dynamic library.

runFinalization   §1.14.13

`public void runFinalization()`

Calling this method suggests that the Java Virtual Machine expend effort toward running the `finalize` methods (**I-§1.12.4**) of objects that have been found to be discarded but whose `finalize` methods have not yet been run. When control returns from the method call, the Java Virtual Machine has made a best effort to complete all outstanding finalizations.

The Java Virtual Machine performs the finalization process automatically as needed if the `runFinalization` method is not invoked explicitly.

totalMemory   §1.14.14

`public long totalMemory()`

Determines the total amount of memory in the Java Virtual Machine.

RETURNS:

the total amount of memory currently available for allocating objects, measured in bytes.

traceInstructions   §1.14.15

`public void traceInstructions(boolean on)`

If the `boolean` argument is `true`, this method asks the Java Virtual Machine to print out a detailed trace of each instruction in the Java Virtual Machine as it is executed. The virtual machine may ignore this request if it does not support this feature. The destination of the trace output is system dependent.

If the `boolean` argument is `false`, this method causes the Java Virtual Machine to stop performing the detailed instruction trace it is performing.

PARAMETERS:

on: `true` to enable instruction tracing; `false` to disable this feature.

traceMethodCalls   §1.14.16

`public void traceMethodCalls(boolean on)`

If the `boolean` argument is `true`, this method asks the Java Virtual Machine to print out a detailed trace of each method in the Java Virtual Machine as it is called. The virtual machine may ignore this request if it does not support this feature. The destination of the trace output is system dependent.

If the `boolean` argument is `false`, this method causes the Java Virtual Machine to stop performing the detailed method trace it is performing.

PARAMETERS:

on: `true` to enable instruction tracing; `false` to disable this feature.

1.15 Class SecurityManager

```
public abstract class java.lang.SecurityManager
    extends java.lang.Object (I-§1.12)
{
    // Fields
    protected boolean inCheck;                              §1.15.1

    // Constructors
    protected SecurityManager();                            §1.15.2

    // Methods
    public void checkAccept(String host, int port);         §1.15.3
    public void checkAccess(Thread g);                      §1.15.4
    public void checkAccess(ThreadGroup g);                 §1.15.5
    public void checkConnect(String host, int port);        §1.15.6
    public void checkConnect(String host, int port,         §1.15.7
                        Object context);
    public void checkCreateClassLoader();                   §1.15.8
    public void checkDelete(String file);                   §1.15.9
    public void checkExec(String cmd);                      §1.15.10
    public void checkExit(int status);                      §1.15.11
    public void checkLink(String lib);                      §1.15.12
    public void checkListen(int port);                      §1.15.13
    public void checkPackageAccess(String pkg);             §1.15.14
    public void checkPackageDefinition(String pkg);         §1.15.15
    public void checkPropertiesAccess();                    §1.15.16
    public void checkPropertyAccess(String key);            §1.15.17
    public void checkRead(FileDescriptor fd);               §1.15.18
    public void checkRead(String file);                     §1.15.19
    public void checkRead(String file, Object context);     §1.15.20
    public void checkSetFactory();                          §1.15.21
    public boolean checkTopLevelWindow(Object window);      §1.15.22
    public void checkWrite(FileDescriptor fd);              §1.15.23
    public void checkWrite(String file);                    §1.15.24
    protected int classDepth(String name);                  §1.15.25
    protected int classLoaderDepth();                       §1.15.26
    protected ClassLoader currentClassLoader();             §1.15.27
    protected Class[] getClassContext();                    §1.15.28
    public boolean getInCheck();                            §1.15.29
    public Object getSecurityContext();                     §1.15.30
    protected boolean inClass(String name);                 §1.15.31
    protected boolean inClassLoader();                      §1.15.32
}
```

The security manager is an abstract class that allows applications to implement a security policy. It allows an application to determine, before performing a possibly unsafe or sensitive operation, what the operation is and whether the operation is being performed by a class created via a class loader (**I-§1.4**) rather than installed locally. Classes loaded via a class loader (especially if they have been downloaded over a network) may be less trustworthy than classes from files installed locally. The application can allow or disallow the operation.

The SecurityManager class contains many methods with names that begin with the word check. These methods are called by various methods in the Java libraries before those methods perform certain potentially sensitive operations. The invocation of such a check method typically looks like this:

```
SecurityManager security = System.getSecurityManager();
if (security != null) {
    security.checkXXX(argument, ... );

}
```

The security manager is thereby given an opportunity to prevent completion of the operation by throwing an exception. A security manager routine simply returns if the operation is permitted, but throws a SecurityException (**I-§1.43**) if the operation is not permitted. The only exception to this convention is check-TopLevelWindow (**I-§1.15.22**), which returns a boolean value.

The current security manager is set by the setSecurityManager method (**I-§1.18.16**) in class System. The current security manager is obtained by the get-SecurityManager method (**I-§1.18.11**).

The default implementation of each of the checkXXX methods is to assume that the caller does *not* have permission to perform the requested operation.

Fields

---

inCheck   §1.15.1

```
protected boolean inCheck
```

This field is true if there is a security check in progress; false otherwise.

Constructors

SecurityManager   **§1.15.2**

```
protected SecurityManager()
```

Constructs a new `SecurityManager`. An application is not allowed to create a new security manager if there is already a current security manager (**I-§1.18.11**).

THROWS:

`SecurityException` (**I-§1.43**)
if a security manager already exists.

Methods

checkAccept   **§1.15.3**

```
public void checkAccept(String host, int port)
```

This method should throw a `SecurityException` if the calling thread is not permitted to accept a socket connection from the specified host and port number.

This method is invoked for the current security manager (**I-§1.18.11**) by the accept method (**I-§4.5.3**) of class `ServerSocket`.

The checkAccept method for class `SecurityManager` always throws a `SecurityException`.

PARAMETERS:

`host`: the host name of the socket connection.
`port`: the port number of the socket connection.

THROWS:

`SecurityException` (**I-§1.43**)
if the caller does not have permission to accept the connection.

checkAccess   §1.15.4

```
public void checkAccess(Thread g)
```

This method should throw a SecurityException if the calling thread is not allowed to modify the thread argument.

This method is invoked for the current security manager (**I-§1.18.11**) by the stop (**I-§1.19.37**), suspend (**I-§1.19.39**), resume (**I-§1.19.29**), setPriority (**I-§1.19.33**), setName (**I-§1.19.32**), and setDaemon (**I-§1.19.31**) methods of class Thread.

The checkAccess method for class SecurityManager always throws a SecurityException.

PARAMETERS:

g: the thread to be checked.

THROWS:

SecurityException (**I-§1.43**)

if the caller does not have permission to modify the thread.

checkAccess   §1.15.5

```
public void checkAccess(ThreadGroup g)
```

This method should throw a SecurityException if the calling thread is not allowed to modify the thread group argument.

This method is invoked for the current security manager (**I-§1.18.11**) when a new child thread or child thread group is created, and by the setDaemon (**I-§1.20.18**), setMaxPriority (**I-§1.20.19**), stop (**I-§1.20.20**), suspend (**I-§1.20.21**), resume (**I-§1.20.17**), and destroy (**I-§1.20.6**) methods of class ThreadGroup.

The checkAccess method for class SecurityManager always throws a SecurityException.

PARAMETERS:

g: the thread group to be checked.

THROWS:

SecurityException (**I-§1.43**)

if the caller does not have permission to modify the thread group.

checkConnect   §1.15.6

    public void checkConnect(String host, int port)

This method should throw a `SecurityException` if the calling thread is not allowed to open a socket connection to the specified host and port number.

A port number of -1 indicates that the calling method is attempting to determine the IP address of the specified host name.

The `checkConnect` method for class `SecurityManager` always throws a `SecurityException`.

PARAMETERS:

`host`: the host name port to connect to.
`port`: the protocol port to connect to.

THROWS:

`SecurityException` **(I-§1.43)**

if the caller does not have permission to open a socket connection to the specified `host` and `port`.

checkConnect   §1.15.7

    public void
    checkConnect(String host, int port, Object context)

This method should throw a `SecurityException` if the specified security context **(I-§1.15.30)** is not allowed to open a socket connection to the specified host and port number.

A port number of -1 indicates that the calling method is attempting to determine the IP address of the specified host name.

The `checkConnect` method for class `SecurityManager` always throws a `SecurityException`.

PARAMETERS:

`host`: the host name port to connect to.
`port`: the protocol port to connect to.
`context`: a system-dependent security context.

THROWS:

`SecurityException` **(I-§1.43)**

if the specified security context does not have permission to open a socket connection to the specified `host` and `port`.

checkCreateClassLoader   §1.15.8

`public void checkCreateClassLoader()`

This method should throw a `SecurityException` if the calling thread is not allowed to create a new class loader (**I-§1.4.1**).

The `checkCreateClassLoader` method for class `SecurityManager` always throws a `SecurityException`.

THROWS:

`SecurityException` (**I-§1.43**)
if the caller does not have permission to create a new class loader.

checkDelete   §1.15.9

`public void checkDelete(String file)`

This method should throw a `SecurityException` if the calling thread is not allowed to delete the specified file.

This method is invoked for the current security manager (**I-§1.18.11**) by the `delete` method (**I-§2.7.10**) of class `File`.

The `checkDelete` method for class `SecurityManager` always throws a `SecurityException`.

PARAMETERS:

`file`: the system-dependent filename.

THROWS:

`SecurityException` (**I-§1.43**)
if the caller does not have permission to delete the file.

checkExec   §1.15.10

`public void checkExec(String cmd)`

This method should throw a `SecurityException` if the calling thread is not allowed to create a subprocss.

This method is invoked for the current security manager (**I-§1.18.11**) by the `exec` methods (**I-§1.14.1–§1.14.4**) of class `Runtime`.

The `checkExec` method for class `SecurityManager` always throws a `SecurityException`.

PARAMETERS:

`cmd`: the specified system command.

THROWS:

`SecurityException` (**I-§1.43**)
if the caller does not have permission to create a subprocess.

checkExit §1.15.11

`public void checkExit(int status)`

This method should throw a `SecurityException` if the calling thread is not allowed to cause the Java Virtual Machine to halt with the specified status code.

This method is invoked for the current security manager (**I-§1.18.11**) by the `exit` method (**I-§1.14.5**) of class `Runtime`. A status of 0 indicates success; other values indicate various errors.

The `checkExit` method for class `SecurityManager` always throws a `SecurityException`.

PARAMETERS:

`status`: the exit status.

THROWS:

`SecurityException` (**I-§1.43**)

if the caller does not have permission to halt the Java Virtual Machine with the specified status.

checkLink §1.15.12

`public void checkLink(String lib)`

This method should throw a `SecurityException` if the calling thread is not allowed to dynamic link the library code specified by the string argument file. The argument is either a simple library name or a complete filename.

This method is invoked for the current security manager (**I-§1.18.11**) by methods `load` (**I-§1.14.11**) and `loadLibrary` (**I-§1.14.12**) of class `Runtime`.

The `checkLink` method for class `SecurityManager` always throws a `SecurityException`.

PARAMETERS:

`lib`: the name of the library.

THROWS:

`SecurityException` (**I-§1.43**)

if the caller does not have permission to dynamically link the library.

checkListen   §1.15.13

```
public void checkListen(int port)
```

This method should throw a SecurityException if the calling thread is not allowed to wait for a connection request on the specified local port number.

The checkListen method for class SecurityManager always throws a SecurityException.

PARAMETERS:

port: the local port.

THROWS:

SecurityException (I-§1.43)

if the caller does not have permission to listen on the specified port.

checkPackageAccess   §1.15.14

```
public void checkPackageAccess(String pkg)
```

This method should throw a SecurityException if the calling thread is allowed to access the package specified by the argument.

This method is used by the loadClass method (I-§1.4.4) of class loaders.

The checkPackageAccess method for class SecurityManager always throws a SecurityException.

PARAMETERS:

pkg: the package name.

THROWS:

SecurityException (I-§1.43)

if the caller does not have permission to access the specified package.

checkPackageDefinition   §1.15.15

```
public void checkPackageDefinition(String pkg)
```

This method should throw a SecurityException if the calling thread is not allowed to define classes in the package specified by the argument.

This method is used by the loadClass method (I-§1.4.4) of some class loaders.

The checkPackageDefinition method for class SecurityManager always throws a SecurityException.

PARAMETERS:

pkg: the package name.

THROWS:

SecurityException (I-§1.43)

if the caller does not have permission to define classes in the specified package.

checkPropertiesAccess §1.15.16

```
public void checkPropertiesAccess()
```

This method should throw a SecurityException if the calling thread is not allowed to access or modify the system properties.

This method is used by the getProperties **(I-§1.18.8)** and setProperties **(I-§1.18.15)** methods of class System.

The checkPropertiesAccess method for class SecurityManager always throws a SecurityException.

THROWS:

SecurityException **(I-§1.43)**

if the caller does not have permission to access or modify the system properties.

checkPropertyAccess §1.15.17

```
public void checkPropertyAccess(String key)
```

This method should throw a SecurityException if the calling thread is not allowed to access the system property with the specified key name.

This method is used by the getProperty **(I-§1.18.9)** method of class System.

The checkPropertiesAccess method for class SecurityManager always throws a SecurityException.

PARAMETERS:

key: a system property key.

THROWS:

SecurityException **(I-§1.43)**

if the caller does not have permission to access the specified system property.

checkRead §1.15.18

```
public void checkRead(FileDescriptor fd)
```

This method should throw a SecurityException if the calling thread is not allowed to read from the specified file descriptor **(I-§2.8)**.

The checkRead method for class SecurityManager always throws a SecurityException.

PARAMETERS:

fd: the system-dependent file descriptor.

THROWS:

SecurityException **(I-§1.43)**

if the caller does not have permission to access the specified file descriptor.

checkRead   §1.15.19

```
public void checkRead(String file)
```

This method should throw a `SecurityException` if the calling thread is not allowed to read the file specified by the string argument.

The `checkRead` method for class `SecurityManager` always throws a `SecurityException`.

PARAMETERS:

`file`: the system-dependent file name.

THROWS:

`SecurityException` **(I-§1.43)**

if the caller does not have permission to access the specified file.

checkRead   §1.15.20

```
public void checkRead(String file, Object context)
```

This method should throw a `SecurityException` if the specified security context is not allowed to read the file specified by the string argument. The context must be a security context returned by a previous call to `get-SecurityContext` **(I-§1.15.30)**.

The `checkRead` method for class `SecurityManager` always throws a `SecurityException`.

PARAMETERS:

`file`: the system-dependent filename.
`context`: a system-dependent security context.

THROWS:

`SecurityException` **(I-§1.43)**

if the specified security context does not have permission to read the specified file.

checkSetFactory   §1.15.21

```
public void checkSetFactory()
```

This method should throw a `SecurityException` if the calling thread is not allowed to set the socket factor used by `ServerSocket` **(I-§4.5.7)** or `Socket` **(I-§4.6.11)**, or the stream handler factory used by URL **(I-§4.8.16)**.

The `checkSetFactory` method for class `SecurityManager` always throws a `SecurityException`.

THROWS:

`SecurityException` **(I-§1.43)**

if the caller does not have permission to specify a socket factory or a stream handler factory.

checkTopLevelWindow   §1.15.22

`public boolean checkTopLevelWindow(Object window)`

This method should return `false` if the calling thread is not trusted to bring up the top-level window indicated by the `window` argument. In this case, the caller can still decide to show the window, but the window should include some sort of visual warning. If the method returns `true`, then the window can be shown without any special restrictions.

See class `Window` **(II-§1.42)** for more information on trusted and untrusted windows.

The `checkSetFactory` method for class `SecurityManager` always returns `false`.

PARAMETERS:

`window`: the new window that is being created.

RETURNS:

`true` if the caller is trusted to put up top-level windows; `false` otherwise.

checkWrite   §1.15.23

`public void checkWrite(FileDescriptor fd)`

This method should throw a `SecurityException` if the calling thread is not allowed to write to the specified file descriptor **(I-§2.8)**.

The `checkWrite` method for class `SecurityManager` always throws a `SecurityException`.

PARAMETERS:

`fd`: the system-dependent file descriptor.

THROWS:

`SecurityException` **(I-§1.43)**

if the caller does not have permission to access the specified file descriptor.

checkWrite   §1.15.24

`public void checkWrite(String file)`

This method should throw a `SecurityException` if the calling thread is not allowed to write to the file specified by the string argument.

The `checkWrite` method for class `SecurityManager` always throws a `SecurityException`.

PARAMETERS:

`file`: the system-dependent filename.

THROWS:

`SecurityException` **(I-§1.43)**

if the caller does not have permission to access the specified file.

classDepth   §1.15.25

> `protected int classDepth(String name)`
>
> Determines the stack depth of a given class.
>
> **PARAMETERS:**
>
> name: the fully qualified name of the class to search for.
>
> **RETURNS:**
>
> the depth on the stack frame of the first occurrence of a method from a class
> with the specified name; -1 if such a frame cannot be found.

classLoaderDepth   §1.15.26

> `protected int classLoaderDepth()`
>
> Determines the stack depth of the most recently executing method from a
> class defined using a class loader.
>
> **RETURNS:**
>
> the depth on the stack frame of the most recent occurrence of a method from
> a class defined using a class loader; returns -1 if there is no occurrence of
> a method from a class defined using a class loader.

currentClassLoader   §1.15.27

> `protected ClassLoader currentClassLoader()`
>
> Determines the most recent class loader executing on the stack.
>
> **RETURNS:**
>
> the class loader of the most recent occurrence on the stack of a method from
> a class defined using a class loader; returns null if there is no occurrence
> on the stack of a method from a class defined using a class loader.

getClassContext   §1.15.28

> `protected Class[] getClassContext()`
>
> Calculates the current execution stack, which is returned as an array of
> classes.
>
> The length of the array is the number of methods on the execution stack.
> The element at index 0 is the class of the currently executing method, the
> element at index 1 is the class of that method's caller, and so on.
>
> **RETURNS:**
>
> the execution stack.

getInCheck   §1.15.29

    public boolean getInCheck()

RETURNS:

the value of the inCheck (**I-§1.15.1**) field. This field should contain true if a
security check is in progress; false otherwise.

getSecurityContext   §1.15.30

    public Object getSecurityContext()

Creates an object that encapsulates the current execution environment.
The result of this method is used by the three-argument checkConnect
method (**I-§1.15.7**) and by the two-argument checkRead method (**I-§1.15.20**).

These methods are needed because a trusted method may be called on to
read a file or open a socket on behalf of another method. The trusted method
needs to determine if the other (possibly untrusted) method would be
allowed to perform the operation on its own.

RETURNS:

an implementation-dependent object that encapsulates sufficient information
about the current execution environment to perform some security checks
later.

inClass   §1.15.31

    protected boolean inClass(String name)

PARAMETERS:

name: the fully qualified name of the class.

RETURNS:

true if a method from a class with the specified name is on the execution
stack; false otherwise.

inClassLoader   §1.15.32

    protected boolean inClassLoader()

RETURNS:

true if a method from a class defined using a class loader is on the execution
stack.

1.16 Class String

```
public final class java.lang.String
    extends java.lang.Object (I-§1.12)
{
    // Constructors
    public String();                                        §1.16.1
    public String(byte ascii[], int hibyte);                §1.16.2
    public String(byte ascii[], int hibyte,                 §1.16.3
                int offset, int count);
    public String(char value[]);                            §1.16.4
    public String(char value[], int offset, int count);     §1.16.5
    public String(String value);                            §1.16.6
    public String(StringBuffer buffer);                     §1.16.7

    // Methods
    public char charAt(int index);                          §1.16.8
    public int compareTo(String anotherString);             §1.16.9
    public String concat(String str);                       §1.16.10
    public static String copyValueOf(char data[]);          §1.16.11
    public static String                                    §1.16.12
        copyValueOf(char data[], int offset, int count);
    public boolean endsWith(String suffix);                 §1.16.13
    public boolean equals(Object anObject);                 §1.16.14
    public boolean equalsIgnoreCase(String anotherString);  §1.16.15
    public void getBytes(int srcBegin, int srcEnd,          §1.16.16
                    byte dst[], int dstBegin);
    public void getChars(int srcBegin, int srcEnd,          §1.16.17
                    char dst[], int dstBegin);
    public int hashCode();                                  §1.16.18
    public int indexOf(int ch);                             §1.16.19
    public int indexOf(int ch, int fromIndex);              §1.16.20
    public int indexOf(String str);                         §1.16.21
    public int indexOf(String str, int fromIndex);          §1.16.22
    public String intern();                                 §1.16.23
    public int lastIndexOf(int ch);                         §1.16.24
    public int lastIndexOf(int ch, int fromIndex);          §1.16.25
    public int lastIndexOf(String str);                     §1.16.26
    public int lastIndexOf(String str,                      §1.16.27
                    int fromIndex);
    public int length();                                    §1.16.28
    public boolean regionMatches(boolean ignoreCase,        §1.16.29
                        int toffset, String other,
                        int ooffset, int len);
    public boolean regionMatches(int toffset,               §1.16.30
                        String other,
                        int ooffset, int len);
    public String replace(char oldChar, char newChar);      §1.16.31
    public boolean startsWith(String prefix);               §1.16.32
```

```
public boolean startsWith(String prefix, int toffset);   §1.16.33
public String substring(int beginIndex);                 §1.16.34
public String substring(int beginIndex, int endIndex);   §1.16.35
public char[] toCharArray();                             §1.16.36
public String toLowerCase();                             §1.16.37
public String toString();                               §1.16.38
public String toUpperCase();                            §1.16.39
public String trim();                                   §1.16.40
public static String valueOf(boolean b);                §1.16.41
public static String valueOf(char c);                   §1.16.42
public static String valueOf(char data[]);              §1.16.43
public static String                                    §1.16.44
    valueOf(char data[], int offset, int count);
public static String valueOf(double d);                 §1.16.45
public static String valueOf(float f);                  §1.16.46
public static String valueOf(int i);                    §1.16.47
public static String valueOf(long l);                   §1.16.48
public static String valueOf(Object obj);               §1.16.49
}
```

The String class represents character strings. All string literals in Java programs, such as "abc", are implemented as instances of this class.

Strings are constant; their values cannot be changed after they are created. String buffers (I-§1.17) support mutable strings.

The class String includes methods for examining individual characters of the sequence, for comparing strings, for searching strings, for extracting substrings, and for creating a copy of a string with all characters translated to uppercase or to lowercase.

Constructors

String   §1.16.1

```
public String()
```

Allocates a new String containing no characters.

String   §1.16.2

```
public String(byte ascii[], int hibyte)
```

Allocates a new String containing characters constructed from an array of 8-bit integer values. Each character c in the resulting string is constructed from the corresponding component b in the byte array such that

$$c == (\text{char})(((hibyte \text{ \& } 0xff) << 8) \mid (b \text{ \& } 0xff))$$

PARAMETERS:

ascii: the bytes to be converted to characters.
hibyte: the top 8 bits of each 16-bit Unicode character.

String   §1.16.3

```
public String(byte ascii[], int hibyte, int offset,
              int count)
```

Allocates a new `String` constructed from a subarray of an array of 8-bit integer values.

The `offset` argument is the index of the first byte of the subarray, and the `count` argument specifies the length of the subarray.

Each `byte` in the subarray is converted to a `char` as specified in the method above (**I-§1.16.2**).

PARAMETERS:

`ascii`: the bytes to be converted to characters.
`hibyte`: the top 8 bits of each 16-bit Unicode character.
`offset`: the initial offset.
`count`: the length.

THROWS:

`StringIndexOutOfBoundsException` (**I-§1.44**)
if the `offset` or `count` argument is invalid.

String   §1.16.4

```
public String(char value[])
```

Allocates a new `String` so that it represents the sequence of characters currently contained in the character array argument.

PARAMETERS:

`value`: the initial value of the string.

String   §1.16.5

```
public String(char value[], int offset, int count)
```

Allocates a new `String` that contains characters from a subarray of the character array argument. The `offset` argument is the index of the first character of the subarray and the `count` argument specifies the length of the subarray.

PARAMETERS:

`value`: array that is the source of characters.
`offset`: the initial offset.
`count`: the length.

THROWS:

`StringIndexOutOfBoundsException` (**I-§1.44**)
if the `offset` and `count` arguments index characters outside the bounds of the `value` array.

String §1.16.6

```
public String(String value)
```

Allocates a new string that contains the same sequence of characters as the string argument.

PARAMETERS:

`value:` a `String`.

String §1.16.7

```
public String(StringBuffer buffer)
```

Allocates a new string that contains the sequence of characters currently contained in the string buffer argument.

PARAMETERS:

`buffer:` a `StringBuffer`.

Methods

charAt §1.16.8

```
public char charAt(int index)
```

RETURNS:

the character at the specified index of this string. The first character is at index 0.

PARAMETERS:

`index:` the index of the character.

THROWS:

`StringIndexOutOfBoundsException` (**I-§1.44**)

if the index is out of range.

compareTo §1.16.9

```
public int compareTo(String anotherString)
```

Compares two strings lexicographically.

PARAMETERS:

`anotherString:` the `String` to be compared.

RETURNS:

the value 0 if the argument string is equal to this string; a value less than 0 if this string is lexicographically less than the string argument; and a value greater than 0 if this string is lexicographically greater than the string argument.

concat   §1.16.10

```
public String concat(String str)
```

Concatenates the string argument to the end of this string.

If the length of the argument string is 0, then this object is returned.

PARAMETERS:

str: the String that is concatenated to the end of this String.

RETURNS:

a string that represents the concatenation of this object's characters followed by the string argument's characters.

copyValueOf   §1.16.11

```
public static String copyValueOf(char data[])
```

RETURNS:

a String that contains the characters of the character array.

PARAMETERS:

data: the character array.

copyValueOf   §1.16.12

```
public static String
copyValueOf(char data[], int offset, int count)
```

PARAMETERS:

data: the character array.
offset: initial offset of the subarray.
count: length of the subarray.

RETURNS:

a String that contains the characters of the specified subarray of the character array.

endsWith   §1.16.13

```
public boolean endsWith(String suffix)
```

PARAMETERS:

suffix: the suffix.

RETURNS:

true if the character sequence represented by the argument is a suffix of the character sequence represented by this object; false otherwise.

equals §1.16.14

```
public boolean equals(Object anObject)
```

The result is `true` if and only if the argument is not `null` and is a `String` object that represents the same sequence of characters as this object.

PARAMETERS:

`anObject`: the object to compare this `String` against.

RETURNS:

`true` if the `String` are equal; `false` otherwise.

OVERRIDES:

`equals` in class `Object` (I-§1.12.3).

SEE ALSO:

`equalsIgnoreCase` (I-§1.16.15).

`compareTo` (I-§1.16.9).

equalsIgnoreCase §1.16.15

```
public boolean equalsIgnoreCase(String anotherString)
```

The result is `true` if and only if the argument is not `null` and is a `String` object that represents the same sequence of characters as this object, where case is ignored.

Two characters are considered the same, ignoring case, if at least one of the following is true:

♦ The two characters are the same (as compared by the == operator).

♦ Applying the method `Character.toUppercase` (I-§1.2.24) to each character produces the same result.

♦ Applying the method `Character.toLowercase` (I-§) to each character produces the same result.

Two sequences of characters are the same, ignoring case, if the sequences have the same length and corresponding characters are the same, ignoring case.

PARAMETERS:

`anotherString`: the `String` to compare this `String` against.

RETURNS:

`true` if the `Strings` are equal, ignoring case; `false` otherwise.

getBytes   §1.16.16

```
public void getBytes(int srcBegin, int srcEnd,
                     byte dst[], int dstBegin)
```

Copies characters from this string into the destination byte array. Each byte receives the 8 low-order bits of the corresponding character.

The first character to be copied is at index srcBegin; the last character to be copied is at index srcEnd-1. The total number of characters to be copied is srcEnd-srcBegin. The characters, converted to bytes, are copied into the subarray of dst starting at index dstBegin and ending at index:

```
dstbegin + (srcEnd-srcBegin) - 1
```

PARAMETERS:

srcBegin: index of the first character in the string to copy.
srcEnd: index after the last character in the string to copy.
dst: the destination array.
dstBegin: the start offset in the destination array.

getChars   §1.16.17

```
public void getChars(int srcBegin, int srcEnd,
                     char dst[], int dstBegin)
```

Copies characters from this string into the destination character array.

The first character to be copied is at index srcBegin; the last character to be copied is at index srcEnd-1 (thus the total number of characters to be copied is srcEnd-srcBegin). The characters are copied into the subarray of dst starting at index dstBegin and ending at index:

```
dstbegin + (srcEnd-srcBegin) - 1
```

PARAMETERS:

srcBegin: index of the first character in the string to copy.
srcEnd: index after the last character in the string to copy.
dst: the destination array.
dstBegin: the start offset in the destination array.

hashCode   §1.16.18

```
public int hashCode()
```

RETURNS:

a hash code value for this object.

OVERRIDES:

hashCode in class Object (I-§1.12.6).

indexOf §1.16.19

```
public int indexOf(int ch)
```

PARAMETERS:

ch: a character.

RETURNS:

the index of the first occurrence of the character in the character sequence represented by this object, or -1 if the character does not occur.

indexOf §1.16.20

```
public int indexOf(int ch, int fromIndex)
```

PARAMETERS:

ch: a character.
fromIndex: the index to start the search from.

RETURNS:

the index of the first occurrence of the character in the character sequence represented by this object that is greater than or equal to fromIndex, or -1 if the character does not occur.

indexOf §1.16.21

```
public int indexOf(String str)
```

PARAMETERS:

str: any string.

RETURNS:

if the string argument occurs as a substring within this object, then the index of the first character of the first such substring is returned; if it does not occur as a substring, -1 is returned.

indexOf §1.16.22

```
public int indexOf(String str, int fromIndex)
```

PARAMETERS:

str: the substring to search for.
fromIndex: the index to start the search from.

RETURNS:

If the string argument occurs as a substring within this object at a starting index no smaller than fromIndex, then the index of the first character of the first such substring is returned. If it does not occur as a substring starting at fromIndex or beyond, -1 is returned.

intern   §1.16.23

    public String intern()

Creates a canonical representation for the string object.

If s and t are strings such that s.equals(t), it is guaranteed that
s.intern() == t.intern().

RETURNS:

a string that has the same contents as this string, but is guaranteed to be from
a pool of unique strings.

lastIndexOf   §1.16.24

    public int lastIndexOf(int ch)

PARAMETERS:

ch: a character.

RETURNS:

the index of the last occurrence of the character in the character sequence
represented by this object, or –1 if the character does not occur.

lastIndexOf   §1.16.25

    public int lastIndexOf(int ch, int fromIndex)

PARAMETERS:

ch: a character.
fromIndex: the index to start the search from.

RETURNS:

the index of the last occurrence of the character in the character sequence
represented by this object that is less than or equal to fromIndex, or –1 if
the character does not occur before that point.

lastIndexOf   §1.16.26

    public int lastIndexOf(String str)

PARAMETERS:

str: the substring to search for.

RETURNS:

if the string argument occurs one or more times as a substring within this
object, then the index of the first character of the last such substring is
returned. If it does not occur as a substring, –1 is returned.

lastIndexOf §1.16.27

`public int lastIndexOf(String str, int fromIndex)`

PARAMETERS:

`str`: the substring to search for.
`fromIndex`: the index to start the search from.

RETURNS:

If the string argument occurs one or more times as a substring within this object at a starting index no greater than `fromIndex` then the index of the first character of the last such substring is returned. If it does not occur as a substring starting at `fromIndex` or earlier, -1 is returned.

length §1.16.28

`public int length()`

RETURNS:

the length of the sequence of characters represented by this object.

regionMatches §1.16.29

```
public boolean
regionMatches(boolean ignoreCase, int toffset,
              String other, int ooffset, int len)
```

Determines if two string regions are equal.

If `toffset` or `ooffset` is negative, or if `toffset+length` is greater than the length of this string, or if `ooffset+length` is greater than the length of the string argument, then this method returns `false`.

PARAMETERS:

`ignoreCase`: if `true`, ignore case when comparing characters.
`toffset`: starting offset of the subregion in this string.
`other`: string argument.
`ooffset`: starting offset of the subregion in the string argument.
`len`: the number of characters to compare.

RETURNS:

`true` if the specified subregion of this string matches the specified subregion of the string argument; `false` otherwise. Whether the matching is exact or case insensitive depends on the `ignoreCase` argument.

regionMatches   §1.16.30

```
public boolean
regionMatches(int toffset, String other,
              int ooffset, int len)
```

Determines if two string regions are equal.

If `toffset` or `ooffset` is negative, or if `toffset+length` is greater than the length of this string, or if `ooffset+length` is greater than the length of the string argument, then this method returns `false`.

PARAMETERS:

`toffset`: starting offset of the subregion in this string.
`other`: string argument.
`ooffset`: starting offset of the subregion in the string argument.
`len`: the number of characters to compare.

RETURNS:

`true` if the specified subregion of this string exactly matches the specified subregion of the string argument; `false` otherwise.

replace   §1.16.31

```
public String replace(char oldChar, char newChar)
```

Returns a new string resulting from replacing all occurrences of `oldChar` in this string with `newChar`.

If the character `oldChar` does not occur in the character sequence represented by this object, then this string is returned.

PARAMETERS:

`oldChar`: the old character.
`newChar`: the new character.

RETURNS:

a string derived from this string by replacing every occurrence of `oldChar` with `newChar`.

startsWith   §1.16.32

```
public boolean startsWith(String prefix)
```

PARAMETERS:

`prefix`: the prefix.

RETURNS:

`true` if the character sequence represented by the argument is a prefix of the character sequence represented by this string; `false` otherwise.

startsWith §1.16.33

```
public boolean startsWith(String prefix, int toffset)
```

PARAMETERS:

prefix: the prefix.

toffset: where to begin looking in the string.

RETURNS:

true if the character sequence represented by the argument is a prefix of the substring of this object starting at index toffset; false otherwise.

substring §1.16.34

```
public String substring(int beginIndex)
```

Creates a new string that is a substring of this string. The substring begins at the specified index and extends to the end of this string.

PARAMETERS:

beginIndex: the beginning index, inclusive.

RETURNS:

the specified substring.

THROWS:

StringIndexOutOfBoundsException (I-§1.44)
if the beginIndex is out of range.

substring §1.16.35

```
public String substring(int beginIndex, int endIndex)
```

Creates a new string that is a substring of this string. The substring begins at the specified beginIndex and extends to the character at index endIndex − 1.

PARAMETERS:

beginIndex: the beginning index, inclusive.

endIndex: the ending index, exclusive.

RETURNS:

the specified substring.

THROWS:

StringIndexOutOfBoundsException (I-§1.44)
if the beginIndex or the endIndex is out of range.

toCharArray §1.16.36

```
public char[] toCharArray()
```

RETURNS:

a newly allocated character array whose length is the length of this string and whose contents are initialized to contain the character sequence represented by this string.

toLowerCase   §1.16.37

`public String toLowerCase()`

Converts a string to lowercase.

If no character in this string has a different lowercase version (**I-§**), then this string is returned.

Otherwise, a new string is allocated, whose length is identical to this string, and such that each character that has a different lowercase version is mapped to this lowercase equivalent.

RETURNS:

the string, converted to lowercase.

toString   §1.16.38

`public String toString()`

This object (which is already a string!) is itself returned.

RETURNS:

the string itself.

OVERRIDES:

`toString` in class `Object` (**I-§1.12.9**).

toUpperCase   §1.16.39

`public String toUpperCase()`

Converts a string to uppercase.

If no character in this string has a different uppercase version (**I-§1.2.24**), then this string is returned.

Otherwise, a new string is allocated, whose length is identical to this string, and such that each character that has a different uppercase version is mapped to this uppercase equivalent.

RETURNS:

the string, converted to uppercase.

trim   §1.16.40

`public String trim()`

Removes white space from both ends of a string.

All characters that have codes less than or equal to `'\u0020'` (the space character) are considered to be white space.

RETURNS:

this string, with white space removed from the front and end.

valueOf §1.16.41

`public static String valueOf(boolean b)`

Creates the string representation of the `boolean` argument.

PARAMETERS:

b: a `boolean`.

RETURNS:

if the argument is `true`, a string equal to `"true"` is returned; otherwise, a string equal to `"false"` is returned.

valueOf §1.16.42

`public static String valueOf(char c)`

Creates the string representation of the `char` argument.

PARAMETERS:

c: a `char`.

RETURNS:

a newly allocated string of length 1 containing as its single character the argument c.

valueOf §1.16.43

`public static String valueOf(char data[])`

Creates the string representation of the `char` array argument.

PARAMETERS:

data: a `char` array.

RETURNS:

a newly allocated string representing the same sequence of characters contained in the character array argument.

valueOf   §1.16.44

```
public static String
valueOf(char data[], int offset, int count)
```

Creates the string representation of a specific subarray of the char array argument.

The offset argument is the index of the first character of the subarray. The count argument specifies the length of the subarray.

PARAMETERS:

data: the character array.
offset: the initial offset into the value of the String.
count: the length of the value of the String.

RETURNS:

a newly allocated string representing the sequence of characters contained in the subarray of the character array argument.

valueOf   §1.16.45

```
public static String valueOf(double d)
```

Creates the string representation of the double argument.

The representation is exactly the one returned by the Double.toString method of one argument (**I-§1.6.21**).

PARAMETERS:

d: a double.

RETURNS:

a newly allocated string containing a string representation of the double argument.

valueOf   §1.16.46

```
public static String valueOf(float f)
```

Creates the string representation of the float argument.

The representation is exactly the one returned by the Float.toString method of one argument (**I-§1.7.22**).

PARAMETERS:

f: a float.

RETURNS:

a newly allocated string containing a string representation of the float argument.

valueOf §1.16.47

```
public static String valueOf(int i)
```

Creates the string representation of the `int` argument.

The representation is exactly the one returned by the `Integer.toString` method of one argument (**I-§1.8.20**).

PARAMETERS:

`i`: an `int`.

RETURNS:

a newly allocated string containing a string representation of the `int` argument.

valueOf §1.16.48

```
public static String valueOf(long l)
```

Creates the string representation of the `long` argument.

The representation is exactly the one returned by the `Long.toString` method of one argument (**I-§1.9.20**).

PARAMETERS:

`l`: a `long`.

RETURNS:

a newly allocated string containing a string representation of the `long` argument.

valueOf §1.16.49

```
public static String valueOf(Object obj)
```

Creates the string representation of the `Object` argument.

PARAMETERS:

`obj`: an `Object`.

RETURNS:

if the argument is `null`, then a string equal to `"null"`; otherwise, the value of `obj.toString()` is returned.

SEE ALSO:

`toString` in class `Object` (**I-§1.12.9**).

1.17 Class StringBuffer

```
public class java.lang.StringBuffer
    extends java.lang.Object (I-§1.12)
{
    // Constructors
    public StringBuffer();                                      §1.17.1
    public StringBuffer(int length);                            §1.17.2
    public StringBuffer(String str);                            §1.17.3

    // Methods
    public StringBuffer append(boolean b);                      §1.17.4
    public StringBuffer append(char c);                         §1.17.5
    public StringBuffer append(char str[]);                     §1.17.6
    public StringBuffer                                         §1.17.7
           append(char str[], int offset, int len);
    public StringBuffer append(double d);                       §1.17.8
    public StringBuffer append(float f);                        §1.17.9
    public StringBuffer append(int i);                          §1.17.10
    public StringBuffer append(long l);                         §1.17.11
    public StringBuffer append(Object obj);                     §1.17.12
    public StringBuffer append(String str);                     §1.17.13
    public int capacity();                                      §1.17.14
    public char charAt(int index);                             §1.17.15
    public void ensureCapacity(int minimumCapacity);            §1.17.16
    public void getChars(int srcBegin, int srcEnd,              §1.17.17
                         char dst[], int dstBegin);
    public StringBuffer insert(int offset, boolean b);          §1.17.18
    public StringBuffer insert(int offset, char c);             §1.17.19
    public StringBuffer insert(int offset, char str[]);         §1.17.20
    public StringBuffer insert(int offset, double d);           §1.17.21
    public StringBuffer insert(int offset, float f);            §1.17.22
    public StringBuffer insert(int offset, int i);              §1.17.23
    public StringBuffer insert(int offset, long l);             §1.17.24
    public StringBuffer insert(int offset, Object obj);         §1.17.25
    public StringBuffer insert(int offset, String str);         §1.17.26
    public int length();                                        §1.17.27
    public StringBuffer reverse();                              §1.17.28
    public void setCharAt(int index, char ch);                  §1.17.29
    public void setLength(int newLength);                       §1.17.30
    public String toString();                                   §1.17.31
}
```

A string buffer implements a mutable sequence of characters.

String buffers are safe for use by multiple threads. The methods are synchronized where necessary so that all the operations on any particular instance behave as if they occur in some serial order.

String buffers are used by the compiler to implement the binary string concatenation operator +. For example, the code

```
x = "a" + 4 + "c"
```

is compiled to the equivalent of:

```
x = new StringBuffer().append("a").append(4).append("c")
                      .toString()
```

The principal operations on a `StringBuffer` are the `append` and `insert` methods, which are overloaded so as to accept data of any type. Each effectively converts a given datum to a string and then appends or inserts the characters of that string to the string buffer. The `append` method always adds these characters at the end of the buffer; the `insert` method adds the characters at a specified point.

For example, if z refers to a string buffer object whose current contents are "start", then the method call `z.append("le")` would cause the string buffer to contain "startle", whereas `z.insert(4, "le")` would alter the string buffer to contain "starlet".

Every string buffer has a capacity. As long as the length of the character sequence contained in the string buffer does not exceed the capacity, it is not necessary to allocate a new internal buffer array. If the internal buffer overflows, it is automatically made larger.

SEE ALSO:
`String` (I-§1.16).
`ByteArrayOutputStream` (I-§2.4).

Constructors

StringBuffer   §1.17.1

```
public StringBuffer()
```

Constructs a string buffer with no characters in it and an initial capacity of 16 characters.

StringBuffer   §1.17.2

```
public StringBuffer(int length)
```

Constructs a string buffer with no characters in it and an initial capacity specified by the `length` argument.

PARAMETERS:
`length`: the initial capacity.

THROWS:
`NegativeArraySizeException` (I-§1.38)
if the `length` argument is less than 0.

StringBuffer   §1.17.3

    `public StringBuffer(String str)`

   Constructs a string buffer so that it represents the same sequence of characters as the string argument. The initial capacity of the string buffer is 16 plus the length of the string argument.

PARAMETERS:

`str:` the initial contents of the buffer.

Methods

---

append   §1.17.4

    `public StringBuffer append(boolean b)`

   Appends the string representation of the `boolean` argument to the string buffer.

   The argument is converted to a string as if by the method `String.valueOf` (**I-§1.16.41**), and the characters of that string are then appended (**I-§1.17.13**) to this string buffer.

PARAMETERS:

`b:` a `boolean`.

RETURNS:

this string buffer.

append   §1.17.5

    `public StringBuffer append(char c)`

   Appends the string representation of the `char` argument to this string buffer.

   The argument is appended to the contents of this string buffer. The length of this string buffer increases by 1.

PARAMETERS:

`ch:` a `char`.

RETURNS:

this string buffer.

append   §1.17.6

```
public StringBuffer append(char str[])
```

Appends the string representation of the char array argument to this string buffer.

The characters of the array argument are appended, in order, to the contents of this string buffer. The length of this string buffer increases by the length of the argument.

PARAMETERS:

str: the characters to be appended.

RETURNS:

this string buffer.

append   §1.17.7

```
public StringBuffer append(char str[], int offset, int len)
```

Appends the string representation of a subarray of the char array argument to this string buffer.

Characters of the character array str, starting at index offset, are appended, in order, to the contents of this string buffer. The length of this string buffer increases by the value of len.

PARAMETERS:

str: the characters to be appended.
offset: the index of the first character to append.
len: the number of characters to append.

RETURNS:

this string buffer.

append   §1.17.8

```
public StringBuffer append(double d)
```

Appends the string representation of the double argument to this string buffer.

The argument is converted to a string as if by the method String.valueOf (**I-§1.16.45**), and the characters of that string are then appended (**I-§1.17.13**) to this string buffer.

PARAMETERS:

d: a double.

RETURNS:

this string buffer.

append   §1.17.9

```
public StringBuffer append(float f)
```

Appends the string representation of the `float` argument to this string buffer.

The argument is converted to a string as if by the method `String.valueOf` (**I-§1.16.46**), and the characters of that string are then appended (**I-§1.17.13**) to this string buffer.

PARAMETERS:

`f:` a `float`.

RETURNS:

this string buffer.

append   §1.17.10

```
public StringBuffer append(int i)
```

Appends the string representation of the `int` argument to this string buffer.

The argument is converted to a string as if by the method `String.valueOf` (**I-§1.16.47**), and the characters of that string are then appended (**I-§1.17.13**) to this string buffer.

PARAMETERS:

`i:` an `int`.

RETURNS:

this string buffer.

append   §1.17.11

```
public StringBuffer append(long l)
```

Appends the string representation of the `long` argument to this string buffer.

The argument is converted to a string as if by the method `String.valueOf` (**I-§1.16.48**), and the characters of that string are then appended (**I-§1.17.13**) to this string buffer.

PARAMETERS:

`l:` a `long`.

RETURNS:

this string buffer.

append   §1.17.12

```
public StringBuffer append(Object obj)
```

Appends the string representation of the `Object` argument to this string buffer.

The argument is converted to a string as if by the method `String.valueOf` **(I-§1.17.3)**, and the characters of that string are then appended **(I-§1.17.13)** to this string buffer.

PARAMETERS:

`obj`: an `Object`.

RETURNS:

this string buffer.

append   §1.17.13

```
public StringBuffer append(String str)
```

Appends the string to this string buffer.

The characters of the `String` argument are appended, in order, to the contents of this string buffer, increasing the length of this string buffer by the length of the argument.

PARAMETERS:

`str`: a string.

RETURNS:

this string buffer.

capacity   §1.17.14

```
public int capacity()
```

RETURNS:

the current capacity of this string buffer.

charAt   §1.17.15

```
public char charAt(int index)
```

Determines the character at a specific index in this string buffer.

The first character of a string buffer is at index 0, the next at index 1, and so on, for array indexing.

The index argument must be greater than or equal to 0, and less than the length (**I-§1.17.27**) of this string buffer.

PARAMETERS:

index: the index of the desired character.

RETURNS:

the character at the specified index of this string buffer.

THROWS:

StringIndexOutOfBoundsException (**I-§1.44**)
if the index is invalid.

ensureCapacity   §1.17.16

```
public void ensureCapacity(int minimumCapacity)
```

If the current capacity of this string buffer is less than the argument, then a new internal buffer is allocated with greater capacity. The new capacity is the larger of:

♦ The minimumCapacity argument.

♦ Twice the old capacity, plus 2.

If the minimumCapacity argument is nonpositive, this method takes no action and simply returns.

PARAMETERS:

minimumCapacity: the minimum desired capacity.

getChars   §1.17.17

```
public void getChars(int srcBegin, int srcEnd,
                     char dst[], int dstBegin)
```

Characters are copied from this string buffer into the destination character array dst. The first character to be copied is at index srcBegin; the last character to be copied is at index srcEnd-1. The total number of characters to be copied is srcEnd-srcBegin. The characters are copied into the subarray of dst starting at index dstBegin and ending at index

```
dstbegin + (srcEnd-srcBegin) - 1.
```

PARAMETERS:

`srcBegin`: begin copy at this offset in the string buffer.
`srcEnd`: stop copying at this offset in the string buffer.
`dst`: the array to copy the data into.
`dstBegin`: offset into `dst`.

THROWS:

`StringIndexOutOfBoundsException` (**I-§1.44**)
if there is an invalid index into the buffer.

`insert`   §1.17.18

`public StringBuffer insert(int offset, boolean b)`

Inserts the string representation of the `boolean` argument into this string buffer.

The second argument is converted to a string as if by the method `String.valueOf` (**I-§1.16.41**), and the characters of that string are then inserted (**I-§1.17.26**) into this string buffer at the indicated offset.

The offset argument must be greater than or equal to `0`, and less than or equal to the length (**I-§1.17.27**) of this string buffer.

PARAMETERS:

`offset`: the offset.
`b`: a `boolean`.

RETURNS:

this string buffer.

THROWS:

`StringIndexOutOfBoundsException` (**I-§1.44**)
if the offset is invalid.

insert   §1.17.19

`public StringBuffer insert(int offset, char c)`

Inserts the string representation of the `char` argument into this string buffer.

The second argument is inserted into the contents of this string buffer at the position indicated by `offset`. The length of this string buffer increases by one.

The offset argument must be greater than or equal to 0, and less than or equal to the length (**I-§1.17.27**) of this string buffer.

PARAMETERS:

`offset`: the offset.
`ch`: a char.

RETURNS:

this string buffer.

THROWS:

`StringIndexOutOfBoundsException` (**I-§1.44**)
if the offset is invalid.

insert   §1.17.20

`public StringBuffer insert(int offset, char str[])`

Inserts the string representation of the `char` array argument into this string buffer.

The characters of the array argument are inserted into the contents of this string buffer at the position indicated by `offset`. The length of this string buffer increases by the length of the argument.

PARAMETERS:

`offset`: the offset.
`ch`: a character array.

RETURNS:

this string buffer.

THROWS:

`StringIndexOutOfBoundsException` (**I-§1.44**)
if the offset is invalid.

insert   §1.17.21

`public StringBuffer insert(int offset, double d)`

Inserts the string representation of the `double` argument into this string buffer.

The second argument is converted to a string as if by the method `String.valueOf` (**I-§1.16.45**), and the characters of that string are then inserted (**I-§1.17.26**) into this string buffer at the indicated offset.

The offset argument must be greater than or equal to 0, and less than or equal to the length (**I-§1.17.27**) of this string buffer.

PARAMETERS:

`offset`: the offset.
`b`: a `double`.

RETURNS:

this string buffer.

THROWS:

`StringIndexOutOfBoundsException` (**I-§1.44**)
if the offset is invalid.

insert   §1.17.22

`public StringBuffer insert(int offset, float f)`

Inserts the string representation of the `float` argument into this string buffer.

The second argument is converted to a string as if by the method `String.valueOf` (**I-§1.16.46**), and the characters of that string are then inserted (**I-§1.17.26**) into this string buffer at the indicated offset.

The offset argument must be greater than or equal to 0, and less than or equal to the length (**I-§1.17.27**) of this string buffer.

PARAMETERS:

`offset`: the offset.
`b`: a `float`.

RETURNS:

this string buffer.

THROWS:

`StringIndexOutOfBoundsException` (**I-§1.44**)
if the offset is invalid.

insert   §1.17.23

`public StringBuffer insert(int offset, int i)`

Inserts the string representation of the second `int` argument into this string buffer.

The second argument is converted to a string as if by the method `String.valueOf` (**I-§1.16.47**), and the characters of that string are then inserted (**I-§1.17.26**) into this string buffer at the indicated offset.

The offset argument must be greater than or equal to 0, and less than or equal to the length (**I-§1.17.27**) of this string buffer.

PARAMETERS:

`offset`: the offset.
`b`: an `int`.

RETURNS:

this string buffer.

THROWS:

`StringIndexOutOfBoundsException` (**I-§1.44**)
if the offset is invalid.

insert   §1.17.24

`public StringBuffer insert(int offset, long l)`

Inserts the string representation of the `long` argument into this string buffer.

The second argument is converted to a string as if by the method `String.valueOf` (**I-§1.16.48**), and the characters of that string are then inserted (**I-§1.17.26**) into this string buffer at the indicated offset.

The offset argument must be greater than or equal to 0, and less than or equal to the length (**I-§1.17.27**) of this string buffer.

PARAMETERS:

`offset`: the offset.
`b`: a `long`.

RETURNS:

this string buffer.

THROWS:

`StringIndexOutOfBoundsException` (**I-§1.44**)
if the offset is invalid.

insert   **§1.17.25**

```
public StringBuffer insert(int offset, Object obj)
```

Inserts the string representation of the `Object` argument into this string buffer.

The second argument is converted to a string as if by the method `String.valueOf` (**I-§1.16.49**), and the characters of that string are then inserted (**I-§1.17.26**) into this string buffer at the indicated offset.

The offset argument must be greater than or equal to 0, and less than or equal to the length (**I-§1.17.27**) of this string buffer.

PARAMETERS:

`offset`: the offset.
`b`: an `Object`.

RETURNS:

this string buffer.

THROWS:

`StringIndexOutOfBoundsException` (**I-§1.44**)
if the offset is invalid.

insert   **§1.17.26**

```
public StringBuffer insert(int offset, String str)
```

Inserts the string into this string buffer.

The characters of the `String` argument are inserted, in order, into this string buffer at the indicated offset. The length of this string buffer is increased by the length of the argument.

The offset argument must be greater than or equal to 0, and less than or equal to the length (**I-§1.17.27**) of this string buffer.

PARAMETERS:

`offset`: the offset.
`str`: a string.

RETURNS:

this string buffer.

THROWS:

`StringIndexOutOfBoundsException` (**I-§1.44**)
if the offset is invalid.

length   **§1.17.27**

```
public int length()
```

RETURNS:

the number of characters in this string buffer.

reverses[31]   §1.17.28

```
public StringBuffer reverse()
```

The character sequence contained in this string buffer is replaced by the reverse of the sequence.

RETURNS:

this string buffer.

setCharAt   §1.17.29

```
public void setCharAt(int index, char ch)
```

The character at the specified index of this string buffer is set to ch.

The offset argument must be greater than or equal to 0, and less than the length **(I-§1.17.27)** of this string buffer.

PARAMETERS:

index: the index of the character to modify.
ch: the new character.

THROWS:

StringIndexOutOfBoundsException **(I-§1.44)**
if the index is invalid.

setLength   §1.17.30

```
public void setLength(int newLength)
```

If the newLength argument is less than the current length **(I-§1.17.27)** of the string buffer, the string buffer is truncated to contain exactly the number of characters given by the newLength argument.

If the newLength argument is greater than or equal to the current length, sufficient null characters ('\u0000') are appended to the string buffer so that length becomes the newLength argument.

The newLength argument must be greater than or equal to 0.

PARAMETERS:

newLength: the new length of the buffer.

THROWS:

StringIndexOutOfBoundsException **(I-§1.44)**
if the newLength argument is invalid.

[31.] This method is new in Java 1.1.

toString §1.17.31

```
public String toString()
```

A new `String` object is allocated and initialized to contain the character sequence currently represented by this string buffer. This `String` is then returned. Subsequent changes to the string buffer do not affect the contents of the `String`.

RETURNS:

a string representation of the string buffer.

OVERRIDES:

toString in class `Object` (**I-§1.12.9**).

1.18 Class System

```
public final class java.lang.System
    extends java.lang.Object (I-§1.12)
{
    // Fields
    public static PrintStream err;                                §1.18.1
    public static InputStream in;                                 §1.18.2
    public static PrintStream out;                                §1.18.3

    // Methods
    public static void                                            §1.18.4
        arraycopy(Object src, int src_position,
                  Object dst, int dst_position,
                  int length);
    public static long currentTimeMillis();                       §1.18.5
    public static void exit(int status);                          §1.18.6
    public static void gc();                                      §1.18.7
    public static Properties getProperties();                     §1.18.8
    public static String getProperty(String key);                §1.18.9
    public static String getProperty(String key, String def); §1.18.10
    public static SecurityManager getSecurityManager();          §1.18.11
    public static void load(String filename);                    §1.18.12
    public static void loadLibrary(String libname);              §1.18.13
    public static void runFinalization();                        §1.18.14
    public static void setProperties(Properties props);         §1.18.15
    public static void setSecurityManager(SecurityManager s); §1.18.16
}
```

The `System` class contains several useful class fields and methods. It cannot be instantiated.

Among the facilities provided by the `System` class are standard input, standard output, and error output streams; access to externally defined "properties"; a means of loading files and libraries; and a utility method for quickly copying a portion of an array.

Fields

err   §1.18.1

```
public static PrintStream err
```

The "standard" output stream. This stream is already open and ready to accept output data.

Typically this stream corresponds to display output or another output destination specified by the host environment or user. By convention, this output stream is used to display error messages or other information that should come to the immediate attention of a user even if the principal output stream, the value of the variable `out`, has been redirected to a file or other destination that is typically not continuously monitored.

in   §1.18.2

```
public static InputStream in
```

The "standard" input stream. This stream is already open and ready to supply input data. Typically this stream corresponds to keyboard input or another input source specified by the host environment or user.

out   §1.18.3

```
public static PrintStream out
```

The "standard" output stream. This stream is already open and ready to accept output data. Typically this stream corresponds to display output or another output destination specified by the host environment or user.

For simple stand-alone Java applications, a typical way to write a line of output data is:

```
System.out.println(data)
```

See the `println` methods (**I-§2.18.15–§2.18.24**) in class `PrintStream`.

Methods

arraycopy §1.18.4

```
public static void
arraycopy(Object src, int src_position, Object dst,
          int dst_position, int length)
```

A subsequence of array components are copied from the source array referenced by `src` to the destination array referenced by `dst`. The number of components copied is equal to the `length` argument. The components at positions `srcOffset` through `srcOffset+length-1` in the source array are copied into positions `dstOffset` through `dstOffset+length-1`, respectively, of the destination array.

If the `src` and `dst` arguments refer to the same array object, then the copying is performed as if the components at positions `srcOffset` through `srcOffset+length-1` were first copied to a temporary array with `length` components and then the contents of the temporary array were copied into positions `dstOffset` through `dstOffset+length-1` of the argument array.

If any of the following is true, an `ArrayStoreException` is thrown and the destination is not modified:

- The `src` argument refers to an object that is not an array.

- The `dst` argument refers to an object that is not an array.

- The `src` argument and `dst` argument refer to arrays whose component types are different primitive types.

- The `src` argument refers to an array with a primitive component type and the `dst` argument refers to an array with a reference component type.

- The `src` argument refers to an array with a reference component type and the `dst` argument refers to an array with a primitive component type.

Otherwise, if any of the following is true, an `ArrayIndexOutOfBounds-Exception` is thrown and the destination is not modified:

- The `srcOffset` argument is negative.

- The `dstOffset` argument is negative.

- The `length` argument is negative.

- `srcOffset+length` is greater than `src.length`, the length of the source array.

- `dstOffset+length` is greater than `dst.length`, the length of the destination array.

Otherwise, if any actual component of the source array from position srcOffset through srcOffset+length-1 cannot be converted to the component type of the destination array by assignment conversion, an Array-StoreException is thrown. In this case, let k be the smallest nonnegative integer less than length such that src[srcOffset+k] cannot be converted to the component type of the destination array; when the exception is thrown, source array components from positions srcOffset through srcOffset+k-1 will already have been copied to destination array positions dstOffset through dstOffset+k-1 and no other positions of the destination array will have been modified.

PARAMETERS:

src: the source array.
srcpos: start position in the source array.
dest: the destination array.
destpos: start position in the destination data.
length: the number of array elements to be copied.

THROWS:

ArrayIndexOutOfBoundsException (I-§1.25)
if copying would cause access of data outside array bounds.

THROWS:

ArrayStoreException (I-§1.26)
if an element in the src array could not be stored into the dest array because of a type mismatch.

currentTimeMillis   §1.18.5

public static long currentTimeMillis()

Gets the current time.

See the description of the class Date (I-§3.2) for a discussion of slight discrepancies that may arise between "computer time" and coordinated universal time (UTC).

RETURNS:

the difference, measured in milliseconds, between the current time and midnight, January 1, 1970 UTC.

exit §1.18.6

```
public static void exit(int status)
```

Terminates the currently running Java Virtual Machine. The argument serves as a status code; by convention, a nonzero status code indicates abnormal termination.

This method calls the `exit` method (**I-§1.14.5**) in class `Runtime`. This method never returns normally.

PARAMETERS:

`status`: exit status.

THROWS:

`SecurityException` (**I-§1.43**)

if the current thread cannot exit with the specified status.

gc §1.18.7

```
public static void gc()
```

This method calls the gc method (**I-§1.14.7**) in class `Runtime`.

Calling the gc method suggests that the Java Virtual Machine expend effort toward recycling unused objects in order to make the memory they currently occupy available for quick reuse. When control returns from the method call, the Java Virtual Machine has made a best effort to reclaim space from all unused objects.

getProperties §1.18.8

```
public static Properties getProperties()
```

Determines the current system properties.

If there is a security manager, its `checkPropertiesAccess` method (**I-§1.15.16**) is called with no arguments. This may result in a security exception (**I-§1.43**).

The current set of system properties is returned as a `Properties` object (**I-§3.6**). If there is no current set of system properties, a set of system properties is first created and initialized.

This set of system properties always includes values for the following keys:

Key	Description of associated value
`java.version`	Java version number
`java.vendor`	Java vendor–specific string
`java.vendor.url`	Java vendor URL
`java.home`	Java installation directory
`java.class.version`	Java class format version number
`java.class.path`	Java class path
`os.name`	Operating system name

os.arch	Operating system architecture
os.version	Operating system version
file.separator	File separator ("/" on UNIX)
path.separator	Path separator (":" on UNIX)
line.separator	Line separator ("\n" on UNIX)
user.name	User's account name
user.home	User's home directory
user.dir	User's current working directory

THROWS:

SecurityException **(I-§1.43)**

if the current thread cannot access the system properties.

getProperty   §1.18.9

```
public static String getProperty(String key)
```

Gets the system property indicated by the specified key.

First, if there is a security manager, its checkPropertyAccess method
(I-§1.15.17) is called with the key as its argument. This may result in a system
exception **(I-§1.43)**.

If there is no current set of system properties, a set of system properties is
first created and initialized in the same manner as for the getProperties
method **(I-§1.18.8)**.

PARAMETERS:

key: the name of the system property.

RETURNS:

the string value of the system property, or null if there is no property with
    that key.

THROWS:

SecurityException **(I-§1.43)**

if the current thread cannot access the system properties or the specified
    property.

getProperty §1.18.10

> `public static String getProperty(String key, String def)`
>
> Gets the system property indicated by the specified key.
>
> First, if there is a security manager, its `checkPropertyAccess` method (**I-§1.15.17**) is called with the key as its argument.
>
> If there is no current set of system properties, a set of system properties is first created and initialized in the same manner as for the `getProperties` method (**I-§1.18.8**).

PARAMETERS:

`key`: the name of the system property.
`def`: a default value.

RETURNS:

> the string value of the system property, or the default value if there is no property with that key.

THROWS:

`SecurityException` (**I-§1.43**)
> if the current thread cannot access the system properties or the specified property.

getSecurityManager §1.18.11

> `public static SecurityManager getSecurityManager()`

RETURNS:

> if a security manager has already been established for the current application, then that security manager is returned; otherwise, `null` is returned.

load §1.18.12

> `public static void load(String filename)`
>
> Loads the given filename as a dynamic library. The filename argument must be a complete pathname.
>
> This method calls the `load` method (**I-§1.14.11**) in class `Runtime`.

PARAMETERS:

`filename`: the file to load.

THROWS:

`UnsatisfiedLinkError` (**I-§1.61**)
if the file does not exist.

THROWS:

`SecurityException` (**I-§1.43**)
if the current thread cannot load the specified dynamic library.

loadLibrary   §1.18.13

`public static void loadLibrary(String libname)`

Loads the system library specified by the `libname` argument. The manner in which a library name is mapped to the actual system library is system dependent.

PARAMETERS:

`libname`: the name of the library.

THROWS:

`UnsatisfiedLinkError` **(I-§1.61)**

if the library does not exist.

THROWS:

`SecurityException` **(I-§1.43)**

if the current thread cannot load the specified dynamic library.

runFinalization   §1.18.14

`public static void runFinalization()`

This method calls the `runFinalization` method **(I-§1.14.13)** in class `Runtime`.

Calling this method suggests that the Java Virtual Machine expend effort toward running the `finalize` methods of objects that have been found to be discarded but whose `finalize` methods have not yet been run. When control returns from the method call, the Java Virtual Machine has made a best effort to complete all outstanding finalizations.

setProperties   §1.18.15

`public static void setProperties(Properties props)`

Sets the system properties to the `Properties` argument.

First, if there is a security manager, its `checkPropertiesAccess` method **(I-§1.15.16)** is called with no arguments. This may result in a security exception **(I-§1.43)**.

The argument becomes the current set of system properties for use by the `getProperty` method. If the argument is `null`, then the current set of system properties is forgotten.

PARAMETERS:

`props`: the new system properties.

THROWS:

`SecurityException` **(I-§1.43)**

if the current thread cannot set the system properties.

setSecurityManager §1.18.16

```
public static void setSecurityManager(SecurityManager s)
```

If a security manager has already been established for the currently running Java application, a `SecurityException` is thrown. Otherwise, the argument is established as the current security manager. If the argument is `null` and no security manager has been established, then no action is taken and the method simply returns.

PARAMETERS:

s : the security manager.

THROWS:

SecurityException (I-§1.43)

if the security manager has already been set.

1.19 Class Thread

```
public class java.lang.Thread
    extends java.lang.Object (I-§1.12)
    implements java.lang.Runnable (I-§1.23)
{
    // Fields
    public final static int MAX_PRIORITY;                    §1.19.1
    public final static int MIN_PRIORITY;                    §1.19.2
    public final static int NORM_PRIORITY;                   §1.19.3

    // Constructors
    public Thread();                                         §1.19.4
    public Thread(Runnable target);                          §1.19.5
    public Thread(Runnable target, String name);             §1.19.6
    public Thread(String name);                              §1.19.7
    public Thread(ThreadGroup group, Runnable target);       §1.19.8
    public Thread(ThreadGroup group,                         §1.19.9
                  Runnable target, String name);
    public Thread(ThreadGroup group, String name);           §1.19.10

    // Methods
    public static int activeCount();                         §1.19.11
    public void checkAccess();                               §1.19.12
    public int countStackFrames();                           §1.19.13
    public static Thread currentThread();                    §1.19.14
    public void destroy();                                   §1.19.15
    public static void dumpStack();                          §1.19.16
    public static int enumerate(Thread tarray[]);            §1.19.17
    public final String getName();                           §1.19.18
    public final int getPriority();                          §1.19.19
    public final ThreadGroup getThreadGroup();               §1.19.20
    public void interrupt();                                 §1.19.21
    public static boolean interrupted();                     §1.19.22
    public final boolean isAlive();                          §1.19.23
    public final boolean isDaemon();                         §1.19.24
    public boolean isInterrupted();                          §1.19.25
    public final void join();                                §1.19.26
    public final void join(long millis);                     §1.19.27
    public final void join(long millis, int nanos)           §1.19.28
    public final void resume();                              §1.19.29
    public void run();                                       §1.19.30
    public final void setDaemon(boolean on);                 §1.19.31
    public final void setName(String name);                  §1.19.32
    public final void setPriority(int newPriority);          §1.19.33
    public static void sleep(long millis);                   §1.19.34
    public static void sleep(long millis, int nanos)         §1.19.35
```

```
    public void start();                                    §1.19.36
    public final void stop();                               §1.19.37
    public final void stop(Throwable obj);                  §1.19.38
    public final void suspend();                            §1.19.39
    public String toString();                               §1.19.40
    public static void yield();                             §1.19.41
}
```

A *thread* is a thread of execution in a program. The Java Virtual Machine allows an application to have multiple threads of executing running concurrently.

Every thread has a priority. Threads with higher priority are executed in preference to threads with lower priority. Each thread may or may not also be marked as a daemon. When code running in some thread creates a new Thread object, the new thread has its priority initially set equal to the priority of the creating thread, and is a daemon thread if and only if the creating thread is a daemon.

When a Java Virtual Machine starts up, there is usually a single non-daemon thread (which typically calls the method named main of some designated class). The Java Virtual Machine continues to execute threads until either of the following occurs:

♦ The exit method (**I-§1.14.5**) of class Runtime has been called and the security manager has permitted the exit operation to take place.

♦ All threads that are not daemon threads have died, either by returning from the call to the run method (**I-§1.19.30**) or by performing the stop method (**I-§1.19.37**).

There are two ways to create a new thread of execution. One is to declare a class to be a subclass of Thread. This subclass should override the run method of class Thread. An instance of the subclass can then be allocated and started. For example, a thread that computes primes larger than a stated value could be written as follows:

```
class PrimeThread extends Thread {
    long minPrime;
    PrimeThread(long minPrime) {
        this.minPrime = minPrime;
    }

    public void run() {
        // compute primes larger than minPrime
        ...
    }
}
```

The following code would then create a thread and start it running:

```
PrimeThread p = new PrimeThread(143);

p.start();
```

The other way to create a thread is to declare a class that implements the Run-nable interface (**I-§1.23**). That class then implements the run method. An instance of the class can then be allocated, passed as an argument when creating Thread, and started. The same example in this other style looks like the following:

```
class PrimeRun implements Runnable {
    long minPrime;
    PrimeRun(long minPrime) {
        this.minPrime = minPrime;
    }

    public void run() {
        // compute primes larger than minPrime
        ...
    }
}
```

The following code would then create a thread and start it running:

```
PrimeRun p = new PrimeRun(143);

new Thread(p).start();
```

Every thread has a name for identification purposes. More than one thread may have the same name. If a name is not specified when a thread is created, a new name is generated for it.

Fields

MAX_PRIORITY   §1.19.1
```
public final static int MAX_PRIORITY = 10
```
The maximum priority that a thread can have.

MIN_PRIORITY   §1.19.2
```
public final static int MIN_PRIORITY = 1
```
The minimum priority that a thread can have.

NORM_PRIORITY   §1.19.3
```
public final static int NORM_PRIORITY = 5
```
The default priority that is assigned to a thread.

Constructors

Thread   §1.19.4

```
public Thread()
```

Allocates a new Thread object. This constructor has the same effect as Thread(null, null, *gname*) (I-§1.19.9) where *gname* is a newly generated name. Automatically generated names are of the form "Thread-"+*n* where *n* is an integer.

Thread   §1.19.5

```
public Thread(Runnable target)
```

Allocates a new Thread object. This constructor has the same effect as Thread(null, target, *gname*) (I-§1.19.9) where *gname* is a newly generated name. Automatically generated names are of the form "Thread-"+*n*, where *n* is an integer.

PARAMETERS:

target: the object whose run method is called.

Thread   §1.19.6

```
public Thread(Runnable target, String name)
```

Allocates a new Thread object. This constructor has the same effect as Thread(null, target, name) (I-§1.19.9).

PARAMETERS:

target: the object whose run method is called.
name: the name of the new thread.

Thread   §1.19.7

```
public Thread(String name)
```

Allocates a new Thread object. This constructor has the same effect as Thread(null, null, name) (I-§1.19.9).

PARAMETERS:

name: the name of the new thread.

Thread   §1.19.8

```
public Thread(ThreadGroup group, Runnable target)
```

Allocates a new Thread object. This constructor has the same effect as Thread(group, target, *gname*) **(I-§1.19.9)** where *gname* is a newly generated name. Automatically generated names are of the form "Thread-"+*n*, where *n* is an integer.

PARAMETERS:

group: the thread group.
target: the object whose run method is called.

THROWS:

SecurityException **(I-§1.43)**

if the current thread cannot create a thread in the specified thread group.

Thread   §1.19.9

```
public Thread(ThreadGroup group, Runnable target,
              String name)
```

Allocates a new Thread object so that it has target as its run object, has the specified name as its name, and belongs to the thread group referred to by group.

If group is not null, the checkAccess method **(I-§1.20.5)** of that thread group is called with no arguments; this may result in throwing a SecurityException; if group is null, the new process belongs to the same group as the thread this is creating new thread.

If the target argument is not null, the run method of the target **(I-§1.23.1)** is called when this thread is started. If the target argument is null, this thread's run method **(I-§1.19.30)** is called when this thread is started.

The priority of the newly created thread is set equal to the priority of the thread creating it, that is, the currently running thread. The method setPriority **(I-§1.19.33)** may be used to change the priority to a new value.

The newly created thread is initially marked as being a daemon thread if and only if the thread creating it is currently marked as a daemon thread. The method setDaemon **(I-§1.19.31)** may be used to change whether or not a thread is a daemon.

PARAMETERS:

group: the thread group.
target: the object whose run method is called.
name: the name of the new thread.

THROWS:

SecurityException **(I-§1.43)**

if the current thread cannot create a thread in the specified thread group.

Thread §1.19.10

```
public Thread(ThreadGroup group, String name)
```

Allocates a new Thread object. This constructor has the same effect as Thread(group, null, name) **(I-§1.19.9)**

PARAMETERS:

group: the thread group.
name: the name of the new thread.

THROWS:

SecurityException **(I-§1.43)**
if the current thread cannot create a thread in the specified thread group.

Methods

activeCount §1.19.11

```
public static int activeCount()
```

RETURNS:

the current number of threads in this thread's thread group.

checkAccess §1.19.12

```
public void checkAccess()
```

Determines if the currently running thread has permission to modify this thread.

If there is a security manager, its checkAccess method **(I-§1.15.4)** is called with this thread as its argument. This may result in throwing a Security-Exception.

THROWS:

SecurityException **(I-§1.43)**
if the current thread is not allowed to access this thread.

countStackFrames §1.19.13

```
public int countStackFrames()
```

Counts the number of stack frames in this thread. The thread must be suspended.

RETURNS:

the number of stack frames in this thread.

THROWS:

IllegalThreadStateException **(I-§1.34)**
if this thread is not suspended.

currentThread   §1.19.14

    `public static Thread currentThread()`

      Finds the currently executing thread.

    RETURNS:

    the currently executing thread.

destroy[32]   §1.19.15

    `public void destroy()`

      Destroys this thread, without any cleanup. Any monitors it has locked remain locked.

dumpStack   §1.19.16

    `public static void dumpStack()`

      Prints a stack trace of the current thread. This method is used only for debugging.

    SEE ALSO:

    `printStackTrace` in class `Throwable` (**I-§1.21.5**).

enumerate   §1.19.17

    `public static int enumerate(Thread tarray[])`

      Copies into the array argument every thread in this thread's thread group. This method simply calls the `enumerate` method (**I-§1.20.7**) of this thread's thread group with the array argument.

    RETURNS:

    the number of threads put into the array.

getName   §1.19.18

    `public final String getName()`

    RETURNS:

    this thread's name.

getPriority   §1.19.19

    `public final int getPriority()`

    RETURNS:

    this thread's current priority.

[32.] Unimplemented in Java 1.1.

getThreadGroup §1.19.20

```
public final ThreadGroup getThreadGroup()
```
RETURNS:

this thread's thread group.

interrupt §1.19.21

```
public void interrupt()
```
Interrupts this thread.

interrupted §1.19.22

```
public static boolean interrupted()
```
RETURNS:

true if the current thread has been interrupted; false otherwise.

isAlive §1.19.23

```
public final boolean isAlive()
```
Determines if this thread is alive. A thread is alive if it has been started and has not yet died.

RETURNS:

true if this thread is alive; false otherwise.

isDaemon §1.19.24

```
public final boolean isDaemon()
```
RETURNS:

true if this thread is a daemon thread; false otherwise.

isInterrupted §1.19.25

```
public boolean isInterrupted()
```
RETURNS:

true if this thread has been interrupted; false otherwise.

join §1.19.26

```
public final void join()
throws InterruptedException
```
Waits for this thread to die.

THROWS:

InterruptedException (I-§1.37)
if another thread has interrupted the current thread.

join   §1.19.27

```
public final void join(long millis)
throws InterruptedException
```

   Waits at most `millis` milliseconds for this thread to die. A timeout of 0 means to wait forever.

PARAMETERS:

`millis`: the time to wait in milliseconds.

THROWS:

`InterruptedException` **(I-§1.37)**
if another thread has interrupted the current thread.

join   §1.19.28

```
public final void join(long millis, int nanos)
throws InterruptedException
```

   Waits at most `millis` milliseconds plus `nanos` nanoseconds for this thread to die.

PARAMETERS:

`millis`: the time to wait in milliseconds.
`nanos`: 0–999999 additional nanoseconds to wait.

THROWS:

`InterruptedException` **(I-§1.37)**
if another thread has interrupted the current thread.

resume   §1.19.29

```
public final void resume()
```

   Resumes a suspended thread.

   First, the `checkAccess` method **(I-§1.19.12)** of this thread is called with no arguments. This may result in throwing a `SecurityException` (in the current thread).

   If the thread is alive **(I-§1.19.23)** but suspended, it is resumed and is permitted to make progress in its execution.

THROWS:

`SecurityException` **(I-§1.43)**
if the current thread cannot modify this thread.

run   §1.19.30

   `public void run()`

   If this thread was constructed using a separate `Runnable` run object (see **I-§1.19.9** on page 138 for more information), then that `Runnable` object's run method (**I-§1.23.1**) is called. Otherwise, this method does nothing and returns.

   Subclasses of `Thread` should override this method.

SEE ALSO:

`start` (**I-§1.19.36**).

`stop` (**I-§1.19.37**).

setDaemon   §1.19.31

   `public final void setDaemon(boolean on)`

   Marks this thread as either a daemon thread or a user thread. The Java Virtual Machine exits when the only threads running are all daemon threads.

   This method must be called before the thread is started.

PARAMETERS:

`on`: if `true`, marks this thread as a daemon thread.

THROWS:

`IllegalThreadStateException` (**I-§1.34**)

if this thread is active.

setName   §1.19.32

   `public final void setName(String name)`

   Changes the name of this thread to be equal to the argument name.

   First the `checkAccess` method (**I-§1.19.12**) of this thread is called with no arguments. This may result in throwing a `SecurityException`.

PARAMETERS:

`name`: the new name for this thread.

THROWS:

`SecurityException` (**I-§1.43**)

if the current thread cannot modify this thread.

setPriority   **§1.19.33**

```
public final void setPriority(int newPriority)
```

Changes the priority of this thread.

First the checkAccess method (**I-§1.19.12**) of this thread is called with no arguments. This may result in throwing a SecurityException.

Otherwise, the priority of this thread is set to the smaller of the specified newPriority and the maximum permitted priority (**I-§1.20.11**) of the thread's thread group (**I-§1.19.20**).

THROWS:

IllegalArgumentException (**I-§1.32**)
If the priority is not in the range MIN_PRIORITY to MAX_PRIORITY.

THROWS:

SecurityException (**I-§1.43**)
if the current thread cannot modify this thread.

sleep   **§1.19.34**

```
public static void sleep(long millis)
throws InterruptedException
```

Causes the currently executing thread to sleep (temporarily cease execution) for the specified number of milliseconds. The thread does not lose ownership of any monitors (see **I-§1.12.7** on page 70 for further discussion of monitors).

PARAMETERS:

millis:the length of time to sleep in milliseconds.

THROWS:

InterruptedException (**I-§1.37**)
if another thread has interrupted this thread.

sleep   **§1.19.35**

```
public static void sleep(long millis, int nanos)
throws InterruptedException
```

Causes the currently executing thread to sleep (cease execution) for the specified number of milliseconds plus the specified number of nanoseconds. The thread does not lose ownership of any monitors (see **I-§1.12.7** on page 70 for further discussion of monitors).

PARAMETERS:

millis:the length of time to sleep in milliseconds.
nanos:0–999999 additional nanoseconds to sleep.

THROWS:

InterruptedException (**I-§1.37**)
if another thread has interrupted this thread.

start   **§1.19.36**

> `public void start()`
>
> Causes this thread to begin execution; the Java Virtual Machine calls the run method (**I-§1.19.30**) of this thread.
>
> The result is that two threads are running concurrently: the current thread (which returns from the call to the `start` method) and the other thread (which executes its run method).
>
> **THROWS:**
>
> `IllegalThreadStateException` (**I-§1.34**)
> if the thread was already started.
>
> **SEE ALSO:**
>
> run (**I-§1.19.30**).
> stop (**I-§1.19.37**).

stop   **§1.19.37**

> `public final void stop()`
>
> Forces the thread to stop executing.
>
> First, the `checkAccess` method (**I-§1.19.12**) of this thread is called with no arguments. This may result in throwing a `SecurityException` (in the current thread).
>
> The thread represented by this thread is forced to stop whatever it is doing abnormally and to throw a newly created `ThreadDeath` (**I-§1.59**) object as an exception.
>
> It is permitted to stop a thread that has not yet been started. If the thread is eventually started, it immediately terminates.
>
> An application should not normally try to catch `ThreadDeath` unless it must do some extraordinary cleanup operation (note that the throwing of `ThreadDeath` causes `finally` clauses of `try` statements to be executed before the thread officially dies). If a `catch` clause catches a `ThreadDeath` object, it is important to rethrow the object so that the thread actually dies.
>
> The top-level error handler that reacts to otherwise uncaught exceptions (**I-§1.20.23**) does not print out a message or otherwise notify the application if the uncaught exception is an instance of `ThreadDeath`.
>
> **SEE ALSO:**
>
> start (**I-§1.19.36**).
> run (**I-§1.19.30**).
>
> **THROWS:**
>
> `SecurityException` (**I-§1.43**)
> if the current thread cannot modify this thread.

stop   §1.19.38

```
public final void stop(Throwable obj)
```

Forces the thread to stop executing.

First, the checkAccess method **(I-§1.19.12)** of this thread is called with no arguments. This may result in throwing a SecurityException (in the current thread).

If the argument obj is null, a NullPointerException is thrown (in the current thread).

The thread represented by this thread is forced to complete whatever it is doing abnormally and to throw the Throwable object obj as an exception. This is an unusual action to take; normally, the stop method that takes no arguments **(I-§1.19.37)** should be used.

It is permitted to stop a thread that has not yet been started. If the thread is eventually started, it immediately terminates.

PARAMETERS:

obj: the Throwable object to be thrown.

THROWS:

SecurityException **(I-§1.43)**
if the current thread cannot modify this thread.

suspend   §1.19.39

```
public final void suspend()
```

Suspends this thread.

First, the checkAccess method **(I-§1.19.12)** of this thread is called with no arguments. This may result in throwing a SecurityException (in the current thread).

If the thread is alive **(I-§1.19.23)**, it is suspended and makes no further progress unless and until it is resumed.

THROWS:

SecurityException **(I-§1.43)**
if the current thread cannot modify this thread.

toString   §1.19.40

```
public String toString()
```

RETURNS:

a string representation of this thread.

OVERRIDES:

toString in class Object **(I-§1.12.9)**.

yield §1.19.41

    `public static void yield()`

    Causes the currently executing thread object to temporarily pause and allow other threads to execute.

1.20 Class ThreadGroup

```
public class java.lang.ThreadGroup
    extends java.lang.Object (I-§1.12)
{
    // Constructors
    public ThreadGroup(String name);                        §1.20.1
    public ThreadGroup(ThreadGroup parent,                  §1.20.2
                    String name);

    // Methods
    public int activeCount();                               §1.20.3
    public int activeGroupCount();                          §1.20.4
    public final void checkAccess();                        §1.20.5
    public final void destroy();                            §1.20.6
    public int enumerate(Thread list[]);                    §1.20.7
    public int enumerate(Thread list[], boolean recurse);   §1.20.8
    public int enumerate(ThreadGroup list[]);               §1.20.9
    public int enumerate(ThreadGroup list[],                §1.20.10
                    boolean recurse);
    public final int getMaxPriority();                      §1.20.11
    public final String getName();                          §1.20.12
    public final ThreadGroup getParent();                   §1.20.13
    public final boolean isDaemon();                        §1.20.14
    public void list();                                     §1.20.15
    public final boolean parentOf(ThreadGroup g);           §1.20.16
    public final void resume();                             §1.20.17
    public final void setDaemon(boolean daemon);            §1.20.18
    public final void setMaxPriority(int pri);              §1.20.19
    public final void stop();                               §1.20.20
    public final void suspend();                            §1.20.21
    public String toString();                               §1.20.22
    public void uncaughtException(Thread t,                 §1.20.23
                    Throwable e);
}
```

    A thread group represents a set of threads. In addition, a thread group can also include other thread groups. The thread groups form a tree in which every thread group except the initial thread group has a parent.

A thread is allowed to access information about its own thread group, but not to access information about its thread group's parent thread group or any other thread groups.

Constructors

ThreadGroup   §1.20.1
```
public ThreadGroup(String name)
```
Constructs a new thread group. The parent of this new group is the thread group of the currently running thread.

PARAMETERS:

name: the name of the new thread group.

ThreadGroup   §1.20.2
```
public ThreadGroup(ThreadGroup parent, String name)
```
Creates a new thread group. The parent of this new group is the specified thread group.

The `checkAccess` method (**I-§1.20.5**) of the parent thread group is called with no arguments; this may result in a security exception (**I-§1.43**).

PARAMETERS:

parent: the parent thread group.
name: the name of the new thread group.

THROWS:

NullPointerException (**I-§1.40**)
if the thread group argument is null.

THROWS:

SecurityException (**I-§1.43**)
if the current thread cannot create a thread in the specified thread group.

Methods

activeCount   §1.20.3
```
public int activeCount()
```
RETURNS:

the number of active threads in this thread group and in any other thread group that has this thread group as an ancestor.

activeGroupCount §1.20.4

```
public int activeGroupCount()
```

RETURNS:

the number of active thread groups with this thread group as an ancestor.

checkAccess §1.20.5

```
public final void checkAccess()
```

Determines if the currently running thread has permission to modify this thread group.

If there is a security manager, its checkAccess method (**I-§1.15.5**) is called with this thread group as its argument. This may result in throwing a SecurityException.

THROWS:

SecurityException (**I-§1.43**)

if the current thread is not allowed to access this thread group.

destroy §1.20.6

```
public final void destroy()
```

Destroys this thread group and all of its subgroups. This thread group must be empty, indicating that all threads that had been in this thread group have since stopped.

THROWS:

IllegalThreadStateException (**I-§1.34**)

if the thread group is not empty or if the thread group has already been destroyed.

THROWS:

SecurityException (**I-§1.43**)

if the current thread cannot modify this thread group.

enumerate §1.20.7

```
public int enumerate(Thread list[])
```

Copies into the specified array every active thread in this thread group and its subgroups.

An application should use the activeCount method (**I-§1.20.3**) to get an estimate of how big the array should be. If the array is too short to hold all the threads, the extra threads are silently ignored.

PARAMETERS:

list: an array into which to place the list of threads.

RETURNS:

the number of threads put into the array.

enumerate   §1.20.8

```
public int enumerate(Thread list[], boolean recurse)
```

Copies into the specified array every active thread in this thread group. If the `recurse` flag is `true`, references to every active thread in this thread's subgroups are also included. If the array is too short to hold all the threads, the extra threads are silently ignored.

An application should use the `activeCount` method (**I-§1.20.3**) to get an estimate of how big the array should be.

PARAMETERS:

`list`: an array into which to place the list of threads.
`recurse`: flag indicating whether also to include threads in thread groups
    that are subgroups of this thread group.

RETURNS:

the number of threads placed into the array.

enumerate   §1.20.9

```
public int enumerate(ThreadGroup list[])
```

Copies into the specified array references to every active subgroup in this thread group.

An application should use the `activeGroupCount` method (**I-§1.20.4**) to get an estimate of how big the array should be. If the array is too short to hold all the thread groups, the extra thread groups are silently ignored.

PARAMETERS:

`list`: an array into which to place the list of thread groups.

RETURNS:

the number of thread groups put into the array.

enumerate   §1.20.10

```
public int enumerate(ThreadGroup list[], boolean recurse)
```

Copies into the specified array references to every active subgroup in this thread group. If the `recurse` flag is `true`, references to all active subgroups of the subgroups and so forth are also included.

An application should use the `activeGroupCount` method (**I-§1.20.4**) to get an estimate of how big the array should be.

PARAMETERS:

`list`: an array into which to place the list of threads.
`recurse`: a flag indicating whether to recursively enumerate all included
    thread groups.

RETURNS:

the number of thread groups put into the array.

getMaxPriority §1.20.11

```
public final int getMaxPriority()
```
RETURNS:

the maximum priority that a thread in this thread group can have.

getName §1.20.12

```
public final String getName()
```
RETURNS:

the name of this thread group.

getParent §1.20.13

```
public final ThreadGroup getParent()
```
RETURNS:

the parent of this thread group. The top-level thread group is the only thread group whose parent is null.

isDaemon §1.20.14

```
public final boolean isDaemon()
```
Determines if this thread group is a daemon thread group. A daemon thread group is automatically destroyed when its last thread is stopped or its last thread group is destroyed.

RETURNS:

true if this thread group is a daemon thread group; false otherwise.

list §1.20.15

```
public void list()
```
Prints information about this thread group to the standard output. This method is useful only for debugging.

parentOf §1.20.16

```
public final boolean parentOf(ThreadGroup g)
```
Determines if this thread group is either the thread group argument or one of its ancestor thread groups.

PARAMETERS:

g: a thread group.

RETURNS:

true if this thread group is the thread group argument or one of its ancestor thread groups; false otherwise.

resume   §1.20.17

```
public final void resume()
```

Resumes all processes in this thread group.

First, the checkAccess method (**I-§1.20.5**) of this thread group is called with no arguments; this may result in a security exception (**I-§1.43**).

This method then calls the resume method (**I-§1.19.29**) on all the threads in this thread group and in all of its sub groups.

THROWS:

SecurityException (**I-§1.43**)

if the current thread is not allowed to access this thread group or any of the threads in the thread group.

setDaemon   §1.20.18

```
public final void setDaemon(boolean daemon)
```

Sets whether this thread group is a daemon thread group.

First, the checkAccess method (**I-§1.20.5**) of this thread group is called with no arguments; this may result in a security exception (**I-§1.43**).

A daemon thread group is automatically destroyed when its last thread is stopped or its last thread group is destroyed.

PARAMETERS:

daemon: if true, marks this thread group as a daemon thread group; otherwise, marks this thread group as normal.

THROWS:

SecurityException (**I-§1.43**)

if the current thread cannot modify this thread.

setMaxPriority   §1.20.19

```
public final void setMaxPriority(int pri)
```

Sets the maximum priority of the group.

First, the checkAccess method (**I-§1.20.5**) of this thread group is called with no arguments; this may result in a security exception (**I-§1.43**).

Threads in the thread group that already have a higher priority are not affected.

PARAMETERS:

pri: the new priority of the thread group.

THROWS:

SecurityException (**I-§1.43**)

if the current thread cannot modify this thread group.

stop   §1.20.20

> `public final void stop()`
>
> Stops all processes in this thread group.
>
> First, the `checkAccess` method (**I-§1.20.5**) of this thread group is called with no arguments; this may result in a security exception (**I-§1.43**).
>
> This method then calls the `stop` method (**I-§1.19.37**) on all the threads in this thread group and in all of its subgroups.
>
> **THROWS:**
>
> `SecurityException` (**I-§1.43**)
>
> if the current thread is not allowed to access this thread group or any of the threads in the thread group.

suspend   §1.20.21

> `public final void suspend()`
>
> Suspends all processes in this thread group.
>
> First, the `checkAccess` method (**I-§1.20.5**) of this thread group is called with no arguments; this may result in a security exception (**I-§1.43**).
>
> This method then calls the `suspend` method (**I-§1.19.39**) on all the threads in this thread group and in all of its subgroups.
>
> **THROWS:**
>
> `SecurityException` (**I-§1.43**)
>
> if the current thread is not allowed to access this thread group or any of the threads in the thread group.

toString   §1.20.22

> `public String toString()`
>
> **RETURNS:**
>
> a string representation of this thread group.
>
> **OVERRIDES:**
>
> `toString` in class `Object` (**I-§1.12.9**).

uncaughtException   §1.20.23

> `public void uncaughtException(Thread t, Throwable e)`
>
> The Java Virtual Machine calls this method when a thread in this thread group stops because of an uncaught exception.
>
> The `uncaughtException` method of `ThreadGroup` does the following:
>
> 1. If this thread group has a parent thread group, the `uncaughtException` method of that parent is called with the same two arguments.
>
> 2. Otherwise, this method determines if the `Throwable` argument is an instance of `ThreadDeath` (**I-§1.59**). If so, nothing special is done. Otherwise, the

Throwable's `printStackTrace` method (**I-§1.21.6**) is called to print a stack backtrace to the standard error stream (**I-§1.18.1**).

Applications can override this method in subclasses of `ThreadGroup` to provide alternative handling of uncaught exceptions.

PARAMETERS:
`t`: the thread that is about to exit.
`e`: the uncaught exception.

1.21 Class Throwable

```
public class java.lang.Throwable
    extends java.lang.Object (I-§1.12)
{
    // Constructors
    public Throwable();                          §1.21.1
    public Throwable(String message);            §1.21.2

    // Methods
    public Throwable fillInStackTrace();         §1.21.3
    public String getMessage();                  §1.21.4
    public void printStackTrace();               §1.21.5
    public void printStackTrace(PrintStream s);  §1.21.6
    public String toString();                    §1.21.7
}
```

The `Throwable` class is the superclass of all errors and exceptions in the Java language. Only objects that are instances of this class (or of one of its subclasses) are thrown by the Java Virtual Machine or can be thrown by the Java `throw` statement. Similarly, only this class or one of its subclasses can be the argument type in a `catch` clause.

A `Throwable` class contains a snapshot of the execution stack of its thread at the time it was created. It can also contain a message string that gives more information about the error.

Here is one example of catching an exception:

```
try {
    int a[] = new int[2];
    a[4];
} catch (ArrayIndexOutOfBoundsException e) {
    System.out.println("exception: " + e.getMessage());
    e.printStackTrace();
}
```

Constructors

Throwable §1.21.1

    public Throwable()

Constructs a new `Throwable` with no detail message. The stack trace is automatically filled in.

Throwable §1.21.2

    public Throwable(String message)

Constructs a new `Throwable` with the specified detail message. The stack trace is automatically filled in.

PARAMETERS:

`message`: the detail message.

Methods

---

fillInStackTrace §1.21.3

    public Throwable fillInStackTrace()

Fills in the execution stack trace. This method is useful when an application is re-throwing an error or exception. For example:

```
try {
    a = b / c;
} catch(ArithmeticThrowable e) {
    a = Number.MAX_VALUE;
    throw e.fillInStackTrace();
}
```

RETURNS:

this `Throwable` object.

SEE ALSO:

`printStackTrace` (I-§1.21.5).

getMessage §1.21.4

    public String getMessage()

RETURNS:

the detail message of this `Throwable`, or `null` if this `Throwable` does not have a detailed message.

printStackTrace   **§1.21.5**
>   public void printStackTrace()

>   Prints this Throwable and its backtrace to the standard error (**I-§1.18.1**) output stream.

printStackTrace   **§1.21.6**
>   public void printStackTrace(PrintStream s)

>   Prints this Throwable and its backtrace to the specified print stream.

toString   **§1.21.7**
>   public String toString()

>   **RETURNS:**

>   a string representation of this Throwable.

>   **OVERRIDES:**

>   toString in class Object (**I-§1.12.9**).

1.22 Interface Cloneable

```
public interface java.lang.Cloneable
{
}
```

   A class implements the Cloneable interface to indicate to the clone method (**I-§1.12.2**) in class Object that it is legal for that method to make a field-for-field copy of instances of that class.

   Attempts to clone instances that do not implement the Cloneable interface result in the exception CloneNotSupportedException (**I-§1.29**) being thrown.

1.23 Interface Runnable

```
public interface java.lang.Runnable
{
    // Methods
    public abstract void run();                                     §1.23.1
}
```

   The Runnable interface should be implemented by any class whose instances are intended to be executed by a thread (**I-§1.19**). The class must define a method of no arguments called run.

   SEE ALSO:

   Thread (**I-§1.19**).

Methods

---

run   §1.23.1

```
public abstract void run()
```

When an object implementing interface Runnable is used to create a thread, starting the thread causes the object's run method to be called in that separately executing thread.

SEE ALSO:

run in class Thread (**I-§1.19.30**).

1.24 Class ArithmeticException

```
public class java.lang.ArithmeticException
    extends java.lang.RuntimeException (I-§1.42)
{
    // Constructors
    public ArithmeticException();                          §1.24.1
    public ArithmeticException(String s);                  §1.24.2
}
```

Thrown when an exceptional arithmetic condition has occurred. For example, an integer "divide by zero" throws an instance of this class.

Constructors

ArithmeticException   §1.24.1

```
public ArithmeticException()
```

Constructs an ArithmeticException with no detail message.

ArithmeticException   §1.24.2

```
public ArithmeticException(String s)
```

Constructs an ArithmeticException with the specified detail message.

PARAMETERS:

s: the detail message.

1.25 Class ArrayIndexOutOfBoundsException

```
public class java.lang.ArrayIndexOutOfBoundsException
    extends java.lang.IndexOutOfBoundsException (I-§1.35)
{
    // Constructors
    public ArrayIndexOutOfBoundsException();            §1.25.1
    public ArrayIndexOutOfBoundsException(int index);   §1.25.2
    public ArrayIndexOutOfBoundsException(String s);    §1.25.3
}
```

Thrown to indicate that an array has been accessed with an illegal index. The index is either negative or greater than or equal to the size of the array.

Constructors

ArrayIndexOutOfBoundsException   §1.25.1

public ArrayIndexOutOfBoundsException()

Constructs an ArrayIndexOutOfBoundsException with no detail message.

ArrayIndexOutOfBoundsException   §1.25.2

public ArrayIndexOutOfBoundsException(int index)

Constructs a new ArrayIndexOutOfBoundsException class with an argument indicating the illegal index.

PARAMETERS:

index: the illegal index.

ArrayIndexOutOfBoundsException   §1.25.3

public ArrayIndexOutOfBoundsException(String s)

Constructs an ArrayIndexOutOfBoundsException class with the specified detail message.

PARAMETERS:

s: the detail message.

1.26 Class ArrayStoreException

```
public class java.lang.ArrayStoreException
    extends java.lang.RuntimeException (I-§1.42)
{
    // Constructors
    public ArrayStoreException();                    §1.26.1
    public ArrayStoreException(String s);            §1.26.2
}
```

Thrown to indicate that an attempt has been made to store the wrong type of object into an array of objects. For example, the following code generates an ArrayStoreException:

```
        Object x[] = new String[3];
        x[0] = new Integer(0);
```

Constructors

ArrayStoreException   §1.26.1

    public ArrayStoreException()

Constructs an ArrayStoreException with no detail message.

ArrayStoreException   §1.26.2

    public ArrayStoreException(String s)

Constructs an ArrayStoreException with the specified detail message.

PARAMETERS:
s: the detail message.

1.27 Class ClassCastException

```
public class java.lang.ClassCastException
    extends java.lang.RuntimeException (I-§1.42)
{
    // Constructors
    public ClassCastException();                     §1.27.1
    public ClassCastException(String s);             §1.27.2
}
```

Thrown to indicate that the code has attempted to cast an object to a subclass of which it is not an instance. For example, the following code generates a Class-CastException:

```
Object x = new Integer(0);
System.out.println((String)x);
```

Constructors

ClassCastException   §1.27.1

    `public ClassCastException()`

        Constructs a `ClassCastException` with no detail message.

ClassCastException   .   §1.27.2

    `public ClassCastException(String s)`

        Constructs a `ClassCastException` with the specified detail message.

    PARAMETERS:

    `s`: the detail message.

1.28 Class ClassNotFoundException

```
public class java.lang.ClassNotFoundException
    extends java.lang.Exception (I-§1.30)
{
    // Constructors
    public ClassNotFoundException();                §1.28.1
    public ClassNotFoundException(String s);        §1.28.2
}
```

Thrown when an application tries to load in a class through its string name using

    ♦ The `forName` method **(I-§1.3.1)** in class `Class`

    ♦ The `findSystemClass` method **(I-§1.4.3)** in class `ClassLoader`

    ♦ The `loadClass` method in class `ClassLoader` **(I-§1.4.4)**

but no definition for the class with the specifed name could be found.

Constructors

ClassNotFoundException   §1.28.1

    `public ClassNotFoundException()`

        Constructs a `ClassNotFoundException` with no detail message.

ClassNotFoundException   §1.28.2

> public ClassNotFoundException(String s)

Constructs a ClassNotFoundException with the specified detail message.

PARAMETERS:
s: the detail message.

1.29 Class CloneNotSupportedException

```
public class java.lang.CloneNotSupportedException
    extends java.lang.Exception (I-§1.30)
{
    // Constructors
    public CloneNotSupportedException();                §1.29.1
    public CloneNotSupportedException(String s);        §1.29.2
}
```

Thrown to indicate that the clone method (I-§1.12.2) in class Object has been called to clone an object, but that the object's class does not implement the Cloneable interface (I-§1.22).

Applications that override the clone method can also throw this exception to indicate that an object could not or should not be cloned.

Constructors

CloneNotSupportedException   §1.29.1

> public CloneNotSupportedException()

Constructs a CloneNotSupportedException with no detail message.

CloneNotSupportedException   §1.29.2

> public CloneNotSupportedException(String s)

Constructs a CloneNotSupportedException with the specified detail message.

PARAMETERS:
s: the detail message.

1.30 Class Exception

```
public class java.lang.Exception
    extends java.lang.Throwable (I-§1.21)
{
    // Constructors
    public Exception();                                           §1.30.1
    public Exception(String s);                                   §1.30.2
}
```

The class Exception and its subclasses are a form of Throwable that indicates conditions that a reasonable application might want to catch.

SEE ALSO:
Error (I-§1.48).

Constructors

Exception   §1.30.1

   public Exception()

   Constructs an Exception with no specified detail message.

Exception   §1.30.2

   public Exception(String s)

   Constructs an Exception with the specified detail message.

   PARAMETERS:
   s: the detail message.

1.31 Class IllegalAccessException

```
public class java.lang.IllegalAccessException
    extends java.lang.Exception (I-§1.30)
{
    // Constructors
    public IllegalAccessException();                              §1.31.1
    public IllegalAccessException(String s);                      §1.31.2
}
```

Thrown when an application tries to load in a class through its string name using

- ◆ The forName method (**I-§1.3.1**) in class Class
- ◆ The findSystemClass method (**I-§1.4.3**) in class ClassLoader
- ◆ The loadClass method in class ClassLoader (**I-§1.4.4**)

but the currently executing method does not have access to the definition of the specified class, because the class is not public and in another package.

An instance of this class can also be thrown when an application tries to create an instance of a class using the newInstance method (**I-§1.3.7**) in class Class, but the current method does not have access to the appropriate zero-argument constructor.

Constructors

IllegalAccessException   **§1.31.1**

    public IllegalAccessException()

    Constructs an IllegalAccessException without a detail message.

IllegalAccessException   **§1.31.2**

    public IllegalAccessException(String s)

    Constructs an IllegalAccessException with a detail message.

    PARAMETERS:

    s: the detail message.

1.32 Class IllegalArgumentException

```
public class java.lang.IllegalArgumentException
    extends java.lang.RuntimeException (I-§1.42)
{
    // Constructors
    public IllegalArgumentException();              §1.32.1
    public IllegalArgumentException(String s);      §1.32.2
}
```

Thrown to indicate that a method has been passed an illegal or inappropriate argument.

Constructors

IllegalArgumentException   §1.32.1

    `public IllegalArgumentException()`

      Constructs an `IllegalArgumentException` with no detail message.

IllegalArgumentException   §1.32.2

    `public IllegalArgumentException(String s)`

      Constructs an `IllegalArgumentException` with the specified detail message.

    PARAMETERS:

    `s`: the detail message.

1.33 Class IllegalMonitorStateException

```
public class java.lang.IllegalMonitorStateException
    extends java.lang.RuntimeException (I-§1.42)
{
    // Constructors
    public IllegalMonitorStateException();              §1.33.1
    public IllegalMonitorStateException(String s);      §1.33.2
}
```

Thrown to indicate that a thread has attempted to wait on an object's monitor (I-§1.12.10–§1.12.12) or to notify other threads waiting on an object's monitor (I-§1.12.7, §1.12.8) without owning the specified monitor.

Constructors

IllegalMonitorStateException   §1.33.1

    `public IllegalMonitorStateException()`

      Constructs an `IllegalMonitorStateException` with no detail message.

IllegalMonitorStateException   §1.33.2

    `public IllegalMonitorStateException(String s)`

      Constructs an `IllegalMonitorStateException` with the specified detail message.

    PARAMETERS:

    `s`: the detail message.

1.34 Class IllegalThreadStateException

```
public class java.lang.IllegalThreadStateException
    extends java.lang.IllegalArgumentException (I-§1.32)
{
    // Constructors
    public IllegalThreadStateException();           §1.34.1
    public IllegalThreadStateException(String s);   §1.34.2
}
```

Thrown to indicate that a thread is not in an appropriate state for the requested operation. See, for example, the suspend (**I-§1.19.39**) and resume (**I-§1.19.29**) methods in class Thread.

Constructors

IllegalThreadStateException   §1.34.1

    public IllegalThreadStateException()

       Constructs an IllegalThreadStateException with no detail message.

IllegalThreadStateException   §1.34.2

    public IllegalThreadStateException(String s)

       Constructs an IllegalThreadStateException with the specified detail message.

       PARAMETERS:

    s: the detail message.

1.35 Class IndexOutOfBoundsException

```
public class java.lang.IndexOutOfBoundsException
    extends java.lang.RuntimeException (I-§1.42)
{
    // Constructors
    public IndexOutOfBoundsException();           §1.35.1
    public IndexOutOfBoundsException(String s);   §1.35.2
}
```

Instances of this class are thrown to indicate that an index of some sort (such as to an array, to a string, or to a vector) is out of range.

Applications can subclass this class to indicate similar exceptions.

Constructors

IndexOutOfBoundsException   §1.35.1

```
public IndexOutOfBoundsException()
```

Constructs an IndexOutOfBoundsException with no detail message.

IndexOutOfBoundsException   §1.35.2

```
public IndexOutOfBoundsException(String s)
```

Constructs an IndexOutOfBoundsException with the specified detail message.

PARAMETERS:

s: the detail message.

1.36 Class InstantiationException

```
public class java.lang.InstantiationException
    extends java.lang.Exception (I-§1.30)
{
    // Constructors
    public InstantiationException();                §1.36.1
    public InstantiationException(String s);        §1.36.2
}
```

Thrown when an application tries to create an instance of a class using the newInstance method (**I-§1.3.7**) in class Class, but the specified class object cannot be instantiated because it is an interface or is an abstract class.

Constructors

InstantiationException   §1.36.1

```
public InstantiationException()
```

Constructs an InstantiationException with no detail message.

InstantiationException   §1.36.2

```
public InstantiationException(String s)
```

Constructs an InstantiationException with the specified detail message.

PARAMETERS:

s: the detail message.

1.37 Class InterruptedException

```
public class java.lang.InterruptedException
    extends java.lang.Exception (I-§1.30)
{
    // Constructors
    public InterruptedException();                    §1.37.1
    public InterruptedException(String s);            §1.37.2
}
```

Thrown when a thread is waiting (**I-§1.12.10–§1.12.12**), sleeping (**I-§1.19.34**), or otherwise paused for a long time and another thread interrupts it using the `interrupt` method (**I-§1.19.21**) in class `Thread`.

Constructors

InterruptedException   §1.37.1

> `public InterruptedException()`
>
> Constructs an `InterruptedException` with no detail message.

InterruptedException   §1.37.2

> `public InterruptedException(String s)`
>
> Constructs an `InterruptedException` with the specified detail message.
>
> **PARAMETERS:**
> `s`: the detail message.

1.38 Class NegativeArraySizeException

```
public class java.lang.NegativeArraySizeException
    extends java.lang.RuntimeException (I-§1.42)
{
    // Constructors
    public NegativeArraySizeException();              §1.38.1
    public NegativeArraySizeException(String s);      §1.38.2
}
```

Thrown if an application tries to create an array with negative size.

Constructors

NegativeArraySizeException   §1.38.1

    `public NegativeArraySizeException()`

      Constructs a `NegativeArraySizeException` with no detail message.

NegativeArraySizeException   §1.38.2

    `public NegativeArraySizeException(String s)`

      Constructs a `NegativeArraySizeException` with the specified detail message.

      PARAMETERS:

    `s`: the detail message.

1.39 Class NoSuchMethodException

```
public class java.lang.NoSuchMethodException
    extends java.lang.Exception (I-§1.30)
{
    // Constructors
    public NoSuchMethodException();                §1.39.1
    public NoSuchMethodException(String s);        §1.39.2
}
```

This exception is obsolete.

Constructors

NoSuchMethodException   §1.39.1

    `public NoSuchMethodException()`

      Constructs a `NoSuchMethodException` without a detail message.

NoSuchMethodException   §1.39.2

    `public NoSuchMethodException(String s)`

      Constructs a `NoSuchMethodException` with a detail message.

      PARAMETERS:

    `s`: the detail message.

1.40 Class NullPointerException

```
public class java.lang.NullPointerException
    extends java.lang.RuntimeException (I-§1.42)
{
    // Constructors
    public NullPointerException();                          §1.40.1
    public NullPointerException(String s);                  §1.40.2
}
```

Thrown when an application attempts to use `null` in a case where an object is required. These include:

◆ Calling the instance method of a `null` object.

◆ Accessing or modifying the field of a `null` object.

◆ Taking the length of `null` as if it were an array.

◆ Accessing or modifying the slots of `null` as if it were an array.

◆ Throwing `null` as if it were a `Throwable` value.

Applications should throw instances of this class to indicate other illegal uses of the `null` object.

Constructors

NullPointerException   §1.40.1

    `public NullPointerException()`

        Constructs a `NullPointerException` with no detail message.

NullPointerException   §1.40.2

    `public NullPointerException(String s)`

        Constructs a `NullPointerException` with the specified detail message.

    PARAMETERS:

    `s`: the detail message.

1.41 Class NumberFormatException

```
public class java.lang.NumberFormatException
    extends java.lang.IllegalArgumentException (I-§1.32)
{
    // Constructors
    public NumberFormatException();                        §1.41.1
    public NumberFormatException(String s);                §1.41.2
}
```

Thrown to indicate that the application has attempted to convert a string to one of the numeric types, but that the string does not have the appropriate format.

Constructors

NumberFormatException   §1.41.1

    public NumberFormatException()

    Constructs a NumberFormatException with no detail message.

NumberFormatException   §1.41.2

    public NumberFormatException(String s)

    Constructs a NumberFormatException with the specified detail message.

    PARAMETERS:
    s: the detail message.

1.42 Class RuntimeException

```
public class java.lang.RuntimeException
    extends java.lang.Exception (I-§1.30)
{
    // Constructors
    public RuntimeException();                             §1.42.1
    public RuntimeException(String s);                     §1.42.2
}
```

RuntimeException is the superclass of those exceptions that can be thrown during the normal operation of the Java Virtual Machine.

A method is not required to declare in its throws clause any subclasses of RuntimeException that might be thrown during the execution of the method but not caught.

Constructors

RuntimeException   §1.42.1

    `public RuntimeException()`

   Constructs a `RuntimeException` with no detail message.

RuntimeException   §1.42.2

    `public RuntimeException(String s)`

   Constructs a `RuntimeException` with the specified detail message.

   PARAMETERS:

   `s:` the detail message.

1.43 Class SecurityException

```
public class java.lang.SecurityException
    extends java.lang.RuntimeException (I-§1.42)
{
    // Constructors
    public SecurityException();                       §1.43.1
    public SecurityException(String s);               §1.43.2
}
```

Thrown by the security manager **(I-§1.15)** to indicate a security violation.

Constructors

SecurityException   §1.43.1

    `public SecurityException()`

   Constructs a `SecurityException` with no detail message.

SecurityException   §1.43.2

    `public SecurityException(String s)`

   Constructs a `SecurityException` with the specified detail message.

   PARAMETERS:

   `s:` the detail message.

1.44 Class StringIndexOutOfBoundsException

```
public class java.lang.StringIndexOutOfBoundsException
    extends java.lang.IndexOutOfBoundsException (I-§1.35)
{
    // Constructors
    public StringIndexOutOfBoundsException();              §1.44.1
    public StringIndexOutOfBoundsException(int index);     §1.44.2
    public StringIndexOutOfBoundsException(String s)       §1.44.3
}
```

Thrown by the charAt method (**I-§1.16.8**) in class class String and by other String methods to indicate that an index is either negative or greater than or equal to the size of the string.

Constructors

StringIndexOutOfBoundsException   §1.44.1

```
public StringIndexOutOfBoundsException()
```

Constructs a StringIndexOutOfBoundsException with no detail message.

StringIndexOutOfBoundsException   §1.44.2

```
public StringIndexOutOfBoundsException(int index)
```

Constructs a new StringIndexOutOfBoundsException class with an argument indicating the illegal index.

PARAMETERS:
index: the illegal index.

StringIndexOutOfBoundsException   §1.44.3

```
public StringIndexOutOfBoundsException(String s)
```

Constructs a StringIndexOutOfBoundsException with the specified detail message.

PARAMETERS:
s: the detail message.

1.45 Class AbstractMethodError

```
public class java.lang.AbstractMethodError
    extends java.lang.IncompatibleClassChangeError (I-§1.50)
{
    // Constructors
    public AbstractMethodError();                        §1.45.1
    public AbstractMethodError(String s);                §1.45.2
}
```

Thrown when an application tries to call an abstract method. Normally, this error is caught by the compiler; this error can only occur at run time if the definition of some class has incompatibly changed since the currently executing method was last compiled.

Constructors

AbstractMethodError   §1.45.1

public AbstractMethodError()

Constructs an AbstractMethodError with no detail message.

AbstractMethodError   §1.45.2

public AbstractMethodError(String s)

Constructs an AbstractMethodError with the specified detail message.

PARAMETERS:

s: the detail message.

1.46 Class ClassCircularityError

```
public class java.lang.ClassCircularityError
    extends java.lang.LinkageError (I-§1.53)
{
    // Constructors
    public ClassCircularityError();                      §1.46.1
    public ClassCircularityError(String s);              §1.46.2
}
```

This error is obsolete.

Constructors

ClassCircularityError   §1.46.1

    public ClassCircularityError()

        Constructs a ClassCircularityError with no detail message.

ClassCircularityError   §1.46.2

    public ClassCircularityError(String s)

        Constructs a ClassCircularityError with the specified detail message.

    PARAMETERS:

    s : the detail message.

1.47 Class ClassFormatError

```
public class java.lang.ClassFormatError
    extends java.lang.LinkageError (I-§1.53)
{
    // Constructors
    public ClassFormatError();                          §1.47.1
    public ClassFormatError(String s);                  §1.47.2
}
```

Thrown when the Java Virtual Machine attempts to read a class file and determines that the file is malformed or otherwise cannot be interpreted as a class file.

Constructors

ClassFormatError   §1.47.1

    public ClassFormatError()

        Constructs a ClassFormatError with no detail message.

ClassFormatError   §1.47.2

    public ClassFormatError(String s)

        Constructs a ClassFormatError with the specified detail message.

    PARAMETERS:

    s : the detail message.

1.48 Class Error

```
public class java.lang.Error
    extends java.lang.Throwable (I-§1.21)
{
    // Constructors
    public Error();                                    §1.48.1
    public Error(String s);                            §1.48.2
}
```

An Error is a subclass of Throwable that indicates serious problems that a reasonable application should not try to catch. Most such errors are abnormal conditions. The ThreadDeath error (I-§1.59), though a "normal" condition, is also a subclass of Error because most applications should not try to catch it.

A method is not required to declare in its throws clause any subclasses of Error that might be thrown during the execution of the method but not caught, since these errors are abnormal conditions that should never occur.

Constructors

Error   §1.48.1

    public Error()

    Constructs an Error with no specified detail message.

Error   §1.48.2

    public Error(String s)

    Constructs an Error with the specified detail message.

    PARAMETERS:
    s: the detail message.

1.49 Class IllegalAccessError

```
public class java.lang.IllegalAccessError
    extends java.lang.IncompatibleClassChangeError (I-§1.50)
{
    // Constructors
    public IllegalAccessError();                       §1.49.1
    public IllegalAccessError(String s);               §1.49.2
}
```

Thrown if an application attempts to access or modify a field, or to call a method that it does not have access to.

Normally, this error is caught by the compiler; this error can only occur at run time if the definition of a class has incompatibly changed.

Constructors

IllegalAccessError   §1.49.1
　　public IllegalAccessError()
　　　Constructs an IllegalAccessError with no detail message.

IllegalAccessError   §1.49.2
　　public IllegalAccessError(String s)
　　　Constructs an IllegalAccessError with the specified detail message.
　　PARAMETERS:
　　s: the detail message.

1.50 Class IncompatibleClassChangeError

```
public class java.lang.IncompatibleClassChangeError
    extends java.lang.LinkageError (I-§1.53)
{
    // Constructors
    public IncompatibleClassChangeError();              §1.50.1
    public IncompatibleClassChangeError(String s);      §1.50.2
}
```

An instance of a subclass of IncompatibleClassChangeError is thrown to indicate that an incompatible class change has occurred to some class definition. The definition of some class, on which the currently executing method depends, has since changed.

Constructors

IncompatibleClassChangeError   §1.50.1
　　public IncompatibleClassChangeError()
　　　Constructs an IncompatibleClassChangeError with no detail message.

IncompatibleClassChangeError §1.50.2

> public IncompatibleClassChangeError(String s)

> Constructs an IncompatibleClassChangeError with the specified detail message.

> **PARAMETERS:**
> s: the detail message.

1.51 Class InstantiationError

```
public class java.lang.InstantiationError
    extends java.lang.IncompatibleClassChangeError (I-§1.50)
{
    // Constructors
    public InstantiationError();                        §1.51.1
    public InstantiationError(String s);                §1.51.2
}
```

Thrown when an application tries to use the Java new construct to instantiate an abstract class or an interface.

Normally, this error is caught by the compiler; this error can only occur at run time if the definition of a class has incompatibly changed.

Constructors

InstantiationError §1.51.1

> public InstantiationError()

> Constructs an InstantiationError with no detail message.

InstantiationError §1.51.2

> public InstantiationError(String s)

> Constructs an InstantiationError with the specified detail message.

> **PARAMETERS:**
> s: the detail message.

1.52 Class InternalError

```
public class java.lang.InternalError
    extends java.lang.VirtualMachineError (I-§1.63)
{
    // Constructors
    public InternalError();                           §1.52.1
    public InternalError(String s);                   §1.52.2
}
```

Thrown to indicate some unexpected internal error has occurred in the Java Virtual Machine.

Constructors

InternalError   §1.52.1

> public InternalError()

> Constructs an InternalError with no detail message.

InternalError   §1.52.2

> public InternalError(String s)

> Constructs an InternalError with the specified detail message.

> **PARAMETERS:**
> s: the detail message.

1.53 Class LinkageError

```
public class java.lang.LinkageError
    extends java.lang.Error (I-§1.48)
{
    // Constructors
    public LinkageError();                            §1.53.1
    public LinkageError(String s);                    §1.53.2
}
```

Subclasses of LinkageError indicate that a class has some dependency on another class; however, the latter class has incompatibly changed after the compilation of the former class.

Constructors

LinkageError §1.53.1

> `public LinkageError()`
>
> Constructs a `LinkageError` with no detail message.

LinkageError §1.53.2

> `public LinkageError(String s)`
>
> Constructs a `LinkageError` with the specified detail message.
>
> **PARAMETERS:**
> `s`: the detail message.

1.54 Class NoClassDefFoundError

```
public class java.lang.NoClassDefFoundError
    extends java.lang.LinkageError (I-§1.53)
{
    // Constructors
    public NoClassDefFoundError();                    §1.54.1
    public NoClassDefFoundError(String s);            §1.54.2
}
```

Thrown if the Java Virtual Machine or a classloader tries to load in the definition of a class (as part of a normal method call or as part of creating a new instance using the new expression) and no definition of the class could be found.

The searched-for class definition existed when the currently executing class was compiled, but the definition can no longer be found.

Constructors

NoClassDefFoundError §1.54.1

> `public NoClassDefFoundError()`
>
> Constructs a `NoClassDefFoundError` with no detail message.

NoClassDefFoundError §1.54.2

> `public NoClassDefFoundError(String s)`
>
> Constructs a `NoClassDefFoundError` with the specified detail message.
>
> **PARAMETERS:**
> `s`: the detail message.

1.55 Class NoSuchFieldError

```
public class java.lang.NoSuchFieldError
    extends java.lang.IncompatibleClassChangeError (I-§1.50)
{
    // Constructors
    public NoSuchFieldError();                                §1.55.1
    public NoSuchFieldError(String s);                        §1.55.2
}
```

Thrown if an application tries to access or modify a specified field of an object, and that object no longer has that field.

Normally, this error is caught by the compiler; this error can only occur at run time if the definition of a class has incompatibly changed.

Constructors

NoSuchFieldError   §1.55.1

   public NoSuchFieldError()

   Constructs a NoSuchFieldException with no detail message.

NoSuchFieldError   §1.55.2

   public NoSuchFieldError(String s)

   Constructs a NoSuchFieldException with the specified detail message.

   PARAMETERS:
   s: the detail message.

1.56 Class NoSuchMethodError

```
public class java.lang.NoSuchMethodError
    extends java.lang.IncompatibleClassChangeError (I-§1.50)
{
    // Constructors
    public NoSuchMethodError();                               §1.56.1
    public NoSuchMethodError(String s);                       §1.56.2
}
```

Thrown if an application tries to call a specified method of a class (either static or instance), and that class no longer has a definition of that method.

Normally, this error is caught by the compiler; this error can only occur at run time if the definition of a class has incompatibly changed.

Constructors

NoSuchMethodError §1.56.1

> `public NoSuchMethodError()`

> Constructs a NoSuchMethodException with no detail message.

NoSuchMethodError §1.56.2

> `public NoSuchMethodError(String s)`

> Constructs a NoSuchMethodException with the specified detail message.

> **PARAMETERS:**

> s : the detail message.

1.57 Class OutOfMemoryError

```
public class java.lang.OutOfMemoryError
    extends java.lang.VirtualMachineError (I-§1.63)
{
    // Constructors
    public OutOfMemoryError();                §1.57.1
    public OutOfMemoryError(String s);        §1.57.2
}
```

Thrown when the Java Virtual Machine cannot allocate an object because it is out of memory, and no more memory could be made available by the garbage collector.

Constructors

OutOfMemoryError §1.57.1

> `public OutOfMemoryError()`

> Constructs an OutOfMemoryError with no detail message.

OutOfMemoryError §1.57.2

> `public OutOfMemoryError(String s)`

> Constructs an OutOfMemoryError with the specified detail message.

> **PARAMETERS:**

> s : the detail message.

1.58 Class StackOverflowError

```
public class java.lang.StackOverflowError
    extends java.lang.VirtualMachineError (I-§1.63)
{
    // Constructors
    public StackOverflowError();                        §1.58.1
    public StackOverflowError(String s);                §1.58.2
}
```

Thrown when a stack overflow occurs because an application recurses too deeply.

Constructors

StackOverflowError   §1.58.1

    public StackOverflowError()

     Constructs a StackOverflowError with no detail message.

StackOverflowError   §1.58.2

    public StackOverflowError(String s)

     Constructs a StackOverflowError with the specified detail message.

     PARAMETERS:

     s: the detail message.

1.59 Class ThreadDeath

```
public class java.lang.ThreadDeath
    extends java.lang.Error (I-§1.48)
{
    // Constructors
    public ThreadDeath();                               §1.59.1
}
```

An instance of ThreadDeath is thrown in the victim thread when the stop method with zero arguments (I-§1.19.37) in class Thread is called.

An application should catch instances of this class only if it must clean up after being terminated asynchronously. If ThreadDeath is caught by a method, it is important that it be rethrown so that the thread actually dies.

The top-level error handler does not print out a message if ThreadDeath is never caught.

The class `ThreadDeath` is specifically a subclass of `Error` rather than `Exception`, even though it is a "normally occurrence," because many applications catch all occurrences of `Exception` and then discard the exception.

Constructors

ThreadDeath   §1.59.1

    `public ThreadDeath()`

        Constructs a new ThreadDeath object.

1.60 Class UnknownError

```
public class java.lang.UnknownError
    extends java.lang.VirtualMachineError (I-§1.63)
{
    // Constructors
    public UnknownError();                                §1.60.1
    public UnknownError(String s);                        §1.60.2
}
```

Thrown when an unknown but serious exception has occurred in the Java Virtual Machine.

Constructors

UnknownError   §1.60.1

    `public UnknownError()`

        Constructs an `UnknownError` with no detail message.

UnknownError   §1.60.2

    `public UnknownError(String s)`

        Constructs an `UnknownError` with the specified detail message.

        PARAMETERS:

    `s`: the detail message.

1.61 Class UnsatisfiedLinkError

```
public class java.lang.UnsatisfiedLinkError
    extends java.lang.LinkageError (I-§1.53)
{
    // Constructors
    public UnsatisfiedLinkError();                          §1.61.1
    public UnsatisfiedLinkError(String s);                  §1.61.2
}
```

Thrown if the Java Virtual Machine cannot find an appropriate native-language definition of a method declared `native`.

Constructors

UnsatisfiedLinkError   §1.61.1

> public UnsatisfiedLinkError()

> Constructs an UnsatisfiedLinkError with no detail message.

UnsatisfiedLinkError   §1.61.2

> public UnsatisfiedLinkError(String s)

> Constructs an UnsatisfiedLinkError with the specified detail message.

> **PARAMETERS:**

> s: the detail message.

1.62 Class VerifyError

```
public class java.lang.VerifyError
    extends java.lang.LinkageError (I-§1.53)
{
    // Constructors
    public VerifyError();                                   §1.62.1
    public VerifyError(String s);                           §1.62.2
}
```

Thrown when the "verifier" detects that a class file, though well formed, contains some sort of internal inconsistency or security problem.

Constructors

VerifyError   **§1.62.1**

  public VerifyError()

   Constructs an VerifyError with no detail message.

VerifyError   **§1.62.2**

  public VerifyError(String s)

   Constructs an VerifyError with the specified detail message.

1.63 Class VirtualMachineError

```
public class java.lang.VirtualMachineError
    extends java.lang.Error (I-§1.48)
{
    // Constructors
    public VirtualMachineError();                   §1.63.1
    public VirtualMachineError(String s);           §1.63.2
}
```

Thrown to indicate that the Java Virtual Machine is broken or has run out of resources necessary for it to continue operating.

Constructors

VirtualMachineError   **§1.63.1**

  public VirtualMachineError()

   Constructs a VirtualMachineError with no detail message.

VirtualMachineError   **§1.63.2**

  public VirtualMachineError(String s)

   Constructs a VirtualMachineError with the specified detail message.

   PARAMETERS:

   s: the detail message.

CHAPTER 2

Package java.io

THE java.io package provides a set of input and output streams used to read and write data to files or other input and output sources.

The classes can be divided into several categories:

♦ **Low-level Input and Output**: The classes InputStream (I-§2.13) and OutputStream (I-§2.15) implement the basic input/output streams in the system. They provide the mechanisms for reading and writing single bytes and arrays of bytes. All other input and output streams are built on top of these.

♦ **Filtered Streams**: The classes FilteredInputStream (I-§2.11) and FilteredOutputStream (I-§2.12) provide extensible mechanisms for adding functionality to input streams and output streams. The filter streams provided in java.io are the following:

  ♦ The class PrintStream (I-§2.18) makes it easier for an application to print objects other than bytes and byte arrays.

  ♦ The class LineNumberInputStream (I-§2.14) keeps track of line numbers in an input stream.

  ♦ The classes BufferedInputStream (I-§2.1) and BufferedOutputStream (I-§2.19) provide an application a means of buffering input and output in order to save system resources.

  ♦ The classes DataInputStream (I-§2.5) and DataOuputStream (I-§2.6) provide a mechanism for reading and writing primitive data types in a portable manner. These two classes implement the DataInput (I-§2.24) and DataOutput (I-§2.25) interfaces, respectively. These two interfaces allow an application to create additional classes that read and write primitive data types.

  ♦ The PushbackInputStream (I-§2.19) provides an "unread" mechanism.

♦ **Files**: The classes `File` (I-§2.7) and `FileDescriptor` (I-§2.8) allow files to be specified as either a pathname or in terms of a system-dependent file descriptor. Using either a file or a file descriptor, an application can read and write from a file using the classes `FileInputStream` (I-§2.9) and `FileOutputStream` (I-§2.10). The class `RandomAccessFile` (I-§2.20) allows an application to both read and write a file. The `FilenameFilter` interface (I-§2.26) provides a means whereby an application can filter the contents of a directory listing.

♦ **Input and Output to Strings**: The classes `ByteArrayInputStream` (I-§2.3), `StringBufferInputStream` (I-§2.23), and `ByteArrayOutputStream` (I-§2.4) implement streams that get their input from a string or from a byte array, or write their output to a string or to a byte array.

♦ **Communication Pipes**: The classes `PipedInputStream` (I-§2.16) and `PipedOutputStream` (I-§2.17) provide a means for two threads to communicate using a string to which one writes and from which the other reads.

♦ **Stream Concatenation**: The class `SequenceInputStream` (I-§2.21) allows an application to create an input from two or more input streams.

♦ **Tokenization**: The class `StreamTokenizer` (I-§2.22) allows an application to parse an input stream into tokens.

♦ **Exceptions**: All exceptions in this package are subclasses of `IOException` (I-§2.29). Under certain circumstances, a more specific exception is thrown. The exception `FileNotFoundException` (I-§2.28) indicates that a specified file could not be opened. The exceptions `UTFDataFormatException` (I-§2.31) and `EOFException` (I-§2.24) indicate that the input stream was malformed when reading primitive data from a data input stream. The `InterruptedIOException` (I-§2.30) indicates that a long-running input operation is interrupted.

Some of the streams implement marks. Stream marks are intended to be used when an application needs to read ahead a little to see what is in the stream. For example, an application might try one of several parsers on an input stream until it finds one that succeeds. An application can determine if a specific stream implements marks by calling the `markSupported` method (I-§2.13.5).

2.1 Class BufferedInputStream

```
public class java.io.BufferedInputStream
    extends java.io.FilterInputStream (I-§2.11)
{
    // Fields
    protected byte buf[];                                    §2.1.1
    protected int count;                                     §2.1.2
    protected int marklimit;                                 §2.1.3
    protected int markpos;                                   §2.1.4
    protected int pos;                                       §2.1.5

    // Constructors
    public BufferedInputStream(InputStream in);              §2.1.6
    public BufferedInputStream(InputStream in, int size);    §2.1.7
    public int available();                                  §2.1.8

    // Methods
    public void mark(int readlimit);                         §2.1.9
    public boolean markSupported();                          §2.1.10
    public int read();                                       §2.1.11
    public int read(byte b[], int off, int len);             §2.1.12
    public void reset();                                     §2.1.13
    public long skip(long n);                                §2.1.14
}
```

The class implements a buffered input stream. By setting up such an input stream, an application can read bytes from a stream without necessarily causing a call to the underlying system for each byte read. The data is read by blocks into a buffer; subsequent reads can access the data directly from the buffer.

Fields

buf   §2.1.1

    `protected byte buf[]`

      The buffer where data is stored.

count   §2.1.2

    `protected int count`

      The index one greater than the index of the last valid byte in the buffer.

marklimit   §2.1.3

```
protected int marklimit
```

The maximum read ahead allowed after a call to the mark method (**I-§2.1.9**) before subsequent calls to the reset method (**I-§2.1.13**) fail.

markpos   §2.1.4

```
protected int markpos
```

The value of the pos field (**I-§2.1.5**) at the time the last mark method (**I-§2.1.9**) was called. The value of this field is –1 if there is no current mark.

pos   §2.1.5

```
protected int pos
```

The current position in the buffer. This is the index of the next character to be read from the buf (**I-§2.1.1**) array.

Constructors

BufferedInputStream   §2.1.6

```
public BufferedInputStream(InputStream in)
```

Creates a new buffered input stream to read data from the specified input stream with a default 512-byte buffer size.

PARAMETERS:
in: the underlying input stream.

BufferedInputStream   §2.1.7

```
public BufferedInputStream(InputStream in, int size)
```

Creates a new buffered input stream to read data from the specified input stream with the specified buffer size.

PARAMETERS:
in: the underlying input stream.
size: the buffer size.

Methods

available   §2.1.8

```
public int available()
throws IOException
```

Determines the number of bytes that can be read from this input stream without blocking.

The `available` method of `BufferedInputStream` returns the sum of the the number of bytes remaining to be read in the buffer (count – pos) and the result of calling the `available` method of the underlying input stream (**I-§2.11.1**).

RETURNS:

the number of bytes that can be read from this input stream without blocking.

THROWS:

`IOException` (**I-§2.29**)
if an I/O error occurs.

OVERRIDES:

`available` in class `FilterInputStream` (**I-§2.11.3**).

mark   §2.1.9

```
public void mark(int readlimit)
```

Marks the current position in this input stream. A subsequent call to the `reset` method (**I-§2.1.13**) repositions the stream at the last marked position so that subsequent reads re-read the same bytes.

The `readlimit` argument tells the input stream to allow that many bytes to be read before the mark position gets invalidated.

PARAMETERS:

`readlimit`: the maximum limit of bytes that can be read before the mark position becomes invalid.

OVERRIDES:

`mark` in class `FilterInputStream` (**I-§2.11.5**).

markSupported   §2.1.10

```
public boolean markSupported()
```

Determines if this input stream supports the mark (I-§2.13.4) and reset (I-§2.13.9) methods. The markSupported method of BufferedInputStream returns true.

RETURNS:

a boolean indicating if this stream type supports the mark and reset methods.

OVERRIDES:

markSupported in class FilterInputStream (I-§2.11.6).

read   §2.1.11

```
public int read()
throws IOException
```

Reads the next byte of data from this buffered input stream. The value byte is returned as an int in the range 0 to 255. If no byte is available because the end of the stream has been reached, the value -1 is returned. This method blocks until input data is available, the end of the stream is detected, or an exception is thrown.

The read method of BufferedInputStream returns the next byte of data from its buffer if the buffer is not empty. Otherwise, it refills the buffer from the underlying input stream (I-§2.11.1) and returns the next character, if the underlying stream has not returned an end-of-stream indicator.

RETURNS:

the next byte of data, or -1 if the end of the stream is reached.

THROWS:

IOException (I-§2.29)
if an I/O error occurs.

OVERRIDES:

read in class FilterInputStream (I-§2.11.7).

read   §2.1.12

```
public int read(byte b[], int off, int len)
throws IOException
```

Reads up to len bytes of data from this buffered input stream into an array of bytes. This method blocks until some input is available.

The read method of BufferedInputStream copies bytes from its buffer into the array argument if the buffer is not empty. Otherwise, it refills the buffer from the underlying input stream (**I-§2.11.1**) and unless the underlying stream returns an end-of-stream indicator, it fills the array argument with characters from the newly filled buffer.

PARAMETERS:

b: the buffer into which the data is read.
off: the start offset of the data.
len: the maximum number of bytes read.

RETURNS:

the total number of bytes read into the buffer, or -1 if there is no more data because the end of the stream has been reached.

THROWS:

IOException (**I-§2.29**)
if an I/O error occurs.

OVERRIDES:

read in class FilterInputStream (**I-§2.11.9**).

reset   §2.1.13

```
public void reset()
throws IOException
```

Repositions this stream to the position at the time the mark method (**I-§2.1.9**) was last called on this input stream.

THROWS:

IOException (**I-§2.29**)
if this stream has not been marked or if the mark has been invalidated.

OVERRIDES:

reset in class FilterInputStream (**I-§2.11.10**).

skip   §2.1.14

```
public long skip(long n)
throws IOException
```

Skips over and discards n bytes of data from the input stream. The `skip` method may, for a variety of reasons, end up skipping over some smaller number of bytes, possibly 0. The actual number of bytes skipped is returned.

The skip method of `BufferedInputStream` compares the number of bytes it has available in its buffer, α, where $\alpha = \text{count} - \text{pos}$, with n. If $n \le \alpha$, then the `pos` field is incremented by n. Otherwise, the `pos` field is incremented to have the value `count`, and the remaining bytes (if any) are skipped by calling the underlying input stream's **(I-§2.11.1)** `skip` method with the argument $n - \alpha$.

PARAMETERS:

n: the number of bytes to be skipped.

RETURNS:

the actual number of bytes skipped.

THROWS:

IOException **(I-§2.29)**

if an I/O error occurs.

OVERRIDES:

skip in class `FilterInputStream` **(I-§2.11.11)**.

2.2 Class BufferedOutputStream

```
public class java.io.BufferedOutputStream
    extends java.io.FilterOutputStream (I-§2.12)
{
    // Fields
    protected byte buf[];                                    §2.2.1
    protected int count;                                     §2.2.2

    // Constructors
    public BufferedOutputStream(OutputStream out);           §2.2.3
    public BufferedOutputStream(OutputStream out,
                                int size);                   §2.2.4

    // Methods
    public void flush();                                     §2.2.5
    public void write(byte b[], int off, int len);           §2.2.6
    public void write(int b);                                §2.2.7
}
```

The class implements a buffered output stream. By setting up such an output stream, an application can write bytes to the underlying output stream without necessarily causing a call to the underlying system for each byte written. The data is written into a buffer, and then written to the underlying stream if the buffer reaches its capacity, the buffer output stream is closed, or the buffer output stream is explicity flushed.

Fields

buf §2.2.1

```
protected byte buf[]
```

The buffer where data is stored.

count §2.2.2

```
protected int count
```

The number of valid bytes in the buffer.

Constructors

BufferedOutputStream §2.2.3

```
public BufferedOutputStream(OutputStream out)
```

Creates a new buffered output stream to write data to the specified underlying output stream with a default 512-byte buffer size.

PARAMETERS:

out: the underlying output stream.

BufferedOutputStream §2.2.4

```
public BufferedOutputStream(OutputStream out, int size)
```

Creates a new buffered output stream to write data to the specified underlying output stream with the specified buffer size.

PARAMETERS:

out: the underlying output stream.
size: the buffer size.

Methods

flush   §2.2.5

```
public void flush()
throws IOException
```

Flushes this buffered output stream. This forces any buffered output bytes to be written out to the underlying output stream (**I-§2.12.1**).

THROWS:

`IOException` (**I-§2.29**)
if an I/O error occurs.

OVERRIDES:

`flush` in class `FilterOutputStream` (**I-§2.12.4**).

write   §2.2.6

```
public void write(byte b[], int off, int len)
throws IOException
```

Writes `len` bytes from the specified byte array starting at offset `off` to this buffered output stream.

PARAMETERS:

`b`: the data.
`off`: the start offset in the data.
`len`: the number of bytes to write.

THROWS:

`IOException` (**I-§2.29**)
if an I/O error occurs.

OVERRIDES:

`write` in class `FilterOutputStream` (**I-§2.12.6**).

write   §2.2.7

```
public void write(int b)
throws IOException
```

Writes the specified byte to this buffered output stream.

PARAMETERS:

`b`: the byte to be written.

THROWS:

`IOException` (**I-§2.29**)
if an I/O error occurs.

OVERRIDES:

`write` in class `FilterOutputStream` (**I-§2.12.7**).

2.3 Class ByteArrayInputStream

```
public class java.io.ByteArrayInputStream
    extends java.io.InputStream (I-§2.13)
{
    // Fields
    protected byte buf[];                                      §2.3.1
    protected int count;                                       §2.3.2
    protected int pos;                                         §2.3.3

    // Constructors
    public ByteArrayInputStream(byte buf[]);                   §2.3.4
    public ByteArrayInputStream(byte buf[], int offset,        §2.3.5
                                int length);
    // Methods
    public int available();                                    §2.3.6
    public int read();                                         §2.3.7
    public int read(byte b[], int off, int len);              §2.3.8
    public void reset();                                       §2.3.9
    public long skip(long n);                                  §2.3.10
}
```

This class allows an application to create an input stream in which the bytes read are supplied by the contents of a byte array. Applications can also read bytes from a string by using a `StringBufferInputStream` (I-§2.23).

Fields

buf   §2.3.1

```
protected byte buf[]
```
The byte array containing the data.

count   §2.3.2

```
protected int count
```
The index one greater than the last valid character in the input stream buffer.

pos   §2.3.3

```
protected int pos
```
The index of the next character to read from the input stream buffer.

Constructors

ByteArrayInputStream   §2.3.4

```
public ByteArrayInputStream(byte buf[])
```

Creates a new byte array input stream that reads data from the specified byte array. The byte array is not copied.

PARAMETERS:

buf: the input buffer.

ByteArrayInputStream   §2.3.5

```
public ByteArrayInputStream(byte buf[], int offset,
                            int length)
```

Creates a new byte array input stream that reads data from the specified byte array. Up to length characters are to be read from the byte array, starting at the indicated offset.

The byte array is not copied.

PARAMETERS:

buf: the input buffer.
offset: the offset in the buffer of the first byte to read.
length: the maximum number of bytes to read from the buffer.

Methods

available   §2.3.6

```
public int available()
```

Determines the number of bytes that can be read from this input stream without blocking.

The available method of ByteArrayInputStream returns the value of count − pos, which is the number of bytes remaining to be read from the input buffer.

RETURNS:

the number of bytes that can be read from the input stream without blocking.

OVERRIDES:

available in class InputStream (I-§2.13.2).

read   §2.3.7

`public int read()`

Reads the next byte of data from this input stream. The value byte is returned as an `int` in the range `0` to `255`. If no byte is available because the end of the stream has been reached, the value `-1` is returned.

The `read` method of `ByteArrayInputStream` cannot block.

RETURNS:

the next byte of data, or `-1` if the end of the stream has been reached.

OVERRIDES:

read in class `InputStream` (**I-§2.13.6**).

read   §2.3.8

`public int read(byte b[], int off, int len)`

Reads up to `len` bytes of data into an array of bytes from this input stream. This `read` method cannot block.

PARAMETERS:

`b`: the buffer into which the data is read.
`off`: the start offset of the data.
`len`: the maximum number of bytes read.

RETURNS:

the total number of bytes read into the buffer, or `-1` if there is no more data because the end of the stream has been reached.

OVERRIDES:

read in class `InputStream` (**I-§2.13.8**).

reset   §2.3.9

`public void reset()`

Resets this input stream to begin reading from the same position at which it first started reading from the buffer.

OVERRIDES:

reset in class `InputStream` (**I-§2.13.9**).

skip   §2.3.10

```
public long skip(long n)
```

Skips n bytes of input from this input stream. Fewer bytes might be skipped if the end of the input stream is reached.

PARAMETERS:

n: the number of bytes to be skipped.

RETURNS:

the actual number of bytes skipped.

OVERRIDES:

`skip` in class `InputStream` (I-§2.13.10).

2.4 Class ByteArrayOutputStream

```
public class java.io.ByteArrayOutputStream
    extends java.io.OutputStream (I-§2.15)
{
    // Fields
    protected byte buf[];                                    §2.4.1
    protected int count;                                     §2.4.2

    // Constructors
    public ByteArrayOutputStream();                          §2.4.3
    public ByteArrayOutputStream(int size);                  §2.4.4

    // Methods
    public void reset();                                     §2.4.5
    public int size();                                       §2.4.6
    public byte[] toByteArray();                             §2.4.7
    public String toString();                                §2.4.8
    public String toString(int hibyte);                      §2.4.9
    public void write(byte b[], int off, int len);           §2.4.10
    public void write(int b);                                §2.4.11
    public void writeTo(OutputStream out);                   §2.4.12
}
```

This class implements an output stream in which the data is written into a byte array. The buffer automatically grows as data is written to it.

Fields

buf   §2.4.1

```
protected byte buf[]
```

The buffer where data is stored.

count §2.4.2

```
protected int count
```

   The number of valid bytes in the buffer.

Constructors

ByteArrayOutputStream §2.4.3

```
public ByteArrayOutputStream()
```

   Creates a new byte array output stream.

ByteArrayOutputStream §2.4.4

```
public ByteArrayOutputStream(int size)
```

   Creates a new byte array output stream. The buffer capacity is initially 32 bytes, though its size increases if necessary.

   PARAMETERS:

   `size`: the initial size.

Methods

reset §2.4.5

```
public void reset()
```

   Resets the `count` field **(I-§2.3.2)** of this byte array output stream to zero, so that all currently accumulated output in the ouput stream is discarded. The output stream can be used again, reusing the already allocated buffer space.

size §2.4.6

```
public int size()
```

   RETURNS:

   the value of the `count` field **(I-§2.4.2)**, which is the number of valid bytes in this output stream.

toByteArray §2.4.7

```
public byte[] toByteArray()
```

   Creates a newly allocated byte array. Its size is the current size of this output stream **(I-§2.4.6)** and the valid contents of the buffer have been copied into it.

   RETURNS:

   the current contents of this output stream, as a byte array.

toString   §2.4.8

```
public String toString()
```

Creates a newly allocated string. Its size is the current size of this output stream **(I-§2.4.6)** and the valid contents of the buffer have been copied into it. Each character *c* in the resulting string is constructed from the corresponding element *b* in the byte array such that

```
c == (char)(b & 0xff)
```

RETURNS:

the current contents of this output stream, as a string.

OVERRIDES:

toString in class Object **(I-§1.12.9)**.

toString   §2.4.9

```
public String toString(int hibyte)
```

Creates a newly allocated string. Its size is the current size of the output stream **(I-§2.4.6)** and the valid contents of the buffer have been copied into it. Each character *c* in the resulting string is constructed from the corresponding element *b* in the byte array such that

```
c == (char)(((hibyte & 0xff) << 8) | (b & 0xff))
```

PARAMETERS:

hibyte: the bits set.

RETURNS:

the current contents of the output stream, as a string.

write   §2.4.10

```
public void write(byte b[], int off, int len)
```

Writes len bytes from the specified byte array starting at offset off to this byte array output stream.

PARAMETERS:

b: the data.
off: the start offset in the data.
len: the number of bytes to write.

OVERRIDES:

write in class OutputStream **(I-§2.15.5)**.

write   **§2.4.11**

> public void write(int b)

> Writes the specified byte to this byte array output stream.

PARAMETERS:

b: the byte to be written.

OVERRIDES:

write in class OutputStream **(I-§2.15.6)**.

writeTo   **§2.4.12**

> public void writeTo(OutputStream out)
> throws IOException

> Writes the complete contents of this byte array output stream to the specified output stream argument, as if by calling the output stream's write method using out.write(buf, 0, count).

PARAMETERS:

out: the output stream to which to write the data.

THROWS:

IOException **(I-§2.29)**
if an I/O error occurs.

2.5 Class DataInputStream

```
public class java.io.DataInputStream
    extends java.io.FilterInputStream (I-§2.11)
    implements java.io.DataInput (I-§2.24)
{
    // Constructors
    public DataInputStream(InputStream in);                §2.5.1

    // Methods
    public final int read(byte b[]);                       §2.5.2
    public final int read(byte b[], int off, int len);     §2.5.3
    public final boolean readBoolean();                    §2.5.4
    public final byte readByte();                          §2.5.5
    public final char readChar();                          §2.5.6
    public final double readDouble();                      §2.5.7
    public final float readFloat();                        §2.5.8
    public final void readFully(byte b[]);                 §2.5.9
    public final void readFully(byte b[], int off,
                                 int len);                 §2.5.10
    public final int readInt();                            §2.5.11
    public final String readLine();                        §2.5.12
    public final long readLong();                          §2.5.13
    public final short readShort();                        §2.5.14
    public final int readUnsignedByte();                   §2.5.15
    public final int readUnsignedShort();                  §2.5.16
    public final String readUTF();                         §2.5.17
    public final static String readUTF(DataInput in);      §2.5.18
    public final int skipBytes(int n);                     §2.5.19
}
```

A data input stream lets an application read primitive Java data types from an underlying input stream in a machine-independent way. An application uses a data output stream (I-§2.6) to write data that can later be read by a data input stream.

Data input streams and data output streams represent Unicode strings in a format that is a slight modification of UTF-8.[33] All characters in the range '\u0001' to '\u007F' are represented by a single byte:

0	bits 0–7

[33.] X/Open Company Ltd., "File System Safe UCS Transformation Format (FSS_UTF)", X/Open Preliminary Specification, Document Number: P316. This information also appears in ISO/IEC 10646, Annex P.

The null character '\u0000' and characters in the range '\u0080' to '\u07FF' are represented by a pair of bytes:

1	1	0	*bits 6–10*

1	0	*bits 0–5*

Characters in the range '\u0800' to '\uFFFF' are represented by 3 bytes:

1	1	1	0	*bits 12–15*

1	0	*bits 6–11*

1	0	*bits 0–5*

The two differences between this format and the "standard" UTF-8 format are the following:

- The null byte '\u0000' is encoded in 2-byte format rather than 1-byte, so that the encoded strings never have embedded nulls.

- Only the 1-byte, 2-byte, and 3-byte formats are used.

Constructors

DataInputStream   §2.5.1

```
public DataInputStream(InputStream in)
```

Creates a new data input stream to read data from the specified input stream.

PARAMETERS:

in: the input stream.

Methods

---

read   §2.5.2

```
public final int read(byte b[])
throws IOException
```

Reads up to byte.length bytes of data from this data input stream into an array of bytes. This method blocks until some input is available.

The read method of DataInputStream calls the read method (**I-§2.13.8**) of its underlying input stream (**I-§2.11.1**) with the three arguments b, 0, and b.length and returns whatever value that method returns.

PARAMETERS:

b: the buffer into which the data is read.

RETURNS:

the total number of bytes read into the buffer, or –1 if there is no more data because the end of the stream has been reached.

THROWS:

IOException (**I-§2.29**)
if an I/O error occurs.

OVERRIDES:

read in class FilterInputStream (**I-§2.11.8**).

read §2.5.3

```
public final int read(byte b[], int off, int len)
throws IOException
```

Reads up to len bytes of data from this data input stream into an array of bytes. This method blocks until some input is available.

The read method of DataInputStream calls the read method (I-§2.13.8) of its underlying input stream (I-§2.11.1) with the same arguments and returns whatever value that method returns.

PARAMETERS:
b: the buffer into which the data is read.
off: the start offset of the data.
len: the maximum number of bytes read.

RETURNS:
the total number of bytes read into the buffer, or -1 if there is no more data
 because the end of the stream has been reached.

THROWS:
IOException (I-§2.29)
if an I/O error occurs.

OVERRIDES:
read in class FilterInputStream (I-§2.11.9).

readBoolean §2.5.4

```
public final boolean readBoolean()
throws IOException
```

Reads a boolean from this data input stream. This method reads a single byte from the underlying input stream (I-§2.11.1). A value of 0 represents false. Any other value represents true. This method blocks until either the byte is read, the end of the stream is detected, or an exception is thrown.

RETURNS:
the boolean value read.

THROWS:
EOFException (I-§2.24)
if this input stream has reached the end.

THROWS:
IOException (I-§2.29)
if an I/O error occurs.

readByte   §2.5.5

```
public final byte readByte()
throws IOException
```

Reads a signed 8-bit value from this data input stream. This method reads a byte from the underlying input stream (**I-§2.11.1**). If the byte read is b, where $0 \le b \le 255$, then the result is

```
(byte)(b)
```

This method blocks until either the byte is read, the end of the stream is detected, or an exception is thrown.

RETURNS:

the next byte of this input stream as a signed 8-bit byte.

THROWS:

IOException (**I-§2.24**)
if this input stream has reached the end.

THROWS:

IOException (**I-§2.29**)
if an I/O error occurs.

readChar   §2.5.6

```
public final char readChar()
throws IOException
```

Reads a Unicode character from this data input stream. This method reads 2 bytes from the underlying input stream (**I-§2.11.1**). If the bytes read, in order, are b1 and b2, where $0 \le b1, b2 \le 255$, then the result is equal to

```
(char)((b1 << 8) | b2)
```

This method blocks until either the 2 bytes are read, the end of the stream is detected, or an exception is thrown.

RETURNS:

the next 2 bytes of this input stream as a Unicode character.

THROWS:

IOException (**I-§2.24**)
if this input stream reaches the end before reading two bytes.

THROWS:

IOException (**I-§2.29**)
if an I/O error occurs.

readDouble §2.5.7

```
public final double readDouble()
throws IOException
```

Reads a double from this data input stream. This method reads a long value as if by the readLong method (**I-§2.5.13**) and then converts that long to a double using the longBitsToDouble method (**I-§1.6.18**) in class Double.

This method blocks until the 8 bytes are read, the end of the stream is detected, or an exception is thrown.

RETURNS:

the next 8 bytes of this input stream, interpreted as a double.

THROWS:

EOFException (**I-§2.24**)
if this input stream reaches the end before reading 8 bytes.

THROWS:

IOException (**I-§2.29**)
if an I/O error occurs.

readFloat §2.5.8

```
public final float readFloat()
throws IOException
```

Reads a float from this data input stream. This method reads an int value as if by the readInt method (**I-§2.5.11**) and then converts that int to a float using the intBitsToFloat method (**I-§1.7.14**) in class Float. This method blocks until the 4 bytes are read, the end of the stream is detected, or an exception is thrown.

RETURNS:

the next 4 bytes of this input stream, interpreted as a float.

THROWS:

EOFException (**I-§2.24**)
if this input stream reaches the end before reading 4 bytes.

THROWS:

IOException (**I-§2.29**)
if an I/O error occurs.

readFully   §2.5.9

```
public final void readFully(byte b[])
throws IOException
```

Reads b.length bytes from this data input stream into the byte array. This method reads repeatedly from the underlying stream (I-§2.11.1) until all the bytes are read. This method blocks until all the bytes are read, the end of the stream is detected, or an exception is thrown.

PARAMETERS:

b: the buffer into which the data is read.

THROWS:

EOFException (I-§2.24)

if this input stream reaches the end before reading all the bytes.

THROWS:

IOException (I-§2.29)

if an I/O error occurs.

readFully   §2.5.10

```
public final void readFully(byte b[], int off, int len)
throws IOException
```

Reads exactly len bytes from this data input stream into the byte array. This method reads repeatedly from the underlying stream (I-§2.11.1) until all the bytes are read. This method blocks until all the bytes are read, the end of the stream is detected, or an exception is thrown.

PARAMETERS:

b: the buffer into which the data is read.
off: the start offset of the data.
len: the number of bytes to read.

THROWS:

EOFException (I-§2.24)

if this input stream reaches the end before reading all the bytes.

THROWS:

IOException (I-§2.29)

if an I/O error occurs.

readInt   §2.5.11

```
public final int readInt()
throws IOException
```

Reads a signed 32-bit integer from this data input stream. This method reads 4 bytes from the underlying input stream (**I-§2.11.1**). If the bytes read, in order, are b1, b2, b3, and b4, where $0 \leq$ b1, b2, b3, b4 ≤ 255, then the result is equal to

```
(b1 << 24) | (b2 << 16) + (b3 << 8) + b4
```

This method blocks until the 4 bytes are read, the end of the stream is detected, or an exception is thrown.

RETURNS:

the next 4 bytes of this input stream, interpreted as an int.

THROWS:

EOFException (**I-§2.24**)
if this input stream reaches the end before reading 2 bytes.

THROWS:

IOException (**I-§2.29**)
if an I/O error occurs.

readLine   §2.5.12

```
public final String readLine()
throws IOException
```

Reads the next line of text from this data input stream. This method successively reads bytes from the underlying input stream (**I-§2.11.1**) until it reaches the end of a line of text.

A line of text is terminated by a carriage return character ('\r'), a newline character ('\n'), a carriage return character immediately followed by a newline character, or the end of the input stream. The line-terminating character(s), if any, are included as part of the string returned.

This method blocks until a newline character is read, a carriage return and the byte following it are read (to see if it is a newline), the end of the stream is detected, or an exception is thrown.

RETURNS:

the next line of text from this input stream.

THROWS:

IOException (**I-§2.29**)
if an I/O error occurs.

readLong   §2.5.13

```
public final long readLong()
throws IOException
```

Reads a signed 64-bit integer from this data input stream. This method reads 8 bytes from the underlying input stream (I-§2.11.1). If the bytes read, in order, are b1, b2, b3, b4, b5, b6, b7, and b8, where

$$0 \leq b1, b2, b3, b4, b5, b6, b7, b8 \leq 255,$$

then the result is equal to

```
((long)b1 << 56) +((long)b2 << 48) +
    ((long)b3 << 40) + ((long)b4 << 32)+
    ((long)b5 << 24) + (b6 << 16) +
    (b7 << 8) + b8
```

This method blocks until the 8 bytes are read, the end of the stream is detected, or an exception is thrown.

RETURNS:

the next 8 bytes of this input stream, interpreted as a `long`.

THROWS:

EOFException (I-§2.24)
if this input stream reaches the end before reading 8 bytes.

THROWS:

IOException (I-§2.29)
if an I/O error occurs.

readShort   §2.5.14

```
public final short readShort()
throws IOException
```

Reads a signed 16-bit number from this data input stream. The method reads 2 bytes from the underlying input stream (I-§2.11.1). If the 2 bytes read, in order, are b1 and b2, where each of the 2 values is between 0 and 255, inclusive, then the result is equal to:

```
(short)((b1 << 8) | b2)
```

This method blocks until the 2 bytes are read, the end of the stream is detected, or an exception is thrown.

RETURNS:

the next 2 bytes of this input stream, interpreted as a signed 16-bit number.

THROWS:

EOFException **(I-§2.24)**
if this input stream reaches the end before reading 2 bytes.

THROWS:

IOException **(I-§2.29)**
if an I/O error occurs.

readUnsignedByte §2.5.15

```
public final int readUnsignedByte()
throws IOException
```

Reads an unsigned 8-bit number from this data input stream. This method reads a byte from this data input stream's underlying input stream **(I-§2.11.1)** and returns that byte. This method blocks until the byte is read, the end of the stream is detected, or an exception is thrown.

RETURNS:

the next byte of this input stream, interpreted as an unsigned 8-bit number.

THROWS:

EOFException **(I-§2.24)**
if this input stream has reached the end.

THROWS:

IOException **(I-§2.29)**
if an I/O error occurs.

readUnsignedShort §2.5.16

```
public final int readUnsignedShort()
throws IOException
```

Reads an unsigned 16-bit number from this data input stream. This method reads 2 bytes from the underlying input stream **(I-§2.11.1)**. If the bytes read, in order, are b1 and b2, where $0 \le b1, b2 \le 255$, then the result is equal to

```
(b1 << 8) | b2
```

This method blocks until the 2 bytes are read, the end of the stream is detected, or an exception is thrown.

RETURNS:

the next 2 bytes of this input stream, interpreted as an unsigned 16-bit integer.

THROWS:

EOFException (I-§2.24)

if this input stream reaches the end before reading 2 bytes.

THROWS:

IOException (I-§2.29)

if an I/O error occurs.

readUTF   §2.5.17

```
public final String readUTF()
throws IOException
```

Reads in a string that has been encoded using a modified UTF-8 format from this data input stream. This method calls readUTF(this). See the following method for a more complete description of the format.

This method blocks until all the bytes are read, the end of the stream is detected, or an exception is thrown.

RETURNS:

a Unicode string.

THROWS:

EOFException (I-§2.24)

if this input stream reaches the end before reading all the bytes.

THROWS:

IOException (I-§2.29)

if an I/O error occurs.

readUTF §2.5.18

```
public final static String readUTF(DataInput in)
throws IOException
```

Reads in a string from the specified data input stream. The string has been encoded using a modified UTF-8 format.

The first 2 bytes are read as if by `readUnsignedShort` **(I-§2.5.16)**. This value gives the number of following bytes that are in the encoded string. (Note: *not* the length of the resulting string). The following bytes are then interpreted as bytes encoding characters in the UTF-8 format (page I-204) and are converted into characters.

This method blocks until all the bytes are read, the end of the stream is detected, or an exception is thrown.

PARAMETERS:

`in`: a data input stream.

RETURNS:

a Unicode string.

THROWS:

`EOFException` **(I-§2.24)**
if the input stream reaches the end before all the bytes.

THROWS:

`UTFDataFormatException` **(I-§2.31)**
if the bytes do not represent a valid UTF-8 encoding of a Unicode string.

THROWS:

`IOException` **(I-§2.29)**
if an I/O error occurs.

skipBytes

```
public final int skipBytes(int n)
throws IOException
```

   Skips exactly n bytes of input in the underlying input stream (**I-§2.11.1**). This method blocks until all the bytes are skipped, the end of the stream is detected, or an exception is thrown.

PARAMETERS:

n: the number of bytes to be skipped.

RETURNS:

the number of bytes skipped, which is always n.

THROWS:

EOFException (**I-§2.24**)
if this input stream reaches the end before skipping all the bytes.

THROWS:

IOException (**I-§2.29**)
if an I/O error occurs.

2.6 Class DataOutputStream

```
public class java.io.DataOutputStream
    extends java.io.FilterOutputStream (I-§2.12)
    implements java.io.DataOutput (I-§2.25)
{
    // Fields
    protected int written;                              §2.6.1

    // Constructors
    public DataOutputStream(OutputStream out);          §2.6.2

    // Methods
    public void flush();                                §2.6.3
    public final int size();                            §2.6.4
    public void write(byte b[], int off, int len);      §2.6.5
    public void write(int b);                           §2.6.6
    public final void writeBoolean(boolean v);          §2.6.7
    public final void writeByte(int v);                 §2.6.8
    public final void writeBytes(String s);             §2.6.9
    public final void writeChar(int v);                 §2.6.10
    public final void writeChars(String s);             §2.6.11
    public final void writeDouble(double v);            §2.6.12
    public final void writeFloat(float v);              §2.6.13
    public final void writeInt(int v);                  §2.6.14
    public final void writeLong(long v);                §2.6.15
    public final void writeShort(int v);                §2.6.16
    public final void writeUTF(String str);             §2.6.17
}
```

A data input stream lets an application write primitive Java data types to an output stream in a portable way. An application can then use a data input stream (**I-§2.5**) to read the data back in.

Fields

written   **§2.6.1**

```
protected int written
```
   The number of bytes written to the data output stream.

Constructors

DataOutputStream   §2.6.2

    public DataOutputStream(OutputStream out)

Creates a new data output stream to write data to the specified underlying output stream **(I-§2.12.1)**.

PARAMETERS:

out: the underlying output stream.

Methods

flush   §2.6.3

    public void flush()
    throws IOException

Flushes this data output stream. This forces any buffered output bytes to be written out to the stream.

The flush method of DataOuputStream calls the flush method **(I-§2.15.3)** of its underlying output stream **(I-§2.12.1)**.

THROWS:

IOException **(I-§2.29)**
if an I/O error occurs.

OVERRIDES:

flush in class FilterOutputStream **(I-§2.12.4)**.

size   §2.6.4

    public final int size()

Determines the number of bytes written to this data output stream.

RETURNS:

the value of the written field **(I-§2.6.1)**.

write   §2.6.5

```
public void write(byte b[], int off, int len)
throws IOException
```

Writes `len` bytes from the specified byte array starting at offset `off` to the underlying output stream **(I-§2.12.1)**.

PARAMETERS:

`b`: the data.
`off`: the start offset in the data.
`len`: the number of bytes to write.

THROWS:

`IOException` **(I-§2.29)**
if an I/O error occurs.

OVERRIDES:

`write` in class `FilterOutputStream` **(I-§2.12.6)**.

write   §2.6.6

```
public void write(int b)
throws IOException
```

Writes the specified byte to the underlying output stream **(I-§2.12.1)**.

PARAMETERS:

`b`: the byte to be written

THROWS:

`IOException` **(I-§2.29)**
if an I/O error occurs.

OVERRIDES:

`write` in class `FilterOutputStream` **(I-§2.12.7)**.

writeBoolean   §2.6.7

```
public final void writeBoolean(boolean v)
throws IOException
```

Writes a `boolean` to the underlying output stream **(I-§2.12.1)** as a 1-byte value. The value `true` is written out as the value `(byte)1`; the value `false` is written out as the value `(byte)0`.

PARAMETERS:

`v`: a `boolean` value to be written.

THROWS:

`IOException` **(I-§2.29)**
if an I/O error occurs.

writeByte   §2.6.8

```
public final void writeByte(int v)
throws IOException
```

Writes out a byte to the underlying output stream (**I-§2.12.1**) as a 1-byte value.

PARAMETERS:

v: a byte value to be written.

THROWS:

IOException (**I-§2.29**)
if an I/O error occurs.

writeBytes   §2.6.9

```
public final void writeBytes(String s)
throws IOException
```

Writes out the string to the underlying output stream (**I-§2.12.1**) as a sequence of bytes. Each character in the string is written out, in sequence, by discarding its high 8 bits.

PARAMETERS:

s: a string of bytes to be written.

THROWS:

IOException (**I-§2.29**)
if an I/O error occurs.

writeChar   §2.6.10

```
public final void writeChar(int v)
throws IOException
```

Writes a char to the underlying output stream (**I-§2.12.1**) as a 2-byte value, high byte first.

PARAMETERS:

v: a char value to be written.

THROWS:

IOException (**I-§2.29**)
if an I/O error occurs.

writeChars §2.6.11

```
public final void writeChars(String s)
throws IOException
```

Writes a string to the underlying output stream (**I-§2.12.1**) as a sequence of characters. Each character is written to the data output stream as if by the writeChar method (**I-§2.6.10**).

PARAMETERS:

s: a String value to be written.

THROWS:

IOException (**I-§2.29**)
if an I/O error occurs.

writeDouble §2.6.12

```
public final void writeDouble(double v)
throws IOException
```

Converts the double argument to a long using the doubleToLongBits method (**I-§1.6.8**) in class Double, and then writes that long value to the underlying output stream (**I-§2.12.1**) as an 8-byte quantity, high byte first.

PARAMETERS:

v: a double value to be written.

THROWS:

IOException (**I-§2.29**)
if an I/O error occurs.

writeFloat §2.6.13

```
public final void writeFloat(float v)
throws IOException
```

Converts the float argument to an int using the floatToIntBits method (**I-§1.7.11**) in class Float, and then writes that int value to the underlying output stream (**I-§2.12.1**) as a 4-byte quantity, high byte first.

PARAMETERS:

v: a float value to be written.

THROWS:

IOException (**I-§2.29**)
if an I/O error occurs.

writeInt   §2.6.14

```
public final void writeInt(int v)
throws IOException
```

Writes an `int` to the underlying output stream **(I-§2.12.1)** as 4 bytes, high-byte first.

PARAMETERS:

v: an `int` to be written.

THROWS:

IOException **(I-§2.29)**
if an I/O error occurs.

writeLong   §2.6.15

```
public final void writeLong(long v)
throws IOException
```

Writes a `long` to the underlying output stream **(I-§2.12.1)** as 8 bytes, high byte first.

PARAMETERS:

v: a `long` to be written.

THROWS:

IOException **(I-§2.29)**
if an I/O error occurs.

writeShort   §2.6.16

```
public final void writeShort(int v)
throws IOException
```

Writes a `short` to the underlying output stream **(I-§2.12.1)** as 2 bytes, high byte first.

PARAMETERS:

v: a `short` to be written.

THROWS:

IOException **(I-§2.29)**
if an I/O error occurs.

writeUTF §2.6.17

```
public final void writeUTF(String str)
throws IOException
```

Writes out a string to the underlying output stream **(I-§2.12.1)** using UTF-8 encoding in a machine-independent manner.

First, 2 bytes are written to the output stream as if by the `writeShort` method **(I-§2.6.16)** giving the number of bytes to follow. This value is the number of bytes actually written out, not the length of the string. Following the length, each character of the string is output, in sequence, using the UTF-8 encoding (page I-204) for the character.

PARAMETERS:

`str:` a string to be written.

THROWS:

`IOException` **(I-§2.29)**
if an I/O error occurs.

2.7 Class File

```
public class java.io.File
    extends java.lang.Object (I-§1.12)
{
    // Fields
    public final static String pathSeparator;        §2.7.1
    public final static char pathSeparatorChar;      §2.7.2
    public final static String separator;            §2.7.3
    public final static char separatorChar;          §2.7.4

    // Constructors
    public File(File dir, String name);              §2.7.5
    public File(String path);                        §2.7.6
    public File(String path, String name);           §2.7.7

    // Methods
    public boolean canRead();                         §2.7.8
    public boolean canWrite();                        §2.7.9
    public boolean delete();                          §2.7.10
    public boolean equals(Object obj);                §2.7.11
    public boolean exists();                          §2.7.12
    public String getAbsolutePath();                  §2.7.13
    public String getName();                          §2.7.14
    public String getParent();                        §2.7.15
    public String getPath();                          §2.7.16
    public int hashCode();                            §2.7.17
    public boolean isAbsolute();                      §2.7.18
    public boolean isDirectory();                     §2.7.19
    public boolean isFile();                          §2.7.20
    public long lastModified();                       §2.7.21
    public long length();                             §2.7.22
    public String[] list();                           §2.7.23
    public String[] list(FilenameFilter filter);      §2.7.24
    public boolean mkdir();                           §2.7.25
    public boolean mkdirs();                          §2.7.26
    public boolean renameTo(File dest);               §2.7.27
    public String toString();                         §2.7.28
}
```

Instances of this class represent the name of a file or directory on the host file system. A file is specified by a pathname, which can either be an absolute pathname or a pathname relative to the current working directory. The pathname must follow the naming conventions of the host platform.

The File class is intended to provide an abstraction that deals with most of the machine dependent complexities of files and pathnames in a machine-independent fashion.

Fields

pathSeparator §2.7.1

`public final static String pathSeparator`

The system-dependent path separator string. This field is initialized to contain the value of the system property **(I-§1.18.9)** "`path.separator.`"

pathSeparatorChar §2.7.2

`public final static char pathSeparatorChar`

The system-dependent path separator character. This field is initialized to contain the first character of the value of the system property **(I-§1.18.9)** `path.separator`. This character is often used to separate filenames in a sequence of files given as a "path list."

separator §2.7.3

`public final static String separator`

The system-dependent path separator string. This field is initialized to contain the value of the system property **(I-§1.18.9)** `file.separator`.

separatorChar §2.7.4

`public final static char separatorChar`

The system-dependent path separator string. This field is initialized to contain the first character of the value of the system property **(I-§1.18.9)** `file.separator`. This character separates the directory and file components in a filename.

Constructors

File §2.7.5

`public File(File dir, String name)`

Creates a `File` instance that represents the file with the specified name in the specified directory.

If the directory argument is `null`, the resulting `File` instance represents a file in the (system-dependent) current directory whose pathname **(I-§2.7.16)** is the `name` argument. Otherwise, the `File` instance represents a file whose pathname is the pathname of the directory, followed by the separator character **(I-§2.7.3)**, followed by the `name` argument.

PARAMETERS:

`dir`: the directory.
`name`: the file pathname.

File   §2.7.6

   `public File(String path)`

   Creates a `File` instance that represents the file whose pathname (**I-§2.7.16**) is the given path argument.

   PARAMETERS:

   `path`: the file pathname.

   THROWS:

   `NullPointerException` (**I-§1.40**)
   if the file path is equal to `null`.

File   §2.7.7

   `public File(String path, String name)`

   Creates a `File` instance whose pathname (**I-§2.7.16**) is the pathname of the specified directory, followed by the separator character (**I-§2.7.3**), followed by the name argument.

   PARAMETERS:

   `path`: the directory pathname.
   `name`: the file pathname.

Methods

canRead   §2.7.8

   `public boolean canRead()`

   Determines if the application can read from the specified file.

   RETURNS:

   `true` if the file specified by this object exists and the application can read the file; `false` otherwise.

   THROWS:

   `SecurityException` (**I-§1.43**)
   if a security manager exists, its `checkRead` method (**I-§1.15.19**) is called with the pathname (**I-§2.7.16**) of this `File` to see if the application is allowed read access to the file.

canWrite §2.7.9

```
public boolean canWrite()
```

Determines if the application can write to this file.

RETURNS:

`true` if the application is allowed to write to a file whose name is specified by this object; `false` otherwise.

THROWS:

`SecurityException` **(I-§1.43)**

if a security manager exists, its `checkWrite` method **(I-§1.15.24)** is called with the pathname **(I-§2.7.16)** of this `File` to see if the application is allowed write access to the file.

delete §2.7.10

```
public boolean delete()
```

Deletes the file specified by this object.

RETURNS:

`true` if the file is successfully deleted; `false` otherwise.

THROWS:

`SecurityException` **(I-§1.43)**

if a security manager exists, its `checkDelete` method **(I-§1.15.9)** is called with the pathname **(I-§2.7.16)** of this `File` to see if the application is allowed to delete the file.

equals §2.7.11

```
public boolean equals(Object obj)
```

The result is `true` if and only if the argument is not `null` and is a `File` object whose pathname is equal to the pathname of this object.

PARAMETERS:

`obj`: the object to compare with.

RETURNS:

`true` if the objects are the same; `false` otherwise.

OVERRIDES:

`equals` in class `Object` **(I-§1.12.3)**.

exists   §2.7.12

```
public boolean exists()
```

Determines if this `File` exists.

RETURNS:

`true` if the file specified by this object exists; `false` otherwise.

THROWS:

`SecurityException (I-§1.43)`

if a security manager exists, its `checkRead` method (I-§1.15.19) is called with the pathname (I-§2.7.16) of this `File` to see if the application is allowed read access to the file.

getAbsolutePath   §2.7.13

```
public String getAbsolutePath()
```

If this object represents an absolute pathname (I-§2.7.18), then return the pathname (I-§2.7.16). Otherwise, return a pathname that is a concatenation of the current user directory, the separator character, and the pathname of this file object.

The system property (I-§1.18.9) `user.dir` contains the current user directory.

RETURNS:

a system-dependent absolute pathname for this `File`.

getName   §2.7.14

```
public String getName()
```

Returns the name of the file represented by this object. The name is everything in the pathame (I-§2.7.16) after the last occurrence of the separator character (I-§2.7.3).

RETURNS:

the name of the file (without any directory components) represented by this `File` object.

getParent   §2.7.15

```
public String getParent()
```

Returns the parent directory of the file represented by this object. The parent directory is everything in the pathname (I-§2.7.16) before the last occurrence of the separator character (I-§2.7.3), or `null` if the separator character does not appear in the pathname.

RETURNS:

the name of the directory of the file represented by this `File` object.

getPath §2.7.16

    public String getPath()

RETURNS:

the pathname represented by this `File` object.

hashCode §2.7.17

    public int hashCode()

RETURNS:

a hash code value for this `File` object.

OVERRIDES:

hashCode in class `Object` (**I-§1.12.6**).

isAbsolute §2.7.18

    public boolean isAbsolute()

Determines if this `File` represents an absolute pathname. The definition of an absolute pathname is system dependent.[34]

RETURNS:

`true` if the pathname (**I-§2.7.16**) indicated by the `File` object is an absolute pathname; `false` otherwise.

isDirectory §2.7.19

    public boolean isDirectory()

Determines if the file represented by this `File` object is a directory.

RETURNS:

`true` if this `File` exists and is a directory; `false` otherwise.

THROWS:

`SecurityException` (**I-§1.43**)

if a security manager exists, its `checkRead` method (**I-§1.15.19**) is called with the pathname (**I-§2.7.16**) of this `File` to see if the application is allowed read access to the file.

[34.] For example, on UNIX, a pathname is absolute if its first character is the separator character (**I-§2.7.3**). On Windows platforms, a pathname is absolute if its first character is an ASCII `'\'`, `'/'`, or if it begins with a letter followed by a colon.

isFile   §2.7.20

```
public boolean isFile()
```

Determines if the file represented by this `File` object is a "normal" file.

A file is "normal" if it is not a directory and, in addition, satisfies other system-dependent criteria. Any non-directory file created by a Java application is guaranteed to be a normal file.

RETURNS:

`true` if the file specified by this object exists and is a "normal" file; `false` otherwise.

THROWS:

`SecurityException` **(I-§1.43)**

If a security manager exists, its `checkRead` method **(I-§1.15.19)** is called with the pathname **(I-§2.7.16)** of this `File` to see if the application is allowed read access to the file.

lastModified   §2.7.21

```
public long lastModified()
```

Determines the time that the file represented by this `File` object was last modified.

The return value is system dependent and should only be used to compare with other values returned by last modified. It should not be interpreted as an absolute time.

RETURNS:

the time the file specified by this object was last modified, or `0L` if the specified file does not exist.

THROWS:

`SecurityException` **(I-§1.43)**

if a security manager exists, its `checkRead` method **(I-§1.15.19)** is called with the pathname **(I-§2.7.16)** of this `File` to see if the application is allowed read access to the file.

length §2.7.22

```
public long length()
```

Determines the length of the file represented by this `File` object.

RETURNS:

the length, in bytes, of the file specified by this object, or `0L` if the specified file does not exist.

THROWS:

`SecurityException` (I-§1.43)

if a security manager exists, its `checkRead` method (I-§1.15.19) is called with the pathname (I-§2.7.16) of this `File` to see if the application is allowed read access to the file.

list §2.7.23

```
public String[] list()
```

Lists the files in the directory specified by this `File`.

RETURNS:

an array of file names in the specified directory. This list does not include the current directory or the parent directory (".'' and "..'' on Unix systems).

THROWS:

`SecurityException` (I-§1.43)

If a security manager exists, its `checkRead` method (I-§1.15.19) is called with the pathname (I-§2.7.16) of this `File` to see if the application is allowed read access to the file.

list §2.7.24

```
public String[] list(FilenameFilter filter)
```

Lists the files in the directory specified by this `File` that satisfy the specified filter (I-§2.26).

PARAMETERS:

`filter`: a filename filter.

RETURNS:

an array of filenames in the specified directory that satisfy the filter. This list does not include the current directory or the parent directory (".'' and "..'' on UNIX systems).

THROWS:

`SecurityException` (I-§1.43)

if a security manager exists, its `checkRead` method (I-§1.15.19) is called with the pathname (I-§2.7.16) of this `File` to see if the application is allowed read access to the file.

mkdir §2.7.25

```
public boolean mkdir()
```

Creates a directory whose pathname is specified by this `File` object.

RETURNS:

`true` if the directory could be created; `false` otherwise.

THROWS:

`SecurityException` (I-§1.43)

if a security manager exists, its `checkWrite` method (I-§1.15.24) is called with the pathname (I-§2.7.16) of this `File` to see if the application is allowed write access to the file.

mkdirs §2.7.26

```
public boolean mkdirs()
```

Creates a directory whose pathname is specified by this `File` object. In addition, create all parent directories as necessary.

RETURNS:

`true` if the directory (or directories) could be created; `false` otherwise.

THROWS:

`SecurityException` (I-§1.43)

if a security manager exists, its `checkWrite` method (I-§1.15.24) is called with the pathname (I-§2.7.16) of each of the directories that is to be created, before any of the directories are created.

renameTo §2.7.27

```
public boolean renameTo(File dest)
```

Renames the file specified by this `File` object to have the pathname given by the `File` argument.

PARAMETERS:

`dest`: the new filename.

RETURNS:

`true` if the renaming succeeds; `false` otherwise.

THROWS:

`SecurityException` (I-§1.43)

if a security manager exists, its `checkWrite` method (I-§1.15.24) is called both with the pathname (I-§2.7.16) of this file object and with the pathname of the destination target object to see if the application is allowed to write to both files.

toString   §2.7.28

    `public String toString()`

      Returns a string representation of this object.

    RETURNS:

    a string giving the pathname (**I-§2.7.16**) of this object.

    OVERRIDES:

    `toString` in class `Object` (**I-§1.12.9**).

2.8 Class FileDescriptor

```
public final class java.io.FileDescriptor
    extends java.lang.Object (I-§1.12)
{
    // Fields
    public final static FileDescriptor err;          §2.8.1
    public final static FileDescriptor in;           §2.8.2
    public final static FileDescriptor out;          §2.8.3

    // Constructors
    public FileDescriptor();                          §2.8.4

    // Methods
    public boolean valid();                           §2.8.5
}
```

    Instances of the file descriptor class serve as an opaque handle to the underlying machine-specific structure representing an open file or an open socket.

    Applications should not create their own file descriptors.

Fields

---

err   §2.8.1

    `public final static FileDescriptor err`

      A handle to the standard error stream.

in   §2.8.2

    `public final static FileDescriptor in`

      A handle to the standard input stream.

out   §2.8.3

    `public final static FileDescriptor out`

      A handle to the standard output stream.

Constructors

FileDescriptor   §2.8.4

    `public FileDescriptor()`

     The default constructor.

Methods

valid   §2.8.5

    `public boolean valid()`

    RETURNS:

    `true` if the file descriptor object represents a valid, open file or socket; `false` otherwise.

2.9 Class FileInputStream

```
public class java.io.FileInputStream
    extends java.io.InputStream (I-§2.13)
{
    // Constructors
    public FileInputStream(File file);              §2.9.1
    public FileInputStream(FileDescriptor fdObj);   §2.9.2
    public FileInputStream(String name);            §2.9.3

    // Methods
    public int available();                         §2.9.4
    public void close();                            §2.9.5
    protected void finalize();                      §2.9.6
    public final FileDescriptor getFD();            §2.9.7
    public int read();                              §2.9.8
    public int read(byte b[]);                      §2.9.9
    public int read(byte b[], int off, int len);    §2.9.10
    public long skip(long n);                       §2.9.11
}
```

A file input stream is an input stream for reading data from a `File` (I-§2.7) or from a `FileDescriptor` (I-§2.8).

Constructors

`FileInputStream`   §2.9.1

```
public FileInputStream(File file)
throws FileNotFoundException
```

Creates an input file stream to read from the specified `File` object.

PARAMETERS:

`file`: the file to be opened for reading.

THROWS:

`FileNotFoundException` **(I-§2.28)**

if the file is not found.

THROWS:

`SecurityException` **(I-§1.43)**

if a security manager exists, its `checkRead` method **(I-§1.15.19)** is called with the pathname **(I-§2.7.16)** of this `File` argument to see if the application is allowed read access to the file.

`FileInputStream`   §2.9.2

```
public FileInputStream(FileDescriptor fdObj)
```

Creates an input file stream to read from the specified file descriptor.

PARAMETERS:

`fdObj`: the file descriptor to be opened for reading.

THROWS:

`SecurityException` **(I-§1.43)**

if a security manager exists, its `checkRead` method **(I-§1.15.18)** is called with the file descriptor to see if the application is allowed to read from the specified file descriptor.

FileInputStream

```
public FileInputStream(String name)
throws FileNotFoundException
```

Creates an input file stream to read from a file with the specified name.

PARAMETERS:

name: the system-dependent file name.

THROWS:

FileNotFoundException **(I-§2.28)**
if the file is not found.

THROWS:

SecurityException **(I-§1.43)**

if a security manager exists, its checkRead method **(I-§1.15.19)** is called with
the name argument to see if the application is allowed read access to the
file.

Methods

available

```
public int available()
throws IOException
```

RETURNS:

the number of bytes that can be read from this file input stream without
blocking.

THROWS:

IOException **(I-§2.29)**
if an I/O error occurs.

OVERRIDES:

available in class InputStream **(I-§2.13.2)**.

close

```
public void close()
throws IOException
```

Closes this file input stream and releases any system resources associated
with the stream.

THROWS:

IOException **(I-§2.29)**
if an I/O error occurs.

OVERRIDES:

close in class InputStream **(I-§2.13.3)**.

finalize   §2.9.6

```
protected void finalize()
throws IOException
```

This `finalize` method ensures that the `close` method (**I-§2.9.5**) of this file input stream is called when there are no more references to it.

THROWS:

`IOException` (**I-§2.29**)
if an I/O error occurs.

OVERRIDES:

`finalize` in class `Object` (**I-§1.12.4**).

getFD   §2.9.7

```
public final FileDescriptor getFD()
throws IOException
```

RETURNS:

the file descriptor object (**I-§2.8**) associated with this stream.

THROWS:

`IOException` (**I-§2.29**)
if an I/O error occurs.

read   §2.9.8

```
public int read()
throws IOException
```

Reads a byte of data from this input stream. This method blocks if no input is yet available.

RETURNS:

the next byte of data, or –1 if the end of the file is reached.

THROWS:

`IOException` (**I-§2.29**)
if an I/O error occurs.

OVERRIDES:

`read` in class `InputStream` (**I-§2.13.6**).

read   §2.9.9

```
public int read(byte b[])
throws IOException
```

   Reads up to b.length bytes of data from this input stream into an array of bytes. This method blocks until some input is available.

PARAMETERS:

b: the buffer into which the data is read.

RETURNS:

the total number of bytes read into the buffer, or -1 if there is no more data because the end of the file has been reached.

THROWS:

IOException (I-§2.29)

if an I/O error occurs.

OVERRIDES:

read in class InputStream (I-§2.13.7).

read   §2.9.10

```
public int read(byte b[], int off, int len)
throws IOException
```

   Reads up to len bytes of data from this input stream into an array of bytes. This method blocks until some input is available.

PARAMETERS:

b: the buffer into which the data is read.
off: the start offset of the data.
len: the maximum number of bytes read.

RETURNS:

the total number of bytes read into the buffer, or -1 if there is no more data because the end of the file has been reached.

THROWS:

IOException (I-§2.29)

if an I/O error occurs.

OVERRIDES:

read in class InputStream (I-§2.13.8).

skip §2.9.11

```
public long skip(long n)
throws IOException
```

Skips over and discards n bytes of data from the input stream. The `skip` method may, for a variety of reasons, end up skipping over some smaller number of bytes, possibly 0. The actual number of bytes skipped is returned.

PARAMETERS:

n: the number of bytes to be skipped.

RETURNS:

the actual number of bytes skipped.

THROWS:

IOException (I-§2.29)

if an I/O error occurs.

OVERRIDES:

skip in class InputStream (I-§2.13.10).

2.10 Class FileOutputStream

```
public class java.io.FileOutputStream
    extends java.io.OutputStream (I-§2.15)
{
    // Constructors
    public FileOutputStream(File file);            §2.10.1
    public FileOutputStream(FileDescriptor fdObj);  §2.10.2
    public FileOutputStream(String name);          §2.10.3

    // Methods
    public void close();                           §2.10.4
    protected void finalize();                     §2.10.5
    public final FileDescriptor getFD();           §2.10.6
    public void write(byte b[]);                   §2.10.7
    public void write(byte b[], int off, int len); §2.10.8
    public void write(int b);                      §2.10.9
}
```

A file output stream is an output stream for writing data to a File (I-§2.7) or to a FileDescriptor (I-§2.8).

Constructors

FileOutputStream   §2.10.1

```
public FileOutputStream(File file)
throws IOException
```

Creates a file output stream to write to the specified `File` object.

PARAMETERS:

`file`: the file to be opened for writing.

THROWS:

`IOException` **(I-§2.29)**
if the file could not be opened for writing.

THROWS:

`SecurityException` **(I-§1.43)**
if a security manager exists, its `checkWrite` method **(I-§1.15.24)** is called with
the pathname **(I-§2.7.16)** of the `File` argument to see if the application is
allowed write access to the file. This may result in a security exception
(I-§1.43)

FileOutputStream   §2.10.2

```
public FileOutputStream(FileDescriptor fdObj)
```

Creates an output file stream to write to the specified file descriptor.

PARAMETERS:

`fdObj`: the file descriptor to be opened for writing.

THROWS:

`SecurityException` **(I-§1.43)**
if a security manager exists, its `checkWrite` method **(I-§1.15.23)** is called with
the file descriptor to see if the application is allowed to write to the specified file descriptor.

FileOutputStream §2.10.3

```
public FileOutputStream(String name)
throws IOException
```

Creates an output file stream to write to the file with the specified name.

PARAMETERS:

`name`: the system-dependent filename.

THROWS:

`IOException` (I-§2.29)

if the file could not be opened for writing.

THROWS:

`SecurityException` (I-§1.43)

if a security manager exists, its `checkWrite` method (I-§1.15.24) is called with the name argument to see if the application is allowed write access to the file.

Methods

close §2.10.4

```
public void close()
throws IOException
```

Closes this file output stream and releases any system resources associated with this stream.

THROWS:

`IOException` (I-§2.29)

if an I/O error occurs.

OVERRIDES:

`close` in class `OutputStream` (I-§2.15.2).

finalize §2.10.5

```
protected void finalize()
throws IOException
```

This `finalize` method ensures that the `close` method (I-§2.9.5) of this file output stream is called when there are no more references to this stream.

THROWS:

`IOException` (I-§2.29)

if an I/O error occurs.

OVERRIDES:

`finalize` in class `Object` (I-§1.12.4).

getFD   §2.10.6

```
public final FileDescriptor getFD()
throws IOException
```

RETURNS:

the file descriptor object (**I-§2.8**) associated with this stream.

THROWS:

IOException (**I-§2.29**)
if an I/O error occurs.

write   §2.10.7

```
public void write(byte b[])
throws IOException
```

Writes b.length bytes from the specified byte array to this file output stream.

PARAMETERS:

b: the data.

THROWS:

IOException (**I-§2.29**)
if an I/O error occurs.

OVERRIDES:

write in class OutputStream (**I-§2.15.4**).

write   §2.10.8

```
public void write(byte b[], int off, int len)
throws IOException
```

Writes len bytes from the specified byte array starting at offset off to this file output stream.

PARAMETERS:

b: the data.
off: the start offset in the data.
len: the number of bytes to write.

THROWS:

IOException (**I-§2.29**)
if an I/O error occurs.

OVERRIDES:

write in class OutputStream (**I-§2.15.5**).

write   §2.10.9

```
public void write(int b)
throws IOException
```

Writes the specified byte to this file output stream.

PARAMETERS:

b: the byte to be written.

THROWS:

IOException **(I-§2.29)**

if an I/O error occurs.

OVERRIDES:

write in class OutputStream **(I-§2.15.6).**

2.11 Class FilterInputStream

```
public class java.io.FilterInputStream
    extends java.io.InputStream (I-§2.13)
{
    // Fields
    protected InputStream in;                                §2.11.1

    // Constructors
    protected FilterInputStream(InputStream in);             §2.11.2

    // Methods
    public int available();                                  §2.11.3
    public void close();                                     §2.11.4
    public void mark(int readlimit);                         §2.11.5
    public boolean markSupported();                          §2.11.6
    public int read();                                       §2.11.7
    public int read(byte b[]);                               §2.11.8
    public int read(byte b[], int off, int len);             §2.11.9
    public void reset();                                     §2.11.10
    public long skip(long n);                                §2.11.11
}
```

This class is the superclass of all classes that filter input streams. These streams sit on top of an already existing input stream (the *underlying* input stream), but provide additional functionality.

The class FilterInputStream itself simply overrides all methods of Input-Stream with versions that pass all requests to the underlying input stream. Sub-classes of FilterInputStream may further override some of these methods as well as provide additional methods and fields.

Fields

in   §2.11.1

    `protected InputStream in`

      The underlying input stream.

Constructors

FilterInputStream   §2.11.2

    `protected FilterInputStream(InputStream in)`

      Creates an input stream filter built on top of the specified input stream.

    PARAMETERS:

    `in`: the underlying input stream.

Methods

available   §2.11.3

    `public int available()`
    `throws IOException`

      Determines the number of bytes that can be read from this input stream without blocking.

      The `available` method of `FilterInputStream` calls the `available` method of its underlying input stream (**I-§2.11.1**) and returns whatever value that method returns.

    RETURNS:

    the number of bytes that can be read from the input stream without blocking.

    THROWS:

    `IOException` (**I-§2.29**)
    if an I/O error occurs.

    OVERRIDES:

    `available` in class `InputStream` (**I-§2.13.2**).

close   §2.11.4

```
public void close()
throws IOException
```

Closes this input stream and releases any system resources associated with the stream. The close method of FilterInputStream calls the close method of its underlying input stream (I-§2.11.1).

THROWS:

IOException (I-§2.29)
if an I/O error occurs.

OVERRIDES:

close in class InputStream (I-§2.13.3).

mark   §2.11.5

```
public void mark(int readlimit)
```

Marks the current position in this input stream. A subsequent call to the reset method (I-§2.11.10) repositions this stream at the last marked position so that subsequent reads re-read the same bytes.

The readlimit argument tells this input stream to allow that many bytes to be read before the mark position gets invalidated.

The mark method of FilterInputStream calls the mark method of its underlying input stream (I-§2.11.1) with the readlimit argument.

PARAMETERS:

readlimit: the maximum limit of bytes that can be read before the mark position becomes invalid.

OVERRIDES:

mark in class InputStream (I-§2.13.4).

markSupported   §2.11.6

```
public boolean markSupported()
```

Determines if this input stream supports the mark (I-§2.13.4) and reset (I-§2.13.9) methods. The markSupported method of FilterInputStream calls the markSupported method of its underlying input stream (I-§2.11.1) and returns whatever value that method returns.

RETURNS:

true if this stream type supports the mark and reset method; false otherwise.

OVERRIDES:

markSupported in class InputStream (I-§2.13.5).

read   §2.11.7

```
public int read()
throws IOException
```

Reads the next byte of data from this input stream. The value byte is returned as an `int` in the range 0 to 255. If no byte is available because the end of the stream has been reached, the value -1 is returned. This method blocks until input data is available, the end of the stream is detected, or an exception is thrown.

The `read` method of `FilterInputStream` calls the `read` method of its underlying input stream (I-§2.11.1) and returns whatever value that method returns.

RETURNS:

the next byte of data, or -1 if the end of the stream is reached.

THROWS:

`IOException` (I-§2.29)
if an I/O error occurs.

OVERRIDES:

read in class `InputStream` (I-§2.13.6).

read §2.11.8

```
public int read(byte b[])
throws IOException
```

Reads up to `byte.length` bytes of data from this input stream into an array of bytes. This method blocks until some input is available.

The `read` method of `FilterInputStream` calls the `read` method of three arguments (I-§2.11.9) with the arguments b, 0, and b.length, and returns whatever value that method returns.

Note that this method does not call the one-argument `read` method of its underlying stream with the single argument b. Subclasses of `FilterInputStream` do not need to override this method if they have overridden the three-argument `read` method.

PARAMETERS:

b: the buffer into which the data is read.

RETURNS:

the total number of bytes read into the buffer, or -1 if there is no more data because the end of the stream has been reached.

THROWS:

`IOException` (I-§2.29)
if an I/O error occurs.

OVERRIDES:

read in class `InputStream` (I-§2.13.7).

read   §2.11.9

```
public int read(byte b[], int off, int len)
throws IOException
```

Reads up to `len` bytes of data from this input stream into an array of bytes. This method blocks until some input is available.

The `read` method of `FilterInputStream` calls the `read` method of its underlying input stream **(I-§2.11.1)** with the same arguments and returns whatever value that method returns.

PARAMETERS:

`b`: the buffer into which the data is read.
`off`: the start offset of the data.
`len`: the maximum number of bytes read.

RETURNS:

the total number of bytes read into the buffer, or -1 if there is no more data because the end of the stream has been reached.

THROWS:

`IOException` **(I-§2.29)**
if an I/O error occurs.

OVERRIDES:

read in class `InputStream` **(I-§2.13.8)**.

reset   §2.11.10

```
public void reset()
throws IOException
```

Repositions this stream to the position at the time the `mark` method **(I-§2.11.5)** was last called on this input stream.

The `reset` method of `FilterInputStream` calls the `reset` method of its underlying input stream **(I-§2.11.1)**.

THROWS:

`IOException` **(I-§2.29)**
if the stream has not been marked or if the mark has been invalidated.

OVERRIDES:

reset in class `InputStream` **(I-§2.13.9)**.

skip   §2.11.11

```
public long skip(long n)
throws IOException
```

Skips over and discards n bytes of data from the input stream. The `skip` method may, for a variety of reasons, end up skipping over some smaller number of bytes, possibly 0. The actual number of bytes skipped is returned.

The `skip` method of `FilterInputStream` calls the `skip` method of its underlying input stream **(I-§2.11.1)** with the same argument, and returns whatever value that method does.

PARAMETERS:

n: the number of bytes to be skipped.

RETURNS:

the actual number of bytes skipped.

THROWS:

IOException **(I-§2.29)**
if an I/O error occurs.

OVERRIDES:

skip in class InputStream **(I-§2.13.10)**.

2.12 Class FilterOutputStream

```
public class java.io.FilterOutputStream
    extends java.io.OutputStream (I-§2.15)
{
    // Fields
    protected OutputStream out;                              §2.12.1

    // Constructors
    public FilterOutputStream(OutputStream out);             §2.12.2

    // Methods
    public void close();                                     §2.12.3
    public void flush();                                     §2.12.4
    public void write(byte b[]);                             §2.12.5
    public void write(byte b[], int off, int len);          §2.12.6
    public void write(int b);                                §2.12.7
}
```

This class is the superclass of all classes that filter output streams. These streams sit on top of an already existing output stream (the *underlying* output stream), but provide additional functionality.

The class `FilterOutputStream` itself simply overrides all methods of `OutputStream` with versions that pass all requests to the underlying output stream. Subclasses of `FilterOutputStream` may further override some of these methods as well as provide additional methods and fields.

Fields

out   §2.12.1

    protected OutputStream out
    The underlying output stream.

Constructors

FilterOutputStream   §2.12.2

    public FilterOutputStream(OutputStream out)

Creates an output stream filter built on top of the specified underlying output stream.

PARAMETERS:

out: the underlying output stream.

Methods

close   §2.12.3

    public void close()
    throws IOException

Closes this output stream and releases any system resources associated with the stream.

The `close` method of `FilterOutputStream` calls its `flush` method **(I-§2.12.4)**, and then calls the `close` method of its underlying output stream **(I-§2.12.1)**.

THROWS:

`IOException` **(I-§2.29)**

if an I/O error occurs.

OVERRIDES:

`close` in class `OutputStream` **(I-§2.15.2)**.

flush §2.12.4

```
public void flush()
throws IOException
```

Flushes this output stream and forces any buffered output bytes to be written out to the stream.

The flush method of FilterOutputStream calls the flush method of its underlying output stream (**I-§2.12.1**).

THROWS:

IOException (**I-§2.29**)
if an I/O error occurs.

OVERRIDES:

flush in class OutputStream (**I-§2.15.3**).

write §2.12.5

```
public void write(byte b[])
throws IOException
```

Writes b.length bytes to this output stream.

The write method of FilterOutputStream calls its write method of three arguments (**I-§2.12.6**) with the arguments b, 0, and b.length.

Note that this method does not call the one-argument write method of its underlying stream with the single argument b.

PARAMETERS:

b: the data to be written.

THROWS:

IOException (**I-§2.29**)
if an I/O error occurs.

OVERRIDES:

write in class OutputStream (**I-§2.15.4**).

252   *Java Application Programming Interface*

write   §2.12.6

```
public void write(byte b[], int off, int len)
throws IOException
```

Writes `len` bytes from the specified `byte` array starting at offset `off` to this output stream.

The `write` method of `FilterOutputStream` calls the `write` method of one argument (I-§2.12.7) on each `byte` to output.

Note that this method does not call the `write` method of its underlying input stream with the same arguments. Subclasses of `FilterOutputStream` should provide a more efficient implementation of this method.

PARAMETERS:

b: the data.
off: the start offset in the data.
len: the number of bytes to write.

THROWS:

IOException (I-§2.29)
if an I/O error occurs.

OVERRIDES:

write in class OutputStream (I-§2.15.5).

write   §2.12.7

```
public void write(int b)
throws IOException
```

Writes the specified `byte` to this output stream.

The `write` method of `FilterOutputStream` calls the `write` method of its underlying output stream (I-§2.12.1).

PARAMETERS:

b: the byte.

THROWS:

IOException (I-§2.29)
if an I/O error occurs.

OVERRIDES:

write in class OutputStream (I-§2.15.6).

2.13 Class InputStream

```
public abstract class java.io.InputStream
    extends java.lang.Object (I-§1.12)
{
    // Constructors
    public InputStream();                               §2.13.1

    // Methods
    public int available();                             §2.13.2
    public void close();                                §2.13.3
    public void mark(int readlimit);                    §2.13.4
    public boolean markSupported();                     §2.13.5
    public abstract int read();                         §2.13.6
    public int read(byte b[]);                          §2.13.7
    public int read(byte b[], int off, int len);        §2.13.8
    public void reset();                                §2.13.9
    public long skip(long n);                           §2.13.10
}
```

This abstract class is the superclass of all classes representing an input stream of bytes.

Applications that need to define a subclass of InputStream must always provide a method that returns the next byte of input (**I-§2.13.6**).

Constructors

InputStream   §2.13.1

```
public InputStream()
```

The default constructor. This constructor is only called by subclasses.

Methods

available   §2.13.2

```
public int available()
throws IOException
```

Determines the number of bytes that can be read from this input stream without blocking. The available method of InputStream returns 0. This method should be overridden by subclasses.

RETURNS:

the number of bytes that can be read from this input stream without blocking.

THROWS:

IOException **(I-§2.29)**
if an I/O error occurs.

close   §2.13.3

```
public void close()
throws IOException
```

Closes this input stream and releases any system resources associated with the stream.

The close method of InputStream does nothing.

THROWS:

IOException **(I-§2.29)**
if an I/O error occurs.

mark   §2.13.4

```
public void mark(int readlimit)
```

Marks the current position in this input stream. A subsequent call to the reset method **(I-§2.13.9)** repositions this stream at the last marked position so that subsequent reads re-read the same bytes.

The readlimit arguments tells this input stream to allow that many bytes to be read before the mark position gets invalidated.

The mark method of InputStream does nothing.

PARAMETERS:

readlimit: the maximum limit of bytes that can be read before the mark position becomes invalid.

markSupported   §2.13.5

```
public boolean markSupported()
```

Determines if this input stream supports the mark (I-§2.13.4) and reset (I-§2.13.9) methods. The markSupported method of InputStream returns false.

RETURNS:

true if this true type supports the mark and reset method; false otherwise.

read   §2.13.6

```
public abstract int read()
throws IOException
```

Reads the next byte of data from this input stream. The value byte is returned as an int in the range 0 to 255. If no byte is available because the end of the stream has been reached, the value -1 is returned. This method blocks until input data is available, the end of the stream is detected, or an exception is thrown.

A subclass must provide an implementation of this method.

RETURNS:

the next byte of data, or -1 if the end of the stream is reached.

THROWS:

IOException (I-§2.29)
if an I/O error occurs.

read   §2.13.7

```
public int read(byte b[])
throws IOException
```

Reads up to b.length bytes of data from this input stream into an array of bytes.

The read method of InputStream calls the read method of three arguments (I-§2.13.8) with the arguments b, 0, and b.length.

PARAMETERS:

b: the buffer into which the data is read.

RETURNS:

the total number of bytes read into the buffer, or -1 is there is no more data because the end of the stream has been reached.

THROWS:

IOException (I-§2.29)
if an I/O error occurs.

read   §2.13.8

```
public int read(byte b[], int off, int len)
throws IOException
```

    Reads up to `len` bytes of data from this input stream into an array of bytes. This method blocks until some input is available. If the first argument is `null`, up to `len` bytes are read and discarded.

    The `read` method of `InputStream` reads a single byte at a time using the read method of zero arguments (I-§2.13.6) to fill in the array. Subclasses are encouraged to provide a more efficient implementation of this method.

PARAMETERS:

`b`: the buffer into which the data is read.
`off`: the start offset of the data.
`len`: the maximum number of bytes read.

RETURNS:

the total number of bytes read into the buffer, or –1 if there is no more data
    because the end of the stream has been reached.

THROWS:

`IOException` (I-§2.29)
if an I/O error occurs.

reset   §2.13.9

```
public void reset()
throws IOException
```

    Repositions this stream to the position at the time the `mark` method (I-§2.13.4) was last called on this input stream.

    The `reset` method of `InputStream` throws an `IOException` (I-§2.29), because input streams, by default, do not support `mark` and `reset`.

THROWS:

`IOException` (I-§2.29)
if this stream has not been marked or if the mark has been invalidated.

skip §**2.13.10**

```
public long skip(long n)
throws IOException
```

Skips over and discards n bytes of data from this input stream. The `skip` method may, for a variety of reasons, end up skipping over some smaller number of bytes, possibly 0. The actual number of bytes skipped is returned.

The `skip` method of `InputStream` creates a byte array of length n and then reads into it until n bytes have been read or the end of the stream has been reached. Subclasses are encouraged to provide a more efficient implementation of this method.

PARAMETERS:

n: the number of bytes to be skipped.

RETURNS:

the actual number of bytes skipped.

THROWS:

IOException (**I-§2.29**)

if an I/O error occurs.

2.14 Class LineNumberInputStream

```
public class java.io.LineNumberInputStream
    extends java.io.FilterInputStream (I-§2.11)
{
    // Constructors
    public LineNumberInputStream(InputStream in);         §2.14.1

    // Methods
    public int available();                               §2.14.2
    public int getLineNumber();                           §2.14.3
    public void mark(int readlimit);                      §2.14.4
    public int read();                                    §2.14.5
    public int read(byte b[], int off, int len);          §2.14.6
    public void reset();                                  §2.14.7
    public void setLineNumber(int lineNumber);            §2.14.8
    public long skip(long n);                             §2.14.9
}
```

This class is an input stream filter that provides the added functionality of keeping track of the current line number.

A line is a sequence of bytes ending with a carriage return character ('\r'), a newline character ('\n'), or a carriage return character followed immediately by a linefeed character. In all three cases, the line terminating character(s) are returned as a single newline character.

The line number begins at 0, and is incremented by 1 when a read returns a newline character.

Constructors

LineNumberInputStream   §2.14.1

```
public LineNumberInputStream(InputStream in)
```

Constructs a newline number input stream that reads its input from the specified input stream.

PARAMETERS:

in: the underlying input stream.

Methods

available   §2.14.2

```
public int available()
throws IOException
```

Determines the number of bytes that can be read from this input stream without blocking.

Note that if the underlying input stream (**I-§2.11.1**) is able to supply k input characters without blocking, the LineNumberInputStream can guarantee only to provide $k/2$ characters without blocking, because the k characters from the underlyhing input stream might consist of $k/2$ pairs of '\r' and '\n', which are converted to just $k/2$ '\n' characters.

RETURNS:

the number of bytes that can be read from this input stream without blocking.

THROWS:

IOException (**I-§2.29**)
if an I/O error occurs.

OVERRIDES:

available in class FilterInputStream (**I-§2.11.3**).

getLineNumber   §2.14.3

```
public int getLineNumber()
```

RETURNS:

the current line number.

mark   §2.14.4

```
public void mark(int readlimit)
```

   Marks the current position in this input stream. A subsequent call to the reset method (**I-§2.14.7**) repositions this stream at the last marked position so that subsequent reads re-read the same bytes.

   The mark method of LineNumberInputStream remembers the current line number in a private variable, and then calls the mark method of the underlying input stream (**I-§2.11.1**).

PARAMETERS:

readlimit: the maximum limit of bytes that can be read before the mark
   position becomes invalid.

OVERRIDES:

mark in class FilterInputStream (**I-§2.11.5**).

read   §2.14.5

```
public int read()
throws IOException
```

   Reads the next byte of data from this input stream. The value byte is returned as an int in the range 0 to 255. If no byte is available because the end of the stream has been reached, the value -1 is returned. This method blocks until input data is available, the end of the stream is detected, or an exception is thrown.

   The read method of LineNumberInputStream calls the read method of the underlying input stream (**I-§2.11.1**). It checks for carriage returns and newline characters in the input, and modifies the current line number (**I-§2.14.3**) as appropriate. A carriage-return character or a carriage return followed by a newline character are both converted into a single newline character.

RETURNS:

the next byte of data, or -1 if the end of this stream is reached.

THROWS:

IOException (**I-§2.29**)
if an I/O error occurs.

OVERRIDES:

read in class FilterInputStream (**I-§2.11.7**).

read   §2.14.6

```
public int read(byte b[], int off, int len)
throws IOException
```

Reads up to `len` bytes of data from this input stream into an array of bytes. This method blocks until some input is available.

The `read` method of `LineNumberInputStream` repeatedly calls the `read` method of zero arguments (**I-§2.14.5**) to fill in the byte array.

PARAMETERS:

`b`: the buffer into which the data is read.
`off`: the start offset of the data.
`len`: the maximum number of bytes read.

RETURNS:

the total number of bytes read into the buffer, or -1 if there is no more data because the end of this stream has been reached.

THROWS:

`IOException` (**I-§2.29**)
if an I/O error occurs.

OVERRIDES:

read in class `FilterInputStream` (**I-§2.11.9**).

reset   §2.14.7

```
public void reset()
throws IOException
```

Repositions this stream to the position at the time the `mark` method (**I-§2.14.4**) was last called on this input stream.

The `reset` method of `LineNumberInputStream` resets the line number to be the line number at the time the `mark` method was called, and then calls the mark method of the underlying input stream (**I-§2.11.1**).

THROWS:

`IOException` (**I-§2.29**)
if an I/O error occurs.

OVERRIDES:

reset in class `FilterInputStream` (**I-§2.11.10**).

setLineNumber   §2.14.8

```
public void setLineNumber(int lineNumber)
```

Sets the line number to the specified argument.

PARAMETERS:

`lineNumber`: the new line number.

skip　　　　　　　　　　　　　　　　　　　　　　　　　　　**§2.14.9**

```
public long skip(long n)
throws IOException
```

Skips over and discards n bytes of data from the input stream. The `skip` method may, for a variety of reasons, end up skipping over some smaller number of bytes, possibly 0. The actual number of bytes skipped is returned.

The `skip` method of `LineNumberInputStream` creates a byte array of length n and then reads into it until n bytes have been read or the end of the stream has been reached.

PARAMETERS:

n: the number of bytes to be skipped.

RETURNS:

the actual number of bytes skipped.

THROWS:

`IOException` (I-§2.29)
if an I/O error occurs.

OVERRIDES:

`skip` in class `FilterInputStream` (I-§2.11.11).

2.15 Class OutputStream

```
public abstract class java.io.OutputStream
    extends java.lang.Object (I-§1.12)
{
    // Constructors
    public OutputStream();                                          §2.15.1

    // Methods
    public void close();                                            §2.15.2
    public void flush();                                            §2.15.3
    public void write(byte b[]);                                    §2.15.4
    public void write(byte b[], int off, int len);                 §2.15.5
    public abstract void write(int b);                              §2.15.6
}
```

This abstract class is the superclass of all classes representing an output stream of bytes.

Applications that need to define a subclass of OutputStream must always provide at least a method that writes 1 byte of output (I-§2.15.6).

Constructors

OutputStream   §2.15.1

    public OutputStream()

The default constructor.

Methods

close   §2.15.2

    public void close()
    throws IOException

Closes this output stream and releases any system resources associated with this stream.

The close method of OutputStream does nothing.

THROWS:

IOException (I-§2.29)
if an I/O error occurs.

flush   §2.15.3

```
public void flush()
throws IOException
```

Flushes this output stream and forces any buffered output bytes to be written out.

The flush method of OutputStream does nothing.

THROWS:

IOException (I-§2.29)
if an I/O error occurs.

write   §2.15.4

```
public void write(byte b[])
throws IOException
```

Writes b.length bytes from the specified byte array to this output stream.

The write method of OutputStream calls the write method of three arguments (I-§2.15.5) with the three arguments b, 0, and b.length.

PARAMETERS:

b: the data.

THROWS:

IOException (I-§2.29)
if an I/O error occurs.

write   §2.15.5

```
public void write(byte b[], int off, int len)
throws IOException
```

Writes len bytes from the specified byte array starting at offset off to this output stream.

The write method of OutputStream calls the write method of one argument on each of the bytes to be written out. Subclasses are encouraged to override this method and provide a more efficient implementation.

PARAMETERS:

b: the data.
off: the start offset in the data.
len: the number of bytes to write.

THROWS:

IOException (I-§2.29)
if an I/O error occurs.

write   §2.15.6

```
public abstract void write(int b)
throws IOException
```

Writes the specified byte to this output stream.

Subclasses of `OutputStream` must provide an implementation for this method.

PARAMETERS:

b: the byte.

THROWS:

IOException **(I-§2.29)**

if an I/O error occurs.

2.16 Class PipedInputStream

```
public class java.io.PipedInputStream
    extends java.io.InputStream (I-§2.13)
{
    // Constructors
    public PipedInputStream();                          §2.16.1
    public PipedInputStream(PipedOutputStream src);     §2.16.2

    // Methods
    public void close();                                §2.16.3
    public void connect(PipedOutputStream src);         §2.16.4
    public int read();                                  §2.16.5
    public int read(byte b[], int off, int len);        §2.16.6
}
```

A piped input stream is the receiving end of a communications pipe. Two threads can communicate by having one thread send data through a piped output stream **(I-§2.17)** and having the other thread read the data through a piped input stream.

Constructors

PipedInputStream   §2.16.1

```
public PipedInputStream()
```

Creates a piped input stream that is not yet connected to a piped output stream. It must be connected to a piped output stream, either by the receiver **(I-§2.16.4)** or the sender **(I-§2.17.4)**, before being used.

PipedInputStream §2.16.2

```
public PipedInputStream(PipedOutputStream src)
throws IOException
```

Creates a piped input stream connected to the specified piped output stream.

PARAMETERS:

src: the stream to connect to.

THROWS:

IOException **(I-§2.29)**
if an I/O error occurs.

Methods

close §2.16.3

```
public void close()
throws IOException
```

Closes this piped input stream and releases any system resources associated with the stream.

THROWS:

IOException **(I-§2.29)**
if an I/O error occurs.

OVERRIDES:

close in class InputStream **(I-§2.13.3)**.

connect §2.16.4

```
public void connect(PipedOutputStream src)
throws IOException
```

Connects this piped input stream to a sender.

PARAMETERS:

src: The piped output stream to connect to.

THROWS:

IOException **(I-§2.29)**
if an I/O error occurs.

read §2.16.5

```
public int read()
throws IOException
```

Reads the next byte of data from this piped input stream. The value byte is returned as an `int` in the range 0 to 255. If no byte is available because this end of the stream has been reached, the value -1 is returned. This method blocks until input data is available, the end of the stream is detected, or an exception is thrown.

RETURNS:

the next byte of data, or -1 if the end of the stream is reached.

THROWS:

IOException (I-§2.29)
if the pipe is broken.

OVERRIDES:

read in class InputStream (I-§2.13.6).

read §2.16.6

```
public int read(byte b[], int off, int len)
throws IOException
```

Reads up to `len` bytes of data from this piped input stream into an array of bytes. This method blocks until at least 1 byte of input is available.

PARAMETERS:

b: the buffer into which the data is read.
off: the start offset of the data.
len: the maximum number of bytes read.

RETURNS:

the total number of bytes read into the buffer, or -1 if there is no more data because the end of the stream has been reached.

THROWS:

IOException (I-§2.29)
if an I/O error occurs.

OVERRIDES:

read in class InputStream (I-§2.13.8).

2.17 Class PipedOutputStream

```
public class java.io.PipedOutputStream
    extends java.io.OutputStream (I-§2.15)
{
    // Constructors
    public PipedOutputStream();                          §2.17.1
    public PipedOutputStream(PipedInputStream snk);      §2.17.2

    // Methods
    public void close();                                 §2.17.3
    public void connect(PipedInputStream snk);           §2.17.4
    public void write(byte b[], int off, int len);       §2.17.5
    public void write(int b);                            §2.17.6
}
```

A piped output stream is the sending end of a communications pipe. Two threads can communicate by having one thread send data through a piped output stream (I-§2.16) and having the other thread read the data through a piped input stream.

Constructors

PipedOutputStream   §2.17.1

```
public PipedOutputStream()
```

Creates a piped output stream that is not yet connected to a piped input stream. It must be connected to a piped input stream, either by the receiver (I-§2.16.4) or the sender (I-§2.17.4), before being used.

PipedOutputStream   §2.17.2

```
public PipedOutputStream(PipedInputStream snk)
throws IOException
```

Creates a piped output stream connected to the specified piped input stream.

PARAMETERS:

snk: The piped input stream to connect to.

THROWS:

IOException (I-§2.29)
if an I/O error occurs.

Methods

close   §2.17.3

```
public void close()
throws IOException
```

Closes this piped output stream and releases any system resources associated with this stream.

THROWS:

IOException (I-§2.29)
if an I/O error occurs.

OVERRIDES:

close in class OutputStream (I-§2.15.2).

connect   §2.17.4

```
public void connect(PipedInputStream snk)
throws IOException
```

Connects this piped output stream to a receiver.

PARAMETERS:

snk: The piped output stream to connect to.

THROWS:

IOException (I-§2.29)
if an I/O error occurs.

write   §2.17.5

```
public void write(byte b[], int off, int len)
throws IOException
```

Writes len bytes from the specified byte array starting at offset off to this piped output stream.

PARAMETERS:

b: the data.
off: the start offset in the data.
len: the number of bytes to write.

THROWS:

IOException (I-§2.29)
if an I/O error occurs.

OVERRIDES:

write in class OutputStream (I-§2.15.5).

write §2.17.6

```
public void write(int b)
throws IOException
```

Writes the specified byte to the piped output stream.

PARAMETERS:

b: the byte to be written.

THROWS:

IOException (I-§2.29)

if an I/O error occurs.

OVERRIDES:

write in class OutputStream (I-§2.15.6).

2.18 Class PrintStream

```
public class java.io.PrintStream
    extends java.io.FilterOutputStream (I-§2.12)
{
    // Constructors
    public PrintStream(OutputStream out);                        §2.18.1
    public PrintStream(OutputStream out,
                       boolean autoflush);                       §2.18.2

    // Methods
    public boolean checkError();                                 §2.18.3
    public void close();                                         §2.18.4
    public void flush();                                         §2.18.5
    public void print(boolean b);                                §2.18.6
    public void print(char c);                                   §2.18.7
    public void print(char s[]);                                 §2.18.8
    public void print(double d);                                 §2.18.9
    public void print(float f);                                  §2.18.10
    public void print(int i);                                    §2.18.11
    public void print(long l);                                   §2.18.12
    public void print(Object obj);                               §2.18.13
    public void print(String s);                                 §2.18.14
    public void println();                                       §2.18.15
    public void println(boolean b);                              §2.18.16
    public void println(char c);                                 §2.18.17
    public void println(char s[]);                               §2.18.18
    public void println(double d);                               §2.18.19
    public void println(float f);                                §2.18.20
    public void println(int i);                                  §2.18.21
    public void println(long l);                                 §2.18.22
    public void println(Object obj);                             §2.18.23
    public void println(String s);                               §2.18.24
    public void write(byte b[], int off, int len);              §2.18.25
    public void write(int b);                                    §2.18.26
}
```

A print stream implements an output stream filter that provides convenient methods for printing types other than bytes and arrays of bytes.

In addition, the print stream overrides many of the InputStream methods so as not to throw an IOException. Instead, an I/O exception causes an internal flag to be set, which the application can check by a call to the checkError method (**I-§2.18.3**).

Only the lower 8 bits of any 16-bit quantity are printed to the stream.

An application can specify at creation time whether a print stream should be flushed every time a newline character is written.

Here are some examples of the use of a print stream:

```
System.out.println("Hello world!");
System.out.print("x = ");
System.out.println(x);
System.out.println("y = " + y);
```

Constructors

PrintStream §2.18.1

```
public PrintStream(OutputStream out)
```

Constructs a new print stream that writes its output to the specified underlying output stream (**I-§2.12.1**).

PARAMETERS:

out: the underlying output stream.

PrintStream §2.18.2

```
public PrintStream(OutputStream out, boolean autoflush)
```

Constructs a new print stream that writes its output to the specified underlying output stream (**I-§2.12.1**). In addition, if the autoflush flag is true, then the underlying output stream's flush method is called any time a newline character is printed.

PARAMETERS:

out: the underlying output stream.
autoflush: if true, the stream automatically flushes its output when a newline character is printed.

Methods

checkError §2.18.3

```
public boolean checkError()
```

Flushes this print stream's underlying output stream, and returns a boolean indicating if there has been an error on the underlying output stream.

Errors are cumulative; once the print stream has encounted an error, this method will continue to return true on all successive calls.

RETURNS:

true if the print stream has ever encountered an error on the output stream; false otherwise.

close   §2.18.4

```
public void close()
```

Closes this print stream and releases any resources associated with the underlying output stream.

The close method of PrintStream calls the close method (**I-§2.15.2**) of its underlying output stream (**I-§2.12.1**). However, if that close method throws an IOException, this method catches that exception and indicates, instead, that the underlying stream has gotten an error (see **I-§2.18.3**).

OVERRIDES:

close in class FilterOutputStream (**I-§2.12.3**).

flush   §2.18.5

```
public void flush()
```

Flushes this print stream. This forces any buffered output bytes to be written to the underlying stream.

The flush method of PrintStream calls the flush method (**I-§2.15.3**) of its underlying output stream (**I-§2.12.1**). However, if that flush method throws an IOException, this method catches that exception and indicates, instead, that the underlying stream has gotten an error (see **I-§2.18.3**).

OVERRIDES:

flush in class FilterOutputStream (**I-§2.12.4**).

print   §2.18.6

```
public void print(boolean b)
```

Prints the string "true" to the underlying output stream (**I-§2.12.1**) if the value of the boolean argument is true; otherwise, prints the string "false" to the underlying output stream.

PARAMETERS:

b: a boolean to be printed.

print   §2.18.7

```
public void print(char c)
```

Prints the low 8 bits of the character argument to this print stream's underlying output stream (**I-§2.12.1**).

PARAMETERS:

c: a char to be printed.

print §2.18.8

```
public void print(char s[])
```

Prints the low 8 bits of each of the characters in the character array to this print stream's underlying output stream **(I-§2.12.1)**.

PARAMETERS:

s: an array of chars to be printed.

print §2.18.9

```
public void print(double d)
```

Prints the string representation of the double to this print stream's underlying output stream **(I-§2.12.1)**. The string representation is identical to the one returned by the toString method **(I-§1.6.21)** of class Double with the argument d.

PARAMETERS:

d: a double to be printed.

print §2.18.10

```
public void print(float f)
```

Prints the string representation of the float to this print stream's underlying output stream **(I-§2.12.1)**. The string representation is identical to the one returned by the toString method **(I-§1.7.22)** of class Float with the argument f.

PARAMETERS:

f: a float to be printed.

print §2.18.11

```
public void print(int i)
```

Prints the string representation of the int to this print stream's underlying output stream **(I-§2.12.1)**. The string representation is identical to the one returned by the toString method **(I-§1.8.20)** of class Integer with the argument i.

PARAMETERS:

i: an int to be printed.

print §2.18.12

```
public void print(long l)
```

Prints the string representation of the long to this print stream's underlying output stream **(I-§2.12.1)**. The string representation is identical to the one returned by the toString method **(I-§1.9.20)** of class Long with the argument l.

PARAMETERS:

l: a long to be printed.

print   **§2.18.13**

>   public void print(Object obj)

>   Prints the string representation of the `Object` to this print stream's underlying output stream **(I-§2.12.1)**. The string representation is identical to the one returned by calling the `Object` argument's `toString` method **(I-§1.12.9)**.

>   **PARAMETERS:**

>   `obj`: an `Object` to be printed.

print   **§2.18.14**

>   public void print(String s)

>   If the string argument is `null`, the string `"null"` is printed to this print stream's underlying output stream. Otherwise, the low 8 bits of each of the characters in the string is printed to the underlying output stream **(I-§2.12.1)**.

>   **PARAMETERS:**

>   `s`: a `String` to be printed.

println   **§2.18.15**

>   public void println()

>   Prints a newline character to this print stream's underlying output stream **(I-§2.12.1)**.

println   **§2.18.16**

>   public void println(boolean b)

>   Prints the string `"true"` followed by a newline character to this print stream's underlying output stream if the value of the `boolean` argument is `true`; otherwise, prints the string `"false"` followed by a newline character to the underlying output stream **(I-§2.12.1)**.

>   **PARAMETERS:**

>   `b`: a `boolean` to be printed.

println   **§2.18.17**

>   public void println(char c)

>   Prints the low 8 bits of the character argument followed by a newline character to this print stream's underlying output stream **(I-§2.12.1)**.

>   **PARAMETERS:**

>   `c`: a `char` to be printed.

println   **§2.18.18**

`public void println(char s[])`

Prints the low 8 bits of each of the characters in the character array, followed by a newline character, to this print stream's underlying output stream **(I-§2.12.1)**.

PARAMETERS:

`s`: an array of characters to be printed.

println   **§2.18.19**

`public void println(double d)`

Prints the string representation of the `double` followed by a newline to this print stream's underlying output stream **(I-§2.12.1)**. The string representation is identical to the one returned by the `toString` method **(I-§1.6.21)** of class `Double` with the argument d.

PARAMETERS:

`d`: a `double` to be printed.

println   **§2.18.20**

`public void println(float f)`

Prints the string representation of the `float` followed by a newline to this print stream's underlying output stream **(I-§2.12.1)**. The string representation is identical to the one returned by the `toString` method **(I-§1.8.20)** of class `Integer` with the argument f.

PARAMETERS:

`f`: a `float` to be printed.

println   **§2.18.21**

`public void println(int i)`

Prints the string representation of the `int` followed by a newline to this print stream's underlying output stream **(I-§2.12.1)**. The string representation is identical to the one returned by the `toString` method **(I-§1.8.20)** of class `Integer` with the argument i.

PARAMETERS:

`i`: an `int` to be printed.

println   §2.18.22

    `public void println(long l)`

Prints the string representation of the `long` followed by a newline to this print stream's underlying output stream (**I-§2.12.1**). The string representation is identical to the one returned by the `toString` method (**I-§1.9.20**) of class Long with the argument `l`.

PARAMETERS:

`l`: a long to be printed.

println   §2.18.23

    `public void println(Object obj)`

Prints the string representation of the `Object` followed by a newline to this print stream's underlying output stream (**I-§2.12.1**). The string representation is identical to the one returned by calling the `Object` argument's `toString` method (**I-§1.12.9**).

PARAMETERS:

`obj`: an Object to be printed.

println   §2.18.24

    `public void println(String s)`

If the string argument is `null`, the string `"null"` followed by a newline character is printed to this print stream's underlying output stream. Otherwise, the low 8 bits of each of the characters in the string, followed by a newline character, is printed to the underlying output stream (**I-§2.12.1**).

PARAMETERS:

`s`: a String to be printed.

write   §2.18.25

    `public void write(byte b[], int off, int len)`

Writes `len` bytes from the specified byte array starting at offset `off` to this print stream's underlying output stream (**I-§2.12.1**).

PARAMETERS:

`b`: the data.
`off`: the start offset in the data.
`len`: the number of bytes to write.

OVERRIDES:

write in class `FilterOutputStream` (**I-§2.12.6**).

write §2.18.26

    public void write(int b)

Writes the specified byte to this print stream.

The `write` method of `PrintStream` calls the `write` method of its underlying stream (**I-§2.12.1**). In addition, if the character is a newline character and autoflush is turned on, then the print stream's `flush` method (**I-§2.18.5**) is called.

If any `IOException` is thrown while writing the byte, the exception is caught, and instead an internal error flag is set; the value of the flag can be checked by a call to the `checkError` method (**I-§2.18.3**).

PARAMETERS:

b: the byte.

OVERRIDES:

`write` in class `FilterOutputStream` (**I-§2.12.7**).

2.19 Class PushbackInputStream

    public class java.io.PushbackInputStream
        extends java.io.FilterInputStream (I-§2.11)
    {
        // Fields
        protected int pushBack;   §2.19.1

        // Constructors
        public PushbackInputStream(InputStream in);   §2.19.2

        // Methods
        public int available();   §2.19.3
        public boolean markSupported();   §2.19.4
        public int read();   §2.19.5
        public int read(byte bytes[], int offset, int length);   §2.19.6
        public void unread(int ch);   §2.19.7
    }

This class is an input stream filter that provides a 1-byte pushback buffer. This feature allows an application to "unread" the last character that it read. The next time that a read is performed on the input stream filter, the "unread" character is re-read.

This functionality is useful when a fragment of code should read an indefinite number of data bytes that are delimited by particular byte values. After reading the terminating byte, the code fragment can "unread" it, so that the next read operation on the input stream will re-read the byte that was pushed back.

Fields

pushBack   §2.19.1

```
protected int pushBack
```

A character that has been "unread" and that will be the next byte read. The value -1 indicates that there is no character in the buffer.

Constructors

PushbackInputStream   §2.19.2

```
public PushbackInputStream(InputStream in)
```

Constructs a new pushback input stream that reads its input from the specified input stream.

PARAMETERS:

in: the underlying input stream.

Methods

available   §2.19.3

```
public int available()
throws IOException
```

Determines the number of bytes that can be read from this input stream without blocking.

The available method of PushbackInputStream calls the available method of its underlying input stream (I-§2.11.1); it returns that value if there is no character that has been pushed back, or that value plus 1 if there is a character that has been pushed back.

RETURNS:

the number of bytes that can be read from the input stream without blocking.

OVERRIDES:

available in class FilterInputStream (I-§2.11.3).

THROWS:

IOException (I-§2.29)
if an I/O error occurs.

markSupported §2.19.4

```
public boolean markSupported()
```

Determines if the input stream supports the mark (**I-§2.13.4**) and reset (**I-§2.13.9**) methods. The markSupported method of PushbackInputStream always returns false.

RETURNS:

true if this stream type supports the mark and reset methods; false otherwise.

OVERRIDES:

markSupported in class FilterInputStream (**I-§2.11.6**).

read §2.19.5

```
public int read()
throws IOException
```

Reads the next byte of data from this input stream. The value byte is returned as an int in the range 0 to 255. If no byte is available because the end of the stream has been reached, the value -1 is returned. This method blocks until input data is available, the end of the stream is detected, or an exception is thrown.

The read method of PushbackInputStream returns the just pushed-back character, if there is one, and otherwise calls the read method of its underlying input stream (**I-§2.13.6**) and returns whatever value that method returns.

RETURNS:

the next byte of data, or -1 if the end of the stream is reached.

THROWS:

IOException (**I-§2.29**)
if an I/O error occurs.

OVERRIDES:

read in class FilterInputStream (**I-§2.11.7**).

read   §2.19.6

```
public int read(byte bytes[], int offset, int length)
throws IOException
```

Reads up to `len` bytes of data from this input stream into an array of bytes. This method blocks until at least 1 byte of input is available.

PARAMETERS:

`b`: the buffer into which the data is read.
`off`: the start offset of the data.
`len`: the maximum number of bytes read.

RETURNS:

the total number of bytes read into the buffer, or `-1` if there is no more data
    because the end of the stream has been reached.

THROWS:

`IOException` (**I-§2.29**)
if an I/O error occurs.

OVERRIDES:

read in class `FilterInputStream` (**I-§2.11.9**).

unread   §2.19.7

```
public void unread(int ch)
throws IOException
```

Pushes back a character so that it is read again by the next call to the `read` method on this input stream.

PARAMETERS:

`ch`: the character to push back.

THROWS:

`IOException` (**I-§2.29**)
if the application attempts to push back a character before the previously
    pushed-back character has been read.

2.20 Class RandomAccessFile

```
public class java.io.RandomAccessFile
    extends java.lang.Object (I-§1.12)
    implements java.io.DataOutput (I-§2.25),
               java.io.DataInput (I-§2.24)
{
    // Constructors
    public RandomAccessFile(File file, String mode);        §2.20.1
    public RandomAccessFile(String name, String mode);      §2.20.2

    // Methods
    public void close();                                    §2.20.3
    public final FileDescriptor getFD();                    §2.20.4
    public long getFilePointer();                           §2.20.5
    public long length();                                   §2.20.6
    public int read();                                      §2.20.7
    public int read(byte b[]);                              §2.20.8
    public int read(byte b[], int off, int len);            §2.20.9
    public final boolean readBoolean();                     §2.20.10
    public final byte readByte();                           §2.20.11
    public final char readChar();                           §2.20.12
    public final double readDouble();                       §2.20.13
    public final float readFloat();                         §2.20.14
    public final void readFully(byte b[]);                  §2.20.15
    public final void readFully(byte b[], int off,
                                int len);                   §2.20.16
    public final int readInt();                             §2.20.17
    public final String readLine();                         §2.20.18
    public final long readLong();                           §2.20.19
    public final short readShort();                         §2.20.20
    public final int readUnsignedByte();                    §2.20.21
    public final int readUnsignedShort();                   §2.20.22
    public final String readUTF();                          §2.20.23
    public void seek(long pos);                             §2.20.24
    public int skipBytes(int n);                            §2.20.25
    public void write(byte b[]);                            §2.20.26
    public void write(byte b[], int off, int len);          §2.20.27
    public void write(int b);                               §2.20.28
    public final void writeBoolean(boolean v);              §2.20.29
    public final void writeByte(int v);                     §2.20.30
    public final void writeBytes(String s);                 §2.20.31
    public final void writeChar(int v);                     §2.20.32
    public final void writeChars(String s);                 §2.20.33
    public final void writeDouble(double v);                §2.20.34
    public final void writeFloat(float v);                  §2.20.35
    public final void writeInt(int v);                      §2.20.36
```

```
    public final void writeLong(long v);                §2.20.37
    public final void writeShort(int v);                §2.20.38
    public final void writeUTF(String str);             §2.20.39
}
```

Instances of this class support both reading and writing to a random access file. An application can modify the position in the file at which the next read or write occurs.

Constructors

RandomAccessFile   §2.20.1

```
    public RandomAccessFile(File file, String mode)
    throws IOException
```

Creates a random access file stream to read from, and optionally to write to, the file specified by the File argument.

The mode argument must either be equal to "r" or to "rw", indicating either to open the file for input, or for both input and output, respectively.

PARAMETERS:

file: the file object.
mode: the access mode.

THROWS:

IOException (I-§2.29)
if an I/O error occurs.

THROWS:

IllegalArgumentException (I-§1.32)
if the mode argument is not equal to "r" or to "rw".

THROWS:

SecurityException (I-§1.43)
if a security manager exists, its checkRead method (I-§1.15.19) is called with the pathname (I-§2.7.16) of the File argument to see if the application is allowed read access to the file. If the mode argument is equal to "rw", its checkWrite method (I-§1.15.19) also is called with the pathname to see if the application is allowed write access to the file.

RandomAccessFile §2.20.2

```
public RandomAccessFile(String name, String mode)
throws IOException
```

Creates a random access file stream to read from, and optionally to write to, a file with the specified name.

The mode argument must either be equal to "r" or "rw", indicating either to open the file for input or for both input and output.

PARAMETERS:

name: the system-dependent filename.
mode: the access mode.

THROWS:

IOException (**I-§2.29**)
if an I/O error occurs.

THROWS:

IllegalArgumentException (**I-§1.32**)
if the mode argument is not equal to "r" or to "rw".

THROWS:

SecurityException (**I-§1.43**)

if a security manager exists, its checkRead method (**I-§1.15.19**) is called with the name argument to see if the application is allowed read access to the file. If the mode argument is equal to "rw", its checkWrite method (**I-§1.15.19**) also is called with the name argument to see if the application is allowed write access to the file. Either of these may result in a security exception (**I-§1.43**).

Methods

close §2.20.3

```
public void close()
throws IOException
```

Closes this random access file stream and releases any system resources associated with the stream.

THROWS:

IOException (**I-§2.29**)
if an I/O error occurs.

getFD   §2.20.4

```
public final FileDescriptor getFD()
throws IOException
```

RETURNS:

the file descriptor object **(I-§2.8)** associated with this stream.

THROWS:

IOException **(I-§2.29)**
if an I/O error occurs.

getFilePointer   §2.20.5

```
public long getFilePointer()
throws IOException
```

Returns the current offset in this file.

RETURNS:

the offset from the beginning of the file, in bytes, at which the next read or
write occurs.

THROWS:

IOException **(I-§2.29)**
if an I/O error occurs.

length   §2.20.6

```
public long length()
throws IOException
```

RETURNS:

the length of this file.

THROWS:

IOException **(I-§2.29)**
if an I/O error occurs.

read   §2.20.7

```
public int read()
throws IOException
```

Reads a byte of data from this file. This method blocks if no input is yet
available.

RETURNS:

the next byte of data, or -1 if the end of the file is reached.

THROWS:

IOException **(I-§2.29)**
if an I/O error occurs.

read §2.20.8

```
public int read(byte b[])
throws IOException
```

Reads up to b.length bytes of data from this file into an array of bytes. This method blocks until at least 1 byte of input is available.

PARAMETERS:

b: the buffer into which the data is read.

RETURNS:

the total number of bytes read into the buffer, or -1 if there is no more data because the end of this file has been reached.

THROWS:

IOException (I-§2.29)
if an I/O error occurs.

read §2.20.9

```
public int read(byte b[], int off, int len)
throws IOException
```

Reads up to len bytes of data from this file into an array of bytes. This method blocks until at least 1 byte of input is available.

PARAMETERS:

b: the buffer into which the data is read.
off: the start offset of the data.
len: the maximum number of bytes read.

RETURNS:

the total number of bytes read into the buffer, or -1 if there is no more data because the end of the file has been reached.

THROWS:

IOException (I-§2.29)
if an I/O error occurs.

readBoolean   §2.20.10

```
public final boolean readBoolean()
throws IOException
```

Reads a boolean from this file. This method reads a single byte from the file. A value of 0 represents false. Any other value represents true. This method blocks until the byte is read, the end of the stream is detected, or an exception is thrown.

RETURNS:

the boolean value read.

THROWS:

EOFException (I-§2.24)
if this file has reached the end.

THROWS:

IOException (I-§2.29)
if an I/O error occurs.

readByte   §2.20.11

```
public final byte readByte()|
throws IOException
```

Reads a signed 8-bit value from this file. This method reads a byte from the file. If the byte read is b, where $0 \leq b \leq 255$, then the result is

```
(byte)(b)
```

This method blocks until the byte is read, the end of the stream is detected, or an exception is thrown.

RETURNS:

the next byte of this file as a signed 8-bit byte.

THROWS:

EOFException (I-§2.24)
if this file has reached the end.

THROWS:

IOException (I-§2.29)
if an I/O error occurs.

readChar   §2.20.12

```
public final char readChar()
throws IOException
```

Reads a Unicode character from this file. This method reads 2 bytes from the file. If the bytes read, in order, are b1 and b2, where $0 \le b1, b2 \le 255$, then the result is equal to

```
(char)((b1 << 8) | b2)
```

This method blocks until the 2 bytes are read, the end of the stream is detected, or an exception is thrown.

RETURNS:

the next 2 bytes of this file as a Unicode character.

THROWS:

EOFException (**I-§2.24**)
if this file reaches the end before reading 2 bytes.

THROWS:

IOException (**I-§2.29**)
if an I/O error occurs.

readDouble   §2.20.13

```
public final double readDouble()
throws IOException
```

Reads a double from this file. This method reads a long value as if by the readLong method (**I-§2.20.19**) and then converts that long to a double using the longBitsToDouble method (**I-§1.6.18**) in class Double.

This method blocks until the 8 bytes are read, the end of the stream is detected, or an exception is thrown.

RETURNS:

the next 8 bytes of this file, interpreted as a double.

THROWS:

EOFException (**I-§2.24**)
if this file reaches the end before reading 8 bytes.

THROWS:

IOException (**I-§2.29**)
if an I/O error occurs.

readFloat   §2.20.14

```
public final float readFloat()
throws IOException
```

Reads a float from this file. This method reads an int value as if by the readInt method (I-§2.20.17) and then converts that int to a float using the intBitsToFloat method (I-§1.7.14) in class Float.

This method blocks until the 4 bytes are read, the end of the stream is detected, or an exception is thrown.

RETURNS:

the next 4 bytes of this file, interpreted as a float.

THROWS:

EOFException (I-§2.24)
if this file reaches the end before reading 4 bytes.

THROWS:

IOException (I-§2.29)
if an I/O error occurs.

readFully   §2.20.15

```
public final void readFully(byte b[])
throws IOException
```

Reads b.length bytes from this file into the byte array. This method reads repeatedly from the file until all the bytes are read. This method blocks until all the bytes are read, the end of the stream is detected, or an exception is thrown.

PARAMETERS:

b: the buffer into which the data is read.

THROWS:

EOFException (I-§2.24)
if this file reaches the end before reading all the bytes.

THROWS:

IOException (I-§2.29)
if an I/O error occurs.

readFully §2.20.16

```
public final void readFully(byte b[], int off, int len)
throws IOException
```

Reads exactly `len` bytes from this file into the byte array. This method reads repeatedly from the file until all the bytes are read. This method blocks until all the bytes are read, the end of the stream is detected, or an exception is thrown.

PARAMETERS:

`b`: the buffer into which the data is read.
`off`: the start offset of the data.
`len`: the number of bytes to read.

THROWS:

EOFException **(I-§2.24)**
if this file reaches the end before reading all the bytes.

THROWS:

IOException **(I-§2.29)**
if an I/O error occurs.

readInt §2.20.17

```
public final int readInt()
throws IOException
```

Reads a signed 32-bit integer from this file. This method reads 4 bytes from the file. If the bytes read, in order, are `b1`, `b2`, `b3`, and `b4`, where $0 \leq b1, b2, b3, b4 \leq 255$, then the result is equal to

```
(b1 << 24) | (b2 << 16) + (b3 << 8) + b4
```

This method blocks until the 4 bytes are read, the end of the stream is detected, or an exception is thrown.

RETURNS:

the next 4 bytes of this file, interpreted as an `int`.

THROWS:

EOFException **(I-§2.24)**
if this file reaches the end before reading 4 bytes.

THROWS:

IOException **(I-§2.29)**
if an I/O error occurs.

readLine   §2.20.18

```
public final String readLine()
throws IOException
```

Reads the next line of text from this file. This method successively reads bytes from the file until it reaches the end of a line of text.

A line of text is terminated by a carriage-return character (`'\r'`), a newline character (`'\n'`), a carriage-return character immediately followed by a newline character, or the end of the input stream. The line-terminating character(s), if any, are included as part of the string returned.

This method blocks until a newline character is read, a carriage return and the byte following it are read (to see if it is a newline), the end of the stream is detected, or an exception is thrown.

RETURNS:

the next line of text from this file.

THROWS:

IOException (I-§2.29)
if an I/O error occurs.

readLong   §2.20.19

```
public final long readLong()
throws IOException
```

Reads a signed 64-bit integer from this file. This method reads 8 bytes from the file. If the bytes read, in order, are b1, b2, b3, b4, b5, b6, b7, and b8, where

$$0 \le b1, b2, b3, b4, b5, b6, b7, b8 \le 255,$$

then the result is equal to

```
((long)b1 << 56) + ((long)b2 << 48)
+ ((long)b3 << 40) + ((long)b4 << 32)
+ ((long)b5 << 24) + ((long)b6 << 16)
+ ((long)b7 << 8) + b8
```

This method blocks until the 8 bytes are read, the end of the stream is detected, or an exception is thrown.

RETURNS:

the next 8 bytes of this file, interpreted as a `long`.

THROWS:

EOFException (I-§2.24)
if this file reaches the end before reading 8 bytes.

THROWS:

IOException (I-§2.29)
if an I/O error occurs.

readShort   §2.20.20

```
public final short readShort()
throws IOException
```

Reads a signed 16-bit number from this file. The method reads 2 bytes from this file. If the 2 bytes read, in order, are b1 and b2, where each of the 2 values is between 0 and 255, inclusive, then the result is equal to

```
(short)((b1 << 8) | b2)
```

This method blocks until the 2 bytes are read, the end of the stream is detected, or an exception is thrown.

RETURNS:

the next 2 bytes of this file, interpreted as a signed 16-bit number.

THROWS:

EOFException **(I-§2.24)**
if this file reaches the end before reading 2 bytes.

THROWS:

IOException **(I-§2.29)**
if an I/O error occurs.

readUnsignedByte   §2.20.21

```
public final int readUnsignedByte()
throws IOException
```

Reads an unsigned 8-bit number from this file. This method reads a byte from this file and returns that byte.

This method blocks until the byte is read, the end of the stream is detected, or an exception is thrown.

RETURNS:

the next byte of this file, interpreted as an unsigned 8-bit number.

THROWS:

EOFException **(I-§2.24)**
if this file has reached the end.

THROWS:

IOException **(I-§2.29)**
if an I/O error occurs.

readUnsignedShort §2.20.22

```
public final int readUnsignedShort()
throws IOException
```

Reads an unsigned 16-bit number from this file. This method reads 2 bytes from the file. If the bytes read, in order, are b1 and b2, where $0 \le b1, b2 \le 255$, then the result is equal to

```
(b1 << 8) | b2
```

This method blocks until the 2 bytes are read, the end of the stream is detected, or an exception is thrown.

RETURNS:

the next 2 bytes of this file, interpreted as an unsigned 16-bit integer.

THROWS:

EOFException **(I-§2.24)**
if this file reaches the end before reading 2 bytes.

THROWS:

IOException **(I-§2.29)**
if an I/O error occurs.

readUTF   §2.20.23

```
public final String readUTF()
throws IOException
```

Reads in a string from this file. The string has been encoded using a modified UTF-8 format.

The first 2 bytes are read as if by `readUnsignedShort` (**I-§2.20.22**). This value gives the number of following bytes that are in the encoded string. (Note: *not* the length of the resulting string). The following bytes are then interpreted as bytes encoding characters in the UTF-8 format (page I-204) and are converted into characters.

This method blocks until all the bytes are read, the end of the stream is detected, or an exception is thrown.

RETURNS:

a Unicode string.

THROWS:

`EOFException` (**I-§2.24**)
if this file reaches the end before reading all the bytes.

THROWS:

`UTFDataFormatException` (**I-§2.31**)
if the bytes do not represent a valid UTF-8 encoding of a Unicode string.

THROWS:

`IOException` (**I-§2.29**)
if an I/O error occurs.

seek   §2.20.24

```
public void seek(long pos)
throws IOException
```

Sets the offset from the beginning of this file at which the next read or write occurs.

PARAMETERS:

`pos`: the absolute position.

THROWS:

`IOException` (**I-§2.29**)
if an I/O error occurs.

skipBytes   §2.20.25

```
public int skipBytes(int n)
throws IOException
```

Skips exactly n bytes of input.

This method blocks until all the bytes are skipped, the end of the stream is detected, or an exception is thrown.

PARAMETERS:

n: the number of bytes to be skipped.

RETURNS:

the number of bytes skipped, which is always n.

THROWS:

EOFException **(I-§2.24)**

if this file reaches the end before skipping all the bytes.

THROWS:

IOException **(I-§2.29)**

if an I/O error occurs.

write   §2.20.26

```
public void write(byte b[])
throws IOException
```

Writes b.length bytes from the specified byte array starting at offset off to this file.

PARAMETERS:

b: the data.

THROWS:

IOException **(I-§2.29)**

if an I/O error occurs.

write   §2.20.27

```
public void write(byte b[], int off, int len)
throws IOException
```

Writes len bytes from the specified byte array starting at offset off to this file.

PARAMETERS:

b: the data.
off: the start offset in the data.
len: the number of bytes to write.

THROWS:

IOException **(I-§2.29)**

if an I/O error occurs.

write §2.20.28

```
public void write(int b)
throws IOException
```

Writes the specified byte to this file.

PARAMETERS:

b: the byte to be written.

THROWS:

IOException **(I-§2.29)**
if an I/O error occurs.

writeBoolean §2.20.29

```
public final void writeBoolean(boolean v)
throws IOException
```

Writes a boolean to the file as a 1-byte value. The value true is written out as the value (byte)1; the value false is written out as the value (byte)0.

PARAMETERS:

v: a boolean value to be written.

THROWS:

IOException **(I-§2.29)**
if an I/O error occurs.

writeByte §2.20.30

```
public final void writeByte(int v)
throws IOException
```

Writes out a byte to the file as a 1-byte value.

PARAMETERS:

v: a byte value to be written.

THROWS:

IOException **(I-§2.29)**
if an I/O error occurs.

writeBytes   §2.20.31

```
public final void writeBytes(String s)
throws IOException
```

   Writes out the string to the file as a sequence of bytes. Each character in the string is written out, in sequence, by discarding its high 8 bits.

PARAMETERS:

s: a string of bytes to be written.

THROWS:

IOException (I-§2.29)
if an I/O error occurs.

writeChar   §2.20.32

```
public final void writeChar(int v)
throws IOException
```

   Writes a char to the file as a 2-byte value, high byte first.

PARAMETERS:

v: a char value to be written.

THROWS:

IOException (I-§2.29)
if an I/O error occurs.

writeChars   §2.20.33

```
public final void writeChars(String s)
throws IOException
```

   Writes a string to the file as a sequence of characters. Each character is written to the data output stream as if by the writeChar method (I-§2.20.32).

PARAMETERS:

s: a String value to be written.

THROWS:

IOException (I-§2.29)
if an I/O error occurs.

writeDouble §2.20.34

```
public final void writeDouble(double v)
throws IOException
```

Converts the double argument to a `long` using the `doubleToLongBits` method (**I-§1.6.8**) in class `Double`, and then writes that `long` value to the file as an 8-byte quantity, high byte first.

PARAMETERS:

v: a `double` value to be written.

THROWS:

IOException (**I-§2.29**)
if an I/O error occurs.

writeFloat §2.20.35

```
public final void writeFloat(float v)
throws IOException
```

Converts the float argument to an `int` using the `floatToIntBits` method (**I-§1.7.11**) in class `Float`, and then writes that `int` value to the file as a 4-byte quantity, high byte first.

PARAMETERS:

v: a `float` value to be written.

THROWS:

IOException (**I-§2.29**)
if an I/O error occurs.

writeInt §2.20.36

```
public final void writeInt(int v)
throws IOException
```

Writes an `int` to the file as 4 bytes, high byte first.

PARAMETERS:

v: an `int` to be written.

THROWS:

IOException (**I-§2.29**)
if an I/O error occurs.

writeLong   §2.20.37

```
public final void writeLong(long v)
throws IOException
```

Writes a long to the file as 8 bytes, high byte first.

PARAMETERS:

v: a long to be written.

THROWS:

IOException (I-§2.29)
if an I/O error occurs.

writeShort   §2.20.38

```
public final void writeShort(int v)
throws IOException
```

Writes a short to the file as 2 bytes, high byte first.

PARAMETERS:

v: a short to be written.

THROWS:

IOException (I-§2.29)
if an I/O error occurs.

writeUTF   §2.20.39

```
public final void writeUTF(String str)
throws IOException
```

Writes out a string to the file using UTF-8 encoding in a machine-independent manner.

First, 2 bytes are written to the file as if by the writeShort method (I-§2.20.38) giving the number of bytes to follow. This value is the number of bytes actually written out, not the length of the string. Following the length, each character of the string is output, in sequence, using the UTF-8 encoding (page I-204) for each character.

PARAMETERS:

str: a string to be written.

THROWS:

IOException (I-§2.29)
if an I/O error occurs.

2.21 Class SequenceInputStream

```
public class java.io.SequenceInputStream
    extends java.io.InputStream (I-§2.13)
{
    // Constructors
    public SequenceInputStream(Enumeration e);        §2.21.1
    public SequenceInputStream(InputStream s1,        §2.21.2
                        InputStream s2);
    // Methods
    public void close();                              §2.21.3
    public int read();                                §2.21.4
    public int read(byte buf[], int pos, int len);    §2.21.5
}
```

The sequence input stream class allows an application to combine several input streams serially and make them appear as if they were a single input stream. Each input stream is read from, in turn, until it reaches the end of the stream. The sequence input stream class then closes that stream and automatically switches to the next input stream.

Constructors

SequenceInputStream   §2.21.1

```
public SequenceInputStream(Enumeration e)
```

Constructs a new sequence input stream initialized to the specified enumeration (I-§3.11) of input streams. Each object in the enumeration must be an InputStream.

PARAMETERS:

e: an enumeration of input streams.

SequenceInputStream   §2.21.2

```
public SequenceInputStream(InputStream s1, InputStream s2)
```

Constructs a new sequence input stream initialized to read first from the input stream s1, and then from the input stream s2.

Methods

close   §2.21.3

```
public void close()
throws IOException
```

Closes this input stream and releases any system resources associated with the stream.

The `close` method of `SequenceInputStream` calls the `close` method of both the substream from which it is currently reading and the `close` method of all the substreams that it has not yet begun to read from.

THROWS:

`IOException` **(I-§2.29)**

if an I/O error occurs.

OVERRIDES:

`close` in class `InputStream` **(I-§2.13.3)**.

read   §2.21.4

```
public int read()
throws IOException
```

Reads the next byte of data from this input stream. The byte is returned as an `int` in the range `0` to `255`. If no byte is available because the end of the stream has been reached, the value `-1` is returned. This method blocks until input data is available, the end of the stream is detected, or an exception is thrown.

The `read` method of `SequenceInputStream` tries to read 1 character from the current substream. If it reaches the end of the stream, it calls the `close` method of the current substream and begins reading from the next substream.

RETURNS:

the next byte of data, or `-1` if the end of the stream is reached.

THROWS:

`IOException` **(I-§2.29)**

if an I/O error occurs.

OVERRIDES:

`read` in class `InputStream` **(I-§2.13.6)**.

read §2.21.5

```
public int read(byte buf[], int pos, int len)
throws IOException
```

Reads up to `len` bytes of data from this input stream into an array of bytes. This method blocks until at least 1 byte of input is available. If the first argument is `null`, up to `len` bytes are read and discarded.

The `read` method of `SequenceInputStream` tries to read the data from the current substream. If it fails to read any characters because the substream has reached the end of the stream, it calls the `close` method of the current substream and begins reading from the next substream.

PARAMETERS:

`b`: the buffer into which the data is read.
`off`: the start offset of the data.
`len`: the maximum number of bytes read.

THROWS:

`IOException` **(I-§2.29)**
if an I/O error occurs.

OVERRIDES:

`read` in class `InputStream` **(I-§2.13.8)**.

2.22 Class StreamTokenizer

```
public class java.io.StreamTokenizer
    extends java.lang.Object (I-§1.12)
{
    // Fields
    public double nval;                                        §2.22.1
    public String sval;                                        §2.22.2
    public int ttype;                                          §2.22.3

    // possible values for the ttype field
    public final static int TT_EOF;                            §2.22.4
    public final static int TT_EOL;                            §2.22.5
    public final static int TT_NUMBER;                         §2.22.6
    public final static int TT_WORD;                           §2.22.7

    // Constructors
    public StreamTokenizer(InputStream I);                     §2.22.8

    // Methods
    public void commentChar(int ch);                           §2.22.9
    public void eolIsSignificant(boolean flag);                §2.22.10
    public int lineno();                                       §2.22.11
    public void lowerCaseMode(boolean fl);                     §2.22.12
    public int nextToken();                                    §2.22.13
    public void ordinaryChar(int ch);                          §2.22.14
    public void ordinaryChars(int low, int hi);                §2.22.15
    public void parseNumbers();                                §2.22.16
    public void pushBack();                                    §2.22.17
    public void quoteChar(int ch);                             §2.22.18
    public void resetSyntax();                                 §2.22.19
    public void slashSlashComments(boolean flag);              §2.22.20
    public void slashStarComments(boolean flag);               §2.22.21
    public String toString();                                  §2.22.22
    public void whitespaceChars(int low, int hi);              §2.22.23
    public void wordChars(int low, int hi);                    §2.22.24
}
```

The StreamTokenizer class takes an input stream and parses it into "tokens," allowing the tokens to be read one at a time. The parsing process is controlled by a table and a number of flags that can be set to various states. The stream tokenizer can recognize identifiers, numbers, quoted strings, and various comment styles.

Each byte read from the input stream is regarded as a character in the range '\u0000' through '\u00FF'. The character value is used to look up five possible attributes of the character: *white space*, *alphabetic*, *numeric*, *string quote*, and *comment character*. Each character can have zero or more of these attributes.

In addition, an instance has 4 flags. These flags indicate:

♦ Whether line terminators are to be returned as tokens or treated as white space that merely separates tokens.

♦ Whether C-style comments are to be recognized and skipped.

♦ Whether C++-style comments are to be recognized and skipped.

♦ Whether the characters of identifiers are converted to lowercase.

A typical application first constructs an instance of this class, sets up the syntax tables, and then repeatedly loops calling the `nextToken` method **(I-§2.22.13)** in each iteration of the loop until it returns the value `TT_EOF` **(I-§2.22.4)**.

Fields

nval   **§2.22.1**

    public double nval

If the current token is a number, this field contains the value of that number. The current token is a number when the value of the `ttype` field **(I-§2.22.3)** is `TT_NUMBER` **(I-§2.22.6)**.

sval   **§2.22.2**

    public String sval

If the current token is a word token, this field contains a string giving the characters of the word token. When the current token is a quoted string token, this field contains the body of the string.

The current token is a word when the value of the `ttype` field **(I-§2.22.3)** is `TT_WORD` **(I-§2.22.7)**. The current token is a quoted string token when the value of the `ttype` field is a quote character (see **I-§2.22.18**).

ttype   **§2.22.3**

    public int ttype

After a call to the `nextToken` method **(I-§2.22.13)**, this field contains the type of the token just read. For a single character token, its value is the single character, converted to an integer. For a quoted string token (see **I-§2.22.18**), its value is the quote character. Otherwise, its value is one of the following:

♦ `TT_WORD` **(I-§2.22.7)** indicates that the token is a word.

♦ `TT_NUMBER` **(I-§2.22.6)** indicates that the token is a number.

♦ TT_EOL (**I-§2.22.5**) indicates that the end of line has been read. The field can only have this value if the `eolIsSignificant` method (**I-§2.22.10**) has been called with the argument `true`.

♦ TT_EOF (**I-§2.22.4**) indicates that the end of the input stream has been reached.

TT_EOF §2.22.4

    `public final static int TT_EOF = -1`

        A constant indicating that the end of the stream has been read.

TT_EOL §2.22.5

    `public final static int TT_EOL = '\n'`

        A constant indicating that the end of the line has been read.

TT_NUMBER §2.22.6

    `public final static int TT_NUMBER = -2`

        A constant indicating that a number token has been read.

TT_WORD §2.22.7

    `public final static int TT_WORD = -3`

        A constant indicating that a word token has been read.

Constructors

StreamTokenizer §2.22.8

    `public StreamTokenizer(InputStream I)`

        Creates a stream tokenizer that parses the specified input stream. The stream tokenizer is initialized to the following default state:

♦ All byte values `'A'` through `'Z'`, `'a'` through `'z'`, and `'\u00A0'` through `'\u00FF'` are considered to be alphabetic.

♦ All byte values `'\u0000'` through `'\u0020'` are considered to be white space.

♦ `'/'` is a comment character.

♦ Single quote `'\''` and double quote `'"'` are string quote characters.

♦ Numbers are parsed.

♦ Ends of lines are treated as white space, not as separate tokens.

♦ C-style and C++-style comments are not recognized.

PARAMETERS:

`I`: the input stream.

Methods

---

commentChar   §2.22.9

    public void commentChar(int ch)

Specified that the character argument starts a single-line comment. All characters from the comment character to the end of the line are ignored by this stream tokenizer.

PARAMETERS:

ch: the character.

eolIsSignificant   §2.22.10

    public void eolIsSignificant(boolean flag)

If the flag argument is true, this tokenizer treats end of lines as tokens; the nextToken method (I-§2.22.13) returns TT_EOL (I-§2.22.5) and also sets the ttype field (I-§2.22.3) to this value when an end of line is read.

A line is a sequence of characters ending with either a carriage-return character ('\r') or a newline character ('\n'). In addition, a carriage-return character followed immediately by a newline character is treated as a single end-of-line token.

If the flag is false, end-of-line characters are treated as white space and serve only to separate tokens.

PARAMETERS:

flag: true indicates that end-of-line characters are separate tokens; false indicates that end-of-line characters are white space.

lineno   §2.22.11

    public int lineno()

RETURNS:

the current line number of this stream tokenizer.

lowerCaseMode   §2.22.12

    public void lowerCaseMode(boolean fl)

If the flag argument is true, then the value in the sval field is lowercased whenever a word token is returned (the ttype field [I-§2.22.3] has the value TT_WORD [I-§2.22.7]) by the nextToken method (I-§2.22.13) of this tokenizer.

If the flag argument is false, then the sval field is not modified.

PARAMETERS:

fl: true indicates that all word tokens should be lowercased.

nextToken   §2.22.13

```
public int nextToken()
throws IOException
```

Parses the next token from the input stream of this tokenizer. The type of the next token is returned in the ttype field (I-§2.22.3). Additional information about the token may be in the nval field (I-§2.22.1) or the sval field (I-§2.22.2) of this tokenizer.

RETURNS:

the value of the ttype field (I-§2.22.3).

THROWS:

IOException (I-§2.29)
if an I/O error occurs.

ordinaryChar   §2.22.14

```
public void ordinaryChar(int ch)
```

Specifies that the character argument is "ordinary" in this tokenizer. It removes any special significance the character has as a comment character, word component, string delimiter, white space, or number character. When such a character is encountered by the parser, the parser treats it as a single-character token and sets ttype field (I-§2.22.3) to the character value.

PARAMETERS:

ch: the character.

ordinaryChars   §2.22.15

```
public void ordinaryChars(int low, int hi)
```

Specifies that all characters c in the range $low \leq c \leq high$ are "ordinary" in this tokenizer. See the ordinaryChar method (I-§2.22.14) for more information on a character being ordinary.

PARAMETERS:

low: the low end of the range.
hi: the high end of the range.

parseNumbers   §2.22.16

```
public void parseNumbers()
```

Specifies that numbers should be parsed by this tokenizer. The syntax table of this tokenizer is modified so that each of the 12 characters

```
0 1 2 3 4 5 6 7 8 9 . -
```

has the "numeric" attribute.

When the parser encounters a word token that has the format of a double precision floating-point number, it treats the token as a number rather than a word, by setting the the `ttype` field (**I-§2.22.3**) to the value `TT_NUMBER` (**I-§2.22.6**) and putting the numeric value of the token into the `nval` field (**I-§2.22.1**).

pushBack §2.22.17

```
public void pushBack()
```

Causes the next call to the `nextToken` method (**I-§2.22.13**) of this tokenizer to return the current value in the `ttype` field (**I-§2.22.3**), and not to modify the value in the `nval` (**I-§2.22.1**) or `sval` (**I-§2.22.2**) field.

quoteChar §2.22.18

```
public void quoteChar(int ch)
```

Specifies that matching pairs of this character delimit string constants in this tokenizer.

When the `nextToken` method (**I-§2.22.13**) encounters a string constant, the `ttype` field (**I-§2.22.3**) is set to the string delimiter and the `sval` field (**I-§2.22.2**) is set to the body of the string.

If a string quote character is encountered, then a string is recognized, consisting of all characters after (but not including) the string quote character, up to (but not including) the next occurrence of that same string quote character, or a line terminator, or end of file. The usual escape sequences such as "\n" and "\t" are recognized and converted to single characters as the string is parsed.

PARAMETERS:

`ch`: the character.

resetSyntax §2.22.19

```
public void resetSyntax()
```

Resets this tokenizer's syntax table so that all characters are "ordinary." See the `ordinaryChar` method (**I-§2.22.14**) for more information on a character being ordinary.

slashSlashComments   §2.22.20

```
public void slashSlashComments(boolean flag)
```

If the flag argument is `true`, this stream tokenizer recognizes C++-style comments. Any occurrence of two consecutive slash characters (`'/'`) is treated as the beginning of a comment that extends to the end of the line.

If the flag argument is `false`, then C++-style comments are not treated specially.

PARAMETERS:

`flag`: true indicates to recognize and ignore C++-style comments.

slashStarComments   §2.22.21

```
public void slashStarComments(boolean flag)
```

If the flag argument is `true`, this stream tokenizer recognizes C-style comments. All text between successive occurrences of `/*` and `*/` are discarded.

If the flag argument is `false`, then C-style comments are not treated specially.

PARAMETERS:

`flag`: true indicates to recognize and ignore C-style comments.

toString   §2.22.22

```
public String toString()
```

Returns the string representation of the current stream token.

RETURNS:

a string representation of the token specified by the `ttype` (**I-§2.22.3**), `nval` (**I-§2.22.1**), and `sval` (**I-§2.22.2**) fields.

OVERRIDES:

`toString` in class `Object` (**I-§1.12.9**).

whitespaceChars   §2.22.23

```
public void whitespaceChars(int low, int hi)
```

Specifies that all characters c in the range $low \leq c \leq high$ are white space characters. White space characters serve only to separate tokens in the input stream.

PARAMETERS:

`low`: the low end of the range.
`hi`: the high end of the range.

wordChars §2.22.24

```
public void wordChars(int low, int hi)
```

Specifies that all characters c in the range $low \le c \le high$ are word constituents. A word token consists of a word constituent followed by zero or more word constituents or number constituents.

PARAMETERS:

low: the low end of the range.
hi: the high end of the range.

2.23 Class StringBufferInputStream

```
public class java.io.StringBufferInputStream
    extends java.io.InputStream (I-§2.13)
{
    // Fields
    protected String buffer;                        §2.23.1
    protected int count;                            §2.23.2
    protected int pos;                              §2.23.3

    // Constructors
    public StringBufferInputStream(String s);       §2.23.4

    // Methods
    public int available();                         §2.23.5
    public int read();                              §2.23.6
    public int read(byte b[], int off, int len);    §2.23.7
    public void reset();                            §2.23.8
    public long skip(long n);                       §2.23.9
}
```

This class allows an application to create an input stream in which the bytes read are supplied by the contents of a string. Applications can also read bytes from a byte array by using a ByteArrayInputStream (I-§2.3).

Only the low 8 bits of each character in the string are used by this class.

Fields

buffer §2.23.1

```
protected String buffer
```

The string from which bytes are read.

count §2.23.2

```
protected int count
```

The number of valid characters in the input stream buffer (I-§2.23.1).

pos   §2.23.3

```
protected int pos
```

The index of the next character to read from the input stream buffer
(I-§2.23.1).

Constructors

StringBufferInputStream   §2.23.4

```
public StringBufferInputStream(String s)
```

Creates a string input stream to read data from the specified string.

PARAMETERS:

s: the underlying input buffer.

Methods

available   §2.23.5

```
public int available()
```

Determines the number of bytes that can be read from the input stream
without blocking.

RETURNS:

the value of count – pos , which is the number of bytes remaining to be read
    from the input buffer.

OVERRIDES:

available in class InputStream **(I-§2.13.2)**.

read   §2.23.6

```
public int read()
```

Reads the next byte of data from this input stream. The value byte is
returned as an int in the range 0 to 255. If no byte is available because the
end of the stream has been reached, the value -1 is returned.

The read method of StringBufferInputStream cannot block. It returns
the low 8 bits of the next character in this input stream's buffer.

RETURNS:

the next byte of data, or -1 if the end of the stream is reached.

OVERRIDES:

read in class InputStream **(I-§2.13.6)**.

read   §2.23.7

```
public int read(byte b[], int off, int len)
```

Reads up to `len` bytes of data from this input stream into an array of bytes.

The `read` method of `StringBufferInputStream` cannot block. It copies the low 8 bits from the characters in this input stream's buffer into the byte array argument.

PARAMETERS:

`b`: the buffer into which the data is read.
`off`: the start offset of the data.
`len`: the maximum number of bytes read.

RETURNS:

the total number of bytes read into the buffer, or -1 if there is no more data
   because the end of the stream has been reached.

OVERRIDES:

`read` in class `InputStream` (**I-§2.13.8**).

reset   §2.23.8

```
public void reset()
```

Resets the input stream to begin reading from the first character of this input stream's underlying buffer.

OVERRIDES:

`reset` in class `InputStream` (**I-§2.13.9**).

skip   §2.23.9

```
public long skip(long n)
```

Skips n bytes of input from this input stream. Fewer bytes might be skipped if the end of the input stream is reached.

PARAMETERS:

`n`: the number of bytes to be skipped.

RETURNS:

the actual number of bytes skipped.

OVERRIDES:

`skip` in class `InputStream` (**I-§2.13.10**).

2.24 Interface DataInput

```
public interface java.io.DataInput
{
    // Methods
    public abstract boolean readBoolean();                    §2.24.1
    public abstract byte readByte();                          §2.24.2
    public abstract char readChar();                          §2.24.3
    public abstract double readDouble();                      §2.24.4
    public abstract float readFloat();                        §2.24.5
    public abstract void readFully(byte b[]);                 §2.24.6
    public abstract void                                      §2.24.7
        readFully(byte b[], int off, int len);
    public abstract int readInt();                            §2.24.8
    public abstract String readLine();                        §2.24.9
    public abstract long readLong();                          §2.24.10
    public abstract short readShort();                        §2.24.11
    public abstract int readUnsignedByte();                   §2.24.12
    public abstract int readUnsignedShort();                  §2.24.13
    public abstract String readUTF();                         §2.24.14
    public abstract int skipBytes(int n);                     §2.24.15
}
```

The data input interface is implemented by streams that can read primitive Java data types from a stream in a machine-independent manner.

SEE ALSO:

DataInputStream (I-§2.5).

DataOutput (I-§2.25).

Methods

readBoolean   §2.24.1

```
public abstract boolean readBoolean()
throws IOException
```

Reads a boolean value from the input stream.

RETURNS:

the boolean value read.

THROWS:

EOFException (I-§2.24)

if this stream reaches the end before reading all the bytes.

THROWS:

IOException (I-§2.29)

if an I/O error occurs.

readByte §2.24.2

```
public abstract byte readByte()
throws IOException
```

Reads a signed 8-bit value from the input stream.

RETURNS:

the 8-bit value read.

THROWS:

EOFException **(I-§2.24)**
if this stream reaches the end before reading all the bytes.

THROWS:

IOException **(I-§2.29)**
if an I/O error occurs.

readChar §2.24.3

```
public abstract char readChar()
throws IOException
```

Reads a Unicode char value from the input stream.

RETURNS:

the Unicode char read.

THROWS:

EOFException **(I-§2.24)**
if this stream reaches the end before reading all the bytes.

THROWS:

IOException **(I-§2.29)**
if an I/O error occurs.

readDouble §2.24.4

```
public abstract double readDouble()
throws IOException
```

Reads a double value from the input stream.

RETURNS:

the double value read.

THROWS:

EOFException **(I-§2.24)**
if this stream reaches the end before reading all the bytes.

THROWS:

IOException **(I-§2.29)**
if an I/O error occurs.

readFloat   §2.24.5

```
public abstract float readFloat()
throws IOException
```

Reads a float value from the input stream.

RETURNS:

the float value read.

THROWS:

EOFException (I-§2.24)
if this stream reaches the end before reading all the bytes.

THROWS:

IOException (I-§2.29)
if an I/O error occurs.

readFully   §2.24.6

```
public abstract void readFully(byte b[])
throws IOException
```

Reads b.length bytes into the byte array. This method blocks until all the bytes are read.

PARAMETERS:

b: the buffer into which the data is read.

THROWS:

EOFException (I-§2.24)
if this stream reaches the end before reading all the bytes.

THROWS:

IOException (I-§2.29)
if an I/O error occurs.

readFully   §2.24.7

```
public abstract void readFully(byte b[], int off, int len)
throws IOException
```

Reads b.length bytes into the byte array. This method blocks until all the bytes are read.

PARAMETERS:

b: the buffer into which the data is read.

THROWS:

EOFException (I-§2.24)
if this stream reaches the end before reading all the bytes.

THROWS:

IOException (I-§2.29)
if an I/O error occurs.

readInt

```
public abstract int readInt()
throws IOException
```

Reads an int value from the input stream.

RETURNS:

the int value read.

THROWS:

EOFException **(I-§2.24)**
if this stream reaches the end before reading all the bytes.

THROWS:

IOException **(I-§2.29)**
if an I/O error occurs.

readLine

```
public abstract String readLine()
throws IOException
```

Reads the next line of text from the input stream.

RETURNS:

if this stream reaches the end before reading all the bytes.

THROWS:

IOException **(I-§2.29)**
if an I/O error occurs.

readLong

```
public abstract long readLong()
throws IOException
```

Reads a long value from the input stream.

RETURNS:

the long value read.

THROWS:

EOFException **(I-§2.24)**
if this stream reaches the end before reading all the bytes.

THROWS:

IOException **(I-§2.29)**
if an I/O error occurs.

readShort   §2.24.11

```
public abstract short readShort()
throws IOException
```

Reads a 16-bit value from the input stream.

RETURNS:

the 16-bit value read.

THROWS:

EOFException **(I-§2.24)**
if this stream reaches the end before reading all the bytes.

THROWS:

IOException **(I-§2.29)**
if an I/O error occurs.

readUnsignedByte   §2.24.12

```
public abstract int readUnsignedByte()
throws IOException
```

Reads an unsigned 8-bit value from the input stream.

RETURNS:

the unsigned 8-bit value read.

THROWS:

EOFException **(I-§2.24)**
if this stream reaches the end before reading all the bytes.

THROWS:

IOException **(I-§2.29)**
if an I/O error occurs.

readUnsignedShort   §2.24.13

```
public abstract int readUnsignedShort()
throws IOException
```

Reads an unsigned 16-bit value from the input stream.

RETURNS:

the unsigned 16-bit value read.

THROWS:

EOFException **(I-§2.24)**
if this stream reaches the end before reading all the bytes.

THROWS:

IOException **(I-§2.29)**
if an I/O error occurs.

readUTF §2.24.14

```
public abstract String readUTF()
throws IOException
```

Reads in a string that has been encoded using a modified UTF-8 format.

RETURNS:

a Unicode string.

THROWS:

EOFException **(I-§2.24)**

if this stream reaches the end before reading all the bytes.

THROWS:

UTFDataFormatException **(I-§2.31)**

if the bytes do not represent a valid UTF-8 encoding of a string.

THROWS:

IOException **(I-§2.29)**

if an I/O error occurs.

skipBytes §2.24.15

```
public abstract int skipBytes(int n)
throws IOException
```

Skips exactly n bytes of input.

PARAMETERS:

n: the number of bytes to be skipped.

RETURNS:

the number of bytes skipped, which is always n.

THROWS:

EOFException **(I-§2.24)**

if this stream reaches the end before skipping all the bytes.

THROWS:

IOException **(I-§2.29)**

if an I/O error occurs.

2.25 Interface DataOutput

```
public interface java.io.DataOutput
{
    // Methods
    public abstract void write(byte b[]);                    §2.25.1
    public abstract void write(byte b[],
                            int off, int len);               §2.25.2
    public abstract void write(int b);                       §2.25.3
    public abstract void writeBoolean(boolean v);            §2.25.4
    public abstract void writeByte(int v);                   §2.25.5
    public abstract void writeBytes(String s);               §2.25.6
    public abstract void writeChar(int v);                   §2.25.7
    public abstract void writeChars(String s);               §2.25.8
    public abstract void writeDouble(double v);              §2.25.9
    public abstract void writeFloat(float v);                §2.25.10
    public abstract void writeInt(int v);                    §2.25.11
    public abstract void writeLong(long v);                  §2.25.12
    public abstract void writeShort(int v);                  §2.25.13
    public abstract void writeUTF(String str);               §2.25.14
}
```

The data output interface is implemented by streams that can write primitive Java data types to an output stream in a machine-independent manner.

SEE ALSO:

DataOutputStream (I-§2.6).
DataInput (I-§2.24).

Methods

write   §2.25.1

```
    public abstract void write(byte b[])
    throws IOException
```

Writes b.length bytes from the specified byte array to this output stream.

PARAMETERS:

b: the data.

THROWS:

IOException (I-§2.29)
if an I/O error occurs.

write   §2.25.2

```
public abstract void write(byte b[], int off, int len)
throws IOException
```

Writes `len` bytes from the specified byte array starting at offset `off` to this output stream.

PARAMETERS:

`b`: the data.
`off`: the start offset in the data.
`len`: the number of bytes to write.

THROWS:

IOException (**I-§2.29**)
if an I/O error occurs.

write   §2.25.3

```
public abstract void write(int b)
throws IOException
```

Writes the specified byte to this data output stream.

PARAMETERS:

`b`: the byte to be written.

THROWS:

IOException (**I-§2.29**)
if an I/O error occurs.

writeBoolean   §2.25.4

```
public abstract void writeBoolean(boolean v)
throws IOException
```

Writes a `boolean` value to this output stream.

PARAMETERS:

`v`: the boolean to be written.

THROWS:

IOException (**I-§2.29**)
if an I/O error occurs.

writeByte   §2.25.5

```
public abstract void writeByte(int v)
throws IOException
```

    Writes an 8-bit value to this output stream.

PARAMETERS:

v: the byte value to be written.

THROWS:

IOException (I-§2.29)
if an I/O error occurs.

writeBytes   §2.25.6

```
public abstract void writeBytes(String s)
throws IOException
```

    Writes out the string to this output stream.

PARAMETERS:

s: the string of bytes to be written.

THROWS:

IOException (I-§2.29)
if an I/O error occurs.

writeChar   §2.25.7

```
public abstract void writeChar(int v)
throws IOException
```

    Writes a char value to this output stream.

PARAMETERS:

v: the char value to be written.

THROWS:

IOException (I-§2.29)
if an I/O error occurs.

writeChars   §2.25.8

```
public abstract void writeChars(String s)
throws IOException
```

    Writes a string to this output stream.

PARAMETERS:

s: the string value to be written.

THROWS:

IOException (I-§2.29)
if an I/O error occurs.

writeDouble §2.25.9

```
public abstract void writeDouble(double v)
throws IOException
```

Writes a double value to this output stream.

PARAMETERS:

v: the double value to be written.

THROWS:

IOException **(I-§2.29)**
if an I/O error occurs.

writeFloat §2.25.10

```
public abstract void writeFloat(float v)
throws IOException
```

Writes a float value to this output stream.

PARAMETERS:

v: the float value to be written.

THROWS:

IOException **(I-§2.29)**
if an I/O error occurs.

writeInt §2.25.11

```
public abstract void writeInt(int v)
throws IOException
```

Writes an int value to this output stream.

PARAMETERS:

v: the int value to be written.

THROWS:

IOException **(I-§2.29)**
if an I/O error occurs.

writeLong §2.25.12

```
public abstract void writeLong(long v)
throws IOException
```

Writes a long value to this output stream.

PARAMETERS:

v: the long value to be written.

THROWS:

IOException **(I-§2.29)**
if an I/O error occurs.

writeShort   §2.25.13

```
public abstract void writeShort(int v)
throws IOException
```

Writes a 16-bit value to this output stream.

PARAMETERS:

v: the short value to be written.

THROWS:

IOException **(I-§2.29)**

if an I/O error occurs.

writeUTF   §2.25.14

```
public abstract void writeUTF(String str)
throws IOException
```

Writes out a Unicode string by encoding it using modified UTF-8 format.

PARAMETERS:

str: the string value to be written.

THROWS:

IOException **(I-§2.29)**

if an I/O error occurs.

2.26 Interface FilenameFilter

```
public interface java.io.FilenameFilter
{
    // Methods
    public abstract boolean accept(File dir, String name);  §2.26.1
}
```

Instances of classes that implement this interface are used to filter filenames. These instances are used to filter directory listings in the list method **(I-§2.7.24)** of class File **(I-§2.7)**, and by the Abstract Window Toolkit's file dialog component **(II-§1.15.13)**.

SEE ALSO:

File **(I-§2.7)**.

Methods

---

accept   §2.26.1

    `public abstract boolean accept(File dir, String name)`

       Determines whether a specified file should be included in a file list.

    PARAMETERS:

    `dir`: the directory in which the file was found.
    `name`: the name of the file.

    RETURNS:

    `true` if the name should be included in the file list; `false` otherwise.

2.27 Class EOFException

```
public class java.io.EOFException
    extends java.io.IOException (I-§2.29)
{
    // Constructors
    public EOFException();                              §2.27.1
    public EOFException(String s);                      §2.27.2
}
```

    Signals that an end of file or end of stream has been reached unexpectedly during input.

    This exception is mainly used by data input streams, which generally expect a binary file in a specific format, and for which an end of stream is an unusual condition. Most other input streams return a special value on end of stream.

Constructors

EOFException   §2.27.1

    `public EOFException()`

       Constructs an EOFException with no detail message.

EOFException   §2.27.2

    `public EOFException(String s)`

       Constructs an EOFException with the specified detail message.

    PARAMETERS:

    `s`: the detail message.

2.28 Class FileNotFoundException

```
public class java.io.FileNotFoundException
    extends java.io.IOException (I-§2.29)
{
    // Constructors
    public FileNotFoundException();                              §2.28.1
    public FileNotFoundException(String s);                      §2.28.2
}
```

Signals that a file could not be found.

Constructors

FileNotFoundException   **§2.28.1**

    public FileNotFoundException()

        Constructs a FileNotFoundException with no detail message.

FileNotFoundException   **§2.28.2**

    public FileNotFoundException(String s)

        Constructs a FileNotFoundException with the specified detail message.

    PARAMETERS:

    s: the detail message.

2.29 Class IOException

```
public class java.io.IOException
    extends java.lang.Exception (I-§1.30)
{
    // Constructors
    public IOException();                                        §2.29.1
    public IOException(String s);                                §2.29.2
}
```

Signals that an I/O exception of some sort has occurred.

Constructors

IOException   **§2.29.1**

    public IOException()

        Constructs an IOException with no detail message.

IOException   §2.29.2

>   public IOException(String s)

>   Constructs an IOException with the specified detail message.

>   **PARAMETERS:**

>   s: the detail message.

2.30 Class InterruptedIOException

```
public class java.io.InterruptedIOException
    extends java.io.IOException (I-§2.29)
{
    // Fields
    public int bytesTransferred;                                        §2.30.1

    // Constructors
    public InterruptedIOException();                                    §2.30.2
    public InterruptedIOException(String s);                            §2.30.3
}
```

>   Signals that an I/O operation has been interrupted.

See Also:

>   InputStream (I-§2.13).
>   OutputStream (I-§2.15).
>   Interrupt in class Thread (I-§1.19.21).

Fields

bytesTransferred   §2.30.1

>   public int bytesTransferred

>   Reports how many bytes had been transferred as part of the I/O operation
>   before it was interrupted.

Constructors

InterruptedIOException   §2.30.2

>   public InterruptedIOException()

>   Constructs an InterruptedIOException with no detail message.

InterruptedIOException   §2.30.3

```
public InterruptedIOException(String s)
```

Constructs an `InterruptedIOException` with the specified detail message.

PARAMETERS:

s : the detail message.

2.31 Class UTFDataFormatException

```
public class java.io.UTFDataFormatException
    extends java.io.IOException (I-§2.29)
{
    // Constructors
    public UTFDataFormatException();                        §2.31.1
    public UTFDataFormatException(String s);                §2.31.2
}
```

Signals that a malformed UTF-8 string has been read in a data input stream (I-§2.24) or by any class that implements the data input interface (I-§2.24). See the writeUTF method (I-§2.5.18) for the format in which UTF-8 strings are read and written. See page I-204 for more information on UTF-8.

Constructors

UTFDataFormatException   §2.31.1

```
public UTFDataFormatException()
```

Constructs a `UTFDataFormatException` with no detail message.

UTFDataFormatException   §2.31.2

```
public UTFDataFormatException(String s)
```

Constructs a `UTFDataFormatException` with the specified detail message.

PARAMETERS:

s : the detail message.

CHAPTER 3

Package java.util

THE java.util package contains a collection of miscellaneous utility classes and interfaces.

- ♦ **Generic Data Structures:** The classes Dictionary (I-§3.3), Hashtable (I-§3.4), Stack (I-§3.8), and Vector (I-§3.10) provide generic data structures that can be used in a wide variety of applications.

- ♦ **Bits:** The class BitSet (I-§3.1) provides the user with an extendable array of bits.

- ♦ **Time and Date:** The class Date (I-§3.2) provides a set of calendar routines for accessing the date and time.

- ♦ **String Manipulation:** The class StringTokenizer (I-§3.9) is a string manipulation class. It is used to parse a string into its components.

- ♦ **Random Numbers:** The class Random (I-§3.7) allows the user to create a variety of pseudorandom numbers. The user can either create a reproducible sequence, or cause a different sequence to be generated each time.

- ♦ **User Environment:** The class Properties (I-§3.6) allows the user to learn in a system-independent way about the environment in which the program is running.

- ♦ **Notification:** The class Observable (I-§3.5) and the corresponding interface Observer (I-§3.12) allow a general interface in which an Object can be informed about changes in other objects.

- ♦ **Enumeration:** The interface Enumeration (I-§3.11) provides a generic interface for enumerating through the elements of data structure such as a Vector or a Hashtable.

3.1 Class BitSet

```
public final class java.util.BitSet
    extends java.lang.Object (I-§1.12)
    implements java.lang.Cloneable (I-§1.22)
{
    // Constructors
    public BitSet();                                    §3.1.1
    public BitSet(int nbits);                           §3.1.2

    // Methods
    public void and(BitSet set);                        §3.1.3
    public void clear(int bit);                         §3.1.4
    public Object clone();                              §3.1.5
    public boolean equals(Object obj);                  §3.1.6
    public boolean get(int bit);                        §3.1.7
    public int hashCode();                              §3.1.8
    public void or(BitSet set);                         §3.1.9
    public void set(int bit);                           §3.1.10
    public int size();                                  §3.1.11
    public String toString();                           §3.1.12
    public void xor(BitSet set);                        §3.1.13
}
```

This class implements a vector of bits that grows as needed. Each component of the bit set has a boolean value. The bits of a BitSet are indexed by nonnegative integers. Individual indexed bits can be examined, set, or cleared.

By default, all bits in the set initially have the value false.

Every bit set has a current size, which is the number of bits currently in the bit set.

Constructors

BitSet   §3.1.1

    public BitSet()

Creates a new bit set. All bits are initially false.

BitSet   §3.1.2

    public BitSet(int nbits)

Creates a bit set whose initial size is the specified number of bits. All bits are initially false.

PARAMETERS:

nbits: the initial size of the bit set.

Methods

and §3.1.3

```
public void and(BitSet set)
```

Performs a logical **AND** of this target bit set with the argument bit set. This bit set is modified so that each bit in it has the value `true` if and only if it both initially had the value `true` and the corresponding bit in the bit set argument also had the value `true`.

PARAMETERS:

`set`: a bit set.

clear §3.1.4

```
public void clear(int bit)
```

Sets the bit specified by the index to `false`.

PARAMETERS:

`bit`: the index of the bit to be cleared.

clone §3.1.5

```
public Object clone()
```

The clone of the bit set is another bit set that has exactly the same bits set to `true` as this bit set and the same current size (I-**§3.1.11**).

RETURNS:

a clone of this bit set.

OVERRIDES:

`clone` in class `Object` (I-**§1.12.2**).

equals §3.1.6

```
public boolean equals(Object obj)
```

The result is `true` if and only if the argument is not `null` and is a `Bitset` object that has exactly the same set of bits set to `true` as this bit set. The current sizes (I-**§3.1.11**) of the two bit sets are not compared.

PARAMETERS:

`obj`: the object to compare with.

RETURNS:

`true` if the objects are the same; `false` otherwise.

OVERRIDES:

`equals` in class `Object` (I-**§1.12.3**).

get   §3.1.7

    `public boolean get(int bit)`
    PARAMETERS:
    `bit`: the bit index.
    RETURNS:
    the value of the bit with the specified index.

hashCode   §3.1.8

    `public int hashCode()`
    RETURNS:
    a hash code value for this bit set.
    OVERRIDES:
    hashCode in class `Object` (**I-§1.12.6**).

or   §3.1.9

    `public void or(BitSet set)`
    Performs a logical **OR** of this bit set with the bit set argument. This bit set is modified so that a bit in it has the value `true` if and only if it either already had the value `true` or the corresponding bit in the bit set argument has the value `true`.
    PARAMETERS:
    `set`: a bit set.

set   §3.1.10

    `public void set(int bit)`
    Sets the bit specified by the index to `true`.
    PARAMETERS:
    `bit`: a bit index.

size   §3.1.11

    `public int size()`
    RETURNS:
    the number of bits currently in this bit set.

toString   §3.1.12

    `public String toString()`
    RETURNS:
    a string representation of this bit set.
    OVERRIDES:
    toString in class `Object` (**I-§1.12.9**).

xor

```
public void xor(BitSet set)
```

Performs a logical **XOR** of this bit set with the bit set argument. This bit set is modified so that a bit in it has the value `true` if and only if one of the following statements holds:

- ♦ The bit initially has the value `true`, and the corresponding bit in the argument has the value `false`.

- ♦ The bit initially has the value `false`, and the corresponding bit in the argument has the value `true`.

PARAMETERS:

`set`: a bit set.

3.2 Class Date

```
public class java.util.Date
    extends java.lang.Object (I-§1.12)
{
    // Constructors
    public Date();                                              §3.2.1
    public Date(int year, int month, int date);                §3.2.2
    public Date(int year, int month, int date,                 §3.2.3
            int hrs, int min);
    public Date(int year, int month, int date,                 §3.2.4
            int hrs, int min, int sec);
    public Date(long date);                                    §3.2.5
    public Date(String s);                                     §3.2.6

    // Methods
    public boolean after(Date when);                           §3.2.7
    public boolean before(Date when);                          §3.2.8
    public boolean equals(Object obj);                         §3.2.9
    public int getDate();                                      §3.2.10
    public int getDay();                                       §3.2.11
    public int getHours();                                     §3.2.12
    public int getMinutes();                                   §3.2.13
    public int getMonth();                                     §3.2.14
    public int getSeconds();                                   §3.2.15
    public long getTime();                                     §3.2.16
    public int getTimezoneOffset();                            §3.2.17
    public int getYear();                                      §3.2.18
    public int hashCode();                                     §3.2.19
    public static long parse(String s);                        §3.2.20
    public void setDate(int date);                             §3.2.21
    public void setHours(int hours);                           §3.2.22
    public void setMinutes(int minutes);                       §3.2.23
    public void setMonth(int month);                           §3.2.24
    public void setSeconds(int seconds);                       §3.2.25
    public void setTime(long time);                            §3.2.26
    public void setYear(int year);                             §3.2.27
    public String toGMTString();                               §3.2.28
    public String toLocaleString();                            §3.2.29
    public String toString();                                  §3.2.30
    public static long UTC(int year, int month, int date,      §3.2.31
                    int hrs, int min, int sec);
}
```

The class Date provides an abstraction of dates and times. Dates may be constructed from a year, month, date (day of month), hour, minute, and second. Those six components, as well as the day of the week, may be extracted from a date. Dates may also be compared and converted to a readable string form. A date is represented to a precision of 1 millisecond.

The following code prints today's date:

```
System.out.println("today = " + new Date());
```

The following code finds out the day of the week for some particular date, for example, January 16, 1963:

```
new Date(63, 0, 16).getDay()
```

Although the Date class is intended to reflect coordinated universal time (UTC), it may not do so exactly, depending on the host environment of the Java Virtual Machine. Nearly all modern operating systems assume that 1 day = $24 \times 60 \times 60$ = 86400 seconds in all cases. In UTC, however, about once every year or two there is an extra second, called a "leap second." The leap second is always added as the last second of the day, and always on December 31 or June 30. For example, the last minute of the year 1995 was 61 seconds long, thanks to an added leap second. Most computer clocks are not accurate enough to be able to reflect the leap-second distinction.

Some computer standards are defined in terms of Greenwich mean time (GMT), which is equivalent to universal time (UT). GMT is the "civil" name for the standard; UT is the "scientific" name for the same standard. The distinction between UTC and UT is that UTC is based on an atomic clock and UT is based on astronomical observations, which for all practical purposes is an invisibly fine hair to split. Because the earth's rotation is not uniform—it slows down and speeds up in complicated ways—UT does not always flow uniformly. Leap seconds are introduced as needed into UTC so as to keep UTC within 0.9 seconds of UT1, which is a version of UT with certain corrections applied. There are other time and date systems as well; for example, the time scale used by the satellite-based global positioning system (GPS) is synchronized to UTC but is *not* adjusted for leap seconds. An interesting source of further information is the U.S. Naval Observatory, particularly the Directorate of Time at

```
http://tycho.usno.navy.mil
```

and their definitions of "Systems of Time" at

```
http://tycho.usno.navy.mil/systime.html
```

In all methods of class Date that accept or return year, month, date, hours, minutes, and seconds values, the following representations are used:

♦ A year y is represented by the integer $y - 1900$.

♦ A month is represented by an integer form 0 to 11; 0 is January, 1 is February, and so on; thus 11 is December.

- A date (day of month) is represented by an integer from 1 to 31 in the usual manner.

- An hour is represented by an integer from 0 to 23. Thus, the hour from midnight to 1 A.M. is hour 0, and the hour from noon to 1 P.M. is hour 12.

- A minute is represented by an integer from 0 to 59 in the usual manner.

- A second is represented by an integer from 0 to 60; the value 60 occurs only for leap seconds and even then only in Java implementations that actually track leap seconds correctly.

In all cases, arguments given to methods for these purposes need not fall within the indicated ranges; for example, a date may be specified as January 32 and is interpreted as meaning February 1.

Constructors

Date   §3.2.1

```
public Date()
```

Allocates a `Date` object and initializes it so that it represents the time at which it was allocated measured to the nearest millisecond.

SEE ALSO:

`currentTimeMillis` (**I-§1.18.5**) in class `System`.

Date   §3.2.2

```
public Date(int year, int month, int date)
```

Allocates a `Date` object and initializes it so that it represents midnight, local time, at the beginning of the day specified by the `year`, `month`, and `date` arguments.

PARAMETERS:

`year`: the year minus 1900.
`month`: a month between 0–11.
`date`: day of the month between 1–31.

Date   **§3.2.3**

```
public Date(int year, int month, int date,
            int hrs, int min)
```

Allocates a Date object and initializes it so that it represents the specified hour and minute, local time, of the date specified by the year, month, and date arguments.

PARAMETERS:

year: the year minus 1900.
month: a month between 0–11.
date: day of the month between 1–31.
hrs: hours between 0–23.
min: minutes between 0–59.

Date   **§3.2.4**

```
public Date(int year, int month, int date, int hrs,
            int min, int sec)
```

Allocates a Date object and initializes it so that it represents the specified hour, minute, and second, local time of the date specified by the year, month, and date arguments.

PARAMETERS:

year: the year minus 1900.
month: a month between 0–11.
date: day of the month between 1–31.
hrs: hours between 0–23.
min: minutes between 0–59.
sec: seconds between 0–59.

Date   **§3.2.5**

```
public Date(long date)
```

Allocates a Date object and initializes it to represent the specified number of milliseconds since January 1, 1970, 00:00:00 GMT.

PARAMETERS:

date: milliseconds since January 1, 1970, 00:00:00 GMT.

SEE ALSO:

currentTimeMillis (**I-§1.18.5**) in class System.

Date   §3.2.6

> `public Date(String s)`

> Allocates a `Date` object and initializes it so that it represents the date and time indicated by the string `s`, which is interpreted as if by the `parse` method (I-§3.2.20).

> **PARAMETERS:**

> `s`: a string representation of the date.

Methods

after   §3.2.7

> `public boolean after(Date when)`

> **PARAMETERS:**

> `when`: a date.

> **RETURNS:**

> `true` if this date is after the argument date; `false` otherwise.

before   §3.2.8

> `public boolean before(Date when)`

> **PARAMETERS:**

> `when`: a date.

> **RETURNS:**

> `true` if this date is before the argument date; `false` otherwise.

equals   §3.2.9

> `public boolean equals(Object obj)`

> The result is `true` if and only if the argument is not `null` and is a `Date` object that represents the same point in time, to the millisecond, as this object.

> Thus, two `Date` objects are equal if and only if the `getTime` method (I-§3.2.16) returns the same `long` value for both.

> **PARAMETERS:**

> `obj`: the object to compare with.

> **RETURNS:**

> `true` if the objects are the same; `false` otherwise.

> **OVERRIDES:**

> `equals` in class `Object` (I-§1.12.3).

getDate §3.2.10

  public int getDate()
  RETURNS:
  the day of the month represented by this date. The value returned is between
    1 and 31.

getDay §3.2.11

  public int getDay()
  RETURNS:
  the day of the week represented by this date. The value returned is between 0
    and 6, where 0 represents Sunday.

getHours §3.2.12

  public int getHours()
  RETURNS:
  the hour represented by this date. The value returned is between 0 and 23,
    where 0 represents midnight.

getMinutes §3.2.13

  public int getMinutes()
  RETURNS:
  the number of minutes past the hour represented by this date. The value
    returned is between 0 and 59.

getMonth §3.2.14

  public int getMonth()
  RETURNS:
  the month represented by this date. The value returned is between 0 and 11,
    with the value 0 representing January.

getSeconds §3.2.15

  public int getSeconds()
  RETURNS:
  the number of seconds past the minute represented by this date. The value
    returned is between 0 and 60. The value 60 can only occur on those Java
    Virtual Machines that take leap seconds into account.

getTime §3.2.16

  public long getTime()
  RETURNS:
  the number of milliseconds since January 1, 1970, 00:00:00 GMT repre-
    sented by this date.

getTimezoneOffset   §3.2.17

```
public int getTimezoneOffset()
```

Determines the local time-zone offset. The time-zone offset is the number of minutes that must be added to GMT to give the local time zone. This value includes the correction, if necessary, for daylight saving time.

RETURNS:

the time-zone offset, in minutes, for the current locale.

getYear   §3.2.18

```
public int getYear()
```

RETURNS:

the year represented by this date, minus 1900.

hashCode   §3.2.19

```
public int hashCode()
```

RETURNS:

a hash code value for this object.

OVERRIDES:

hashCode in class Object (**I-§1.12.6**).

parse   §3.2.20

```
public static long parse(String s)
```

Given a string representing a time, parse it and return the time value. This method recognizes most standard syntaxes.

It accepts many syntaxes; in particular, it recognizes the IETF standard date syntax: "Sat, 12 Aug 1995 13:30:00 GMT". It also understands the continental U.S. time-zone abbreviations, but for general use, a time-zone offset should be used: "Sat, 12 Aug 1995 13:30:00 GMT+0430" (4 hours, 30 minutes west of the Greenwich meridian). If no time zone is specified, the local time zone is assumed. GMT and UTC are considered equivalent.

PARAMETERS:

s: a string to be parsed as a date.

RETURNS:

the number of milliseconds since January 1, 1970, 00:00:00 GMT represented by the string argument.

setDate §3.2.21

   `public void setDate(int date)`

     Sets the day of the month of this date to the specified value.

    PARAMETERS:

    `date`: the day value.

setHours §3.2.22

   `public void setHours(int hours)`

     Sets the hour of this date to the specified value.

    PARAMETERS:

    `hours`: the hour value.

setMinutes §3.2.23

   `public void setMinutes(int minutes)`

     Sets the minutes of this date to the specified value.

    PARAMETERS:

    `minutes`: the value of the minutes.

setMonth §3.2.24

   `public void setMonth(int month)`

     Sets the month of this date to the specified value.

    PARAMETERS:

    `month`: the month value (0–11).

setSeconds §3.2.25

   `public void setSeconds(int seconds)`

     Sets the seconds of this date to the specified value.

    PARAMETERS:

    `seconds`: the second value.

setTime §3.2.26

   `public void setTime(long time)`

     Sets this date to represent the specified number of milliseconds since January 1, 1970 00:00:00 GMT.

    PARAMETERS:

    `time`: A number of milliseconds.

setYear   §3.2.27

```
public void setYear(int year)
```

Sets the year of this date to be the specified value plus 1900.

PARAMETERS:

year: the year value.

toGMTString   §3.2.28

```
public String toGMTString()
```

Creates a string representation of this date. The result is of the form

```
"12 Aug 1995 02:30:00 GMT"
```

in which the day of the month is always one or two digits. The other fields have exactly the width shown. The time zone is always given as "GMT."

RETURNS:

a string representation of this date, using the Internet GMT conventions.

toLocaleString   §3.2.29

```
public String toLocaleString()
```

Creates a string representation of this date in an implementation-dependent form. The intent is that the form should be familiar to the user of the Java application, wherever it may happen to be running. The intent is comparable to that of the %c format supported by the strftime() function of ISO C.

RETURNS:

a string representation of this date, using the locale conventions.

toString   §3.2.30

```
public String toString()
```

CREATES A CANONICAL STRING REPRESENTATION OF THE DATE. THE RESULT IS OF THE FORM "Sat Aug 12 02:30:00 PDT 1995".

RETURNS:

a string representation of this date.

OVERRIDES:

toString in class Object (I-§1.12.9).

UTC   §3.2.31

```
public static long UTC(int year, int month, int date,
                       int hrs, int min, int sec)
```

Determines the date and time based on the arguments. The arguments are interpreted in UTC, not in the local time zone.

PARAMETERS:

year: the year minus 1900.
month: a month between 0–11.
date: day of the month between 1–31.
hrs: hours between 0–23.
min: minutes between 0–59.
sec: seconds between 0–59.

RETURNS:

the number of seconds since January 1, 1970, 00:00:00 GMT for the date and time specified by the arguments.

3.3 Class Dictionary

```
public abstract class java.util.Dictionary
    extends java.lang.Object (I-§1.12)
{
    // Constructors
    public Dictionary();                                    §3.3.1

    // Methods
    public abstract Enumeration elements();                 §3.3.2
    public abstract Object get(Object key);                 §3.3.3
    public abstract boolean isEmpty();                      §3.3.4
    public abstract Enumeration keys();                     §3.3.5
    public abstract Object put(Object key, Object value)    §3.3.6
    public abstract Object remove(Object key);              §3.3.7
    public abstract int size();                             §3.3.8
}
```

The Dictionary class is the abstract parent of any class, such as Hashtable (I-§3.4), which maps keys to values. Any non-null object can be used as a key and as a value.

As a rule, the equals method (I-§1.12.3) should be used by implementations of this class to decide if two keys are the same.

SEE ALSO:

hashCode in class Object (I-§1.12.6).

Constructors

Dictionary   §3.3.1

    `public Dictionary()`

      The default constructor.

Methods

---

elements   §3.3.2

    `public abstract Enumeration elements()`

    RETURNS:

    an enumeration (I-§3.11) of the values in the dictionary.

    SEE ALSO:

    keys (I-§3.3.5).

get   §3.3.3

    `public abstract Object get(Object key)`

    PARAMETERS:

    key: a key in this dictionary.

    RETURNS:

    the value to which the key is mapped in this dictionary; `null` if the key is not mapped to any value in this dictionary.

    SEE ALSO:

    put (I-§3.3.6).

isEmpty   §3.3.4

    `public abstract boolean isEmpty()`

    RETURNS:

    true if this dictionary maps no keys to values; `false` otherwise.

keys   §3.3.5

    `public abstract Enumeration keys()`

    RETURNS:

    an enumeration (I-§3.11) of the keys in this dictionary.

    SEE ALSO:

    elements (I-§3.3.2).

put §3.3.6

```
public abstract Object put(Object key, Object value)
```

Maps the specified key to the specified value in this dictionary. Neither the key nor the value can be null.

The value can be retrieved by calling the get method (**I-§3.3.3**) with a key that is equal (**I-§1.12.3**) to the original key.

PARAMETERS:

key: the hashtable key.
value: the value.

RETURNS:

the previous value to which the key was mapped in the dictionary, or null if the key did not have a previous mapping.

THROWS:

NullPointerException (**I-§1.40**)
if the key or value is null.

remove §3.3.7

```
public abstract Object remove(Object key)
```

Removes the key (and its corresponding value) from this dictionary. This method does nothing if the key is not in this dictionary.

PARAMETERS:

key: the key that needs to be removed.

RETURNS:

the value to which the key had been mapped in this dictionary, or null if the key did not have a mapping.

size §3.3.8

```
public abstract int size()
```

RETURNS:

the number of keys in this dictionary.

3.4 Class Hashtable

```
public class java.util.Hashtable
    extends java.util.Dictionary (I-§3.3)
    implements java.lang.Cloneable (I-§1.22)
{
    // Constructors
    public Hashtable();                                    §3.4.1
    public Hashtable(int initialCapacity);                 §3.4.2
    public Hashtable(int initialCapacity,
                      float loadFactor);                   §3.4.3

    // Methods
    public void clear();                                   §3.4.4
    public Object clone();                                 §3.4.5
    public boolean contains(Object value);                 §3.4.6
    public boolean containsKey(Object key);                §3.4.7
    public Enumeration elements();                         §3.4.8
    public Object get(Object key);                         §3.4.9
    public boolean isEmpty();                              §3.4.10
    public Enumeration keys();                             §3.4.11
    public Object put(Object key, Object value);           §3.4.12
    protected void rehash();                               §3.4.13
    public Object remove(Object key);                      §3.4.14
    public int size();                                     §3.4.15
    public String toString();                              §3.4.16
}
```

This class implements a hashtable, which maps keys to values. Any non-null object can be used as a key or as a value.

To successfully store and retrieve objects from a hashtable, the objects used as keys must implement the hashCode method (I-§1.12.6) and the equals method (I-§1.12.3).

An instance of Hashtable has two parameters that affect its efficiency: its *capacity* and its *load factor*. The load factor should be between 0.0 and 1.0. When the number of entries in the hashtable exceeds the product of the load factor and the current capacity, the capacity is increased by calling the rehash method (I-§3.4.13). Larger load factors use memory more efficiently, at the expense of larger expected time per lookup.

If many entries are to be made into a Hashtable, creating it with a sufficiently large capacity may allow the entries to be inserted more efficiently than letting it perform automatic rehashing as needed to grow the table.

This example creates a hashtable of numbers. It uses the names of the numbers as keys:

```
Hashtable numbers = new Hashtable();
numbers.put("one", new Integer(1));
numbers.put("two", new Integer(2));
numbers.put("three", new Integer(3));
```

To retrieve a number use the following code:

```
Integer n = (Integer)numbers.get("two");
if (n != null) {
    System.out.println("two = " + n);
}
```

Constructors

Hashtable   §3.4.1

```
public Hashtable()
```

Constructs a new empty hashtable.

Hashtable   §3.4.2

```
public Hashtable(int initialCapacity)
```

Constructs a new, empty hashtable with the specified initial capacity.

PARAMETERS:

`initialCapacity`: the initial capacity of the hashtable.

Hashtable   §3.4.3

```
public Hashtable(int initialCapacity,
                 float loadFactor)
```

Constructs a new, empty hashtable with the specified initial capacity and the specified load factor.

PARAMETERS:

`initialCapacity`: the initial size of the hashtable.
`loadFactor`: a number between 0.0 and 1.0.

THROWS:

`IllegalArgumentException` (I-§1.32)
if the initial capacity is less than or equal to zero, or if the load factor is less than or equal to zero.

Methods

clear   §3.4.4

```
public void clear()
```

Clears this hashtable so that it contains no keys.

clone   §3.4.5

```
public Object clone()
```

Creates a shallow copy of this hashtable. The keys and values themselves are not cloned.

RETURNS:

a clone of the hashtable.

OVERRIDES:

`clone` in class `Object` (**I-§1.12.2**).

contains   §3.4.6

```
public boolean contains(Object value)
```

PARAMETERS:

`value`: a value to search for.

RETURNS:

`true` if some key maps to the `value` argument in this hashtable; `false` otherwise.

THROWS:

`NullPointerException` (**I-§1.40**)
if the value is `null`.

SEE ALSO:

`containsKey` (**I-§3.4.7**).

containsKey   §3.4.7

```
public boolean containsKey(Object key)
```

PARAMETERS:

`key`: possible key.

RETURNS:

`true` if the specified object is a key in this hashtable; `false` otherwise.

SEE ALSO:

`contains` (**I-§3.4.6**).

elements   §3.4.8

    `public Enumeration elements()`

    RETURNS:

    an enumeration (I-§3.11) of the values in this hashtable.

    OVERRIDES:

    `elements` in class `Dictionary` (I-§3.3.2).

    SEE ALSO:

    keys (I-§3.4.11).

get   §3.4.9

    `public Object get(Object key)`

    PARAMETERS:

    `key`: a key in the hashtable.

    RETURNS:

    the value to which the key is mapped in this hashtable; `null` if the key is not
        mapped to any value in this hashtable.

    OVERRIDES:

    `get` in class `Dictionary` (I-§3.3.3).

    SEE ALSO:

    put (I-§3.4.12).

isEmpty   §3.4.10

    `public boolean isEmpty()`

    RETURNS:

    `true` if this hashtable maps no keys to values; `false` otherwise.

    OVERRIDES:

    `isEmpty` in class `Dictionary` (I-§3.3.4).

keys   §3.4.11

    `public Enumeration keys()`

    RETURNS:

    an enumeration (I-§3.11) of the keys in this hashtable.

    OVERRIDES:

    `keys` in class `Dictionary` (I-§3.3.5).

    SEE ALSO:

    elements (I-§3.4.8).

put   §3.4.12

```
public Object put(Object key, Object value)
```

Maps the specified key to the specified value in this hashtable. Neither the key nor the value can be null.

The value can be retrieved by calling the get method (I-§3.4.9) with a key that is equal (I-§1.12.3) to the original key.

PARAMETERS:

key: the hashtable key.
value: the value.

RETURNS:

the previous value of the specified key in this hashtable, or null if it did not have one.

THROWS:

NullPointerException (I-§1.40)
if the key or value is null.

OVERRIDES:

put in class Dictionary (I-§3.3.6).

rehash   §3.4.13

```
protected void rehash()
```

Rehashes the contents of the hashtable into a hashtable with a larger capacity. This method is called automatically when the number of keys in the hashtable exceeds this hashtable's capacity and load factor.

remove   §3.4.14

```
public Object remove(Object key)
```

Removes the key (and its corresponding value) from this hashtable. This method does nothing if the key is not in the hashtable.

PARAMETERS:

key: the key that needs to be removed.

RETURNS:

the value to which the key had been mapped in this hashtable, or null if the key did not have a mapping.

OVERRIDES:

remove in class Dictionary (I-§3.3.7).

size §3.4.15

```
public int size()
```
RETURNS:

the number of keys in this hashtable.

OVERRIDES:

size in class Dictionary (I-§3.3.8).

toString §3.4.16

```
public String toString()
```
RETURNS:

a string representation of this hashtable.

OVERRIDES:

toString in class Object (I-§1.12.9).

3.5 Class Observable

```
public class java.util.Observable
    extends java.lang.Object (I-§1.12)
{
    // Constructors
    public Observable();                                §3.5.1

    // Methods
    public void addObserver(Observer o);               §3.5.2
    protected void clearChanged();                     §3.5.3
    public int countObservers();                       §3.5.4
    public void deleteObserver(Observer o);            §3.5.5
    public void deleteObservers();                     §3.5.6
    public boolean hasChanged();                       §3.5.7
    public void notifyObservers();                     §3.5.8
    public void notifyObservers(Object arg);           §3.5.9
    protected void setChanged();                       §3.5.10
}
```

This class represents an observable object, or "data" in the model-view paradigm. It can be subclassed to represent an object that the application wants to have observed.

An observable object can have one or more observers (I-§3.12). After an observable instance changes, an application calling the Observable's notify-Observers method (I-§3.5.8, §3.5.9) causes all of its observers to be notified of the change by a call to their update method (I-§3.12.1).

Constructors

Observable   §3.5.1

    `public Observable()`

      The default constructor.

Methods

addObserver   §3.5.2

    `public void addObserver(Observer o)`

      Adds an observer to the set of observers for this object.

    PARAMETERS:

    `o`: an observer to be added.

clearChanged   §3.5.3

    `protected void clearChanged()`

      Indicates that this object has no longer changed, or that it has already notified all of its observers of its most recent change. This method is called automatically by the `notifyObservers` methods (**I-§3.5.8, §3.5.9**).

countObservers   §3.5.4

    `public int countObservers()`

    RETURNS:

    the number of observers of this object.

deleteObserver   §3.5.5

    `public void deleteObserver(Observer o)`

      Deletes an observer from the set of observers of this object.

    PARAMETERS:

    `o`: the observer to be deleted.

deleteObservers   §3.5.6

    `public void deleteObservers()`

      Clears the observer list so that this object no longer has any observers.

hasChanged   §3.5.7

    `public boolean hasChanged()`

      Determines if this object has changed.

    RETURNS:

    `true` if the `setChanged` method (**I-§3.5.10**) has been called more recently than the `clearChanged` (**I-§3.5.3**) method on this object; `false` otherwise.

notifyObservers §3.5.8

```
public void notifyObservers()
```

If this object has changed, as indicated by the `hasChanged` method (**I-§3.5.7**), then notify all of its observers and then call the `clearChanged` method (**I-§3.5.3**) to indicate that this object has no longer changed.

Each observer has its `update` method (**I-§3.12.1**) called with 2 arguments: this observable object and `null`.

notifyObservers §3.5.9

```
public void notifyObservers(Object arg)
```

If this object has changed, as indicated by the `hasChanged` method (**I-§3.5.7**), then notify all of its observers and then call the `clearChanged` method (**I-§3.5.3**) to indicate that this object has no longer changed.

Each observer has its `update` method (**I-§3.12.1**) called with 2 arguments: this observable object and the `arg` argument.

PARAMETERS:
`arg`: any object.

setChanged §3.5.10

```
protected void setChanged()
```

Indicates that this object has changed.

3.6 Class Properties

```
public class java.util.Properties
    extends java.util.Hashtable (I-§3.4)
{
    // Fields
    protected Properties defaults;                        §3.6.1

    // Constructors
    public Properties();                                  §3.6.2
    public Properties(Properties defaults);               §3.6.3

    // Methods
    public String getProperty(String key);               §3.6.4
    public String getProperty(String key,                §3.6.5
                        String defaultValue);
    public void list(PrintStream out);                    §3.6.6
    public void load(InputStream in);                     §3.6.7
    public Enumeration propertyNames();                   §3.6.8
    public void save(OutputStream out, String header);    §3.6.9
}
```

The `Properties` class represents a persistent set of properties. The `Properties` can be saved to a stream or loaded from a stream. Each key and its corresponding value in the property list is a string.

A property list can contain another property list as its "defaults"; this second property list is searched if the property key is not found in the original property list.

Fields

defaults   §3.6.1

    `protected Properties defaults`

      A property list that contains default values for any keys not found in this property list.

Constructors

Properties   §3.6.2

    `public Properties()`

      Creates an empty property list with no default values.

Properties   §3.6.3

    `public Properties(Properties defaults)`

      Creates an empty property list with the specified defaults.

    PARAMETERS:

    `defaults`: the defaults.

Methods

getProperty   §3.6.4

    `public String getProperty(String key)`

      Searches for the property with the specified key in this property list.

    PARAMETERS:

    `key`: the property key.

    RETURNS:

    the value in this property list with the specified key value. If the key is not found in this property list, the default property list (**I-§3.6.1**), and its defaults, recursively, are then checked. The method returns `null` if the property is not found.

getProperty §3.6.5

```
public String getProperty(String key, String defaultValue)
```

Searches for the property with the specified key in this property list.

PARAMETERS:

key: the hashtable key.
defaultValue: a default value.

RETURNS:

the value in this property list with the specified key value. If the key is not found in this property list, the default property list (**I-§3.6.1**), and its defaults, recursively, are then checked. The method returns the default value argument if the property is not found.

list §3.6.6

```
public void list(PrintStream out)
```

Prints this property list out to the specified output stream. This method is useful for debugging.

PARAMETERS:

out: an output stream.

load §3.6.7

```
public void load(InputStream in)
throws IOException
```

Reads a property list from an input stream.

PARAMETERS:

in: the input stream.

THROWS:

IOException (**I-§2.29**)
if an error occurred when reading from the input stream.

propertyNames §3.6.8

```
public Enumeration propertyNames()
```

RETURNS:

An enumeration (**I-§3.11**) of all the keys in this property list, including the keys in the default property list (**I-§3.6.1**).

save   §3.6.9

```
public void save(OutputStream out, String header)
```

Stores this property list to the specified output stream. The string header is printed as a comment at the beginning of the stream.

PARAMETERS:

out: an output stream.
header: a description of the property list.

3.7 Class Random

```
public class java.util.Random
    extends java.lang.Object (I-§1.12)
{
    // Constructors
    public Random();                                                §3.7.1
    public Random(long seed);                                       §3.7.2

    // Methods
    public double nextDouble();                                     §3.7.3
    public float nextFloat();                                       §3.7.4
    public double nextGaussian();                                   §3.7.5
    public int nextInt();                                           §3.7.6
    public long nextLong();                                         §3.7.7
    public void setSeed(long seed);                                 §3.7.8
}
```

An instance of this class is used to generate a stream of pseudorandom numbers. The class uses a 48-bit seed, which is modified using a linear congruential formula. (See Donald Knuth, *The Art of Computer Programming, Volume 2*, Section 3.2.1.)

If two instances of Random are created with the same seed, and the same sequence of method calls is made for each, they will generate and return identical sequences of numbers.

Many applications will find the random method (I-§1.10.26) in class Math simpler to use.

Constructors

Random   §3.7.1

```
public Random()
```

Creates a new random number generator. Its seed is initialized to a value based on the current time (I-§1.18.5).

Random §3.7.2

    public Random(long seed)

Creates a new random number generator using a single long seed.

PARAMETERS:

seed: the initial seed.

SEE ALSO:

setSeed (I-§3.7.8).

Methods

nextDouble §3.7.3

    public double nextDouble()

RETURNS:

the next pseudorandom, uniformly distributed double value between 0.0 and 1.0 from this random number generator's sequence.

nextFloat §3.7.4

    public float nextFloat()

RETURNS:

the next pseudorandom, uniformly distributed float value between 0.0 and 1.0 from this random number generator's sequence.

nextGaussian §3.7.5

    public double nextGaussian()

RETURNS:

the next pseudorandom, Gaussian ("normally") distributed double value with mean 0.0 and standard deviation 1.0 from this random number generator's sequence.

nextInt §3.7.6

    public int nextInt()

RETURNS:

the next pseudorandom, uniformly distributed int value from this random number generator's sequence.

nextLong §3.7.7

    public long nextLong()

RETURNS:

the next pseudorandom, uniformly distributed long value from this random number generator's sequence.

setSeed   §3.7.8

    `public void setSeed(long seed)`

       Sets the seed of this random number generator using a single `long` seed.

    PARAMETERS:

    `seed`: the initial seed.

3.8 Class Stack

```
public class java.util.Stack
    extends java.util.Vector (I-§3.10)
{
    // Constructors
    public Stack();                                                §3.8.1

    // Methods
    public boolean empty();                                        §3.8.2
    public Object peek();                                          §3.8.3
    public Object pop();                                           §3.8.4
    public Object push(Object item);                               §3.8.5
    public int search(Object o);                                   §3.8.6
}
```

       The `Stack` class represents a last-in-first-out (LIFO) stack of objects.

Constructors

Stack   §3.8.1

    `public Stack()`

       Creates a new stack with no elements.

Methods

empty   §3.8.2

    `public boolean empty()`

    RETURNS:

    `true` if this stack is empty; `false` otherwise.

peek §3.8.3

```
public Object peek()
```

Looks at the object at the top of this stack without removing it from the stack.

RETURNS:

the object at the top of this stack.

THROWS:

`EmptyStackException` (I-§3.13)
if this stack is empty.

pop §3.8.4

```
public Object pop()
```

Removes the object at the top of this stack and returns that object as the value of this function.

RETURNS:

The object at the top of this stack.

THROWS:

`EmptyStackException` (I-§3.13)
if this stack is empty.

push §3.8.5

```
public Object push(Object item)
```

Pushes an item onto the top of this stack.

PARAMETERS:

`item`: the item to be pushed onto this stack.

RETURNS:

the `item` argument.

search §3.8.6

```
public int search(Object o)
```

Determines if an object is on this stack.

PARAMETERS:

`o`: the desired object.

RETURNS:

The distance from the top of the stack where the object is located; the return value -1 indicates that the object is not on the stack.

3.9 Class StringTokenizer

```
public class java.util.StringTokenizer
    extends java.lang.Object (I-§1.12)
    implements java.util.Enumeration (I-§3.11)
{
    // Constructors
    public StringTokenizer(String str);                    §3.9.1
    public StringTokenizer(String str, String delim);      §3.9.2
    public StringTokenizer(String str, String delim,       §3.9.3
                    boolean returnTokens);
    // Methods
    public int countTokens();                              §3.9.4
    public boolean hasMoreElements();                      §3.9.5
    public boolean hasMoreTokens();                        §3.9.6
    public Object nextElement();                           §3.9.7
    public String nextToken();                             §3.9.8
    public String nextToken(String delim);                 §3.9.9
}
```

The string tokenizer class allows an application to break a string into tokens. The tokenization method is much simpler than the one used by the StreamTokenizer class (I-§2.22). The StringTokenizer methods do not distinguish among identifiers, numbers, and quoted strings, nor does it recognize and skip comments.

The set of delimiters (the characters that separate tokens) may be specified either at creation time or on a per-token basis.

An instance of StringTokenizer behaves in one of two ways, depending on whether it was created with the returnTokens flag having the value true or false:

♦ If the flag is false, delimiter characters merely serve to separate tokens. A token is a maximal sequence of consecutive characters that are delimiters.

♦ If the flag is true, delimiter characters are considered to be tokens. A token is either one delimiter character, or a maximal sequence of consecutive characters that are not delimiters.

The following is one example of the use of the tokenizer. The code

```
StringTokenizer st = new StringTokenizer("this is a test");
while (st.hasMoreTokens()) {
    println(st.nextToken());
}
```

prints the following output:

```
this
is
a
test
```

Constructors

StringTokenizer §3.9.1

`public StringTokenizer(String str)`

Constructs a string tokenizer for the specified string. The tokenizer uses the default delimiter set, which is `"\t\n\r"`: the space character, the tab character, the newline character, and the carriage-return character.

PARAMETERS:

`str`: a string to be parsed.

StringTokenizer §3.9.2

`public StringTokenizer(String str, String delim)`

Constructs a string tokenizer for the specified string. The characters in the `delim` argument are the delimiters for separating tokens.

PARAMETERS:

`str`: a string to be parsed.
`delim`: the delimiters.

StringTokenizer §3.9.3

```
public StringTokenizer(String str, String delim,
                       boolean returnTokens)
```

Constructs a string tokenizer for the specified string. The characters in the `delim` argument are the delimiters for separating tokens.

If the `returnTokens` flag is `true`, then the delimiter characters are also returned as tokens. Each delimiter is returned as a string of length one. If the flag is `false`, the delimiter characters are skipped and only serve as separators between tokens.

PARAMETERS:

`str`: a string to be parsed.
`delim`: the delimiters.
`returnTokens`: flag indicating whether to return the delimiters as tokens.

Methods

countTokens §3.9.4

`public int countTokens()`

Calculates the number of times that this tokenizer's `nextToken` method (I-§3.9.8) can be called before it generates an exception.

RETURNS:

the number of tokens remaining in the string using the current delimiter set.

hasMoreElements   §3.9.5

```
public boolean hasMoreElements()
```

This method returns the same value as the following hasMoreTokens method. It exists so that this class can implement the enumeration (**I-§3.11**) interface.

RETURNS:

true if there are more tokens; false otherwise.

hasMoreTokens   §3.9.6

```
public boolean hasMoreTokens()
```

RETURNS:

true if there are more tokens available from this tokenizer's string; false otherwise.

nextElement   §3.9.7

```
public Object nextElement()
```

This method returns the same value as the following nextToken method, except that its declared return value is Object rather than String. It exists so that this class can implement the enumeration (**I-§3.11**) interface.

RETURNS:

the next token in the string.

THROWS:

NoSuchElementException (**I-§3.14**)
if there are no more tokens in this tokenizer's string.

nextToken   §3.9.8

```
public String nextToken()
```

RETURNS:

the next token from this string tokenizer.

THROWS:

NoSuchElementException (**I-§3.14**)
if there are no more tokens in this tokenizer's string.

nextToken

```
public String nextToken(String delim)
```

Gets the next token in this string tokenizer's string. The new delimiter set remains the default after this call.

PARAMETERS:

`delim`: the new delimiters.

RETURNS:

the next token, after switching to the new delimiter set.

THROWS:

`NoSuchElementException` **(I-§3.14)**

if there are no more tokens in the string.

3.10 Class Vector

```
public class java.util.Vector
    extends java.lang.Object (I-§1.12)
    implements java.lang.Cloneable (I-§1.22)
{
    // Fields
    protected int capacityIncrement;                          §3.10.1
    protected int elementCount;                               §3.10.2
    protected Object elementData[];                           §3.10.3

    // Constructors
    public Vector();                                          §3.10.4
    public Vector(int initialCapacity);                       §3.10.5
    public Vector(int initialCapacity,                        §3.10.6
                int capacityIncrement);

    // Methods
    public final void addElement(Object obj);                 §3.10.7
    public final int capacity();                              §3.10.8
    public Object clone();                                    §3.10.9
    public final boolean contains(Object elem);               §3.10.10
    public final void copyInto(Object anArray[]);             §3.10.11
    public final Object elementAt(int index);                 §3.10.12
    public final Enumeration elements();                      §3.10.13
    public final void ensureCapacity(int minCapacity)         §3.10.14
    public final Object firstElement();                       §3.10.15
    public final int indexOf(Object elem);                    §3.10.16
    public final int indexOf(Object elem, int index);         §3.10.17
    public final void insertElementAt(Object obj,
                                int index);                   §3.10.18
    public final boolean isEmpty();                           §3.10.19
    public final Object lastElement();                        §3.10.20
    public final int lastIndexOf(Object elem);                §3.10.21
    public final int lastIndexOf(Object elem, int index);     §3.10.22
    public final void removeAllElements();                    §3.10.23
    public final boolean removeElement(Object obj);           §3.10.24
    public final void removeElementAt(int index);             §3.10.25
    public final void setElementAt(Object obj, int index);    §3.10.26
    public final void setSize(int newSize);                   §3.10.27
    public final int size();                                  §3.10.28
    public final String toString();                           §3.10.29
    public final void trimToSize();                           §3.10.30
}
```

The Vector class implements a growable array of objects. Like an array, it contains components that can be accessed using an integer index. However, the size of a `Vector` can grow or shrink as needed to accommodate adding and removing items after the `Vector` has been created.

Each vector tries to optimize storage management by maintaining a capacity and a `capacityIncrement`. The `capacity` is always at least as large as the vector size; it is usually larger because as components are added to the vector, the vector's storage increases in chunks the size of `capacityIncrement`. An application can increase the capacity of a vector before inserting a large number of components; this reduces the amount of incremental reallocation.

Fields

capacityIncrement §3.10.1

    `protected int capacityIncrement`

    The amount by which the capacity of the vector is automatically incremented when its size becomes greater than its capacity. If the capacity is 0, the capacity of the vector is doubled each time it needs to grow.

elementCount §3.10.2

    `protected int elementCount`

    The number of valid components in the vector.

elementData §3.10.3

    `protected Object elementData[]`

    The array buffer into which the components of the vector are stored. The capacity of the vector is the length of this array buffer.

Constructors

Vector §3.10.4

    `public Vector()`

    Constructs an empty vector.

Vector §3.10.5

    `public Vector(int initialCapacity)`

    Constructs an empty vector. Its initial capacity is the specified argument size.

    PARAMETERS:

    `initialCapacity`: the initial capacity of the vector.

Vector   §3.10.6

>   public Vector(int initialCapacity, int capacityIncrement)

     Constructs an empty vector with the specified capacity and the specified capacity increment.

PARAMETERS:

initialCapacity: the initial capacity of the vector.
capacityIncrement: the amount by which the capacity is increased when the vector overflows.

Methods

addElement   §3.10.7

>   public final void addElement(Object obj)

     Adds the specified component to the end of this vector, increasing its size by one. The capacity of this vector is increased if its size becomes greater than its capacity.

PARAMETERS:

obj: the component to be added.

capacity   §3.10.8

>   public final int capacity()

RETURNS:

the current capacity of this vector.

clone   §3.10.9

>   public Object clone()

RETURNS:

a clone of this vector.

OVERRIDES:

clone() in class Object (I-§1.12.2).

contains   §3.10.10

>   public final boolean contains(Object elem)

PARAMETERS:

elem: an object.

RETURNS:

true if the specified object is a component in this vector; false otherwise.

copyInto §3.10.11

```
public final void copyInto(Object anArray[])
```

Copies the components of this vector into the specified array. The array must be big enough to hold all the objects in this vector.

PARAMETERS:

`anArray`: the array into which the components get copied.

elementAt §3.10.12

```
public final Object elementAt(int index)
```

PARAMETERS:

`index`: an index into this vector.

RETURNS:

the component at the specified index.

THROWS:

`ArrayIndexOutOfBoundsException` (I-§1.25)
if an invalid index was given.

elements §3.10.13

```
public final Enumeration elements()
```

RETURNS:

an enumeration (I-§3.11) of the components of this vector.

ensureCapacity §3.10.14

```
public final void ensureCapacity(int minCapacity)
```

Increases the capacity of this vector, if necessary, to ensure that it can hold at least the number of components specified by the minimum capacity argument.

PARAMETERS:

`minCapacity`: the desired minimum capacity.

firstElement §3.10.15

```
public final Object firstElement()
```

RETURNS:

the first component of this vector.

THROWS:

`NoSuchElementException` (I-§3.14)
if this vector has no components.

indexOf   §3.10.16

```
public final int indexOf(Object elem)
```

PARAMETERS:

elem: an object.

RETURNS:

the index of the first occurrence of the argument in this vector; returns -1 if the object is not found.

indexOf   §3.10.17

```
public final int indexOf(Object elem, int index)
```

PARAMETERS:

elem: an object.
index: the index to start searching from.

RETURNS:

the index of the first occurrence of the object argument in this vector at position index or later in the vector; returns -1 if the object is not found.

insertElementAt   §3.10.18

```
public final void insertElementAt(Object obj, int index)
```

Inserts the specified object as a component in this vector at the specified index. Each component in this vector with an index greater or equal to the specified index is shifted upward to have an index one greater than the value it had previously.

The index must be a value greater than or equal to 0 and less than or equal to the current size (**I-§3.10.28**) of the vector.

PARAMETERS:

obj: the component to insert.
index: where to insert the new component.

THROWS:

ArrayIndexOutOfBoundsException (**I-§1.25**)
if the index was invalid.

isEmpty   §3.10.19

```
public final boolean isEmpty()
```

RETURNS:

true if this vector has no components; false otherwise.

lastElement §3.10.20

    `public final Object lastElement()`

    RETURNS:

    the last component of the vector, i.e., the component at index `size()` -1 .

    THROWS:

    `NoSuchElementException` **(I-§3.14)**
    if this vector is empty.

lastIndexOf §3.10.21

    `public final int lastIndexOf(Object elem)`

    PARAMETERS:

    `elem`: the desired component.

    RETURNS:

    the index of the last occurrence of the argument in this vector; returns `-1` if
        the object is not found.

lastIndexOf §3.10.22

    `public final int lastIndexOf(Object elem, int index)`

    Searches backwards for the specified object, starting from the specified
    index, and returns an index to it.

    PARAMETERS:

    `elem`: the desired component.
    `index`: the index to start searching from.

    RETURNS:

    the index of the last occurrence of the object argument in this vector at posi-
        tion less than `index` in the vector; returns `-1` if the object is not found.

removeAllElements §3.10.23

    `public final void removeAllElements()`

    Removes all components from this vector and sets its size to zero.

removeElement   §3.10.24
    `public final boolean removeElement(Object obj)`

Removes the first occurrence of the argument from this vector. If the object is found in this vector, each component in the vector with an index greater or equal to the object's index is shifted downward to have an index one smaller than the value it had previously.

PARAMETERS:

`obj`: the component to be removed.

RETURNS:

`true` if the argument was a component of this vector; `false` otherwise.

removeElementAt   §3.10.25
    `public final void removeElementAt(int index)`

Deletes the component at the specified index. Each component in this vector with an index greater or equal to the specified `index` is shifted downward to have an index one smaller than the value it had previously.

The index must be a value greater than or equal to 0 and less than the current size (**I-§3.10.28**) of the vector.

PARAMETERS:

`index`: the index of the object to remove.

THROWS:

`ArrayIndexOutOfBoundsException` (**I-§1.25**)
if the index was invalid.

setElementAt   §3.10.26
    `public final void setElementAt(Object obj, int index)`

Sets the component at the specified `index` of this vector to be the specified object. The previous component at that position is discarded.

The index must be a value greater than or equal to 0 and less than the current size (**I-§3.10.28**) of the vector.

PARAMETERS:

`obj`: what the component is to be set to.
`index`: the specified index.

THROWS:

`ArrayIndexOutOfBoundsException` (**I-§1.25**)
if the index was invalid.

setSize §3.10.27

```
public final void setSize(int newSize)
```

Sets the size of this vector. If the new size is greater than the current size, new null items are added to the end of the vector. If the new size is less than the current size, all components at index newSize and greater are discarded.

PARAMETERS:

newSize: the new size of this vector.

size §3.10.28

```
public final int size()
```

RETURNS:

the number of components in this vector.

toString §3.10.29

```
public final String toString()
```

Creates a string representation of this vector.

RETURNS:

a string representation of this vector.

OVERRIDES:

toString in class Object **(I-§1.12.9)**.

trimToSize §3.10.30

```
public final void trimToSize()
```

Trims the capacity of this vector to be the vector's current size **(I-§3.10.28)**. An application can use this operation to minimize the storage of a vector.

3.11 Interface Enumeration

```
public interface java.util.Enumeration
{
    // Methods
    public abstract boolean hasMoreElements();        §3.11.1
    public abstract Object nextElement();             §3.11.2
}
```

An object that implements the Enumeration interface generates a series of elements, one at a time. Successive calls to the nextElement method **(I-§3.11.2)** return successive elements of the series.

For example, to print all elements of a vector *v*:

```
for (Enumeration e = v.elements() ; e.hasMoreElements() ;)
{

        System.out.println(e.nextElement());
}
```

Methods are provided to enumerate through the elements of a vector **(I-§3.10.13)**, the keys of a hashtable **(I-§3.4.11)**, and the values in a hashtable **(I-§3.4.8)**. Enumerations are also used to specify the input streams to a Sequence-InputStream **(I-§2.21)**.

Methods

hasMoreElements   **§3.11.1**

  `public abstract boolean hasMoreElements()`

  RETURNS:

  `true` if this enumeration contains more elements; `false` otherwise.

nextElement   **§3.11.2**

  `public abstract Object nextElement()`

  RETURNS:

  the next element of this enumeration.

  THROWS:

  `NoSuchElementException` **(I-§3.14)**
  if no more elements exist.

3.12 Interface Observer

```
public interface java.util.Observer
{
    // Methods
    public abstract void update(Observable o, Object arg); §3.12.1
}
```

A class can implement the `Observer` interface when it wants to be informed of changes in observable **(I-§3.5)** objects.

Methods

---

update   §3.12.1

> `public abstract void update(Observable o, Object arg)`

> This method is called whenever the observed object is changed. An application calls an observable object's `notifyObservers` method (**I-§3.5.8, §3.5.9**) to have all the object's observers notified of the change.

> **PARAMETERS:**
> o: the observable object.
> arg: an argument passed to the `notifyObservers` method.

3.13 Class EmptyStackException

```
public class java.util.EmptyStackException
    extends java.lang.RuntimeException (I-§1.42)
{
    // Constructors
    public EmptyStackException();                                   §3.13.1
}
```

Thrown by methods in the `Stack` class (**I-§3.8**) to indicate that the stack is empty.

Constructors

EmptyStackException   §3.13.1

> `public EmptyStackException()`

> Constructs a new `EmptyStackException` with no detail message.

3.14 Class NoSuchElementException

```
public class java.util.NoSuchElementException
    extends java.lang.RuntimeException (I-§1.42)
{
    // Constructors
    public NoSuchElementException();                                §3.14.1
    public NoSuchElementException(String s);                        §3.14.2
}
```

Thrown by the `nextElement` method (**I-§3.11.2**) of an `Enumeration` to indicate that there are no more elements in the enumeration.

Constructors

NoSuchElementException   **§3.14.1**

    public NoSuchElementException()

       Constructs a NoSuchElementException with no detail message.

NoSuchElementException   **§3.14.2**

    public NoSuchElementException(String s)

       Constructs a NoSuchElementException with the specified detail message.

       PARAMETERS:

    s: the detail message.

CHAPTER 4

Package java.net

THE java.net package contains networking classes and interfaces that make it easy for an application to transfer information across a network. There is support for both TCP and UDP datagrams. Information on the World Wide Web can easily be accessed using Uniform Resource Locators (URLs).

The classes and interfaces in this package can be divided into several groups:

♦ **Uniform Resource Locators:** All URLs are represented by an object of class URL **(I-§4.8)**. The class URLStreamHandler **(I-§4.11)** provides the mechanism for parsing the URL string into its components. The class URL-Connection **(I-§4.9)** represents an actual connection to the remote object or data represented by the URL. The class ContentHandler **(I-§4.1)** implements the mechanism for converting the stream of bytes returned by the URL connection into a Java object.

The java.net package makes it easy to customize an application. An application can install a URLStreamHandlerFactory **(I-§4.14)** to indicate how this application wants to parse and implement the various URL protocols. The application can install a ContentHandlerFactory **(I-§4.12)** to indicate how it wants to interpret the various MIME types returned by a URL connection. The default stream handler factory and content handler factory provide implementations of the most popular protocols and MIME types.

A MalformedURLException **(I-§4.15)** indicates a badly formed URL string or an unknown protocol type. An UnknownServiceException **(I-§4.18)** indicates that the remote object's MIME type is not understood.

♦ **TCP:** The classes Socket **(I-§4.6)** and ServerSocket **(I-§4.5)** allow an application to create client sockets and server sockets, respectively. In order to allow applications to deal easily with firewalls, the actual work of both

373

types of sockets is done through a `SocketImpl` (I-§4.7) object, which represents the actual implementation of a socket.

An application can either use the default socket implementation provided by the `java.net` package, or it can install its own `SocketImplFactory` (I-§4.13) to create its own actual socket implementations.

A `ProtocolException` (I-§4.16) or `SocketException` (I-§4.17) indicates an error when reading or writing a socket.

♦ **UDP:** The classes `DatagramPacket` (I-§4.2) and `DatagramSocket` (I-§4.3) together allow an application to send and receive datagram packets, which implement a connectionless packet delivery service.

♦ **IP Addresses:** The class `InetAddress` (I-§4.4) represents the address of a host on the Internet. A host can either be referenced by name, such as `"java.sun.com"`, or by its address, such as `"206.26.48.100"`. An `UnknownHostException` (I-§4.18) indicates that a host name could not be converted into an IP address.

♦ **Miscellaneous:** The class `URLEncoder` (I-§4.10) contains a method for converting arbitrary binary data into text containing only printable ASCII characters.

4.1 Class ContentHandler

```
public abstract class java.net.ContentHandler
    extends java.lang.Object (I-§1.12)
{
    // Constructors
    public ContentHandler();                                    §4.1.1

    // Methods
    public abstract Object getContent(URLConnection urlc);  §4.1.2
}
```

The abstract class `ContentHandler` is the superclass of all classes that read an `Object` from a `URLConnection` (I-§4.9).

An application does not generally call the `getContentHandler` method (I-§4.1.2) in this class directly. Instead, an application calls the `getContent` method in class `URL` (I-§4.8.6) or in `URLConnection` (I-§4.9.11). The application's content handler factory (an instance of a class that implements the interface `ContentHandlerFactory` (I-§4.12) set up by a call to `setContentHandler` (I-§4.9.37)) is called with a `String` giving the MIME type of the object being received on the socket. The factory returns an instance of a subclass of `ContentHandler`, and its `getContent` method is called to create the object.

Constructors

ContentHandler   §4.1.1

    `public ContentHandler()`

      The default constructor for class `ContentHandler`.

Methods

---

getContent   §4.1.2

    `public abstract Object getContent(URLConnection urlc)`
    `throws IOException`

      Given a URL connect stream positioned at the beginning of the representation of an object, this method reads that stream and creates an object from it.

PARAMETERS:

`urlc`: a URL connection.

RETURNS:

the object read by the `ContentHandler`.

THROWS:

`IOException` **(I-§2.29)**
if an I/O error occurs while reading the object.

4.2 Class DatagramPacket

```
public final class java.net.DatagramPacket
    extends java.lang.Object (I-§1.12)
{
    // Constructors
    public DatagramPacket(byte ibuf[], int ilength);           §4.2.1
    public DatagramPacket(byte ibuf[], int ilength,            §4.2.2
                        InetAddress iaddr, int iport);

    // Methods
    public InetAddress getAddress();                           §4.2.3
    public byte[] getData();                                   §4.2.4
    public int getLength();                                    §4.2.5
    public int getPort();                                      §4.2.6
}
```

    This class represents a datagram packet.

Datagram packets are used to implement a connectionless packet delivery service. Each message is routed from one machine to another based solely on information contained within that packet. Multiple packets sent from one machine to another might be routed differently, and might arrive in any order.

Constructors

DatagramPacket   §4.2.1

```
public DatagramPacket(byte ibuf[], int ilength)
```

Constructs a DatagramPacket for receiving packets of length ilength. The length argument must be less than or equal to ibuf.length.

PARAMETERS:
ibuf: buffer for holding the incoming datagram.
ilength: the number of bytes to read.

DatagramPacket   §4.2.2

```
public DatagramPacket(byte ibuf[], int ilength,
                      InetAddress iaddr, int iport)
```

Constructs a datagram packet for sending packets of length ilength to the specified port number on the specified host. The length argument must be less than or equal to ibuf.length.

PARAMETERS:
ibuf: the packet data.
ilength: the packet length.
iaddr: the destination address (§4.4).
iport: the destination port number.

Methods

getAddress   §4.2.3

```
public InetAddress getAddress()
```
RETURNS:
the IP address (§4.4) of the machine to which this datagram is being sent, or from which the datagram was received.

getData   §4.2.4

```
public byte[] getData()
```
RETURNS:
the data received, or the data to be sent.

getLength §4.2.5

```
public int getLength()
```

RETURNS:

the length of the data to be sent, or the length of the data received.

getPort §4.2.6

```
public int getPort()
```

RETURNS:

the port number on the remote host to which this datagram is being sent, or from which the datagram was received.

4.3 Class DatagramSocket

```
public class java.net.DatagramSocket
    extends java.lang.Object (I-§1.12)
{
    // Constructors
    public DatagramSocket();                        §4.3.1
    public DatagramSocket(int port);                §4.3.2

    // Methods
    public void close();                            §4.3.3
    protected void finalize();                      §4.3.4
    public int getLocalPort();                      §4.3.5
    public void receive(DatagramPacket p);          §4.3.6
    public void send(DatagramPacket p);             §4.3.7
}
```

This class represents a socket for sending and receiving datagram packets (§4.2).

A datagram socket is the sending or receiving point for a connectionless packet delivery service. Each packet sent or received on a datagram socket is individually addressed and routed. Multiple packets sent from one machine to another may be routed differently, and may arrive in any order.

Constructors

DatagramSocket   §4.3.1

```
public DatagramSocket()
throws SocketException
```

Constructs a datagram socket and binds it to any available port on the local host machine.

THROWS:

SocketException (I-§4.17)

if the socket could not be opened, or the socket could not bind to the specified local port.

DatagramSocket   §4.3.2

```
public DatagramSocket(int port)
throws SocketException
```

Constructs a datagram socket and binds it to the specified port on the local host machine.

PARAMETERS:

local: port to use.

THROWS:

SocketException (I-§4.17)

if the socket could not be opened, or the socket could not bind to the specified local port.

Methods

close   §4.3.3

```
public void close()
```

Closes this datagram socket.

finalize   §4.3.4

```
protected void finalize()
```

Ensures that this socket is closed if there are no longer any references to this socket.

OVERRIDES:

finalize in class Object (I-§1.12.4).

getLocalPort §4.3.5

```
public int getLocalPort()
```
RETURNS:

the port number on the local host to which this socket is bound.

receive §4.3.6

```
public void receive(DatagramPacket p)
throws IOException
```

Receives a datagram packet from this socket. When this method returns, the DatagramPacket's buffer is filled with the data received. The datagram packet also contains the sender's IP address, and the port number on the sender's machine.

This method blocks until a datagram is received. The length field of the datagram packet object contains the length of the received message. If the message is longer than the buffer length, the message is truncated.

PARAMETERS:

p: the DatagramPacket into which to place the incoming data.

THROWS:

IOException (**I-§2.29**)
if an I/O error occurs.

send §4.3.7

```
public void send(DatagramPacket p)
throws IOException
```

Sends a datagram packet from this socket. The DatagramPacket (**I-§4.2**) includes information indicating the data to be sent, its length, the IP address of the remote host, and the port number on the remote host.

PARAMETERS:

p: the DatagramPacket to be sent.

THROWS:

IOException (**I-§2.29**)
if an I/O error occurs.

4.4 Class InetAddress

```
public final class java.net.InetAddress
    extends java.lang.Object (I-§1.12)
{
    // Methods
    public boolean equals(Object obj);                        §4.4.1
    public byte[] getAddress();                               §4.4.2
    public static InetAddress[] getAllByName(String host);    §4.4.3
    public static InetAddress getByName(String host);         §4.4.4
    public String getHostName();                              §4.4.5
    public static InetAddress getLocalHost();                 §4.4.6
    public int hashCode();                                    §4.4.7
    public String toString();                                 §4.4.8
}
```

This class represents an Internet Protocol (IP) address.

Applications should use the methods getLocalHost (I-§4.4.6), getByName (I-§4.4.4), or getAllByName (I-§4.4.3) to create a new InetAddress instance.

Methods

equals §4.4.1

```
public boolean equals(Object obj)
```

The result is true if and only if the argument is not null and it represents the same IP address as this object.

Two instances of InetAddress represent the same IP address if the length of the byte arrays returned by getAddress (I-§4.4.2) is the same for both, and each of the array components is the same for the byte arrays.

PARAMETERS:

obj: the object to compare against.

RETURNS:

true if the objects are the same; false otherwise.

OVERRIDES:

equals in class Object (I-§1.12.3).

getAddress   §4.4.2

```
public byte[] getAddress()
```

Determines the raw IP address of this `InetAddress` object. The result is in network byte order: the highest order byte of the address is in `getAddress()[0]`.

RETURNS:

the raw IP address of this object.

getAllByName   §4.4.3

```
public static InetAddress[] getAllByName(String host)
throws UnknownHostException
```

Determines all the IP addresses of a host, given the host's name. The host name can either be a machine name, such as "java.sun.com" or a string representing its IP address, such asw "206.26.48.100".

PARAMETERS:

`host`: the name of the host.

RETURNS:

an array of all the IP addresses for a given host name.

THROWS:

`UnknownHostException` **(I-§4.18)**
if no IP address for the `host` could be found.

getByName   §4.4.4

```
public static InetAddress getByName(String host)
throws UnknownHostException
```

Determines the IP address of a host, given the host's name. The host name can either be a machine name, such as "java.sun.com" or a string representing its IP address, such as "206.26.48.100".

PARAMETERS:

`host`: the specified host, or `null` for the local host.

RETURNS:

an IP address for the given host name.

THROWS:

`UnknownHostException` **(I-§4.18)**
if no IP address for the `host` could be found.

getHostName   §4.4.5

```
public String getHostName()
```
RETURNS:

the host name for this IP address.

getLocalHost   §4.4.6

```
public static InetAddress getLocalHost()
throws UnknownHostException
```
RETURNS:

the IP address of the local host.

THROWS:

UnknownHostException (**I-§4.18**)
if no IP address for the host could be found.

hashCode   §4.4.7

```
public int hashCode()
```
RETURNS:

a hash code value for this IP address.

OVERRIDES:

hashCode in class Object (**I-§1.12.6**).

toString   §4.4.8

```
public String toString()
```
RETURNS:

a string representation of this IP address.

OVERRIDES:

toString in class Object (**I-§1.12.9**).

4.5 Class ServerSocket

```
public final class java.net.ServerSocket
    extends java.lang.Object (I-§1.12)
{
    // Constructors
    public ServerSocket(int port);                          §4.5.1
    public ServerSocket(int port, int count);               §4.5.2

    // Methods
    public Socket accept();                                 §4.5.3
    public void close();                                    §4.5.4
    public InetAddress getInetAddress();                    §4.5.5
    public int getLocalPort();                              §4.5.6
    public static void                                      §4.5.7
        setSocketFactory(SocketImplFactory fac);
    public String toString();                               §4.5.8
}
```

This class implements server sockets. A server socket waits for requests to come in over the network. It performs some operation based on that request, and then possibly returns a result to the requester.

The actual work of the server socket is performed by an instance of the SocketImpl class (**I-§4.7**). An application can change the socket factory that creates the socket implementation (**I-§4.5.7**) to configure itself to create sockets appropriate to the local firewall.

Constructors

ServerSocket   **§4.5.1**

```
public ServerSocket(int port)
throws IOException
```

Creates a server socket on a specified port. A port of 0 creates a socket on any free port.

The maximum queue length for incoming connection indications (a request to connect) is set to 50. If a connection indication arrives when the queue is full, the connection is refused.

If the application has specified a server socket factory (**I-§4.5.7**), that factory's `createSocketImpl` method (**I-§4.13.1**) is called to create the actual socket implementation. Otherwise a "plain" socket (see **I-§4.7**) is created.

PARAMETERS:

`port`: the port number, or 0 to use any free port.

THROWS:

`IOException` (**I-§2.29**)

if an I/O error occurs when opening the socket.

ServerSocket   **§4.5.2**

```
public ServerSocket(int port, int count)
throws IOException
```

Creates a server socket and binds it to the specified local port number. A port number of 0 creates a socket on any free port.

The maximum queue length for incoming connection indications (a request to connect) is set to the `count` parameter. If a connection indication arrives when the queue is full, the connection is refused.

If the application has specified a server socket factory (**I-§4.5.7**), that factory's `createSocketImpl` method (**I-§4.13.1**) is called to create the actual socket implementation. Otherwise a "plain" socket (see **I-§4.7**) is created.

PARAMETERS:

`port`: the specified port, or 0 to use any free port.
`count`: the maximum length of the queue.

THROWS:

`IOException` (**I-§2.29**)

if an I/O error occurs when opening the socket.

Methods

accept   §4.5.3

```
public Socket accept()
throws IOException
```

Listens for a connection to be made to this socket and accepts it. The method blocks until a connection is made.

THROWS:

IOException **(I-§2.29)**

if an I/O error occurs when waiting for a connection.

close   §4.5.4

```
public void close()
throws IOException
```

Closes this socket.

THROWS:

IOException **(I-§2.29)**

if an I/O error occurs when closing the socket.

getInetAddress   §4.5.5

```
public InetAddress getInetAddress()
```

RETURNS:

the address to which this socket is connected, or null if the socket is not yet connected.

getLocalPort   §4.5.6

```
public int getLocalPort()
```

RETURNS:

the port number to which this socket is listening.

setSocketFactory   §4.5.7

```
public static void setSocketFactory(SocketImplFactory fac)
throws IOException
```

Sets the server socket implementation factory for the application. The factory can be specified only once.

When an application creates a new server socket, the socket implementation factory's `createSocketImpl` method (**I-§4.13.1**) is called to create the actual socket implementation.

PARAMETERS:

`fac`: the desired factory.

THROWS:

`SocketException` (**I-§4.17**)
if the factory has already been defined.

THROWS:

`IOException` (**I-§2.29**)
if an I/O error occurs when setting the socket factory.

toString   §4.5.8

```
public String toString()
```

RETURNS:

a string representation of this socket.

OVERRIDES:

`toString` in class `Object` (**I-§1.12.9**).

4.6 Class Socket

```
public final class java.net.Socket
    extends java.lang.Object (I-§1.12)
{
    // Constructors
    public Socket(InetAddress address, int port);              §4.6.1
    public Socket(InetAddress address, int port,               §4.6.2
                boolean stream);
    public Socket(String host, int port);                      §4.6.3
    public Socket(String host, int port, boolean stream);      §4.6.4

    // Methods
    public void close();                                       §4.6.5
    public InetAddress getInetAddress();                       §4.6.6
    public InputStream getInputStream();                       §4.6.7
    public int getLocalPort();                                 §4.6.8
    public OutputStream getOutputStream();                     §4.6.9
    public int getPort();                                      §4.6.10
    public static void                                         §4.6.11
        setSocketImplFactory(SocketImplFactory fac);
    public String toString();                                  §4.6.12
}
```

This class implements client sockets (also called just "sockets"). A socket is an endpoint for communication between two machines.

The actual work of the socket is performed by an instance of the SocketImpl class (I-§4.7). An application, by changing the socket factory that creates the socket implementation (I-§4.6.11), can configure itself to create sockets appropriate to the local firewall.

Constructors

Socket   §4.6.1

```
public Socket(InetAddress address, int port)
throws IOException
```

Creates a stream socket and connects it to the specified port number at the specified IP address.

If the application has specified a socket factory (**I-§4.6.11**), that factory's `createSocketImpl` method (**I-§4.13.1**) is called to create the actual socket implementation. Otherwise a "plain" socket (see **I-§4.7**) is created.

PARAMETERS:

`address`: the IP address.
`port`: the port number.

THROWS:

`IOException` (**I-§2.29**)
if an I/O error occurs when creating the socket.

Socket   §4.6.2

```
public Socket(InetAddress address, int port, boolean stream)
throws IOException
```

Creates a socket and connects it to the specified port number at the specified IP address.

If the stream argument is `true`, this creates a stream socket. If the stream argument is `false`, it creates a datagram socket.

If the application has specified a server socket factory (**I-§4.6.11**), that factory's `createSocketImpl` method (**I-§4.13.1**) is called to create the actual socket implementation. Otherwise a "plain" socket (see **I-§4.7**) is created.

PARAMETERS:

`address`: the IP address.
`port`: the port number.
`stream`: if `true`, create a stream socket; if `false`, create a datagram socket.

THROWS:

`IOException` (**I-§2.29**)
if an I/O error occurs when creating the socket.

Socket   §4.6.3

```
public Socket(String host, int port)
throws UnknownHostException, IOException
```

Creates a stream socket and connects it to the specified port number on the named host.

If the application has specified a server socket factory (**I-§4.6.11**), that factory's `createSocketImpl` method (**I-§4.13.1**) is called to create the actual socket implementation. Otherwise a "plain" socket (see **I-§4.7**) is created.

PARAMETERS:

`host`: the host name.
`port`: the port number.

THROWS:

`IOException` (**I-§2.29**)
if an I/O error occurs when creating the socket.

Socket   §4.6.4

```
public Socket(String host, int port, boolean stream)
throws IOException
```

Creates a stream socket and connects it to the specified port number on the named host.

If the stream argument is `true`, this creates a stream socket. If the stream argument is `false`, it creates a datagram socket.

If the application has specified a server socket factory (**I-§4.6.11**), that factory's `createSocketImpl` method (**I-§4.13.1**) is called to create the actual socket implementation. Otherwise a "plain" socket (see **I-§4.7**) is created.

PARAMETERS:

`host`: the host name.
`port`: the port number.
`stream`: a `boolean` indicating whether this is a stream socket or a datagram socket.

THROWS:

`IOException` (**I-§2.29**)
if an I/O error occurs when creating the socket.

Methods

close   §**4.6.5**

```
public void close()
throws IOException
```
   Closes this socket.

THROWS:

IOException (**I-§2.29**)
if an I/O error occurs when closing this socket.

getInetAddress   §**4.6.6**

```
public InetAddress getInetAddress()
```
RETURNS:

the remote IP address to which this socket is connected.

getInputStream   §**4.6.7**

```
public InputStream getInputStream()
throws IOException
```
RETURNS:

an input stream for reading bytes from this socket.

THROWS:

IOException (**I-§2.29**)
if an I/O error occurs when creating the input stream.

getLocalPort   §**4.6.8**

```
public int getLocalPort()
```
RETURNS:

the local port number to which this socket is connected.

getOutputStream   §**4.6.9**

```
public OutputStream getOutputStream()
throws IOException
```
RETURNS:

an output stream for writing bytes to this socket.

THROWS:

IOException (**I-§2.29**)
if an I/O error occurs when creating the output stream.

getPort §4.6.10

```
public int getPort()
```

RETURNS:

the remote port number to which this socket is connected.

setSocketImplFactory §4.6.11

```
public static void
setSocketImplFactory(SocketImplFactory fac)
throws IOException
```

Sets the client socket implementation factory for the application. The factory can be specified only once.

When an application creates a new client socket, the socket implementation factory's `createSocketImpl` method (I-§4.13.1) is called to create the actual socket implementation.

PARAMETERS:

`fac`: the desired factory.

THROWS:

`SocketException` (I-§4.17)
if the factory is already defined.

THROWS:

`IOException` (I-§2.29)
if an I/O error occurs when setting the socket factory.

toString §4.6.12

```
public String toString()
```

RETURNS:

a string representation of this socket.

OVERRIDES:

`toString` in class `Object` (I-§1.12.9).

4.7 Class SocketImpl

```
public abstract class java.net.SocketImpl
    extends java.lang.Object (I-§1.12)
{
    // Fields
    protected InetAddress address;                              §4.7.1
    protected FileDescriptor fd;                                §4.7.2
    protected int localport;                                    §4.7.3
    protected int port;                                         §4.7.4

    // Constructors
    public SocketImpl();                                        §4.7.5

    // Methods
    protected abstract void accept(SocketImpl s);               §4.7.6
    protected abstract int available();                         §4.7.7
    protected abstract void bind(InetAddress host,
                                 int port);                     §4.7.8
    protected abstract void close();                            §4.7.9
    protected abstract void                                     §4.7.10
        connect(InetAddress address, int port);
    protected abstract void connect(String host, int port);    §4.7.11
    protected abstract void create(boolean stream);             §4.7.12
    protected FileDescriptor getFileDescriptor();               §4.7.13
    protected InetAddress getInetAddress();                     §4.7.14
    protected abstract InputStream getInputStream();            §4.7.15
    protected int getLocalPort();                               §4.7.16
    protected abstract OutputStream getOutputStream();          §4.7.17
    protected int getPort();                                    §4.7.18
    protected abstract void listen(int count);                  §4.7.19
    public String toString();                                   §4.7.20
}
```

The abstract class SocketImpl is a common superclass of all classes that actually implement sockets. It is used to create both client and server sockets.

A "plain" socket implements these methods exactly as described, without attempting to go through a firewall or proxy.

Fields

address   §4.7.1

```
    protected InetAddress address
```

The IP address of the remote end of this socket.

fd   §4.7.2

> protected FileDescriptor fd
>
> > The file descriptor object for this socket.

localport   §4.7.3

> protected int localport
>
> > The local port number to which this socket is connected.

port   §4.7.4

> protected int port
>
> > The port number on the remote host to which this socket is connected.

Constructors

SocketImpl   §4.7.5

> public SocketImpl()
>
> > The default constructor for a socket implementation.

Methods

accept   §4.7.6

> protected abstract void accept(SocketImpl s)
> throws IOException
>
> > Accepts a connection.
>
> **PARAMETERS:**
>
> s: the accepted connection.
>
> **THROWS:**
>
> IOException (I-§2.29)
> if an I/O error occurs when accepting the connection.

available   §4.7.7

> protected abstract int available()
> throws IOException
>
> **RETURNS:**
>
> the number of bytes that can be read from this socket without blocking.
>
> **THROWS:**
>
> IOException (I-§2.29)
> if an I/O error occurs when determining the number of bytes available.

bind   §4.7.8

```
protected abstract void bind(InetAddress host, int port)
throws IOException
```

Binds this socket to the specified port number on the specified host.

PARAMETERS:

host: the IP address of the remote host.
port: the port number.

THROWS:

IOException (I-§2.29)
if an I/O error occurs when binding this socket.

close   §4.7.9

```
protected abstract void close()
throws IOException
```

Closes this socket.

THROWS:

IOException (I-§2.29)
if an I/O error occurs when closing this socket.

connect   §4.7.10

```
protected abstract void
connect(InetAddress address, int port)
throws IOException
```

Connects this socket to the specified port number on the specified host.

PARAMETERS:

address: the IP address of the remote host.
port: the port number.

THROWS:

IOException (I-§2.29)
if an I/O error occurs when attempting a connection.

connect   §4.7.11

```
protected abstract void connect(String host, int port)
throws IOException
```

Connects this socket to the specified port on the named host.

PARAMETERS:

host: the name of the remote host.
port: the port number.

THROWS:

IOException (I-§2.29)
if an I/O error occurs when connecting to the remote host.

create §4.7.12

```
protected abstract void create(boolean stream)
throws IOException
```

Creates a socket.

PARAMETERS:

`stream`: if `true`, create a stream socket; otherwise, create a datagram socket.

THROWS:

`IOException` (I-§2.29)

if an I/O error occurs while creating the socket.

getFileDescriptor §4.7.13

```
protected FileDescriptor getFileDescriptor()
```

RETURNS:

the value of this socket's `fd` field (I-§4.7.2).

getInetAddress §4.7.14

```
protected InetAddress getInetAddress()
```

RETURNS:

the value of this socket's `address` field (I-§4.7.1).

getInputStream §4.7.15

```
protected abstract InputStream getInputStream()
throws IOException
```

RETURNS:

a stream for reading from this socket.

THROWS:

`IOException` (I-§2.29)

if an I/O error occurs when creating the input stream.

getLocalPort §4.7.16

```
protected int getLocalPort()
```

RETURNS:

the value of this socket's `localport` field (I-§4.7.3).

getOutputStream   §4.7.17

```
protected abstract OutputStream getOutputStream()
throws IOException
```

RETURNS:

an output stream for writing to this socket.

THROWS:

IOException **(I-§2.29)**
if an I/O error occurs when creating the output stream.

getPort   §4.7.18

```
protected int getPort()
```

RETURNS:

the value of this socket's port field **(I-§4.7.4)**.

listen   §4.7.19

```
protected abstract void listen(int count)
throws IOException
```

Sets the maximum queue length for incoming connection indications (a request to connect) to the count argument. If a connection indication arrives when the queue is full, the connection is refused.

PARAMETERS:

count: the maximum length of the queue.

THROWS:

IOException **(I-§2.29)**
if an I/O error occurs when creating the queue.

toString   §4.7.20

```
public String toString()
```

RETURNS:

a string representation of this socket.

OVERRIDES:

toString in class Object **(I-§1.12.9)**.

4.8 Class URL

```
public final class java.net.URL
    extends java.lang.Object (I-§1.12)
{
    // Constructors
    public URL(String spec);                                §4.8.1
    public URL(String protocol, String host,               §4.8.2
            int port, String file);
    public URL(String protocol, String host, String file); §4.8.3
    public URL(URL context, String spec);                   §4.8.4

    // Methods
    public boolean equals(Object obj);                      §4.8.5
    public final Object getContent();                       §4.8.6
    public String getFile();                                §4.8.7
    public String getHost();                                §4.8.8
    public int getPort();                                   §4.8.9
    public String getProtocol();                            §4.8.10
    public String getRef();                                 §4.8.11
    public int hashCode();                                  §4.8.12
    public URLConnection openConnection();                  §4.8.13
    public final InputStream openStream();                  §4.8.14
    public boolean sameFile(URL other);                     §4.8.15
    public static void                                      §4.8.16
        setURLStreamHandlerFactory(URLStreamHandlerFactory fac);
    public String toExternalForm();                         §4.8.17
    public String toString();                               §4.8.18
}
```

Class URL represents a Uniform Resource Locator—a pointer to a "resource" on the World Wide Web. A resource can be something as simple as a file or a directory, or it can be a reference to a more complicated object, such as a query to a database or to a search engine. More information on the types of URLs and their formats can be found at:

```
http://www.ncsa.uiuc.edu/demoweb/url-primer.html
```

In general, a URL can be broken into several parts. The previous example of a URL indicates that the protocol to use is http (HyperText Transport Protocol) and that the information resides on a host machine named www.ncsa.uiuc.edu. The information on that host machine is named demoweb/url-primer.html. The exact meaning of this name on the host machine is both protocol dependent and host dependent. The information normally resides in a file, but it could be generated on the fly. This component of the URL is called the *file* component, even though the information is not necessarily in a file.

A URL can optionally specify a "port," which is the port number to which the TCP connection is made on the remote host machine. If the port is not specified, the default port for the protocol is used instead. For example, the default port for `http` is 80. An alternative port could be specified as:

```
http://www.ncsa.uiuc.edu:8080/demoweb/url-primer.html
```

A URL may have appended to it an "anchor," also known as a "ref" or a "reference." The anchor is indicated by the sharp sign character "#" followed by more characters. For example,

```
http://java.sun.com/index.html#chapter1
```

This anchor is not technically part of the URL. Rather, it indicates that after the specified resource is retrieved, the application is specifically interested in that part of the document that has the tag `myinfo` attached to it. The meaning of a tag is resource specific.

An application can also specify a "relative URL," which contains only enough information to reach the resource relative to another URL. Relative URLs are frequently used within HTML pages. For example, if the contents of the URL

```
http://java.sun.com/index.html
```

contained within it the relative URL

```
FAQ.html
```

it would be a shorthand for

```
http://java/sun.com/FAQ.html
```

The relative URL need not specify all the components of a URL. If the protocol, host name, or port number is missing, the value is inherited from the fully specified URL. The file component must be specified. The optional anchor is not inherited.

Constructors

URL §4.8.1

```
public URL(String spec)
throws MalformedURLException
```

Creates a URL object from the String representation.

This constructor is equivalent to a call to the two-argument constructor (I-§4.8.4) with a null first argument.

PARAMETERS:

spec: the String to parse as a URL.

THROWS:

MalformedURLException (I-§4.15)
If the string specifies an unknown protocol.

URL §4.8.2

```
public URL(String protocol, String host, int port,
           String file)
throws MalformedURLException
```

Creates a URL object from the specified protocol, host, port number, and file. Specifying a port number of –1 indicates that the URL should use the default port for the protocol.

If this is the first URL object being created with the specified protocol, a stream protocol handler object, an instance of class URLStreamHandler (I-§4.11), is created for that protocol:

1. If the application has previously set up an instance of URLStream-HandlerFactory as the stream handler factory (I-§4.8.16), then the createURLStreamHandler (I-§4.14.1) method of that instance is called with the protocol string as an argument to create the stream protocol handler.

2. If no URLStreamHandlerFactory has yet been set up, or if the factory's createURLStreamHandler method returns null, then the constructor finds the value of the system property (I-§1.18.9)

   java.handler.protol.pkgs

   If the value of that system property is not null, it is interpreted as a list of packages separated by a vertical slash character ' | '. The constructor tries to load the class named

   <package>.<protocol>.Handler

   where <package> is replaced by the name of the package and <protocol> is replaced by the name of the protocol. If this class does not exist, or if the class exists but it is not a subclass of URLStreamHandler, then the next package in the list is tried.[35]

3. If the previous step fails to find a protocol handler, then the constructor tries to load the class named

    sun.net.www.protocol.*<protocol>*.Handler

If this class does not exist, or if the class exists but it is not a subclass of URLStreamHandler, then a MalformedURLException is thrown.

PARAMETERS:

protocol: the name of the protocol.
host: the name of the host.
port: the port number.
file: the host file.

THROWS:

MalformedURLException (**I-§4.15**)
if an unknown protocol is specified.

URL   **§4.8.3**

```
public URL(String protocol, String host, String file)
throws MalformedURLException
```

Creates an absolute URL from the specified protocol name, host name, and file name. The default port for the specified protocol is used.

This method is equivalent to calling the four-argument constructor (**I-§4.8.2**) with the arguments being protocol, host, –1, and file.

PARAMETERS:

protocol: the protocol to use.
host: the host to connect to.
file: the file on that host.

THROWS:

MalformedURLException (**I-§4.15**)
if an unknown protocol is specified.

---

[35] Step 2 is new in Java 1.1.

URL   §4.8.4

```
public URL(URL context, String spec)
throws MalformedURLException
```

Creates a URL by parsing the specification `spec` within a specified context: If the `context` argument is not `null` and the `spec` argument is a partial URL specification, then any of the strings missing components are inherited from the `context` argument.

The specification given by the `String` argument is parsed to determine if it specifies a protocol. If the `String` contains an ASCII colon `':'` character before the first occurrence of an ASCII slash character `'/'`, then the characters before the colon comprise the protocol.

♦ If the `spec` argument does not specify a protocol:

  • If the context argument is not `null`, then the protocol is copied from the context argument.

  • If the context argument is `null`, then a `MalformedURLException` is thrown.

♦ If the `spec` argument does specify a protocol:

  • If the context argument is `null`, or specifies a different protocol than the specification argument, the context argument is ignored.

  • If the context argument is not `null` and specifies the same protocol as the specification, the `host`, `port` number, and `file` are copied from the context argument into the newly created `URL`.

The constructor then searches for an appropriate stream protocol handler of type `URLStreamHandler` **(I-§4.11)** as outlined above in **I-§4.8.2**. The stream protocol handler's `parseURL` method **(I-§4.11.3)** is called to parse the remaining fields of the specification that override any defaults set by the context argument.

PARAMETERS:
`context`: the context in which to parse the specification.
`spec`: a `String` representation of a URL.

THROWS:
`MalformedURLException` **(I-§4.15)**
if no protocol is specified, or an unknown protocol is found.

Methods

---

equals   §4.8.5

```
public boolean equals(Object obj)
```

The result is `true` if and only if the argument is not `null` and is a URL object that represents the same URL as this object. Two URL objects are equal if they have the same protocol and reference the same host, the same port number on the host, and the same file on the host. The anchors of the URL objects are not compared.

This method is equivalent to

```
(obj instanceof URL) && sameFile((URL)obj)
```

PARAMETERS:

`obj`: the URL to compare against.

RETURNS:

`true` if the objects are the same; `false` otherwise.

OVERRIDES:

`equals` in class `Object` (**I-§1.12.3**).

getContent   §4.8.6

```
public final Object getContent()
throws IOException
```

Gets the contents of this URL. This method is a shorthand for

```
openConnection().getContent()
```

RETURNS:

the contents of this URL.

THROWS:

`IOException` (**I-§2.29**)
if an I/O exception occurs.

SEE ALSO:

`getContent` in class `URLConnection` (**I-§4.9.11**).

getFile   §4.8.7

```
public String getFile()
```

RETURNS:

the file name of this URL.

getHost §4.8.8

    `public String getHost()`
    RETURNS:
    the host name of this URL.

getPort §4.8.9

    `public int getPort()`
    RETURNS:
    the port number of this URL.

getProtocol §4.8.10

    `public String getProtocol()`
    RETURNS:
    the protocol of this URL.

getRef §4.8.11

    `public String getRef()`
    RETURNS:
    the anchor (also known as the "reference") of this URL.

hashCode §4.8.12

    `public int hashCode()`
    RETURNS:
    a hash code for this URL.
    OVERRIDES:
    hashCode in class `Object` **(I-§1.12.6)**.

openConnection §4.8.13

    `public URLConnection openConnection()`
    `throws IOException`

    Returns a `URLConnection` object that represents a connection to the remote object referred to by the URL.

    If there is not already an open connection, the connection is opened by calling the `openConnection` method **(I-§4.11.2)** of the protocol handler **(I-§4.8.2)** for this URL.

    RETURNS:
    a `URLConnection` **(I-§4.9)** to the URL.
    THROWS:
    `IOException` **(I-§2.29)**
    if an I/O exception occurs.

openStream   §4.8.14

```
public final InputStream openStream()
throws IOException
```

Opens a connection to this URL and returns an InputStream for reading from that connection. This method is a shorthand for

```
openConnection().getInputStream()
```

RETURNS:

an input stream for reading from the URL connection.

THROWS:

IOException **(I-§2.29)**
if an I/O exception occurs.

sameFile   §4.8.15

```
public boolean sameFile(URL other)
```

Returns true if this URL and the other argument both refer to the same resource; the two URLs might not both contain the same anchor.

PARAMETERS:

other: the URL to compare against.

RETURNS:

true if they reference the same remote object; false otherwise.

setURLStreamHandlerFactory   §4.8.16

```
public static void
setURLStreamHandlerFactory(URLStreamHandlerFactory fac)
```

Sets an application's URLStreamHandlerFactory **(I-§4.14)**. This method can be called at most once by an application.

The URLStreamHandlerFactory instance is used to construct a stream protocol handler **(I-§4.8.2)** from a protocol name.

PARAMETERS:

fac: the desired factory.

THROWS:

Error **(I-§1.48)**
if the application has already set a factory.

toExternalForm §4.8.17

`public String toExternalForm()`

Constructs a string representation of this URL. The string is created by calling the `toExternalForm` method (**I-§4.11.5**) of the stream protocol handler (**I-§4.8.2**) for this object.

RETURNS:

a string representation of this object.

toString §4.8.18

`public String toString()`

Creates a string representation of this object. This method calls the `toExternalForm` method (**I-§4.8.17**) and returns its value.

RETURNS:

a string representation of this object.

OVERRIDES:

`toString` in class `Object` (**I-§1.12.9**).

4.9 Class URLConnection

```
public abstract class java.net.URLConnection
    extends java.lang.Object (I-§1.12)
{
    // Fields
    protected boolean allowUserInteraction;                    §4.9.1
    protected boolean connected;                               §4.9.2
    protected boolean doInput;                                 §4.9.3
    protected boolean doOutput;                                §4.9.4
    protected long ifModifiedSince;                            §4.9.5
    protected URL url;                                         §4.9.6
    protected boolean useCaches;                               §4.9.7

    // Constructors
    protected URLConnection(URL url);                          §4.9.8

    // Methods
    public abstract void connect();                            §4.9.9
    public boolean getAllowUserInteraction();                  §4.9.10
    public Object getContent();                                §4.9.11
    public String getContentEncoding();                        §4.9.12
    public int getContentLength();                             §4.9.13
    public String getContentType();                            §4.9.14
    public long getDate();                                     §4.9.15
    public static boolean
      getDefaultAllowUserInteraction();                        §4.9.16
    public static String                                       §4.9.17
      getDefaultRequestProperty(String key);
    public boolean getDefaultUseCaches();                      §4.9.18
    public boolean getDoInput();                               §4.9.19
    public boolean getDoOutput();                              §4.9.20
    public long getExpiration();                               §4.9.21
    public String getHeaderField(int n);                       §4.9.22
    public String getHeaderField(String name);                 §4.9.23
    public long getHeaderFieldDate(String name,                §4.9.24
                              long Default);
    public int getHeaderFieldInt(String name,                  §4.9.25
                              int Default);
    public String getHeaderFieldKey(int n);                    §4.9.26
    public long getIfModifiedSince();                          §4.9.27
    public InputStream getInputStream();                       §4.9.28
    public long getLastModified();                             §4.9.29
    public OutputStream getOutputStream();                     §4.9.30
    public String getRequestProperty(String key);             §4.9.31
    public URL getURL();                                       §4.9.32
    public boolean getUseCaches();                             §4.9.33
    protected static String                                    §4.9.34
      guessContentTypeFromName(String fname);
```

```
    protected static String                              §4.9.35
        guessContentTypeFromStream(InputStream is);
    public void                                          §4.9.36
        setAllowUserInteraction(boolean allowuserinteraction);
    public static void                                   §4.9.37
        setContentHandlerFactory(ContentHandlerFactory fac);
    public static void                                   §4.9.38
        setDefaultAllowUserInteraction(
            boolean defaultallowuserinteraction);
    public static void                                   §4.9.39
        setDefaultRequestProperty(String key, String value);
    public void                                          §4.9.40
        setDefaultUseCaches(boolean defaultusecaches);
    public void setDoInput(boolean doinput);             §4.9.41
    public void setDoOutput(boolean dooutput);           §4.9.42
    public void setIfModifiedSince(long ifmodifiedsince);  §4.9.43
    public void setRequestProperty(String key,           §4.9.44
                                    String value);
    public void setUseCaches(boolean usecaches);         §4.9.45
    public String toString();                            §4.9.46
}
```

The abstract class URLConnection is the superclass of all classes that represent a communications link between the application and a URL. Instances of this class can be used both to read from and to write to the resource referenced by the URL. In general, creating a connection to a URL is a multistep process:

```
openConnection()connect()
    (I-§4.8.13)                        (I-§4.9.9)
```

	Manipulate parameters that affect the connection to the remote resource.	Interact with the resource: query header fields and contents
	time	

1. The connection object is created by invoking the openConnection method on a URL.

2. The setup parameters and general request properties are manipulated.

3. The actual connection to the remote object is made, using the connect method.

4. The remote object becomes available. The header fields and the contents of the remote object can be accessed.

The setup parameters are modified using the following methods:

setAllowUserInteraction **(I-§4.9.36)**   setDoInput **(I-§4.9.41)**
setUseCaches **(I-§4.9.45)**   setDoOutput **(I-§4.9.42)**
                                                                        setIfModifiedSince **(I-§4.9.43)**

and the general request properties are modified using the method

setRequestProperty **(I-§4.9.44)**

Default values for the AllowUserInteraction and UseCaches parameters can be set using the methods setDefaultAllowUserInteraction **(I-§4.9.39)** and setDefaultUseCaches **(I-§4.9.40)**. Default values for general request properties can be set using the setDefaultRequestProperty method **(I-§4.9.39)**.

Each of the above set methods has a corresponding get method to retrieve the value of the parameter or general request property. The specific parameters and general request properties that are applicable are protocol specific.

The following methods are used to access the header fields and the contents after the connection is made to the remote object.

getContent **(I-§4.9.11)**   getInputStream **(I-§4.9.28)**
getHeaderField **(I-§4.9.22, §4.9.23)**   getOutputStream **(I-§4.9.30)**

Certain header fields are accessed frequently. The methods

getContentEncoding **(I-§4.9.12)**   getDate **(I-§4.9.15)**
getContentLength **(I-§4.9.13)**   getLastModifed **(I-§4.9.29)**
getContentType **(I-§4.9.14)**   getExpiration **(I-§4.9.21)**

provide convenient access to these fields. The getContentType method is used by the getContent method to determine the type of the remote object; subclasses may find it convenient to override the getContentType method.

In the common case, all of the pre-connection parameters and general request properties can be ignored: the pre-connection parameters and request properties default to sensible values. For most clients of this interface, there are only two interesting methods: getInputStream and getObject, which are mirrored in the URL class by convenience methods.

More information on the request properties and header fields of an http connection can be found at

http://www.w3.org/hypertext/WWW/Protocols/HTTP1.0/
        draft-ietf-http-spec.html

Fields

---

allowUserInteraction   §4.9.1

`protected boolean allowUserInteraction`

If `true`, this URL is being examined in a context in which it makes sense to allow user interactions such as popping up an authentication dialog. If `false`, then no user interaction is allowed.

The value of this field can be set by the `setAllowUserInteraction` method (**I-§4.9.36**). Its value is returned by the `getAllowUserInteraction` method (**I-§4.9.10**). Its default value is the value of the argument in the last invocation of the `setDefaultAllowUserInteraction` method (**I-§4.9.38**).

connected   §4.9.2

`protected boolean connected`

If `false`, this connection object has not created a communications link to the specified URL. If `true`, the communications link has been established.

doInput   §4.9.3

`protected boolean doInput`

This variable is set by the `setDoInput` method (**I-§4.9.41**). Its value is returned by the `getDoInput` method (**I-§4.9.19**).

A URL connection can be used for input and/or output. Setting the `doInput` flag to `true` indicates that the application intends to read data from the URL connection.

The default value of this field is `true`.

doOutput   §4.9.4

`protected boolean doOutput`

This variable is set by the `setDoOutput` method (**I-§4.9.42**). Its value is returned by the `getDoInput` method (**I-§4.9.20**).

A URL connection can be used for input and/or output. Setting the `doOutput` flag to `true` indicates that the application intends to write data to the URL connection.

The default value of this field is `false`.

ifModifiedSince   §4.9.5

`    protected long ifModifiedSince`

Some protocols support skipping the fetching of the object unless the object has been modified more recently than a certain time.

A nonzero value gives a time as the number of seconds since January 1, 1970, GMT. The object is fetched only if it has been modified more recently than that time.

This variable is set by the `setIfModifiedSince` method (**I-§4.9.43**). Its value is returned by the `getIfModifiedSince` method (**I-§4.9.27**).

The default value of this field is `0`, indicating that the fetching must always occur.

url   §4.9.6

`    protected URL url`

The URL represents the remote object on the World Wide Web to which this connection is opened.

The value of this field can be accessed by the `getURL` method (**I-§4.9.32**).

The default value of this variable is the value of the URL argument in the `URLConnection` constructor (**I-§4.9.6**).

useCaches   §4.9.7

`    protected boolean useCaches`

If `true`, the protocol is allowed to use caching whenever it can. If `false`, the protocol must always try to get a fresh copy of the object.

This field is set by the `setUseCaches` method (**I-§4.9.45**). Its value is returned by the `getUseCaches` method (**I-§4.9.33**). Its default value is the value given in the last invocation of the `setDefaultUseCaches` method (**I-§4.9.40**).

Constructors

URLConnection   §4.9.8

`    protected URLConnection(URL url)`

Constructs a URL connection to the specified URL. A connection to the object referenced by the URL is not created.

PARAMETERS:

`url`: the specified URL.

Methods

connect §4.9.9

```
public abstract void connect()
throws IOException
```

Opens a communications link to the resource referenced by this URL, if such a connection has not already been established.

If the `connect` method is called when the connection has already been opened (indicated by the `connected` **(I-§4.9.2)** field having the value `true`), the call is ignored.

THROWS:

`IOException` **(I-§2.29)**
if an I/O error occurs while opening the connection.

getAllowUserInteraction §4.9.10

```
public boolean getAllowUserInteraction()
```
RETURNS:

the value of the `allowUserInteraction` **(I-§4.9.1)** field for this object.

getContent §4.9.11

```
public Object getContent()
throws IOException
```

Retrieves the contents of this URL connection.

This method first determines the content type of the object by calling the `getContentType` method **(I-§4.9.1)**. If this is the first time that the application has seen that specific content type, a content handler for that content type is created:

1. If the application has set up a content handler factory instance using the `setContentHandlerFactory` **(I-§4.9.37)** method, the `createContent-Handler` **(I-§4.12.1)** method of that instance is called with the content type as an argument; the result is a content handler for that content type.

2. If no content handler factory has yet been set up, or if the factory's `createContentHandler` method returns `null`, then the application loads the class named

    `sun.net.www.content.`*<contentType>*

where *<contentType>* is formed by taking the content-type string, replacing all slash characters with `a period '.'`, and all other non-alphanumeric characters with the underscore character `'_'`. The alphanumeric characters are specifically the 26 uppercase ASCII letters `'A'` through `'Z'`, the 26 lowercase ASCII letters `'a'` through `'z'`, and the 10 ASCII digits `'0'` through `'9'`. If the specified class does not exist, or is not a subclass of `ContentHandler`, then an `UnknownServiceException` is thrown.

RETURNS:

the object fetched. The `instanceOf` operation should be used to determine the specific kind of object returned.

THROWS:

`IOException` **(I-§2.29)**

if an I/O error occurs while getting the content.

THROWS:

`UnknownServiceException` **(I-§4.19)**

if the protocol does not support the content type.

getContentEncoding   §4.9.12

```
public String getContentEncoding()
```

Determines the value of the `content-encoding` header field **(I-§4.9.23)**.

RETURNS:

the content encoding of the resource that the URL references, or `null` if not known.

getContentLength   §4.9.13

```
public int getContentLength()
```

Determines the value of the `content-length` header field.

RETURNS:

the content length of the resource that this connection's URL references, or −1 if the content length is not known.

getContentType   §4.9.14

```
public String getContentType()
```

Determines the value of the `content-type` header field **(I-§4.9.23)**.

RETURNS:

the content type of the resource that the URL references, or `null` if not known.

getDate   §4.9.15

```
public long getDate()
```

Determines the value of the `date` header field **(I-§4.9.23)**.

RETURNS:

the sending date of the resource that the URL references, or 0 if not known. The value returned is the number of seconds since January 1, 1970 GMT.

getDefaultAllowUserInteraction §4.9.16

    public static boolean getDefaultAllowUserInteraction()
RETURNS:

The default value of the allowUserInteraction (**I-§4.9.1**) field.

getDefaultRequestProperty §4.9.17

    public static String getDefaultRequestProperty(String key)

Gets the value of the default request property. Default request properties are set for every connection.
RETURNS:

the value of the default request property for the specified key.
SEE ALSO:

setDefaultRequestProperty (**I-§4.9.39**).

getDefaultUseCaches §4.9.18

    public boolean getDefaultUseCaches()
RETURNS:

the default value of a URLConnection's useCaches (**I-§4.9.7**) flag.

getDoInput §4.9.19

    public boolean getDoInput()
RETURNS:

the value of this URLConnection's doInput (**I-§4.9.3**) flag.

getDoOutput §4.9.20

    public boolean getDoOutput()
RETURNS:

the value of this URLConnection's doOutput (**I-§4.9.4**) flag.

getExpiration §4.9.21

    public long getExpiration()

Determines the value of the expires header field (**I-§4.9.23**).
RETURNS:

the expiration date of the resource that this URL references, or 0 if not known. The value is the number of seconds since January 1, 1970 GMT.

getHeaderField   §4.9.22

```
public String getHeaderField(int n)
```

Gets the value for the nth header field. It returns `null` if there are fewer than n fields.

This method can be used in conjunction with the `getHeaderFieldKey` method (**I-§4.9.26**) to iterate through all the headers in the message.

PARAMETERS:

n: an index.

RETURNS:

the value of the nth header field.

getHeaderField   §4.9.23

```
public String getHeaderField(String name)
```

PARAMETERS:

name: the name of a header field.

RETURNS:

the value of the named header field, or `null` if there is no such field in the header.

getHeaderFieldDate   §4.9.24

```
public long getHeaderFieldDate(String name, long Default)
```

The named header field is parsed as a date. The result is the number of seconds since January 1, 1970 GMT represented by the named field.

This form of `getHeaderField` exists because some connection types (e.g., `http-ng`) have pre-parsed headers. Classes for that connection type can override this method and short-circuit the parsing.

PARAMETERS:

name: the name of the header field.
Default: a default value.

RETURNS:

the value of the field, parsed as a date. The value of the `Default` argument is returned if the field is missing or malformed.

getHeaderFieldInt §4.9.25

```
public int getHeaderFieldInt(String name, int Default)
```

The named header field is parsed as a number. The value is returned.

This form of `getHeaderField` exists because some connection types (e.g., `http-ng`) have pre-parsed headers. Classes for that connection type can override this method and short-circuit the parsing.

PARAMETERS:

name: the name of the header field.
Default: the default value.

RETURNS:

the value of the named field, parsed as an integer. The `Default` value is returned if the field is missing or malformed.

getHeaderFieldKey §4.9.26

```
public String getHeaderFieldKey(int n)
```

PARAMETERS:

n: an index.

RETURNS:

the key for the nth header field, or `null` if there are fewer than n fields.

getIfModifiedSince §4.9.27

```
public long getIfModifiedSince()
```

RETURNS:

the value of this object's `ifModifiedSince` (**I-§4.9.5**) field.

getInputStream §4.9.28

```
public InputStream getInputStream()
throws IOException
```

RETURNS:

an input stream that reads from this open connection.

THROWS:

IOException (**I-§2.29**)
if an I/O error occurs while creating the input stream.

THROWS:

UnknownServiceException (**I-§4.19**)
if the protocol does not support input.

getLastModified   §4.9.29

> `public long getLastModified()`

Determines the value of the `last-modified` header field (**I-§4.9.23**).

RETURNS:

the date the resource referenced by this `URLConnection` was last modified, or 0 if not known. The result is the number of seconds since January 1, 1970 GMT.

getOutputStream   §4.9.30

> `public OutputStream getOutputStream()`
> `throws IOException`

RETURNS:

an output stream that writes to this connection.

THROWS:

`IOException` (**I-§2.29**)
if an I/O error occurs while creating the output stream.

THROWS:

`UnknownServiceException` (**I-§4.19**)
if the protocol does not support output.

getRequestProperty   §4.9.31

> `public String getRequestProperty(String key)`

RETURNS:

the value of the named general request property for this connection.

getURL   §4.9.32

> `public URL getURL()`

RETURNS:

the value of this `URLConnection`'s URL (**I-§4.9.6**) field.

getUseCaches   §4.9.33

> `public boolean getUseCaches()`

RETURNS:

the value of this `URLConnection`'s useCaches (**I-§4.9.7**) field

guessContentTypeFromName §4.9.34

```
protected static String
guessContentTypeFromName(String fname)
```

Makes a guess as to what the content type of an object is, based on the argument, which should be the "file" component of a URL. This is a convenience method that can be used by subclasses that override the getContentType method (**I-§4.9.14**).

PARAMETERS:

fname: a filename.

RETURNS:

a guess as to what the content type of the object is, based upon its file name.

guessContentTypeFromStream §4.9.35

```
protected static String
guessContentTypeFromStream(InputStream is)
throws IOException
```

Tries to determine the type of an input stream based on the characters at the beginning of the input stream. This method can be used by subclasses that override the getContentType method (**I-§4.9.14**).

Ideally, this routine would not be needed. But many http servers return the incorrect content type; in addition, there are many nonstandard extensions. Direct inspection of the bytes to determine the content type is often more accurate than believing the content type claimed by the http server.

PARAMETERS:

is: an input stream that supports marks (see page I-xxv).

RETURNS:

a guess at the content type, or null if none can be determined.

THROWS:

IOException (**I-§2.29**)
if an I/O error occurs while reading the input stream.

setAllowUserInteraction §4.9.36

```
public void
setAllowUserInteraction(boolean allowuserinteraction)
```

Set the value of the allowUserInteraction (**I-§4.9.1**) field of this URLConnection.

PARAMETERS:

allowuserinteraction: the new value.

setContentHandlerFactory   §4.9.37

```
public static void
setContentHandlerFactory(ContentHandlerFactory fac)
```

Sets the ContentHandlerFactory (**I-§4.12**) of an application. It can be called at most once by an application.

The ContentHandlerFactory instance is used to construct a content handler (**I-§4.9.11**) from a content type

PARAMETERS:

fac: the desired factory.

THROWS:

Error (**I-§1.48**)
if the factory has already been defined.

setDefaultAllowUserInteraction   §4.9.38

```
public static void setDefaultAllowUserInteraction(
    boolean defaultallowuserinteraction)
```

Sets the default value of the allowUserInteraction (**I-§4.9.1**) field for this URLConnection to the specified value.

PARAMETERS:

defaultallowuserinteraction: the new value.

setDefaultRequestProperty   §4.9.39

```
public static void
setDefaultRequestProperty(String key, String value)
```

Sets the default value of a general request property. When a URLConnection is created, it is initialized with these properties.

PARAMETERS:

key: the keyword by which the request is known (e.g., "accept").
value: the value associated with the key.

setDefaultUseCaches   §4.9.40

```
public void setDefaultUseCaches(boolean defaultusecaches)
```

Sets the default value of the useCaches (**I-§4.9.7**) field to the specified value.

PARAMETERS:

defaultusecaches: the new value.

setDoInput §4.9.41

```
public void setDoInput(boolean doinput)
```

Sets the value of the doInput (**I-§4.9.3**) field for this URLConnection to the specified value.

PARAMETERS:

value: the new value.

setDoOutput §4.9.42

```
public void setDoOutput(boolean dooutput)
```

Sets the value of the doOutput (**I-§4.9.4**) field for this URLConnection to the specified value.

PARAMETERS:

value: the new value.

setIfModifiedSince §4.9.43

```
public void setIfModifiedSince(long ifmodifiedsince)
```

Sets the value of the ifModifiedSince (**I-§4.9.5**) field of this URLConnection to the specified value

PARAMETERS:

value: the new value.

setRequestProperty §4.9.44

```
public void setRequestProperty(String key, String value)
```

Sets the general request property.

PARAMETERS:

key: the keyword by which the request is known (e.g., "accept").
value: the value associated with it.

setUseCaches §4.9.45

```
public void setUseCaches(boolean usecaches)
```

Sets the value of the useCaches (**I-§4.9.7**) field of this URLConnection to the specified value.

toString §4.9.46

```
public String toString()
```

RETURNS:

a string representation of this URLConnection.

OVERRIDES:

toString in class Object (**I-§1.12.9**).

4.10 Class URLEncoder

```
public class java.net.URLEncoder
    extends java.lang.Object (I-§1.12)
{
    // Methods
    public static String encode(String s);                    §4.10.1
}
```

The class contains a utility method for converting a String into a MIME format called "x-www-form-urlencoded" format.

To convert a String, each character is examined in turn:

♦ The ASCII characters 'a' through 'z', 'A' through 'Z', and '0' through '9' remain the same.

♦ The space character ' ' is converted into a plus sign '+'.

♦ All other characters are converted into the 3-character string "%xy" where xy is the two-digit hexadecimal representation of the lower 8-bits of the character.

Methods

encode   §4.10.1

```
public static String encode(String s)
```

Translates a string into x-www-form-urlencoded format.

PARAMETERS:

s: String to be translated.

RETURNS:

the translated String.

4.11 Class URLStreamHandler

```
public abstract class java.net.URLStreamHandler
    extends java.lang.Object (I-§1.12)
{
    // Constructors
    public URLStreamHandler();                          §4.11.1

    // Method
    protected abstract URLConnection
        openConnection(URL u);                          §4.11.2
    protected void parseURL(URL u, String spec,         §4.11.3
                            int start, int limit);
    protected void setURL(URL u, String protocol,       §4.11.4
                          String host, int port,
                          String file,
                          String ref);
    protected String toExternalForm(URL u);             §4.11.5
}
```

The abstract class URLStreamHandler is the common superclass for all stream protocol handlers. A stream protocol handler knows how to make a connection for a particular protocol type, such as http, ftp, or gopher.

In most cases, an instance of a URLStreamHandler subclass is not created directly by an application. Rather, the first time a protocol name is encountered when constructing a URL, the appropriate stream protocol handler is automatically loaded. See **I-§4.8.2** for complete details.

Constructors

URLStreamHandler   §4.11.1

```
public URLStreamHandler()
```
The default constructor.

Methods

openConnection   §4.11.2

```
protected abstract URLConnection openConnection(URL u)
throws IOException
```

Opens a connection to the object referenced by the URL argument.

PARAMETERS:

u: the URL that this connects to.

RETURNS:

a URLConnection object for the URL.

THROWS:

IOException (I-§2.29)
if an I/O error occurs while opening the connection.

parseURL   §4.11.3

```
protected void
parseURL(URL u, String spec, int start, int limit)
```

Parses the string representation of a URL into a URL object.

If there is any inherited context, then it has already been copied into the URL argument.

The parseURL method of URLStreamHandler parses the string representation as if it were an http specification. Most URL protocol families have a similar parsing. A stream protocol handler for a protocol that has a different syntax must override this routine.

PARAMETERS:

u: the URL to receive the result of parsing the spec.
spec: the String representing the URL that must be parsed.
start: the character index at which to begin parsing. This is just past the ':'
   (if there is one) that specifies the determination of the protocol name.
limit: the character position to stop parsing at. This is the end of the string
   or the position of the "#" character, if present. All information after the
   sharp sign indicates an anchor.

setURL §4.11.4

```
protected void setURL(URL u, String protocol, String host,
                      int port, String file, String ref)
```

Sets the fields of the URL argument to the indicated values.

PARAMETERS:

u: the URL to modify.
protocol: the protocol name.
host: the remote host value for the URL.
port: the port on the remote machine.
file: the file.
ref: the reference.

toExternalForm §4.11.5

```
protected String toExternalForm(URL u)
```

Converts a URL of a specific protocol to a String.

PARAMETERS:

u: the URL.

RETURNS:

a string representation of the URL argument.

4.12 Interface ContentHandlerFactory

```
public interface java.net.ContentHandlerFactory
{
    // Methods
    public abstract ContentHandler                    §4.12.1
        createContentHandler(String mimetype);
}
```

This interface defines a factory for content handlers. An implementation of this interface should map a MIME type into an instance of Content-Handler (**I-§4.1**).

This interface is used by the URLStreamHandler class (**I-§4.11**) to create a ContentHandler for a MIME type.

Methods

createContentHandler   §4.12.1

```
public abstract ContentHandler
createContentHandler(String mimetype)
```

Creates a new ContentHandler to read an object from a URLStreamHandler.

PARAMETERS:

mimetype: the MIME type for which a content handler is desired.

RETURNS:

a new ContentHandler (**I-§4.1**) to read an object from a URLStreamHandler (**I-§4.11**).

4.13 Interface SocketImplFactory

```
public interface java.net.SocketImplFactory
{
    // Methods
    public abstract SocketImpl createSocketImpl();          §4.13.1
}
```

This interface defines a factory for socket implementations. It is used by the classes Socket (**I-§4.6**) and ServerSocket (**I-§4.5**) to create actual socket implementations.

Methods

createSocketImpl   §4.13.1

```
public abstract SocketImpl createSocketImpl()
```

RETURNS:

a new instance of SocketImpl (**I-§4.7**).

4.14 Interface URLStreamHandlerFactory

```
public interface java.net.URLStreamHandlerFactory
{
    // Methods
    public abstract URLStreamHandler                        §4.14.1
        createURLStreamHandler(String protocol);
}
```

This interface defines a factory for URL stream protocol handlers.

It is used by the URL class (**I-§4.8**) to create a URLStreamHandler (**I-§4.11**) for a specific protocol.

Methods

createURLStreamHandler   §4.14.1

    public abstract URLStreamHandler
    createURLStreamHandler(String protocol)

    PARAMETERS:

    protocol: the protocol ("ftp", "http", "nntp", etc.)

    RETURNS:

    a URLStreamHandler (**I-§4.11**) for the specific protocol.

4.15 Class MalformedURLException

```
public class java.net.MalformedURLException
    extends java.io.IOException (I-§2.29)
{
    // Constructors
    public MalformedURLException();                    §4.15.1
    public MalformedURLException(String msg);          §4.15.2
}
```

Thrown to indicate that a malformed URL has occurred. Either no legal protocol could be found in a specification string, or the string could not be parsed.

Constructors

MalformedURLException   §4.15.1

    public MalformedURLException()

    Constructs a MalformedURLException with no detail message.

MalformedURLException   §4.15.2

    public MalformedURLException(String msg)

    Constructs a MalformedURLException with the specified detail message.

    PARAMETERS:

    msg: the detail message.

4.16 Class ProtocolException

```
public class java.net.ProtocolException
    extends java.io.IOException (I-§2.29)
{
    // Constructors
    public ProtocolException();                              §4.16.1
    public ProtocolException(String host);                   §4.16.2
}
```

Thrown to indicate that there is an error in the underlying protocol, such as a TCP error.

Constructors

ProtocolException   §4.16.1

> public ProtocolException()

> Constructs a new ProtocolException with no detail message.

ProtocolException   §4.16.2

> public ProtocolException(String host)

> Constructs a new ProtocolException with the specified detail message.

> PARAMETERS:
> host: the detail message.

4.17 Class SocketException

```
public class java.net.SocketException
    extends java.io.IOException (I-§2.29)
{
    // Constructors
    public SocketException();                                §4.17.1
    public SocketException(String msg);                      §4.17.2
}
```

Thrown to indicate that some error occurred while attempting to use a socket.

Constructors

SocketException §4.17.1

    `public SocketException()`

      Constructs a new `SocketException` with no detail message.

SocketException §4.17.2

    `public SocketException(String msg)`

      Constructs a new `SocketException` with the specified detail message.

    PARAMETERS:

    `msg`: the detail message.

4.18 Class UnknownHostException

```
public class java.net.UnknownHostException
    extends java.io.IOException (I-§2.29)
{
    // Constructors
    public UnknownHostException();                    §4.18.1
    public UnknownHostException(String host);         §4.18.2
}
```

    Thrown to indicate that the IP address of a host could not be determined.

Constructors

UnknownHostException §4.18.1

    `public UnknownHostException()`

      Constructs a new `UnknownHostException` with no detail message.

UnknownHostException §4.18.2

    `public UnknownHostException(String host)`

      Constructs a new `UnknownHostException` with the specified detail message.

    PARAMETERS:

    `host`: the detail message.

4.19 Class UnknownServiceException

```
public class java.net.UnknownServiceException
    extends java.io.IOException (I-§2.29)
{
    // Constructors
    public UnknownServiceException();                    §4.19.1
    public UnknownServiceException(String msg);          §4.19.2
}
```

Thrown to indicate that an unknown service exception has occurred. Either the MIME type returned by a URL connection does not make sense, or the application is attempting to write to a read-only URL connection.

Constructors

UnknownServiceException   §4.19.1

```
public UnknownServiceException()
```

Constructs a new UnknownServiceException with no detail message.

UnknownServiceException   §4.19.2

```
public UnknownServiceException(String msg)
```

Constructs a new UnknownServiceException with the specified detail message.

PARAMETERS:

msg: the detail message.

Index

A

ABORT, II-291
    static int ABORT in interface Image-
        Observer, II-291
ABORTED, II-170
    static int ABORTED in class
        MediaTracker, II-170
abs, I-58
    static double abs(double) in class Math,
        I-58
    static float abs(float) in class Math, I-59
    static int abs(int) in class Math, I-59
    static long abs(long) in class Math, I-59
AbstractMethodError, I-173
    AbstractMethodError() in class Abstract-
        MethodError, I-173
    AbstractMethodError(String) in class
        AbstractMethodError, I-173
    Class in package java.lang, I-173
accept
    boolean accept(File, String) in interface
        FilenameFilter, I-323
    FilenameFilter, I-323
    ServerSocket, I-386
    Socket accept() in class ServerSocket,
        I-386
    SocketImpl, I-394
    void accept(SocketImpl) in class
        SocketImpl, I-394
ack, I-278
acos, I-60
    static double acos(double) in class Math,
        I-60

action, II-37
    boolean action(Event, Object) in class
        Component, II-37
ACTION_EVENT, II-79
    static int ACTION_EVENT in class
        Event, II-79
activeCount
    int activeCount() in class ThreadGroup,
        I-148
    static int activeCount() in class Thread,
        I-139
    Thread, I-139
    ThreadGroup, I-148
activeGroupCount, I-149
    int activeGroupCount() in class Thread-
        Group, I-149
add
    Component add(Component) in class
        Container, II-63
    Component add(Component, int) in class
        Container, II-64
    Component add(String, Component) in
        class Container, II-64
    Container, II-63
    Menu, II-178
    Menu add(Menu) in class MenuBar,
        II-181
    MenuBar, II-181
    MenuItem add(MenuItem) in class Menu,
        II-178
    Rectangle, II-196
    void add(int, int) in class Rectangle,
        II-196

void add(Point) in class Rectangle, II-197
void add(Rectangle) in class Rectangle,
II-197
void add(String) in class Menu, II-179
addConsumer
FilteredImageSource, II-250
interface, II-294
MemoryImageSource, II-268
void addConsumer(ImageConsumer)
in class FilteredImageSource, II-250
in class MemoryImageSource, II-268
in interface ImageProducer, II-294
addElement, I-364
void addElement(Object) in class Vector,
I-364
addHelpMenu, II-315
void addHelpMenu(Menu) in interface
MenuBarPeer, II-315
addImage, II-171
void addImage(Image, int) in class
MediaTracker, II-171
void addImage(Image, int, int, int) in class
MediaTracker, II-171
addItem
in class List, II-160
Choice, II-24
ChoicePeer, II-300
List, II-160
ListPeer, II-312
MenuPeer, II-317
void addItem(MenuItem)
in class Choice, II-24
in class List, II-160
in interface ChoicePeer, II-300
in interface ListPeer, II-312
in interface MenuPeer, II-317
addLayoutComponent, II-5, II-12
BorderLayout, II-4
FlowLayout, II-93
GridBagLayout, II-140
GridLayout, II-145
interface, II-233
void addLayoutComponent(String,
Component)
in class CardLayout, II-12
in class FlowLayout, II-93

in class GridBagLayout, II-140
in class GridLayout, II-145
in interface LayoutManager, II-233
void addLayoutComponent(String,
Component) in class BorderLayout,
II-5
addMenu, II-315
void addMenu(Menu) in interface
MenuBarPeer, II-315
addNotify
Button, II-8
Canvas, II-10
Checkbox, II-17
CheckboxMenuItem, II-22
Choice, II-24
Component, II-37
Container, II-64
Dialog, II-72
FileDialog, II-88
Frame, II-108
Label, II-155
List, II-160
MenuItem, II-186
Panel, II-188
Scrollbar, II-204
TextArea, II-209
TextField, II-217
void addNotify() in class
Button, II-8
Canvas, II-10
Checkbox, II-17
CheckboxMenuItem, II-22
Choice, II-24
Component, II-37
Container, II-64
Dialog, II-72
FileDialog, II-88
Frame, II-108
Label, II-155
List, II-160
Menu, II-178, II-179
MenuBar, II-181, II-182
MenuItem, II-186
Panel, II-188
Scrollbar, II-204
TextArea, II-209

TextField, II-217
    Window, II-231
    Window, II-231
addObserver
    Observable, I-350
    void addObserver(Observer) in class
        Observable, I-350
addPoint, II-192
    void addPoint(int, int) in class Polygon,
        II-192
address, I-393
    InetAddress address in class SocketImpl,
        I-393
addSeparator
    Menu, II-179
    MenuPeer, II-317
    void addSeparator()
        in class Menu, II-179
        in interface MenuPeer, II-317
after, I-336
    boolean after(Date) in class Date, I-336
algorithms, I-58
ALLBITS, II-291
    static int ALLBITS in interface Image-
        Observer, II-291
allowsMultipleSelections, II-160
    boolean allowsMultipleSelections() in
        class List, II-160
allowUserInteraction, I-410
    boolean allowUserInteraction in class
        URLConnection, I-410
ALT_MASK, II-83
    static int ALT_MASK in class Event,
        II-83
anchor, II-132
    int anchor in class GridBagConstraints,
        II-132
and, I-329
    void and(BitSet) in class BitSet, I-329
append, I-114
    StringBuffer append(boolean) in class
        StringBuffer, I-114
    StringBuffer append(char) in class String-
        Buffer, I-114
    StringBuffer append(char[]) in class
        StringBuffer, I-115

StringBuffer append(char[], int, int) in
    class StringBuffer, I-115
StringBuffer append(double) in class
    StringBuffer, I-115
StringBuffer append(float) in class String-
    Buffer, I-116
StringBuffer append(int) in class String-
    Buffer, I-116
StringBuffer append(long) in class String-
    Buffer, I-116
StringBuffer append(Object) in class
    StringBuffer, I-117
StringBuffer append(String) in class
    StringBuffer, I-117
appendText
    TextArea, II-209
    void appendText(String) in class Text-
        Area, II-209
Applet
    Applet() in class Applet, II-326
    Class in package java.applet, II-326
    constructors, II-326
    methods, II-326
    role of, II-326
AppletContext, II-334
    Interface in package java.applet, II-334
appletResize, II-337
    void appletResize(int, int) in interface
        AppletStub, II-337
AppletStub, II-336
    Interface in package java.applet, II-336
arg, II-78
    Object arg in class Event, II-78
ArithmeticException
    ArithmeticException() in class
        ArithmeticException, I-157
    ArithmeticException(String) in class
        ArithmeticException, I-157
    Class in package java.lang, I-157
    Exceptions, java.lang, I-157
arrayCopy, I-127
    static void arraycopy(Object, int, Object,
        int, int) in class System, I-127
ArrayIndexOutOfBoundsException, I-158

ArrayIndexOutOfBoundsException() in
    class ArrayIndexOutOfBounds-
    Exception, I-158
ArrayIndexOutOfBoundsException(int)
    in class ArrayIndexOutOf-
    BoundsException, I-158
ArrayIndexOutOfBounds-
    Exception(String) in class Array-
    IndexOutOfBoundsException,
    I-158
    Class in package java.lang, I-158
ArrayStoreException, I-159
    ArrayStoreException() in class Array-
      StoreException, I-159
    ArrayStoreException(String) in class
      ArrayStoreException, I-159
    Class in package java.lang, I-159
asin, I-60
    static double asin(double) in class Math,
      I-60
atan, I-60
    static double atan(double) in class Math,
      I-60
atan2, I-60
    static double atan2(double, double) in
      class Math, I-60
AudioClip, II-338
    Interface in package java.applet, II-338
available
    ByteArrayInputStream, I-198
    FileInputStream, I-236
    FilterInputStream, I-244
    int available() in class
      BufferedInputStream, I-191
      ByteArrayInputStream, I-198
      FileInputStream, I-236
      FilterInputStream, I-244
      InputStream, I-254
      LineNumberInputStream, I-258
      PushbackInputStream, I-278
      SocketImpl, I-394
      StringBufferInputStream, I-310
    LineNumberInputStream, I-258
    PushbackInputStream, I-278
    SocketImpl, I-394
    StringBufferInputStream, I-310

availablr
    InputStream, I-254
AWTError, II-236
    AWTError(String) in class AWTError,
      II-236
    Class in package java.awt, II-236
AWTException, II-235
    AWTException(String) in class AWT-
      Exception, II-235
    Class in package java.awt, II-235

B
before, I-336
    boolean before(Date) in class Date, I-336
bind, I-395
    void bind(InetAddress, int) in class
      SocketImpl, I-395
BitSet
    BitSet() in class BitSet, I-328
    Class in package java.util, I-328
    constructors, I-328
    methods, I-329
    role of, I-328
black, II-28
blue, II-28
BOLD, II-96
    static int BOLD in class Font, II-96
Boolean
    Boolean(boolean) in class Boolean, I-3
    Boolean(String) in class Boolean, I-3
    Class in package java.lang, I-2
    constructors, I-3
    fields, I-2
    methods, I-3
    role of, I-2
booleanValue, I-3
    boolean booleanValue() in class Boolean,
      I-3
BorderLayout
    BorderLayout() in class BorderLayout,
      II-4
    BorderLayout(int, int) in class Border-
      Layout, II-4
    Class in package java.awt, II-3
    constructors, II-3
    methods, II-3

role of, II-3
BOTH, II-135
  static int BOTH in class GridBag-
      Constraints, II-135
bottom, II-151
  int bottom in class Insets, II-151
bounds, II-37
  Rectangle bounds() in class Component,
      II-37
brighter, II-30
  Color brighter() in class Color, II-30
buf, I-189, I-195, I-197, I-200
  byte buf[] in class
    BufferedInputStream, I-189
    BufferedOutputStream, I-195
    ByteArrayInputStream, I-197
    ByteArrayOutputStream, I-200
buffer, I-309
  String buffer in class StringBufferInput-
      Stream, I-309
BufferedInputStream
  BufferedInputStream(InputStream) in
      class BufferedInputStream, I-190
  BufferedInputStream(InputStream, int) in
      class BufferedInputStream, I-190
  Class in package java.io, I-189
  constructors, I-190, I-195
  fields, I-189, I-195
  methods, I-191
  role of, I-189, I-194
BufferedOutputStream
  BufferedInputStream, I-194
  BufferedOutputStream(OutputStream) in
      class BufferedOutputStream, I-195
  BufferedOutputStream(OutputStream,
      int) in class BufferedOutputStream,
      I-195
  Class in package java.io, I-194
Button
  Button() in class Button, II-8
  Button(String) in class Button, II-8
  Class in package java.awt, II-7
  constructors, II-7
  methods, II-7
  role of, II-7
ButtonPeer, II-297

Interface in package java.awt.peer, II-297
ByteArrayInputStream
  ByteArrayInputStream(byte[]) in class
      ByteArrayInputStream, I-198
  ByteArrayInputStream(byte[], int, int) in
      class ByteArrayInputStream, I-198
  Class in package java.io, I-197
  constructors, I-198
  Fields, I-197
  methods, I-198
  role of, I-197
ByteArrayOutputStream
  ByteArrayOutputStream() in class Byte-
      ArrayOutputStream, I-201
  ByteArrayOutputStream(int) in class
      ByteArrayOutputStream, I-201
  Class in package java.io, I-200
  constructors, I-201
  Fields, I-200
  methods, I-201
  role of, I-200
bytesTransferred
  int bytesTransferred in class Interrupted-
      IOException, I-325
bytesWidth, II-101
  int bytesWidth(byte[], int, int) in class
      FontMetrics, II-102

C
canFilterIndexColorModel, II-278
  boolean canFilterIndexColorModel in
      class RGBImageFilter, II-278,
      II-279
canRead, I-226
  boolean canRead() in class File, I-226
Canvas
  Canvas() in class Canvas, II-10
  Class in package java.awt, II-9
  constructors, II-9
  methods, II-9
  role of, II-9
CanvasPeer, II-298
  Interface in package java.awt.peer, II-298
canWrite, I-227
  boolean canWrite() in class File, I-227
capacity

int capacity()
   in class StringBuffer, I-117
   in class Vector, I-364
StringBuffer, I-117
Vector, I-364
capacityIncrement, I-363
   int capacityIncrement in class Vector,
      I-363
CardLayout
   CardLayout() in class CardLayout, II-11
   Class in package java.awt, II-11
   constructors, II-11
   methods, II-11
   role of, II-11
ceil, I-60
   static double ceil(double) in class Math,
      I-60
CENTER
   FlowLayout, II-91
   GridBagConstraints, II-134
   Label, II-154
   static int CENTER
      in class FlowLayout, II-91
      in class GridBagConstraints, II-134
      in class Label, II-154
Character
   Character(char) in class Character, I-6
   Class in package java.lang, I-5
   constructors, I-6
   fields, I-6
   methods, I-7
   role of, I-5
charAt
   char charAt(int)
      in class String, I-99
      in class StringBuffer, I-118
   String, I-99
   StringBuffer, I-118
charsWidth, II-102
   , II-102
charValue, I-7
   char charValue() in class Character, I-7
charWidth, II-102
   int charWidth(char) in class FontMetrics,
      II-102–II-103
checkAccept, I-85

void checkAccept(String, int) in class
      SecurityManager, I-85
checkAccess
   SecurityManager, I-86
   Thread, I-139
   ThreadGroup, I-149
   void checkAccess()
      in class Thread, I-139
      in class ThreadGroup, I-149
   void checkAccess(Thread) in class
      SecurityManager, I-86
   void checkAccess(ThreadGroup) in class
      SecurityManager, I-86
checkAll, II-171
   boolean checkAll() in class Media
      Tracker, II-171
   boolean checkAll(boolean) in class
      MediaTracker, II-172
Checkbox
   Checkbox() in class Checkbox, II-16
   Checkbox(String) in class Checkbox,
      II-16
   Checkbox(String, CheckboxGroup,
      boolean) in class Checkbox, II-17
   Class in package java.awt, II-15
   constructors, II-15
   methods, II-15
   role of, II-15
CheckboxGroup
   CheckboxGroup() in class Checkbox-
      Group, II-20
   Class in package java.awt, II-19
   constructors, II-19
   methods, II-19
   role of, II-19
CheckboxMenuItem
   CheckboxMenuItem(String) in class
      CheckboxMenuItem, II-21
   Class in package java.awt, II-21
CheckboxMenuItemPeer, II-298
   Interface in package java.awt.peer, II-298
CheckboxPeer, II-299
   Interface in package java.awt.peer, II-299
checkConnect, I-87
   void checkConnect(String, int) in class
      SecurityManager, I-87

checkCreateClassLoader, I-88
    void checkCreateClassLoader() in class
        SecurityManager, I-88
checkDelete, I-88
    void checkDelete(String) in class
        SecurityManager, I-88
checkError, I-271
    boolean checkError() in class Print-
        Stream, I-271
checkExec, I-88
    void checkExec(String) in class Security-
        Manager, I-88
checkExit, I-89
    void checkExit(int) in class Security-
        Manager, I-89
checkID, II-172
    boolean checkID(int) in class
        MediaTracker, II-172
    boolean checkID(int, boolean) in class
        MediaTracker, II-173
checkImage
    Component, II-38
    ComponentPeer, II-302
    int checkImage(Image, ImageObserver)
        in class Component, II-38
    int checkImage(Image, int, int, Image
        Observer)
        in class Component, II-39
        in class Toolkit, II-223
        in interface ComponentPeer, II-302
    Toolkit, II-223
checkLink, I-89
checkListen, I-90
checkPackageAccess, I-90
checkPackageDefinition, I-90
checkPropertiesAccess, I-91
checkPropertyAccess, I-91
checkRead, I-91
    void checkRead(FileDescriptor) in class
        SecurityManager, I-91
    void checkRead(String) in class Security-
        Manager, I-92
    void checkRead(String, Object) in class
        SecurityManager, I-92
checkSetFactory, I-92
checkTopLevelWindow, I-93

checkWrite, I-93
    void checkWrite(FileDescriptor) in class
        SecurityManager, I-93
    void checkWrite(String) in class Security-
        Manager, I-93
Choice
    Choice() in class Choice, II-24
    Class in package java.awt, II-23
    constructors, II-23
    methods, II-23
    role of, II-23
ChoicePeer, II-300
    Interface in package java.awt.peer, II-300
clase
    FilterInputStream, I-245
    PipedInputStream, I-265
Class
    BitSet, I-328
    ByteArrayInputStream, I-197
    ByteArrayOutputStream, I-200
    Class in package java.lang, I-16
    ContentHandler, I-374
    DatagramPacket, I-376
    DatagramSocket, I-378
    DataInputStream, I-204
    DataOutputStream, I-217
    Date, I-332
    Dictionary, I-341
    File, I-224
    FileDescriptor, I-233
    FileInputStream, I-234
    FileOutputStream, I-239
    FilterInputStream, I-243
    FilterOutputStream, I-249
    Hashtable, I-344
    InetAddress, I-381
    InputStream, I-253
    LineNumberInputStream, I-257
    methods, I-16
    Observable, I-349
    OutputStream, I-262
    PipedInputStream, I-264
    PipedOutputStream, I-267
    PrintStream, I-270
    Properties, I-351
    PushbackInputStream, I-277

Random, I-354
RandomAccessFile, I-281
SequenceInputStream, I-299
ServerSocket, I-384
Socket, I-388
SocketImpl, I-393
Stack, I-356
StreamTokenizer, I-302
StringBufferInputStream, I-309
StringTokenizer, I-358
Thread, I-134
ThreadGroup, I-147
Throwable, I-154
URL, I-398
URLConnection, I-407
URLEncoder, I-421
URLStreamHandler, I-422
Vector, I-362
ClassCastException, I-159
    Class in package java.lang, I-159
    ClassCastException()
        in class ClassCastException, I-160
ClassCircularityError, I-173
    Class in package java.lang, I-173
    ClassCircularityError()
        in class ClassCircularityError, I-174
classDepth, I-94
    int classDepth(String) in class Security-
        Manager, I-94
Classes
    java.applet.Applet, II-326
    java.awt.AWTError, II-236
    java.awt.AWTException, II-235
    java.awt.BorderLayout, II-3
    java.awt.Button, II-7
    java.awt.Canvas, II-9
    java.awt.CardLayout, II-11
    java.awt.Checkbox, II-15
    java.awt.CheckboxGroup, II-19
    java.awt.CheckboxMenuItem, II-21
    java.awt.Choice, II-23
    java.awt.Color, II-27
    java.awt.Component, II-35
    java.awt.Container, II-63
    java.awt.Dialog, II-71
    java.awt.Dimension, II-74

    java.awt.Event, II-76
    java.awt.FileDialog, II-87
    java.awt.FlowLayout, II-90
    java.awt.Font, II-95
    java.awt.FontMetrics, II-100
    java.awt.Frame, II-106
    java.awt.Graphics, II-112
    java.awt.GridBagConstraints,
        II-131
    java.awt.GridBagLayout, II-137
    java.awt.GridLayout, II-143
    java.awt.Image, II-148
    java.awt.image.ColorModel, II-238
    java.awt.image.CropImageFilter,
        II-241
    java.awt.image.DirectColorMod-
        el, II-245
    java.awt.image.FilteredImage-
        Source, II-249
    java.awt.image.ImageFilter,
        II-252
    java.awt.image.IndexColorModel,
        II-257
    java.awt.image.MemoryImage-
        Source, II-264
    java.awt.image.PixelGrabber,
        II-270
    java.awt.image.RGBImageFilter,
        II-277
    java.awt.Insets, II-151
    java.awt.Label, II-153
    java.awt.List, II-157
    java.awt.MediaTracker, II-167
    java.awt.Menu, II-177
    java.awt.MenuBar, II-180
    java.awt.MenuComponent, II-183
    java.awt.MenuItem, II-185
    java.awt.Panel, II-188
    java.awt.Point, II-189
    java.awt.Polygon, II-191
    java.awt.Rectangle, II-194
    java.awt.Scrollbar, II-200
    java.awt.TextArea, II-207
    java.awt.TextComponent, II-213
    java.awt.TextField, II-215
    java.awt.Toolkit, II-221

java.awt.Window, II-230

java.io.BufferedInputStream, I-189

java.io.BufferedOutputStream, I-194

java.io.ByteArrayInputStream, I-197

java.io.ByteArrayOutputStream, I-200

java.io.DataInputStream, I-204

java.io.DataOutputStream, I-217

java.io.EOFException, I-312

java.io.File, I-224

java.io.FileDescriptor, I-233

java.io.FileInputStream, I-234

java.io.FileNotFoundException, I-324

java.io.FileOutputStream, I-239

java.io.FilterInputStream, I-243

java.io.FilterOutputStream, I-249

java.io.InputStream, I-253

java.io.InterruptedIOException, I-325

java.io.IOException, I-324

java.io.LineNumberInputStream, I-257

java.io.OutputStream, I-262

java.io.PipedInputStream, I-264

java.io.PipedOutputStream, I-267

java.io.PrintStream, I-270

java.io.PushbackInputStream, I-277

java.io.RandomAccessFile, I-281

java.io.SequenceInputStream, I-299

java.io.StreamTokenizer, I-302

java.io.StringBufferInput-Stream, I-309

java.io.UTFDataFormatException, I-326

java.lang.AbstractMethodError, I-173

java.lang.ArithmeticException, I-157

java.lang.ArrayIndexOutOfBounds-sException, I-158

java.lang.ArrayStoreException, I-159

java.lang.Boolean, I-2

java.lang.Character, I-5

java.lang.Class, I-16

java.lang.ClassCastException, I-159

java.lang.ClassCircularity-Error, I-173

java.lang.ClassFormatError, I-174

java.lang.ClassLoader, I-19

java.lang.ClassNotFound-Exception, I-160

java.lang.CloneNotSupported-Exception, I-161

java.lang.Compiler, I-23

java.lang.Double, I-25

java.lang.Error, I-175

java.lang.Exception, I-162

java.lang.Float, I-32

java.lang.IllegalAccessError, I-175

java.lang.IllegalAccess-Exception, I-162

java.lang.IllegalArgument-Exception, I-163

java.lang.IllegalMonitorState-Exception, I-164

java.lang.IllegalThreadState-Exception, I-165

java.lang.IncompatibleClass-ChangeError, I-176

java.lang.IndexOutOfBounds-Exception, I-165

java.lang.InstantiationError, I-177

java.lang.Instantiation-Exception, I-166

java.lang.Integer, I-39

java.lang.InternalError, I-178

java.lang.InterruptedException, I-167

java.lang.LinkageError, I-178

java.lang.Long, I-48

java.lang.Math, I-57

java.lang.NegativeArraySize-
Exception, I-167
java.lang.NoClassDefFoundError,
I-179
java.lang.NoSuchFieldError, I-180
java.lang.NoSuchMethodError,
I-180
java.lang.NoSuchMethod-
Exception, I-168
java.lang.NullPointerException,
I-169
java.lang.Number, I-66
java.lang.NumberFormat-
Exception, I-170
java.lang.Object, I-67
java.lang.OutOfMemoryError, I-181
java.lang.Process, I-74
java.lang.Runtime, I-76
java.lang.RuntimeException, I-170
java.lang.SecurityException,
I-171
java.lang.SecurityManager, I-83
java.lang.StackOverflowError,
I-182
java.lang.String, I-96
java.lang.StringBuffer, I-112
java.lang.StringIndexOutOf-
BoundsException, I-172
java.lang.System, I-125
java.lang.Thread, I-134
java.lang.Thread, I-134
java.lang.ThreadDeath, I-182
java.lang.ThreadGroup, I-147
java.lang.Throwable, I-154
java.lang.UnknownError, I-183
java.lang.UnsatisfiedLinkError,
I-184
java.lang.VerifyError, I-184
java.lang.VirtualMachineError,
I-185
java.net.ContentHandler, I-374
java.net.DatagramPacket, I-376
java.net.DatagramSocket, I-378
java.net.InetAddress, I-381
java.net.MalformedURLException,
I-426

java.net.ProtocolException, I-427
java.net.ServerSocket, I-384
java.net.Socket, I-388
java.net.SocketException, I-427
java.net.SocketImpl, I-393
java.net.UnknownHostException,
I-428
java.net.UnknownService-
Exception, I-429
java.net.URL, I-398
java.net.URLConnection, I-407
java.net.URLEncoder, I-421
java.net.URLStreamHandler, I-422
java.util.BitSet, I-328
java.util.Date, I-332
java.util.Dictionary, I-341
java.util.EmptyStackException,
I-371
java.util.Hashtable, I-344
java.util.NoSuchElement-
Exception, I-371
java.util.Observable, I-349
java.util.Properties, I-351
java.util.Random, I-354
java.util.Stack, I-356
java.util.StringTokenizer, I-358
java.util.Vector, I-362
Classes, java.applet class
Applet, II-326
Classes, java.awt
BorderLayout, II-3
Button, II-7
Canvas, II-9
Classes, java.awt class
CardLayout, II-11
Checkbox, II-15
CheckboxGroup, II-19
Choice, II-23
Color, II-27
Component, II-35
Container, II-63
Dialog, II-71
Dimension, II-74
Event, II-76
FileDialog, II-87
FlowLayout, II-90

font, II-95
FontMetrics, II-99
Frame, II-106
Graphics, II-112
GridBagConstraints, II-131
GridBagLayout, II-137
GridLayout, II-143
Image, II-148
insets, II-151
Label, II-153
List, II-157
MediaTracker, II-167
Menu, II-177
MenuBar, II-180
MenuComponent, II-183
MenuItem, II-185
Panel, II-188
Point, II-189
Polygon, II-191
Rectangle, II-194
Scrollbar, II-200
TextArea, II-207
TextComponent, II-213
TextField, II-215
Toolkit, II-221
Window, II-230
Classes, java.awt.image
ColorModel, II-238
Classes, java.awt.image class
CropImageFilter, II-241
DirectColorModel, II-245
FilteredImageSource, II-249
ImageFilter, II-252
IndexColorModel, II-257
MemoryImageSource, II-264
PixelGrabber, II-270
RGBImageFilter, II-277
Classes, java.io
BufferedInputStream, I-189
Classes, java.lang
Boolean, I-2
Character, I-5
Class
    role of, I-16
Compiler, I-23
Double, I-25

Float, I-32
Integer, I-39
Long, I-48
Math, I-57
Number, I-66
Object, I-67
Process, I-74
Runtime, I-76
SecurityManager, I-83
String, I-96
StringBuffer, I-112
System, I-125
Thread, I-134
Classes, java.lang class
ClassLoader, I-19
ClassFormatError, I-174
Class in package java.lang, I-174
ClassFormatError() in class Class-
    FormatError, I-174
ClassLoader
Class in package java.lang, I-19
ClassLoader() in class ClassLoader, I-20
constructors, I-20
methods, I-21
role of, I-19
classLoaderDepth, I-94
int classLoaderDepth() in class Security-
    Manager, I-94
ClassNotFoundException, I-160
Class in package java.lang, I-160
ClassNotFoundException() in class Class-
    NotFoundException, I-160–I-161
clear
BitSet, I-329
Hashtable, I-346
List, II-160
ListPeer, II-312
void clear()
    in class BitSet, I-329
    in class Hashtable, I-346
    in class List, II-160
    in interface ListPeer, II-312
clearChanged, I-350
void clearChanged() in class Observable,
    I-350
clearRect, II-114

void clearRect(int, int, int, int) in class
    Graphics, II-114
clickCount, II-78
    int clickCount in class Event, II-78
clipRect, II-115
    void clipRect(int, int, int, int) in class
        Graphics, II-115
clone
    BitSet, I-329
    GridBagConstraints, II-136
    Hashtable, I-346
    ImageFilter, II-253
    Insets, II-152
    Object, I-68
    Object clone()
        in class BitSet, I-329
        in class GridBagConstraints, II-136
        in class Hashtable, I-346
        in class ImageFilter, II-253
        in class Insets, II-152
        in class Object, I-68
        in class Vector, I-364
    Vector, I-364
Cloneable
    Interface in package java.lang, I-156
CloneNotSupportedException, I-161
    Class in package java.lang, I-161
    CloneNotSupportedException() in class
        CloneNotSupportedException,
        I-161
close, I-395
    DatagramSocket, I-379
    FileInputStream, I-236
    FileOutputStream, I-241
    FilterOutputStream, I-250
    in class PipedInputStream, I-265
    InputStream, I-254
    OutputStream, I-262
    PipedOutputStream, I-268
    PrintStream, I-272
    RandomAccessFile, I-283
    SequenceInputStream, I-300
    ServerSocket, I-386
    Socket, I-391
    void close()
        in class DatagramSocket, I-379

    in class FileInputStream, I-236
    in class FileOutputStream, I-241
    in class FilterInputStream, I-245
    in class FilterOutputStream, I-250
    in class InputStream, I-254
    in class OutputStream, I-262
    in class PipedOutputStream, I-268
    in class PrintStream, I-272
    in class RandomAccessFile, I-283
    in class SequenceInputStream, I-300
    in class ServerSocket, I-386
    in class Socket, I-391
    in class SocketImpl, I-395
Color
    Class in package java.awt, II-27
    Color(float, float, float) in class Color,
        II-29
    Color(int) in class Color, II-30
    Color(int, int, int) in class Color, II-30
    constructors, II-27
    fields, II-27
    methods, II-27
    role of, II-27
ColorModel
    Class in package java.awt.image, II-238
    ColorModel(int) in class ColorModel,
        II-239
    constructors, II-238
    fields, II-238
    methods, II-238
    role of, II-238
command, I-23
commentChar, I-305
compareTo, I-99
compileClass, I-24
compileClasses, I-24
Compiler
    Class in package java.lang, I-23
    methods, I-23
    role of, I-23
COMPLETE, II-170
COMPLETESCANLINES, II-285
Component, II-49
    Class in package java.awt, II-35
    methodd, II-35
    role of, II-35

ComponentPeer, II-301

concat, I-100

Concatenation, streams, I-188

connect

    PipedInputStream, I-265

    PipedOutputStream, I-268

    SocketImpl, I-395

    URLConnection, I-412

    void connect() in class URLConnection, I-412

    void connect(InetAddress, int) in class SocketImpl, I-395

    void connect(PipedInputStream) in class PipedOutputStream, I-268

    void connect(PipedOutputStream) in class PipedInputStream, I-265

    void connect(String, int) in class SocketImpl, I-395

connected, I-410

    boolean connected in class URL-Connection, I-410

Constructors

    ByteArrayInputStream, I-198

Constructors, java.applet class

    Applet, II-326

Constructors, java.awt class

    BorderLayout, II-4

    Button, II-8

    canvas, II-10

    CardLayout, II-11

    Checkbox, II-16

    CheckboxGroup, II-20

    CheckboxMenuItem, II-21

    Choice, II-24

    Color, II-29

    Dialog, II-72

    Dimension, II-74

    Event, II-84

    FileDialog, II-88

    FlowLayout, II-92

    Font, II-96

    FontMetrics, II-101

    Frame, II-108

    Graphics, II-114

    GridBagConstraints, II-136

    GridBagLayout, II-140

    GridLayout, II-144

    Image, II-148

    Insets, II-152

    Label, II-154

    List, II-159

    MediaTracker, II-170

    Menu, II-178

    MenuBar, II-181

    MenuComponent, II-183

    MenuItem, II-186

    Panel, II-188

    Point, II-189

    Polygon, II-192

    Rectangle, II-195

    Scrollbar, II-202

    TextArea, II-208

    TextField, II-217

    Toolkit, II-222

    Window, II-230

Constructors, java.awt.image class

    ColorModel, II-239

    CropImageFilter, II-242

    DirectColorModel, II-246

    FilteredImageSource, II-250

    ImageFilter, II-253

    IndexColorModel, II-258

    MemoryImageSource, II-265

    PixelGrabber, II-272

    RGBImageFilter, II-279

Constructors, java.io

    BufferedInputStream, I-190, I-195

Constructors, java.io class, I-278

    ByteArrayOutputStream, I-201

    DataInputStream, I-205

    DataOutputStream, I-218

    File, I-225

    FileDescriptor, I-234

    FileInputStream, I-235

    FileOutputStream, I-240

    FilterInputStream, I-244

    FilterOutputStream, I-250

    InputStream, I-253

    LineNumberInputStream, I-258

    OutputStream, I-262

    PipedInputStream, I-264

    PipedOutputStream, I-267

PrintStream, I-271
RandomAccessFile, I-282
StreamTokenizer, I-304
StringBufferInputStream, I-310
Constructors, java.io classSequenceInput-
Stream, I-299
Constructors, java.lang class
Boolean, I-3
Character, I-6
ClassLoader, I-20
Double, I-26
Float, I-33
Integer, I-40
Long, I-49
Object, I-68
Process, I-74
SecurityManager, I-85
String, I-97
StringBuffer, I-113
Thread, I-137
ThreadGroup, I-148
Throwable, I-155
Constructors, java.net class
ContentHandler, I-375
DatagramPacket, I-376
DatagramSocket, I-378
ServerSocket, I-385
Socket, I-389
SocketImpl, I-394
URL, I-400
URLConnection, I-411
URLStreamHandler, I-422
Constructors, java.util class
BitSet, I-328
Date, I-334
Dictionary, I-342
Hashtable, I-345
Observable, I-350
Properties, I-352
Random, I-354
Stack, I-356
StringTokenizer, I-359
Vector, I-363
consumer, II-253
ImageConsumer consumer in class
ImageFilter, II-253

Container
Class in package java.awt, II-63
methods, II-63
role of, II-63
ContainerPeer, II-307
Interface in package java.awt.peer, II-307
contains
boolean contains(Object) in class
Hashtable, I-346
boolean contains(Object) in class Vector,
I-364
Hashtable, I-346
Vector, I-364
containsKey
boolean containsKey(Object) in class
Hashtable, I-346
Hashtable, I-346
ContentHandler
Class in package java.net, I-374
constructor, I-375
ContentHandler() in class
ContentHandler, I-375
methods, I-375
role of, I-374
ContentHandlerFactory, I-424
ContentHandlerFactory, I-424
Interface in package java.net, I-424
controlDown, II-85
coordinated universal time (UTC), I-128
copyArea, II-115
copyInto, I-365
copyValueOf, I-100
cos, I-61
static double cos(double) in class Math,
I-61
count, I-189, I-195, I-197, I-201, I-309
int count in class
BufferedInputStream, I-189
BufferedOutputStream, I-195
ByteArrayInputStream, I-197
ByteArrayOutputStream, I-201
StringBufferInputStream, I-309
countComponents, II-65
int countComponents() in class Container,
II-65
countItems

Choice, II-25
int countItems()
    in class Choice, II-25
    in class List, II-161
    in class Menu, II-179
    List, II-160
    Menu, II-179
countMenus, II-182
    int countMenus() in class MenuBar,
        II-182
countObserver, I-350
countStackFrames, I-139
    int countStackFrames() in class Thread,
        I-139
    Thread, I-139
countTokens, I-359
create
    Graphics, II-115
    Graphics create() in class Graphics, II-115
    Graphics create(int, int, int, int) in class
        Graphics, II-116
    SocketImpl, I-396
    void create(boolean) in class SocketImpl,
        I-396
createButton, II-223
createCanvas, II-223
createCheckbox, II-223
    CheckboxPeer createCheckbox
        (Checkbox) in class Toolkit, II-224
createCheckboxMenuItem, II-223
    CheckboxMenuItemPeer create
        CheckboxMenuItem(Checkbox-
        MenuItem) in class Toolkit, II-224
createChoice, II-223
    ChoicePeer createChoice(Choice) in class
        Toolkit, II-224
createContentHandler, I-425
createDialog, II-223
    DialogPeer createDialog(Dialog) in class
        Toolkit, II-224
createFileDialog, II-224
createFrame, II-224
    FramePeer createFrame(Frame) in class
        Toolkit, II-225
createImage
    Component, II-39

ComponentPeer, II-302
Image createImage(ImageProducer)
    in class Component, II-39
    in class Toolkit, II-225
    in interface ComponentPeer, II-302
    Toolkit, II-224
createLabel, II-224
    LabelPeer createLabel(Label) in class
        Toolkit, II-225
createList, II-224
    ListPeer createList(List) in class Toolkit,
        II-225
createMenu, II-225
createMenuBar, II-225
    MenuBarPeer createMenuBar(MenuBar)
        in class Toolkit, II-226
createMenuItem, II-225
    MenuItemPeer createMenuItem(Menu-
        Item) in class Toolkit, II-226
createPanel, II-225
    PanelPeer createPanel(Panel) in class
        Toolkit, II-226
createScrollbar, II-225
    ScrollbarPeer createScrollbar(Scrollbar)
        in class Toolkit, II-226
createSocketImpl, I-425
createTextArea, II-226
createTextField, II-226
    TextFieldPeer createTextField(TextField)
        in class Toolkit, II-227
createURLStreamHandler, I-426
createWindow, II-226
    WindowPeer createWindow(Window) in
        class Toolkit, II-227
CropImageFilter
    Class in package java.awt.image, II-241
    constructors, II-241
    CropImageFilter(int, int, int, int) in class
        CropImageFilter, II-242
    methods, II-241
    role of, II-241
CROSSHAIR_CURSOR, II-107
CTRL_MASK, II-83
currentClassLoader, I-94
currentThread, I-140
currentTimeMillis, I-128

cyan, II-28

D
daemon, I-135
darker, II-30
darkGray, II-28
DatagramPacket
    Class in package java.net, I-376
    constructors, I-376
    DatagramPacket(byte[], int) in class
        DatagramPacket, I-376
    DatagramPacket(byte[], int, InetAddress,
        int) in class DatagramPacket, I-377
    methods, I-377
    role of, I-376
DatagramSocket
    Class in package java.net, I-378
    constructors, I-378
    DatagramSocket() in class Datagram-
        Socket, I-378
    DatagramSocket(int) in class Datagram-
        Socket, I-379
    methods, I-379
    role of, I-378
DataInput
    Interface in package java.io, I-312
DataInputStream
    Class in package java.io, I-204
    constructors, I-205
    DataInputStream(InputStream) in class
        DataInputStream, I-205
    methods, I-206
    role of, I-204
DataOutput
    Interface in package java.io, I-318
DataOutputStream
    Class in package java.io, I-217
    constructors, I-218
    DataOutputStream(OutputStream) in
        class DataOutputStream, I-218
    Fields, I-217
    Methods, I-218
    role of, I-217
Date
    Class in package java.util, I-332
    constructors, I-334

Date() in class Date, I-334–I-336
    Date(long) in class Date, I-335
    Date(String) in class Date, I-336
    methods, I-336
    role of, I-332
DEFAULT_CURSOR, II-107
defaults, I-352
defineClass, I-21
delete, I-227
deleteObserver, I-350
deleteObservers, I-350
delItem
    List, II-160
    MenuPeer, II-317
    void delItem(int)
        in class List, II-161
        in interface MenuPeer, II-317
delItems
    ListPeer, II-313
    void delItems(int, int)
        in class List, II-161
        in interface ListPeer, II-313
deliverEvent
    Component, II-40
    Container, II-65
    void deliverEvent(Event)
        in class Component, II-40
        in class Container, II-65
delMenu, II-315
deselect
    List, II-161
    ListPeer, II-313
    void deselect(int)
        in class List, II-161
        in interface ListPeer, II-313
destroy
    Applet, II-327
    in class Process, I-75
    Process, I-75
    Thread, I-140
    ThreadGroup, I-149
    void destroy()
        in class Applet, II-327
        in class Thread, I-140
        in class ThreadGroup, I-149
Dialog

Class in package java.awt, II-71
    constructors, II-71
    Dialog(Frame, boolean) in class Dialog,
        II-72
    Dialog(Frame, String, boolean) in class
        Dialog, II-72
    methods, II-71
    role of, II-71
DialogPeer, II-308
Dictionary
    Class in package java.util, I-341
    constructors, I-342
    Dictionary() in class Dictionary, I-342
    methods, I-342
    role of, I-341
digit, I-7
Dimension
    Class in package java.awt, II-74
    Dimension() in class Dimension, II-74
    Dimension(Dimension) in class
        Dimension, II-75
    Dimension(int, int) in class Dimension,
        II-75
DirectColorModel
    Class in package java.awt.image, II-245
    constructors, II-245
    DirectColorModel(int, int, int, int) in class
        DirectColorModel, II-246
    methods, II-245
    role of, II-245
disable
    Compiler, I-24
    Component, II-40
    ComponentPeer, II-303
    MenuItem, II-186
    MenuItemPeer, II-316
    static void disable() in class Compiler,
        I-24
    void disable()
        in class Component, II-40
        in class MenuItem, II-186
        in interface ComponentPeer, II-303
        in interface MenuItemPeer, II-316
dispose, II-116
    ComponentPeer, II-303
    Frame, II-108

MenuComponentPeer, II-315
    void dispose()
        in class Frame, II-109
        in class Graphics, II-116
        in class Window, II-231
        in interface ComponentPeer, II-303
        in interface MenuComponentPeer,
            II-315
    Window, II-231
doInput, I-410
doOutput, I-410
Double
    Class in package java.lang, I-25
    constructors, I-26
    Double(double) in class Double, I-26
    Double(String) in class Double, I-27
    fields, I-26
    methods, I-27
    role of, I-25
doubleToLongBits, I-27
    static long doubleToLongBits(double) in
        class Double, I-27
doubleValue, I-27
    double doubleValue()
        in class Double, I-27
        in class Float, I-34
        in class Integer, I-40
        in class Long, I-49
        in class Number, I-67
    Float, I-34
    Integer, I-40
    Long, I-49
    Number, I-67
DOWN, II-81
draw3DRect, II-116
drawArc, II-117
drawBytes, II-117
drawChars, II-118
drawImage, II-118
    boolean drawImage(Image, int, int,
        ImageObserver) in class Graphics,
        II-119
    boolean drawImage(Image, int, int, int,
        int, Color, ImageObserver) in class
        Graphics, II-120

boolean drawImage(Image, int, int, int, int, ImageObserver) in class Graphics, II-121
drawLine, II-121
drawOval, II-122
drawPolygon, II-122
drawRect, II-123
drawRoundRect, II-123
drawString, II-123
   void drawString(String, int, int) in class Graphics, II-124
dumpStack, I-140

E
E, I-58
E_RESIZE_CURSOR, II-107
EAST, II-135
echoCharIsSet, II-217
   boolean echoCharIsSet() in class Text-Field, II-218
elementAt, I-365
elementCount, I-363
elementData, I-363
elements
   Dictionary, I-342
   Enumeration elements()
      in class Dictionary, I-342
      in class Hashtable, I-347
      in class Vector, I-365
   Hashtable, I-347
   Vector, I-365
empty, I-356
EmptyStackException, I-371
   Class in package java.util, I-371
   EmptyStackException() in class Empty-StackException, I-371
enable
   Compiler, I-24
   Component, II-40
   ComponentPeer, II-303
   MenuItem, II-186
   MenuItemPeer, II-316
   void enable
      in class Compiler, I-24
      in class Component, II-40
      in class MenuItem, II-186, II-187

      in interface ComponentPeer, II-303
      in interface MenuItemPeer, II-316
   void enable(boolean)
      in class Component, II-40
encode, I-421
END, II-81
endsWith, I-100
ensureCapacity
   StringBuffer, I-118
   Vector, I-365
   void ensureCapacity(int)
      in class StringBuffer, I-118
      in class Vector, I-365
enumerate
   int enumerate(Thread[]) in class Thread-Group, I-149
   int enumerate(Thread[], boolean) in class ThreadGroup, I-150
   int enumerate(ThreadGroup[]) in class ThreadGroup, I-150
   int enumerate(ThreadGroup[], boolean) in class ThreadGroup, I-150
   static int enumerate(Thread[]) in class Thread, I-140
   Thread, I-140
   ThreadGroup, I-149
Enumeration
   Interface in package java.util, I-369
EOFException, I-323
   Class in package java.io, I-312
   EOFException() in class EOFException, I-323
eolIsSignificant, I-305
   void eolIsSignificant(boolean) in class StreamTokenizer, I-305
equals
   BitSet, I-329
   Boolean, I-3
   boolean equals(Object)
      in class BitSet, I-329
      in class Boolean, I-3
      in class Character, I-7
      in class Color, II-31
      in class Date, I-336
      in class Double, I-28
      in class File, I-227

in class Float, I-34
in class Font, II-97
in class InetAddress, I-381
in class Integer, I-41
in class Long, I-50
in class Object, I-69
in class Point, II-190
in class Rectangle, II-197
in class String, I-101
in class URL, I-403
Character, I-7
Color, II-31
Date, I-336
Double, I-28
File, I-227
Float, I-34
InetAddress, I-381
Integer, I-41
Long, I-50
Object, I-69
Point, II-190
Rectangle, II-197
String, I-101
URL, I-403
equalsIgnoreCase, I-101
eradUnsighnedShort, I-316
err, I-126, I-233
static FileDescriptor err in class File-
Descriptor, I-233
static PrintStream err in class System,
I-126
ERROR, II-291
Error, I-175
AbstractMethodError, I-173
Class in package java.lang, I-175
ClassFormatError, I-174
Error, I-175
Error() in class Error, I-175
Error(String) in class Error, I-175
IllegalAccessError, I-175
ERRORED, II-170
Errors, java.awt
AWTError, II-236
Event
Class in package java.awt, II-76
constructors, II-76

Event(Object, int, Object) in class Event,
II-84
Event(Object, long, int, int, int, int, int) in
class Event, II-84
Event(Object, long, int, int, int, int, int,
Object) in class Event, II-85
fields, II-76
methods, II-76
role of, II-76
evt, II-78
Exception, I-162
Class in package java.lang, I-162
EOFException, I-323
Exception() in class Exception, I-162
Exception(String) in class Exception,
I-162
Exceptions
ArrayIndexOutOfBoundsException,
I-158
ArrayStoreException, I-159
ClassCastException, I-159
ClassNotFoundException, I-160
CloneNotSupportedException, I-161
IllegalAccessException, I-162
IllegalArgumentException, I-163
IllegalMonitorStateException, I-164
IllegalThreadStateException, I-165
IndexOutOfBoundsException, I-165
InstantiationException, I-166
InterruptedException, I-167
NegativeArraySizeException, I-167
NoSuchMethodException, I-168
NullPointerException, I-169
NumberFormatException, I-170
RuntimeException, I-170
SecurityException, I-171
Exceptions, java.awt
AWTException, II-235
Exceptions, java.io, I-188
Exceptions, java.lang
Exception, I-162
exec, I-77
Process exec(String) in class Runtime,
I-77
Process exec(String, String[]) in class
Runtime, I-77

Process exec(String[]) in class Runtime,
    I-78
Process exec(String[], String[]) in class
    Runtime, I-78
exists
    boolean exists() in class File, I-228
    File, I-228
exit
    Runtime, I-79
    static void exit(int) in class System, I-129
    System, I-129
    void exit(int) in class Runtime, I-79
exitValue
    int exitValue() in class Process, I-75
    Process, I-75
exp, I-61
    static double exp(double) in class Math,
        I-61

F
F1, II-82
F10, II-82
F11, II-82
F12, II-83
F2, II-82
F3, II-82
F4, II-82
F5, II-82
F6, II-82
F7, II-82
F8, II-82
F9, II-82
FALSE, I-2
fd, I-394
Fields, I-84
    Frame, II-107
Fields, jav.lang
    SecurityManager, I-84
Fields, java.awt, II-87
    Color, II-28
    FlowLayout, II-91
    Font, II-95
    FontMetrics, II-101
    GridBagConstraints, II-132
    GridBagLayout, II-140
    Image, II-148

Insets, II-151
Label, II-154
MediaTracker, II-170
Point, II-189
Polygon, II-191
Rectangle, II-195
Scrollbar, II-202
Fields, java.awt class
    Dimension, II-74
    Event, II-78
Fields, java.awt.image
    ColorModel, II-238
    ImageFilter, II-253
    RGBImageFilter, II-278
Fields, java.io
    BufferedInputStream, I-189, I-195
    ByteArrayInputStream, I-197
    ByteArrayOutputStream, I-200
    DataOutputStream, I-217
    File, I-225
    FileDescriptor, I-233
    FilterInputStream, I-244
    FilterOutputStream, I-250
    PushbackInputStream, I-278
    StreamTokenizer, I-303
    StringBufferInputStream, I-309
Fields, java.lang
    Boolean, I-2
    Character, I-6
    Double, I-26
    Float, I-33
    Integer, I-39
    Long, I-48
    Math, I-58
    System, I-126
    Thread, I-136
Fields, java.net
    SocketImpl, I-393
    URLConnection, I-410
Fields, java.util
    Properties, I-352
    Vector, I-363
File
    Class in package java.io, I-224
    constructors, I-225
    fields, I-225

File(File, String) in class File, I-225
File(String) in class File, I-226
File(String, String) in class File, I-226
methods, I-226
role of, I-224
file.separator, I-130
FileDescriptor
    Class in package java.io, I-233
    FileDescriptor() in class FileDescriptor, I-234
    role of, I-233
FileDialog
    Class in package java.awt, II-87
    constructors, II-87
    fields, II-87
    FileDialog(Frame, String) in class File-Dialog, II-88
    FileDialog(Frame, String, int) in class FileDialog, II-88
    methods, II-87
    role of, II-87
FileDialogPeer, II-308
    Interface in package java.awt.peer, II-308
FileInputStream
    Class in package java.io, I-234
    constructors, I-235
    FileInputStream(File) in class FileInput-Stream, I-235
    FileInputStream(FileDescriptor) in class FileInputStream, I-235
    FileInputStream(String) in class File-InputStream, I-236
    methods, I-236
    role of, I-234
FilenameFilter
    Interface in package java.io, I-322
FileNotFoundException
    Class in package java.io, I-324
    Exception, I-324
    FileNotFoundException() in class File-NotFoundException, I-324
    FileNotFoundException(String) in class FileNotFoundException, I-324
FileOutputStream
    Class in package java.io, I-239
    constructors, I-240

FileOutputStream(File) in class FileOut-putStream, I-240
FileOutputStream(FileDescriptor) in class FileOutputStream, I-240
FileOutputStream(String) in class File-OutputStream, I-241
methods, I-241
role of, I-239
fill, II-132
fill3DRect, II-124
fillArc, II-124
    void fillArc(int, int, int, int, int, int) in class Graphics, II-125
fillInStackTrace
    Throwable, I-155
    Throwable fillInStackTrace() in class Throwable, I-155
fillOval, II-125
fillPolygon, II-125
    void fillPolygon(int[], int[], int) in class Graphics, II-126
    void fillPolygon(Polygon) in class Graphics, II-126
fillRect, II-127
fillRoundRect, II-127
FilteredImageSource
    Class in package java.awt.image, II-249
    constructors, II-249
    FilteredImageSource(ImageProducer, ImageFilter) in class FilteredImage-Source, II-250
    methods, II-249
    role of, II-249
filterIndexColorModel, II-279
FilterInputStream
    Class in package java.io, I-243
    constructors, I-244
    fields, I-244
    FilterInputStream(InputStream) in class FilterInputStream, I-244
    methods, I-244
    role of, I-243
FilterOutputStream
    Class in package java.io, I-249
    constructors, I-250
    fields, I-250

FilterOutputStream(OutputStream) in
   class FilterOutputStream, I-250
   methods, I-250
   role of, I-249
filterRGB, II-279
filterRGBPixels, II-279
finalize, II-127
   DatagramSocket, I-379
   FileInputStream, I-237
   FileOutputStream, I-241
   Object, I-69
   void finalize()
      in class DatagramSocket, I-379
      in class FileInputStream, I-237
      in class FileOutputStream, I-241
      in class Graphics, II-127
      in class Object, I-69
findSystemClass, I-21
   in class ClassLoader, I-21
first, II-12
firstElement, I-365
Float
   Class in package java.lang, I-32
   constructors, I-33
   fields, I-33
   Float(double) in class Float, I-33
   Float(float) in class Float, I-34
   Float(String) in class Float, I-34
   methods, I-34
   role of, I-32
floatToIntBits, I-35
   static int floatToIntBits(float) in class
      Float, I-35
floatValue, I-35
   Double, I-28
   float floatValue()
      in class Double, I-28
      in class Float, I-35
      in class Integer, I-41
      in class Long, I-50
      in class Number, I-67
   Integer, I-41
   Long, I-50
   Number, I-67
floor, I-61
   in class Math, I-61

FlowLayout
   Class in package java.awt, II-90
   constructors, II-90
   fields, II-90
   FlowLayout() in class FlowLayout, II-92
   FlowLayout(int) in class FlowLayout,
      II-92
   FlowLayout(int, int, int) in class Flow-
      Layout, II-92
   methods, II-90
   role of, II-90
flush, I-196
   DataOutputStream, I-218
   FilterOutputStream, I-251
   Image, II-149
   OutputStream, I-263
   PrintStream, I-272
   void flush()
      in class BufferedOutputStream, I-196
      in class DataOutputStream, I-218
      in class FilterOutputStream, I-251
      in class Image, II-149
      in class OutputStream, I-263
      in class PrintStream, I-272
font, II-101
   Class in package java.awt, II-95
   constructors, II-95
   fields, II-95
   Font font in class FontMetrics, II-101
   Font(String, int, int) in class Font, II-96
   methods, II-95
   role of, II-95
FontMetrics
   Class in package java.awt, II-100
   constructors, II-99
   fields, II-99
   FontMetrics(Font) in class FontMetrics,
      II-101
   methods, II-99
   role of, II-99
forDigit, I-8
forName, I-16
Frame
   Class in package java.awt, II-106
   constructors, II-106
   fields, II-106

Frame() in class Frame, II-108
Frame(String) in class Frame, II-108
methods, II-106
role of, II-106
FRAMEBITS, II-291
    static int FRAMEBITS in interface
        ImageObserver, II-291
FramePeer, II-309
Freely Distributable Math Library (fdlibm),
    I-58
freeMemory, I-79

G
Garbage collector, I-79
    Runtime, I-79
    static void gc() in class System, I-129
    System, I-129
    void gc() in class Runtime, I-79
get
    BitSet, I-330
    boolean get(int) in class BitSet, I-330
    Dictionary, I-342
    Hashtable, I-347
    Object get(Object)
        in class Dictionary, I-342
        in class Hashtable, I-347
getAbsolutePath, I-228
getAddress
    byte getAddress()[] in class InetAddress,
        I-382
    DatagramPacket, I-377
    InetAddress, I-382
    InetAddress getAddress() in class
        DatagramPacket, I-377
getAlignment, II-155
getAllByName, I-382
getAllowUserInteraction, I-412
getAlpha
    ColorModel, II-239
    DirectColorModel, II-246
    IndexColorModel, II-260
    int getAlpha(int)
        in class ColorModel, II-239
        in class DirectColorModel, II-246
        in class IndexColorModel, II-260
getAlphaMask, II-246

getAlphas, II-260
    void getAlphas(byte[]) in class Index-
        ColorModel, II-260
getApplet, II-334
getAppletContext
    Applet, II-327
    AppletContext getAppletContext()
        in class Applet, II-327
        in interface AppletStub, II-337
    AppletStub, II-337
getAppletInfo
    Applet, II-327
    String getAppletInfo() in class Applet, II-
        327
getApplets, II-334
getAscent, II-103
getAudioClip
    Applet, II-328
    AppletContext, II-335
    AudioClip getAudioClip(URL)
        in class Applet, II-328
    AudioClip getAudioClip(URL, String)
        in class Applet, II-328
    in interface AppletContext, II-335
getBackground, II-40
getBlue
    Color, II-31
    ColorModel, II-239
    DirectColorModel, II-246
    IndexColorModel, II-260
    int getBlue() in class Color, II-31
    int getBlue(int)
        in class ColorModel, II-239
        in class DirectColorModel, II-247
        in class IndexColorModel, II-261
    void getBlues(byte[])
        in class IndexColorModel, II-261
getBlueMask, II-246
getBlues, II-261
getBoolean, I-4
getBoundingBox, II-192
getByName, I-382
getBytes, I-102
getChars
    String, I-102
    StringBuffer, I-118

void getChars(int, int, char[], int)
in class String, I-102
in class StringBuffer, I-118
getCheckboxGroup
Checkbox, II-17
CheckboxGroup getCheckboxGroup() in
class Checkbox, II-17
getClass, I-70
getClassContext, I-94
getClassLoader, I-17
getClipRect, II-127
Rectangle getClipRect() in class
Graphics, II-128
getCodeBase
Applet, II-328
AppletStub, II-337
URL getCodeBase()
in class Applet, II-328
in interface AppletStub, II-337
getColor
Color, II-31
Color getColor() in class Graphics, II-128
Graphics, II-127
static Color getColor(String) in class
Color, II-31
static Color getColor(String, Color) in
class Color, II-32
static Color getColor(String, int) in class
Color, II-32
getColorModel
ColorModel getColorModel()
in class Component, II-41
in class Toolkit, II-227
in interface ComponentPeer, II-303
Component, II-41
ComponentPeer, II-303
Toolkit, II-226
getColumns
int getColumns()
in class TextArea, II-209
in class TextField, II-218
TextArea, II-209
TextField, II-217
getComponent, II-65
getConstraints

GridBagConstraints getConstraints
(Component) in class GridBag-
Layout, II-140
GridBagLayout, II-140
getContent
ContentHandler, I-375
in class URLConnection, I-412
Object getContent()
in class URL, I-403
Object getContent(URLConnection)
in class ContentHandler, I-375
URL, I-403
URLConnection, I-412
getContentEncoding, I-413
getContentLength, I-413
getContentType, I-413
getCurrent, II-20
getCursorType, II-108
int getCursorType() in class Frame, II-109
getData, I-377
getDate
Date, I-337
int getDate() in class Date, I-337
long getDate() in class URLConnection,
I-413
URLConnection, I-413
getDay
Date, I-337
int getDay() in class Date, I-337
getDefaultAllowUserInteraction, I-414
getDefaultRequestProperty, I-414
getDefaultToolkit, II-227
getDefaultUseCaches, I-414
getDescent, II-103
getDirectory, II-88
getDocumentBase
Applet, II-328
AppletStub, II-337
URL getDocumentBase()
in class Applet, II-328
in interface AppletStub, II-337
getDoInput, I-414
getDoOutput, I-414
boolean getDoOutput() in class URL-
Connection, I-414
getEchoChar

char getEchoChar() in class TextField,
II-218
TextField, II-218
getErrorsAny, II-173
getErrorsID, II-173
getErrorStream
InputStream getErrorStream() in class
Process, I-75
Process, I-75
getExpiration, I-414
getFamily, II-97
getFD
FileDescriptor getFD()
in class FileInputStream, I-237
in class FileOutputStream, I-242
in class RandomAccessFile, I-284
FileInputStream, I-237
FileOutputStream, I-242
RandomAccessFile, I-284
getFile
FileDialog, II-89
String getFile()
in class FileDialog, II-89
in class URL, I-403
URL, I-403
getFileDescriptor, I-396
getFilenameFilter, II-89
getFilePointer
long getFilePointer() in class Random-
AccessFile, I-284
RandomAccessFile, I-284
getFilterInstance, II-253
getFont
Component, II-41
Font, II-97
Font getFont()
in class Component, II-41
in class FontMetrics, II-103
in class Graphics, II-128
in class MenuComponent, II-184
in interface MenuContainer, II-235
FontMetrics, II-103
Graphics, II-128
interface, II-235
MenuComponent, II-183

static Font getFont(String) in class Font,
II-97
static Font getFont(String, Font) in class
Font, II-97
getFontList, II-227
String getFontList()[] in class Toolkit,
II-228
getFontMetrics
Component, II-41
ComponentPeer, II-303
FontMetrics getFontMetrics()
in class Graphics, II-128
in class Toolkit, II-228
in interface ComponentPeer, II-303
FontMetrics getFontMetrics(Font) in
class Component, II-41
Graphics, II-128
Toolkit, II-227
getForeground
Color getForeground() in class
Component, II-42
Component, II-42
getGraphics
Component, II-42
ComponentPeer, II-303
Graphics getGraphics()
in class Component, II-42
in class Image, II-149
in interface ComponentPeer, II-303
Image, II-149
getGreen
Color, II-32
ColorModel, II-240
DirectColorModel, II-247
IndexColorModel, II-261
int getGreen(int)
in class ColorModel, II-240
in class DirectColorModel, II-247
in class IndexColorModel, II-261
int getGreen() in class Color, II-32
getGreenMask, II-247
getGreens, II-261
getHeaderField, I-415
String getHeaderField(int) in class URL-
Connection, I-415

String getHeaderField(String) in class
    URLConnection, I-415
getHeaderFieldDate, I-415
getHeaderFieldInt, I-416
getHeaderFieldKey, I-416
getHeight
    FontMetrics, II-103
    Image, II-149
    int getHeight() in class FontMetrics,
        II-104
    int getHeight(ImageObserver) in class
        Image, II-149
getHelpMenu, II-182
getHost, I-404
getHostName, I-383
getHours
    Date, I-337
    int getHours() in class Date, I-337
getHSBColor, II-33
getIconImage, II-108
    Image getIconImage() in class Frame,
        II-109
getIfModifiedSince, I-416
getImage
    Applet, II-329
    AppletContext, II-335
    Image getImage(String)
        in class Toolkit, II-228
    Image getImage(URL)
        in class Applet, II-329
        in class Toolkit, II-228
        in interface AppletContext, II-335
    Image getImage(URL, String) in class
        Applet, II-329
    Toolkit, II-227
getInCheck, I-95
getInetAddress
    in class Socket, I-391
    in class SocketImpl, I-396
    InetAddress getInetAddress() in class
        ServerSocket, I-386
    ServerSocket, I-386
    Socket, I-391
    SocketImpl, I-396
getInputStream
    InputStream getInputStream()

    in class Process, I-75
    in class Socket, I-391
    in class SocketImpl, I-396
    in class URLConnection, I-416
    Process, I-75
    Socket, I-391
    SocketImpl, I-396
    URLConnection, I-416
getInteger, I-41
    static Integer getInteger(String) in class
        Integer, I-41
    static Integer getInteger(String, int) in
        class Integer, I-42
    static Integer getInteger(String, Integer) in
        class Integer, I-42
getInterfaces, I-17
    Class getInterfaces()[] in class Class, I-17
getItem
    Choice, II-25
    List, II-161
    Menu, II-179
    MenuItem getItem(int)
        in class List, II-161
        in class Menu, II-179
    String getItem(int) in class Choice, II-25
getLabel
    Button, II-8
    Checkbox, II-17
    MenuItem, II-187
    String getLabel()
        in class Button, II-8
        in class Checkbox, II-17
        in class MenuItem, II-187
getLastModified, I-417
getLayout, II-66
getLeading, II-104
getLength, I-377
getLineIncrement, II-204
getLineNumber, I-258
getLocalHost, I-383
getLocalizedInputStream, I-80
getLocalizedOutputStream, I-80
getLocalPort
    DatagramSocket, I-379
    int getLocalPort()
        in class DatagramSocket, I-379

in class ServerSocket, I-386
in class Socket, I-391
in class SocketImpl, I-396
ServerSocket, I-386
Socket, I-391
SocketImpl, I-396
getLong
Long, I-50
static Long getLong(String) in class Long, I-50
static Long getLong(String, Long) in class Long, I-51, I-52
getMapSize
IndexColorModel, II-261
int getMapSize() in class IndexColor-Model, II-262
getMaxAdvance, II-104
getMaxAscent, II-104
getMaxDescent, II-104
int getMaxDescent() in class FontMetrics, II-105
getMaximum, II-204
getMaxPriority, I-151
getMenu, II-182
getMenuBar, II-108
MenuBar getMenuBar() in class Frame, II-109
getMessage, I-155
getMinimum, II-204
getMinutes
Date, I-337
int getMinutes() in class Date, I-337
getMode, II-89
getMonth
Date, I-337
int getMonth() in class Date, I-337
getName
Class, I-17
File, I-228
Font, II-98
String getName()
in class Class, I-17
in class File, I-228
in class Font, II-98
in class Thread, I-140
in class ThreadGroup, I-151

Thread, I-140
ThreadGroup, I-151
getOrientation, II-204
int getOrientation() in class Scrollbar, II-205
getOutputStream, I-417
OutputStream getOutputStream()
in class Process, I-75
in class Socket, I-391
in class SocketImpl, I-397
in class URLConnection, I-417
Process, I-75
Socket, I-391
SocketImpl, I-397
getParameter
Applet, II-330
AppletStub, II-337
String getParameter(String)
in class Applet, II-330
in interface AppletStub, II-337
getParameterInfo
Applet, II-330
String getParameterInfo()[][] in class Applet, II-330
getParent
Component, II-42
Container getParent() in class Component, II-42
File, I-228
MenuComponent, II-184
MenuContainer getParent() in class MenuComponent, II-184
String getParent() in class File, I-228
ThreadGroup, I-151
ThreadGroup getParent() in class Thread-Group, I-151
getPath, I-229
getPeer
Component, II-42
ComponentPeer getPeer() in class Component, II-42
MenuComponent, II-184
MenuComponentPeer getPeer() in class MenuComponent, II-184
getPixelSize
ColorModel, II-240

int getPixelSize() in class ColorModel,
II-240
getPort
DatagramPacket, I-377
int getPort()
in class DatagramPacket, I-377
in class Socket, I-392
in class SocketImpl, I-397
in class URL, I-404
Socket, I-392
SocketImpl, I-397
URL, I-404
getPriority, I-140
getProperties, I-129
getProperty
Image, II-150
Object getProperty(String, Image-
Observer) in class Image, II-150
Properties, I-352
static String getProperty(String) in class
System, I-130
static String getProperty(String, String) in
class System, I-131
String getProperty(String) in class
Properties, I-352
String getProperty(String, String) in class
Properties, I-353
System, I-130
getProtocol, I-404
getRed
Color, II-33
ColorModel, II-240
DirectColorModel, II-247
IndexColorModel, II-262
int getRed() in class Color, II-33
int getRed(int)
in class ColorModel, II-240
in class DirectColorModel, II-248
in class IndexColorModel, II-262
getRedMask, II-247
getReds, II-262
getRef, I-404
getRequestProperty, I-417
getRGB
Color, II-33
ColorModel, II-240

DirectColorModel, II-248
IndexColorModel, II-262
int getRGB() in class Color, II-33
int getRGB(int)
in class ColorModel, II-240
in class DirectColorModel, II-248
in class IndexColorModel, II-263
getRGBdefault, II-240
getRows
int getRows() in class List, II-162
int getRows() in class TextArea, II-210
List, II-161
TextArea, II-209
getRuntime, I-80
getScreenResolution, II-228
getScreenSize, II-228
getSeconds, I-337
getSecurityContext, I-95
getSecurityManager, I-131
getSelectedIndex
Choice, II-25
int getSelectedIndex()
in class Choice, II-25
in class List, II-162
List, II-161
getSelectedIndexes
int getSelectedIndexes()[]
in class List, II-162
in interface ListPeer, II-313
ListPeer, II-313
getSelectedItem
String getSelectedItem()
in class Choice, II-25
in class List, II-162
getSelectedItems
String getSelectedItems()[] in class List,
II-163
getSelectedText, II-213
getSelectionEnd, II-213
int getSelectionEnd()
in class TextComponent, II-213
in interface TextComponentPeer,
II-320
getSelectionStart, II-213
int getSelectionStart()
in class TextComponent, II-213

in interface TextComponentPeer,
II-320

getSize, II-98

getSource, II-150

getState
boolean getState()
in class Checkbox, II-18
in class CheckboxMenuItem, II-22
Checkbox, II-18
CheckboxMenuItem, II-22

getStyle, II-98

getSuperclass, I-17

getText
Label, II-155
String getText()
in class Label, II-155
in class TextComponent, II-214
in interface TextComponentPeer,
II-321
TextComponent, II-213

getThreadGroup, I-141

getTime, I-337

getTimezoneOffset, I-338

getTitle
Dialog, II-72
Frame, II-109
String getTitle()
in class Dialog, II-72
in class Frame, II-109

getToolkit
Component, II-42
ComponentPeer, II-303
Toolkit getToolkit()
in class Component, II-42
in class Window, II-231
in interface ComponentPeer, II-304
Window, II-231

getTransparentPixel, II-263

getURL, I-417

getUseCaches, I-417

getWarningString, II-231

getWidth, II-150

getWidths, II-104
int getWidths()[] in class FontMetrics,
II-105

getYear, I-338

GMT Greenwich Mean Time, I-333

GOT_FOCUS, II-79

gotFocus, II-43

grabPixels, II-273
boolean grabPixels() in class Pixel-
Grabber, II-273
boolean grabPixels(long) in class Pixel-
Grabber, II-274

Graphics
Class in package java.awt, II-112
constructors, II-112
Graphics() in class Graphics, II-114
methods, II-112
role of, II-112

gray, II-28

green, II-28

GridBagConstraints, II-135
Class in package java.awt, II-131
constructors, II-131
fields, II-131
GridBagConstraints() in class GridBag-
Constraints, II-136
methods, II-131
role of, II-131

GridBagLayout
Class in package java.awt, II-137
constructors, II-137
fields, II-137
GridBagLayout() in class GridBag-
Layout, II-140
methods, II-137
role of, II-137

gridheight, II-133

GridLayout
Class in package java.awt, II-143
constructors, II-143
GridLayout(int, int) in class GridLayout,
II-144
GridLayout(int, int, int, int) in class Grid-
Layout, II-144
methods, II-143
role of, II-143

gridwidth, II-133

gridx, II-133

gridy, II-133

grow, II-197

guessContentTypeFromName, I-418
guessContentTypeFromStream, I-418

H

HAND_CURSOR, II-107
handleEvent
    boolean handleEvent(Event) in class
        Component, II-43
    boolean handleEvent(Event) in interface
        ComponentPeer, II-304
    Component, II-43
    ComponentPeer, II-303
hasChanged, I-350
hashCode, I-35
    BitSet, I-330
    Boolean, I-4
    Character, I-8
    Color, II-33
    Date, I-338
    Double, I-28
    File, I-229
    Font, II-98
    InetAddress, I-383
    int hashCode()
        in class BitSet, I-330
        in class Boolean, I-4
        in class Character, I-8
        in class Color, II-33
        in class Date, I-338
        in class Double, I-28
        in class File, I-229
        in class Float, I-35
        in class Font, II-99
        in class InetAddress, I-383
        in class Integer, I-43
        in class Long, I-52
        in class Object, I-70
        in class Point, II-190
        in class Rectangle, II-198
        in class String, I-102
        in class URL, I-404
    Integer, I-43
    Long, I-52
    Object, I-70
    Point, II-190
    Rectangle, II-198

    String, I-102
    URL, I-404
Hashtable
    Class in package java.util, I-344
    constructors, I-345
    Hashtable() in class Hashtable, I-345
    Hashtable(int) in class Hashtable, I-345
    Hashtable(int, float) in class Hashtable,
        I-345
    methods, I-346
    role of, I-344
hasMoreElements
    boolean hasMoreElements() in class
        StringTokenizer, I-360
    boolean hasMoreElements() in interface
        Enumeration, I-370
    Enumeration, I-370
    StringTokenizer, I-360
hasMoreTokens
    boolean hasMoreTokens() in class String-
        Tokenizer, I-360
    StringTokenizer, I-360
HEIGHT, II-291
height
    Dimension, II-74
    int height in class Dimension, II-74
    int height in class Rectangle, II-195
    Rectangle, II-195
hide
    Component, II-44
    ComponentPeer, II-303
    void hide()
        in class Component, II-44
        in interface ComponentPeer, II-304
HOME, II-83
    static int HOME in class Event, II-83
HORIZONTAL, II-135
    Scrollbar, II-202
    static int HORIZONTAL
        in class GridBagConstraints, II-135
        in class Scrollbar, II-202
HSBtoRGB, II-34
    static int HSBtoRGB(float, float, float) in
        class Color, II-34

I

id, II-78

IEEEremainder, I-61

ifModifiedSince, I-411

II-§1.12, II-2

IllegalAccessError, I-175
  Class in package java.lang, I-175
  IllegalAccessError() in class Illegal-
    AccessError, I-176
  IllegalAccessError(String) in class
    IllegalAccessError, I-176

IllegalAccessException, I-162
  Class in package java.lang, I-162
  IllegalAccessException() in class
    IllegalAccessException, I-163
  IllegalAccessException(String) in class
    IllegalAccessException, I-163

IllegalArgumentException, I-163
  Class in package java.lang, I-163
  IllegalArgumentException() in class
    IllegalArgumentException, I-164
  IllegalArgumentException(String) in
    class IllegalArgumentException,
    I-164

IllegalMonitorStateException, I-164
  Class in package java.lang, I-164
  IllegalMonitorStateException() in class
    IllegalMonitorStateException,
    I-164
  IllegalMonitorStateException(String) in
    class IllegalMonitorState
    Exception, I-164

IllegalThreadStateException, I-165
  Class in package java.lang, I-165
  IllegalThreadStateException() in class Il-
    legalThreadStateException, I-165
  IllegalThreadStateException(String) in
    class IllegalThreadStateException,
    I-165

Image
  Class in package java.awt, II-148
  constructors, II-148
  fields, II-148
  Image() in class Image, II-148
  methods, II-148
  role of, II-148

IMAGEABORTED, II-285

imageComplete
  ImageFilter, II-254
  interface, II-286
  PixelGrabber, II-274
  void imageComplete(int)
    in class ImageFilter, II-254
    in class PixelGrabber, II-274
    in interface ImageConsumer, II-286

ImageConsumer, II-284

IMAGEERROR, II-285

ImageFilter
  Class in package java.awt.image, II-252
  constructors, II-252
  fields, II-252
  ImageFilter() in class ImageFilter, II-253
  methods, II-252
  role of, II-252

ImageObserver, II-290

ImageProducer, II-294

imageUpdate
  boolean imageUpdate(Image, int, int, int,
    int, int)
    in class Component, II-44
    in interface ImageObserver, II-293
  Component, II-44
  interface, II-293

in, I-126, I-233, I-244
  InputStream in in class FilterInputStream,
    I-244
  static FileDescriptor in in class File-
    Descriptor, I-233
  static InputStream in in class System,
    I-126

inCheck, I-84

inClass, I-95

inClassLoader, I-95

IncompatibleClassChangeError
  Class in package java.lang, I-176
  Error, I-176
  IncompatibleClassChangeError() in class
    IncompatibleClassChangeError,
    I-176
  IncompatibleClassChangeError(String) in
    class IncompatibleClassChange-
    Error, I-177

IndexColorModel
  Class in package java.awt.image, II-257
  constructors, II-257
  IndexColorModel(int, int, byte[], byte[],
      byte[]) in class IndexColorModel,
      II-258
  IndexColorModel(int, int, byte[], byte[],
      byte[], byte[]) in class IndexColor-
      Model, II-258
  IndexColorModel(int, int, byte[], byte[],
      byte[], int) in class IndexColor-
      Model, II-259
  IndexColorModel(int, int, byte[], int,
      boolean) in class IndexColorModel,
      II-259
  IndexColorModel(int, int, byte[], int,
      boolean, int) in class IndexColor-
      Model, II-260
  methods, II-257
  role of, II-257
indexOf
  int indexOf(int) in class String, I-103
  int indexOf(int, int) in class String, I-103
  int indexOf(Object) in class Vector, I-366
  int indexOf(Object, int) in class Vector,
      I-366
  int indexOf(String) in class String, I-103
  int indexOf(String, int) in class String,
      I-103
  String, I-103
  Vector, I-366
IndexOutOfBoundsException, I-165
  Class in package java.lang, I-165
  IndexOutOfBoundsException() in class
      IndexOutOfBoundsException,
      I-166
  IndexOutOfBoundsException(String) in
      class IndexOutOfBounds-
      Exception, I-166
InetAddress
  Class in package java.net, I-381
init
  Applet, II-331
  void init() in class Applet, II-331
InputStream
  Class in package java.io, I-253

constructors, I-253
InputStream() in class InputStream, I-253
methods, I-254
role of, I-253
insert, I-119
  StringBuffer insert(int, boolean) in class
      StringBuffer, I-119
  StringBuffer insert(int, char) in class
      StringBuffer, I-120
  StringBuffer insert(int, char[]) in class
      StringBuffer, I-120
  StringBuffer insert(int, double) in class
      StringBuffer, I-121
  StringBuffer insert(int, float) in class
      StringBuffer, I-121
  StringBuffer insert(int, int) in class
      StringBuffer, I-122
  StringBuffer insert(int, long) in class
      StringBuffer, I-122
  StringBuffer insert(int, Object) in class
      StringBuffer, I-123
  StringBuffer insert(int, String) in class
      StringBuffer, I-123
insertElementAt, I-366
  void insertElementAt(Object, int) in class
      Vector, I-366
insertImage
  TextArea, II-209
insertText
  void insertText(String, int) in class
      TextArea, II-210
  void insertText(String, int) in interface
      TextAreaPeer, II-319
insets
  Class in package java.awt, II-151
  constructors, II-151
  Container, II-66
  ContainerPeer, II-307
  fields, II-151
  GridBagConstraints, II-133
  Insets insets in class GridBagConstraints,
      II-133
  Insets insets() in class Container, II-66
  Insets insets() in interface ContainerPeer,
      II-307

insets(int, int, int, int) in class Insets,
II-152
methods, II-151
role of, II-151
inside
boolean inside(int, int)
in class Component, II-45
in class Polygon, II-193
in class Rectangle, II-198
Component, II-45
Polygon, II-193
Rectangle, II-198
InstantiationError
Class in package java.lang, I-177
Error, I-177
InstantiationError() in class
InstantiationError, I-177
InstantiationError(String) in class
InstantiationError, I-177
InstantiationException, I-166
Class in package java.lang, I-166
InstantiationException() in class
InstantiationException, I-166
InstantiationException(String) in class
InstantiationException, I-166
int read()
in class ByteArrayInputStream, I-199
in class FileInputStream, I-238
in class InputStream, I-255
in class PipedInputStream, I-266
in class RandomAccessFile, I-285
in class SequenceInputStream, I-301
intBitsToFloat, I-36
static float intBitsToFloat(int) in class
Float, I-36
Integer
Class in package java.lang, I-39
constructors, I-40
fields, I-39
Integer(int) in class Integer, I-40
Integer(String) in class Integer, I-40
methods, I-40
role of, I-39
Interface
Cloneable, I-156
DataInput, I-312

DataOutput, I-318
Enumeration, I-369
FilenameFilter, I-322
Observer, I-370
Runnable, I-156
Interfaces
java.applet.AppletContext, II-334
java.applet.AppletStub, II-336
java.applet.AudioClip, II-338
java.awt.image.ImageConsumer,
II-284
java.awt.image.ImageObserver,
II-290
java.awt.image.ImageProducer,
II-294
java.awt.LayoutManager, II-232
java.awt.MenuContainer, II-234
java.awt.peer.ButtonPeer, II-297
java.awt.peer.CanvasPeer, II-298
java.awt.peer.CheckboxMenu-
ItemPeer, II-298
java.awt.peer.CheckboxPeer,
II-299
java.awt.peer.ChoicePeer, II-300
java.awt.peer.ComponentPeer,
II-301
java.awt.peer.ContainerPeer,
II-307
java.awt.peer.DialogPeer, II-308
java.awt.peer.FileDialogPeer,
II-308
java.awt.peer.FramePeer, II-309
java.awt.peer.LabelPeer, II-311
java.awt.peer.ListPeer, II-312
java.awt.peer.MenuBarPeer, II-314
java.awt.peer.MenuComponent-
Peer, II-315
java.awt.peer.MenuItemPeer,
II-316
java.awt.peer.MenuPeer, II-316
java.awt.peer.PanelPeer, II-317
java.awt.peer.ScrollbarPeer,
II-317
java.awt.peer.TextAreaPeer,
II-319

`java.awt.peer.TextComponent-`
    `Peer`, II-320
`java.awt.peer.TextFieldPeer`,
    II-321
`java.awt.peer.WindowPeer`, II-323
`java.io.DataInput`, I-312
`java.io.DataOutput`, I-318
`java.io.FilenameFilter`, I-322
`java.lang.Cloneable`, I-156
`java.lang.Runnable`, I-156
`java.net.ContentHandlerFactory`,
    I-424
`java.net.SocketImplFactory`, I-425
`java.net.URLStreamHandler-`
    `Factory`, I-425
`java.util.Enumeration`, I-369
`java.util.Observer`, I-370
Interfaces, java.applet
    AppletContext, II-334
    AppletStub, II-336
    AudioClip, II-338
Interfaces, java.awt
    LayoutManager, II-232
    MenuContainer, II-234
Interfaces, java.awt.image
    ImageConsumer, II-284
    ImageObserver, II-290
    ImageProducer, II-294
Interfaces, java.awt.peer
    ButtonPeer, II-297
    CanvasPeer, II-298
    CheckboxMenuItemPeer, II-298
    CheckboxPeer, II-299
    ChoicePeer, II-300
    ComponentPeer, II-301
    ContainerPeer, II-307
    DialogPeer, II-308
    FileDialogPeer, II-308
    FramePeer, II-309
    LabelPeer, II-311
    ListPeer, II-312
    MenuBarPeer, II-314
    MenuComponentPeer, II-315
    MenuItemPeer, II-316
    MenuPeer, II-316
    PanelPeer, II-317

    ScrollbarPeer, II-317
    TextAreaPeer, II-319
intern, I-104
    String intern() in class String, I-104
InternalError
    Class in package java.lang, I-178
    Error, I-178
    InternalError() in class InternalError,
        I-178
    InternalError(String) in class Internal-
        Error, I-178
interrupt, I-141
    void interrupt() in class Thread, I-141
interrupted, I-141
    static boolean interrupted() in class
        Thread, I-141
InterruptedException, I-167
    Class in package java.lang, I-167
    InterruptedException() in class
        InterruptedException, I-167
    InterruptedException(String) in class
        InterruptedException, I-167
InterruptedIOException
    Class in package java.io, I-325
    Exception, I-325
    InterruptedIOException() in class
        InterruptedIOException, I-325
    InterruptedIOException(String) in class
        InterruptedIOException, I-326
intersection, II-198
intersects, II-198
intValue
    Double, I-29
    Float, I-36
    int intValue()
        in class Double, I-29
        in class Float, I-36
        in class Integer, I-43
        in class Long, I-52
        in class Number, I-67
    Integer, I-43
    Long, I-52
    Number, I-67
invalidate, II-46
IOException
    Class in package java.io, I-324

Exception, I-324
IOException() in class IOException,
 I-324
IOException(String) in class IO
 Exception, I-325
IP addresses, I-374
ipadx, II-134
ipady, II-134
isAbsolute, I-229
isActive
 Applet, II-331
 AppletStub, II-337
 boolean isActive()
  in class Applet, II-331
  in interface AppletStub, II-338
isAlive, I-141
isBold, II-98
 boolean isBold() in class Font, II-99
isConsumer
 boolean isConsumer(ImageConsumer)
  in class FilteredImageSource, II-250
  in class MemoryImageSource, II-268
  in interface ImageProducer, II-294
 FilteredImageSource, II-250
 interface, II-294
 MemoryImageSource, II-268
isDaemon
 boolean isDaemon()
  in class Thread, I-141
  in class ThreadGroup, I-151
 Thread, I-141
 ThreadGroup, I-151
isDefined, I-9
isDigit, I-9
isDirectory, I-229
isEditable
 boolean isEditable() in class Text-
  Component, II-214
 TextComponent, II-213
isEmpty
 boolean isEmpty()
  in class Dictionary, I-342
  in class Hashtable, I-347
  in class Rectangle, II-198
  in class Vector, I-366
 Dictionary, I-342

Hashtable, I-347
 Rectangle, II-198
 Vector, I-366
isEnabled
 boolean isEnabled()
  in class Component, II-46
  in class MenuItem, II-187
 Component, II-46
 MenuItem, II-187
isErrorAny, II-173
 boolean isErrorAny()
  in class MediaTracker, II-174
isErrorID, II-173
 boolean isErrorID(int)
  in class MediaTracker, II-174
isFile, I-230
isInfinite, I-29
 boolean isInfinite()
  in class Double, I-29
  in class Float, I-36
 Float, I-36
 static boolean isInfinite(double) in class
  Double, I-29
 static boolean isInfinite(float) in class
  Float, I-36
isInterface, I-18
isInterrupted, I-141
isItalic, II-98
 boolean isItalic() in class Font, II-99
isJavaLetter, I-10
isJavaLetterOrDigit, I-10
isLetter, I-11
isLetterOrDigit, I-11
isLowerCase, I-11
isModal, II-72
 boolean isModal() in class Dialog, II-73
isNaN
 boolean isNaN() in class Double, I-29
 Double, I-29
 Float, I-37
 static boolean isNaN(double)
  in class Double, I-29
  in class Float, I-37
 static boolean isNaN(float) in class Float,
  I-37
isPlain, II-98

boolean isPlain() in class Font, II-99
isResizable
    boolean isResizable()
        in class Dialog, II-73
        in class Frame, II-109
    Dialog, II-72
    Frame, II-109
isSelected, II-163
isShowing, II-46
isSpace, I-12
isTearOff, II-179
isTitleCase, I-12
isUpperCase, I-13
    static boolean isUpperCase(char) in class
        Character, I-13, I-14, I-15
isValid, II-46
isVisible, II-47
ITALIC, II-96

J

java.applet
    overview of, II-325
java.awt
    basic graphic concepts, II-1
    classes, II-3
    containers, II-2
    errors, II-2
    events, II-2
    exceptions, II-2
    graphical elements, II-1
    images, II-2
    layout managers, II-2
    menu bars, II-1
    overview of, II-1
    text input, II-1
    Toolkit, II-2
java.awt.image
    color, II-237
    image consumers, II-237
    image filters, II-237
    image observers, II-238
    image producers, II-237
    overview of, II-237
java.awt.peer
    overview of, II-297
java.class.patch, I-129

java.class.version, I-129
java.home, I-129
java.io
    communication pipes, I-188
    Exceptions, I-188
    files, I-188
    filtered streams, I-187
    input and output to strings, I-188
    input/output streams, I-187
    overview of, I-187
    stream concatenation, I-188
    Tokenization, I-188
java.lang
    basic classes, I-1
    classes, I-2
    compiler, I-1
    container classes, I-1
    errors, I-1
    exceptions, I-1
    system resources, I-1
    thread classes, I-1
java.net
    overview of, I-373
java.util
    bits, I-327
    enumeration, I-327
    generic data structures, I-327
    notification, I-327
    overview of, I-327
    random numbers, I-327
    string manipulation, I-327
    time and date, I-327
    user environment, I-327
java.vendor, I-129
java.vendor.url, I-129
java.version, I-129
join, I-141
    void join() in class Thread, I-141
    void join(long) in class Thread, I-142
    void join(long, int) in class Thread, I-142

K

key, II-78
KEY_ACTION, II-79
KEY_ACTION_RELEASE, II-79
KEY_PRESS, II-79

KEY_RELEASE, II-79
keyDown, II-47
keys
    Dictionary, I-342
    Enumeration keys()
        in class Dictionary, I-342
        in class Hashtable, I-347
    Hashtable, I-347
keyUp, II-48

L
Label
    Class in package java.awt, II-153
    constructors, II-153
    fields, II-153
    Label() in class Label, II-154
    Label(String) in class Label, II-154
    Label(String, int) in class Label, II-154
    methods, II-153
    role of, II-153
LabelPeer, II-311
last, II-12
lastElement, I-367
lastIndexOf
    int lastIndexOf(int) in class String, I-104
    int lastIndexOf(int, int) in class String,
        I-104
    int lastIndexOf(Object) in class Vector,
        I-367
    int lastIndexOf(Object, int) in class
        Vector, I-367
    int lastIndexOf(String) in class String,
        I-104
    int lastIndexOf(String, int) in class String,
        I-105
    String, I-104
    Vector, I-367
lastModified, I-230
layout
    Component, II-48
    Container, II-66
    void layout()
        in class Component, II-48
        in class Container, II-66
layoutContainer
    BorderLayout, II-5

CardLayout, II-12
FlowLayout, II-93
GridBagLayout, II-141
GridLayout, II-145
interface, II-233
void layoutContainer(Container)
    in class BorderLayout, II-5
    in class CardLayout, II-12
    in class FlowLayout, II-93
    in class GridBagLayout, II-141
    in class GridLayout, II-145
    in interface LayoutManager, II-233
LayoutManager, II-232
LEFT
    Event, II-83
    FlowLayout, II-91
    Label, II-154
    static int LEFT
        in class Event, II-83
        in class FlowLayout, II-92
        in class Label, II-154
left, II-151
length
    File, I-231
    int length()
        in class String, I-105
        in class StringBuffer, I-123
    long in class StringBuffer length()
        in class File, I-231
        in class RandomAccessFile, I-284
    RandomAccessFile, I-284
    StringBuffer, I-123
lightGray, II-28
line.separator, I-130
lineno, I-305
LineNumberInputStream
    Class in package java.io, I-257
    constructors, I-258
    LineNumberInputStream(InputStream)
        in class LineNumberInputStream,
        I-258
    methods, I-258
    role of, I-257
LinkageError
    Class in package java.lang, I-178
    Error, I-178

LinkageError() in class LinkageError,
    I-179
LinkageError(String) in class Linkage-
    Error, I-179
List
    Class in package java.awt, II-157
    constructors, II-157
    List() in class List, II-159
    List(int, boolean) in class List, II-159
    methods, II-157
    role of, II-157
list
    Component, II-48
    Container, II-67
    File, I-231
    in class Container, II-67
    in class Properties, I-353
    Properties, I-353
    String list()[] in class File, I-231
    String list(FilenameFilter)[] in class File,
        I-231
    ThreadGroup, I-151
    void list()
        in class Component, II-48
        in class ThreadGroup, I-151
    void list(PrintStream)
        in class Component, II-48
    void list(PrintStream, int) in class
        Component, II-49
LIST_DESELECT, II-79
LIST_SELECT, II-79
listen, I-397
ListPeer, II-312
LOAD, II-87
load
    Properties, I-353
    Runtime, I-81
    static void load(String) in class System,
        I-131
    System, I-131
    void load(InputStream) in class
        Properties, I-353
    void load(String) in class Runtime, I-81
LOAD_FILE, II-79
loadClass, I-22
LOADING, II-170

loadLibrary
    Runtime, I-81
    static void loadLibrary(String) in class
        System, I-132
    System, I-132
    void loadLibrary(String) in class
        Runtime, I-81
localport, I-394
locate, II-49
    Component locate(int, int)
        in class Component, II-49
        in class Container, II-67
    Container, II-67
location, II-49
log, I-62
Long
    Class in package java.lang, I-48
    constructors, I-49
    fields, I-48
    Long(long) in class Long, I-49
    Long(String) in class Long, I-49
    methods, I-49
    role of, I-48
longBitsToDouble, I-30
longValue
    Double, I-30
    Float, I-37
    IntegerparseInt
        Integer, I-43
    Long, I-53
    long longValue()
        in class Double, I-30
        in class Float, I-37
        in class Integer, I-43
        in class Long, I-53
        in class Number, I-67
    Number, I-67
lookupConstraints
    GridBagConstraints lookup-
        Constraints(Component) in class
        GridBagLayout, II-141
lookupConstraints, II-141
loop, II-338
LOST_FOCUS, II-80
lostFocus, II-50
lowerCaseMode, I-305

M

magenta, II-28

makeVisible
  List, II-163
  ListPeer, II-313
  void makeVisible(int)
      in class List, II-163
      in interface ListPeer, II-313

MalformedURLException, I-426
  Class in package java.net, I-426
  MalformedURLException, I-426
  MalformedURLException() in class
      MalformedURLException, I-426
  MalformedURLException(String) in
      class MalformedURLException,
      I-426

mark
  BufferedInputStream, I-191
  FilterInputStream, I-245
  InputStream, I-254
  LineNumberInputStream, I-259
  void mark(int)
      in class BufferedInputStream, I-191
      in class FilterInputStream, I-245
      in class InputStream, I-254
      in class LineNumberInputStream,
          I-259

marklimit, I-190

markpos, I-190

markSupported
  boolean markSupported()
      in class BufferedInputStream, I-192
      in class FilterInputStream, I-245
      in class InputStream, I-255
      in class PushbackInputStream, I-279
  BufferedInputStream, I-192
  FilterInputStream, I-245
  InputStream, I-255
  PushbackInputStream, I-279

Math
  Class in package java.lang, I-57
  fields, I-58
  methods, I-58
  role of, I-57

max, I-62

static double max(double, double) in class
    Math, I-62
static float max(float, float) in class Math,
    I-62
static int max(int, int) in class Math, I-62
static long max(long, long) in class Math,
    I-63

MAX_PRIORITY, I-136

MAX_RADIX
  Character, I-6

MAX_VALUE
  Character, I-6
  Double, I-26
  Float, I-33
  Integer, I-39
  Long, I-48
  static char MAX_VALUE in class
      Character, I-6
  static double MAX_VALUE in class
      Double, I-26
  static float MAX_VALUE in class Float,
      I-33
  static int MAX_VALUE in class Integer,
      I-39
  static long MAX_VALUE in class Long,
      I-48

MAXGRIDSIZE, II-140

MediaTracker
  Class in package java.awt, II-167
  constructors, II-167
  fields, II-167
  MediaTracker(Component) in class
      MediaTracker, II-170
  methods, II-167
  role of, II-167

MemoryImageSource
  Class in package java.awt.image, II-264
  constructors, II-264
  MemoryImageSource(int, int, Color-
      Model, byte[], int, int) in class
      MemoryImageSource, II-265–
      II-267
  MemoryImageSource(int, int, ColorMod-
      el, byte[], int, int, Hashtable) in
      class MemoryImageSource,
      II-265–II-267

MemoryImageSource(int, int, int[], int, int) in class MemoryImageSource, II-267

MemoryImageSource(int, int, int[], int, int, Hashtable) in class Memory-ImageSource, II-267

methods, II-264

role of, II-264

Menu

    Class in package java.awt, II-177

    constructors, II-177

    Menu(String) in class Menu, II-178

    Menu(String, boolean) in class Menu, II-178

    methods, II-177

    role of, II-177

MenuBar

    Class in package java.awt, II-180

    constructors, II-180

    MenuBar() in class MenuBar, II-181

    methods, II-180

    role of, II-180

MenuBarPeer, II-314

MenuComponent

    Class in package java.awt, II-183

    constructors, II-183

    MenuComponent() in class Menu-Component, II-183

    methods, II-183

    role of, II-183

MenuComponentPeer, II-315

MenuContainer, II-234

MenuItem

    Class in package java.awt, II-185

    constructors, II-185

    MenuItem(String) in class MenuItem, II-186

    methods, II-185

    role of, II-185

MenuItemPeer, II-316

MenuPeer, II-316

META_MASK, II-84

metaDown, II-85

Methods, II-5

    BorderLayout, II-4

    BufferedInputStream, I-196

Container, II-63

DataOutputStream, I-218

Dimension, II-75

GridBagConstraints, II-136

InetAddress, I-381

LineNumberInputStream, I-258

Methods, java.applet class

    Applet, II-327

Methods, java.awt class

    Button, II-8

    Canvas, II-10

    CardLayout, II-12

    Checkbox, II-17

    CheckboxGroup, II-20

    CheckboxMenuItem, II-22

    Choice, II-24

    Color, II-30

    Component, II-37

    Event, II-85

    FileDialog, II-88

    FlowLayout, II-93

    Font, II-97

    FontMetrics, II-101

    Frame, II-108

    Graphics, II-114

    GridBagLayout, II-140

    GridLayout, II-145

    Image, II-149

    Insets, II-152

    Label, II-155

    List, II-160

    MediaTracker, II-171

    Menu, II-178

    MenuBar, II-181

    MenuComponent, II-183

    MenuItem, II-186

    Panel, II-188

    Point, II-190

    Polygon, II-192

    Rectangle, II-196

    Scrollbar, II-204

    TextArea, II-209

    TextComponent, II-213

    TextField, II-217

    Toolkit, II-223

    Window, II-231

Methods, java.awt classs
    Dialog, II-72
Methods, java.awt.image class
    ColorModel, II-239
    CropImageFilter, II-242
    DirectColorModel, II-246
    FilteredImageSource, II-250
    ImageFilter, II-253
    IndexColorModel, II-260
    MemoryImageSource, II-268
    PixelGrabber, II-273
    RGBImageFilter, II-279
Methods, java.io
    BufferedInputStream, I-191, I-196
    ByteArrayInputStream, I-198
Methods, java.io class
    ByteArrayOutputStream, I-201
    DataInputStream, I-206
    File, I-226
    FileDescriptor, I-234
    FileInputStream, I-236
    FileOutputStream, I-241
    FilterInputStream, I-244
    FilterOutputStream, I-250
    InputStream, I-254
    OutputStream, I-262
    PipedInputStream, I-265
    PipedOutputStream, I-268
    PrintStream, I-271
    PushbackInputStream, I-278
    RandomAccessFile, I-283
    SequenceInputStream, I-300
    StreamTokenizer, I-305
    StringBufferInputStream, I-310
Methods, java.lang class
    Boolean, I-3
    Character, I-7
    Class, I-16
    ClassLoader, I-21
    Compiler, I-23
    Double, I-27
    Float, I-34
    Integer, I-40
    Long, I-49
    Math, I-58
    Number, I-67

    Object, I-68
    Process, I-75
    Runtime, I-77
    SecurityManager, I-85
    String, I-99
    StringBuffer, I-114
    System, I-127
    Thread, I-139
    ThreadGroup, I-148
    Throwable, I-155
Methods, java.net class
    ContentHandler, I-375
    DatagramPacket, I-377
    DatagramSocket, I-379
    ServerSocket, I-386
    Socket, I-391
    SocketImpl, I-394
    URL, I-403
    URLConnection, I-412
    URLEncoder, I-421
    URLStreamHandler, I-423
Methods, java.util class
    BitSet, I-329
    Date, I-336
    Dictionary, I-342
    Hashtable, I-346
    Observable, I-350
    Properties, I-352
    Random, I-355
    Stack, I-356
    StringTokenizer, I-359
    Vector, I-364
min, I-63
    static double min(double, double) in class
        Math, I-63
    static float min(float, float) in class Math,
        I-63
    static int min(int, int) in class Math, I-63
    static long min(long, long) in class Math,
        I-63
MIN_PRIORITY, I-136
MIN_RADIX
    Character, I-6
    static int MIN_RADIX in class Character,
        I-6
MIN_VALUE

Character, I-6
Double, I-26
Float, I-33
Integer, I-40
Long, I-49
static char MIN_VALUE in class
    Character, I-6
static double MIN_VALUE in class
    Double, I-26
static float MIN_VALUE in class Float,
    I-33
static int MIN_VALUE in class Integer,
    I-40
static long MIN_VALUE in class Long,
    I-49
minimumLayoutSize
    BorderLayout, II-6
    CardLayout, II-13
    Dimension minimumLayoutSize
        (Container)
        in class BorderLayout, II-6
        in class CardLayout, II-13
        in class FlowLayout, II-93
        in class GridBagLayout, II-141
        in class GridLayout, II-146
        in interface LayoutManager, II-233
    FlowLayout, II-93
    GridBagLayout, II-141
    GridLayout, II-146
    interface, II-233
minimumSize
    Component, II-50
    ComponentPeer, II-303
    Container, II-68
    Dimension minimumSize()
        in class Component, II-50
        in class Container, II-68
        in class List, II-164
        in class TextArea, II-210
        in class TextField, II-218, II-219
        in interface ComponentPeer, II-304
    Dimension minimumSize(int)
        in class List, II-164
        in interface ListPeer, II-313
        in interface TextFieldPeer, II-322
    Dimension minimumSize(int, int)

    in class TextArea, II-211
        in interface TextAreaPeer, II-319
    ListPeer, II-313
    TextArea, II-209
    TextField, II-218
minimumSize4
    List, II-163
MINSIZE, II-140
mkdir, I-232
mkdirs, I-232
modifiers, II-78
MOUSE_DOWN, II-80
MOUSE_DRAG, II-80
MOUSE_ENTER, II-80
MOUSE_EXIT, II-80
MOUSE_MOVE, II-80
mouseDown, II-51
mouseDrag, II-51
mouseEnter, II-52
mouseExit, II-52
mouseMove, II-53
mouseUp, II-53
move
    Component, II-54
    Point, II-190
    Rectangle, II-198
    void move(int, int)
        in class Component, II-54
        in class Point, II-190
        in class Rectangle, II-199
MOVE_CURSOR, II-107

N
N_RESIZE_CURSOR, II-107
name
    String name in class Font, II-95
NaN
    Double, I-26
    Float, I-33
    static double NaN in class Double, I-26
    static float NaN in class Float, I-33
NE_RESIZE_CURSOR, II-107
NEGATIVE_INFINITY
    Double, I-26
    Float, I-33

static double NEGATIVE_INFINITY in class Double, I-26

static float NEGATIVE_INFINITY in class Float, I-33

NegativeArraySizeException, I-167

    Class in package java.lang, I-167

    NegativeArraySizeException() in class NegativeArraySizeException, I-168

    NegativeArraySizeException(String) in class NegativeArraySizeException, I-168

netlib, I-58

newInstance, I-18

newmodel, II-278

next, II-13

nextDouble, I-355

nextElement

    Enumeration, I-370

    Object nextElement()

        in class StringTokenizer, I-360

        in interface Enumeration, I-370

    StringTokenizer, I-360

nextFloat, I-355

nextFocus

    Component, II-54

    ComponentPeer, II-304

    void nextFocus()

        in class Component, II-54

        in interface ComponentPeer, II-304

nextGaussian, I-355

nextInt, I-355

nextLong, I-355

nextToken

    int nextToken() in class StreamTokenizer, I-306

    StreamTokenizer, I-306

    String nextToken() in class StringTokenizer, I-360

    String nextToken(String) in class StringTokenizer, I-361

    StringTokenizer, I-360

NoClassDefFoundError

    Class in package java.lang, I-179

    Error, I-179

NoClassDefFoundError() in class NoClassDefFoundError, I-179

NoClassDefFoundError(String) in class NoClassDefFoundError, I-179

NONE, II-136

NORM_PRIORITY, I-136

NORTH, II-135

NORTHEAST, II-135

NORTHWEST, II-135

NoSuchElementException, I-371

    Class in package java.util, I-371

    NoSuchElementException() in class NoSuchElementException, I-372

    NoSuchElementException(String) in class NoSuchElementException, I-372

NoSuchFieldError

    Class in package java.lang, I-180

    Error, I-180

    NoSuchFieldError() in class NoSuchFieldError, I-180

    NoSuchFieldError(String) in class NoSuchFieldError, I-180

NoSuchMethodError

    Class in package java.lang, I-180

    Error, I-180

    NoSuchMethodError() in class NoSuchMethodError, I-181

    NoSuchMethodError(String) in class NoSuchMethodError, I-181

NoSuchMethodException, I-168

    Class in package java.lang, I-168

    NoSuchMethodException() in class NoSuchMethodException, I-168

    NoSuchMethodException(String) in class NoSuchMethodException, I-168

notify

    void notify() in class Object, I-70

notifyAll, I-71

notifyObservers, I-351

    void notifyObservers() in class Observable, I-351

    void notifyObservers(Object) in class Observable, I-351

notufy, I-70

npoints, II-191

NullPointerException, I-169
    Class in package java.lang, I-169
    NullPointerException() in class
        NullPointerException, I-169
    NullPointerException(String) in class
        NullPointerException, I-169
Number
    Class in package java.lang, I-66
    methods, I-67
    role of, I-66
NumberFormatException, I-170
    Class in package java.lang, I-170
    NumberFormatException() in class
        NumberFormatException, I-170
    NumberFormatException(String) in class
        NumberFormatException, I-170
nval, I-303
    double nval in class StreamTokenizer,
        I-303
NW_RESIZE_CURSOR, II-107
    static int NW_RESIZE_CURSOR in class
        Frame, II-107

O

Object
    Class in package java.lang, I-67
    constructors, I-68
    methods, I-68
    Object() in class Object, I-68
    role of, I-68
Observable
    Class in package java.util, I-349
    constructors, I-350
    methods, I-350
    Observable() in class Observable, I-350
    role of, I-349
Observer
    Interface in package java.util, I-370
openConnection
    URL, I-404
    URLConnection openConnection() in
        class URL, I-404
    URLConnection openConnection(URL)
        in class URLStreamHandler, I-423
    URLStreamHandler, I-423
openStream, I-405

or, I-330
orange, II-29
ordinaryChar, I-306
ordinaryChars, I-306
origmodel, II-278
os.arch, I-130
os.name, I-129
os.version, I-130
out, I-126, I-233, I-250
    OutputStream out in class FilterOutput-
        Stream, I-250
    static FileDescriptor out in class File-
        Descriptor, I-233
    static PrintStream out in class System,
        I-126
OutOfMemoryError
    Class in package java.lang, I-181
    Error, I-181
    OutOfMemoryError() in class Out-
        OfMemoryError, I-181
    OutOfMemoryError(String) in class
        OutOfMemoryError, I-181
OutputStream
    Class in package java.io, I-262
    constructors, I-262
    methods, I-262
    OutputStream() in class OutputStream,
        I-262
    role of, I-262

P

pack
    void pack() in class Window, II-232
paint
    Canvas, II-10
    Component, II-54
    ComponentPeer, II-304
    void paint(Graphics)
        in class Canvas, II-10
        in class Component, II-54
        in interface ComponentPeer, II-305
paintAll, II-55
paintComponents
    Container, II-68
    void paintComponents(Graphics) in class
        Container, II-68

Panel
  Class in package java.awt, II-188
  Panel() in class Panel, II-188
PanelPeer, II-317
paramString
  Button, II-9
  Checkbox, II-18
  CheckboxMenuItem, II-22
  Choice, II-25
  Component, II-55
  Container, II-68
  Dialog, II-72
  Event, II-86
  FileDialog, II-89
  Frame, II-109
  Label, II-155
  List, II-164
  MenuComponent, II-184
  MenuItem, II-187
  String paramString()
    in class Button, II-9
    in class Checkbox, II-18
    in class CheckboxMenuItem, II-22
    in class Choice, II-25
    in class Component, II-55
    in class Container, II-68
    in class Dialog, II-73
    in class Event, II-86
    in class FileDialog, II-89
    in class Frame, II-110
    in class Label, II-155
    in class List, II-164
    in class MenuComponent, II-184
    in class MenuItem, II-187
    in class Scrollbar, II-205
    in class TextArea, II-211
    in class TextComponent, II-214
    in class TextField, II-219
  TextArea, II-211
  TextComponent, II-213
  TextField, II-219
parentOf, I-151
parse
  Date, I-338
  static long parse(String) in class Date,
    I-338

parseInt
  static int parseInt(String) in class Integer,
    I-43
  static int parseInt(String, int) in class
    Integer, I-44
parseLong, I-53
  static long parseLong(String) in class
    Long, I-53
  static long parseLong(String, int) in class
    Long, I-53
parseNumbers, I-306
parseURL, I-423
path.separator, I-130
pathSeparator
  File, I-225
  static String pathSeparator in class File,
    I-225
pathSeparatorChar
  File, I-225
  static char pathSeparatorChar in class
    File, I-225
peek, I-357
PGDN, II-83
PGUP, II-83
PI, I-58
pink, II-29
PipedInputStream
  Class in package java.io, I-264
  constructors, I-264
  methods, I-265
  PipedInputStream() in class PipedInput-
    Stream, I-264
  PipedInputStream(PipedOutputStream) in
    class PipedInputStream, I-265
  role of, I-264
PipedOutputStream
  Class in package java.io, I-267
  constructor, I-267
  methods, I-268
  PipedOutputStream() in class Piped-
    OutputStream, I-267
  PipedOutputStream(PipedInputStream) in
    class PipedOutputStream, I-267
  role of, I-267
pixel_bits, II-238
PixelGrabber

Class in package java.awt.image, II-270
 constructors, II-270
 methods, II-270
 PixelGrabber(Image, int, int, int, int, int[],
  int, int) in class PixelGrabber,
  II-272
 PixelGrabber(ImageProducer, int, int, int,
  int, int[], int, int) in class Pixel-
  Grabber, II-273
 role of, II-270
PLAIN, II-96
 static int PLAIN in class Font, II-96
play
 Applet, II-331
 AudioClip, II-338
 void play() in interface AudioClip, II-339
 void play(URL) in class Applet, II-331
 void play(URL, String) in class Applet, II-
  331
Point
 Class in package java.awt, II-189
 constructors, II-189
 fields, II-189
 methods, II-189
 Point(int, int) in class Point, II-189
 role of, II-189
Polygon
 Class in package java.awt, II-191
 constructors, II-191
 fields, II-191
 methods, II-191
 Polygon() in class Polygon, II-192
 Polygon(int[], int[], int) in class Polygon,
  II-192
 role of, II-191
pop, I-357
 Object pop() in class Stack, I-357
port, I-394
pos, I-190, I-197, I-310
 int pos
  in class BufferedInputStream, I-190
  in class ByteArrayInputStream, I-197
  in class StringBufferInputStream,
   I-310
POSITIVE_INFINITY
 Double, I-26

Float, I-33
 static double POSITIVE_INFINITY in
  class Double, I-26
 static float POSITIVE_INFINITY in class
  Float, I-33
postEvent
 boolean postEvent(Event)
  in class Component, II-55
  in class MenuComponent, II-184
  in interface MenuContainer, II-235
 Component, II-55
 interface, II-235
 MenuComponent, II-184
pow, I-64
preferredLayoutSize, II-14
 BorderLayout, II-6
 Dimension preferredLayoutSize
  (Container)
  in class BorderLayout, II-6
  in class CardLayout, II-14
  in class FlowLayout, II-94
  in class GridBagLayout, II-142
  in class GridLayout, II-147
  in interface LayoutManager, II-234
 FlowLayout, II-94
 GridBagLayout, II-142
 GridLayout, II-147
 interface, II-233
preferredSize
 Component, II-56
 ComponentPeer, II-304
 Container, II-69
 Dimension preferredSize()
  in class Component, II-56
  in class Container, II-69
  in class List, II-165
  in class TextArea, II-211
  in class TextField, II-219, II-220
  in interface ComponentPeer, II-305
  in interface ListPeer, II-314
  in interface TextAreaPeer, II-319
  in interface TextFieldPeer, II-322
 Dimension preferredSize(int) in class
  List, II-165
 Dimension preferredSize(int, int)
  in class TextArea, II-212

List, II-164
ListPeer, II-314
TextArea, II-211
TextField, II-219
prepareImage
boolean prepareImage(Image, Image-
Observer) in class Component,
II-56
boolean prepareImage(Image, int, int,
ImageObserver)
in class Component, II-57
in class Toolkit, II-229
in interface ComponentPeer, II-305
Component, II-56
ComponentPeer, II-304
Toolkit, II-228
previous, II-14
print
Component, II-57
ComponentPeer, II-306
PrintStream, I-272
void print(boolean) in class PrintStream,
I-272
void print(char) in class PrintStream,
I-272
void print(char[]) in class PrintStream,
I-273
void print(double) in class PrintStream,
I-273
void print(float) in class PrintStream,
I-273
void print(Graphics)
in class Component, II-57
in interface ComponentPeer, II-306
void print(int) in class PrintStream, I-273
void print(long) in class PrintStream,
I-274
void print(Object) in class PrintStream,
I-274
void print(String) in class PrintStream,
I-274
printAll, II-57
printComponents, II-69
printIn
PrintStream, I-274
println

void println() in class PrintStream, I-274
void println(boolean) in class Print-
Stream, I-274
void println(char) in class PrintStream,
I-275
void println(char[]) in class PrintStream,
I-275
void println(double) in class PrintStream,
I-275
void println(float) in class PrintStream,
I-275
void println(int) in class PrintStream,
I-275
void println(long) in class PrintStream,
I-276
void println(Object) in class PrintStream,
I-276
void println(String) in class PrintStream,
I-276
printStackTrace, I-156
void printStackTrace() in class
Throwable, I-156
void printStackTrace(PrintStream) in
class Throwable, I-156
PrintStream
Class in package java.io, I-270
constructors, I-271
methods, I-271
PrintStream(OutputStream) in class Print-
Stream, I-271
PrintStream(OutputStream, boolean) in
class PrintStream, I-271
role of, I-270
Process
Class in package java.lang, I-74
constructors, I-74
methods, I-75
Process() in class Process, I-74
role of, I-74
PROPERTIES, II-292
Properties
Class in package java.util, I-351
constructors, I-352
fields, I-352
methods, I-352
Properties() in class Properties, I-352

Properties(Properties) in class Properties, I-352
    role of, I-351
propertyNames, I-353
ProtocolException, I-427
    Class in package java.net, I-427
    ProtocolException, I-427
    ProtocolException() in class Protocol-
        Exception, I-427
    ProtocolException(String) in class
        ProtocolException, I-427
push, I-357
pushBack, I-278, I-307
    int pushBack in class PushbackInput-
        Stream, I-278
    void pushBack() in class Stream-
        Tokenizer, I-307
PushbackInputStream
    Class in package java.io, I-277
    constructors, I-278
    fields, I-278
    methods, I-278
    PushbackInputStream(InputStream) in
        class PushbackInputStream, I-278
    role of, I-277
put
    Dictionary, I-343
    Hashtable, I-348
    Object put(Object, Object)
        in class Dictionary, I-343
        in class Hashtable, I-348

Q
quoteChar, I-307

R
Random
    Class in package java.util, I-354
    constructors, I-354
    methods, I-355
    Random() in class Random, I-354
    Random(long) in class Random, I-355
    role of, I-354
random, I-64
    static double random() in class Math, I-64
RandomAccessFile

Class in package java.io, I-281
    constructors, I-282
    methods, I-283
    RandomAccessFile(File, String) in class
        RandomAccessFile, I-282
    RandomAccessFile(String, String) in
        class RandomAccessFile, I-283
    role of, I-281
RANDOMPIXELORDER, II-285
    static int RANDOMPIXELORDER in
        interface ImageConsumer, II-285
read
    BufferedInputStream, I-192
    ByteArrayInputStream, I-199
    DataInputStream, I-206
    FileInputStream, I-237
    FilterInputStream, I-246
    InputStream, I-255
    int read()
        in class BufferedInputStream, I-192
        in class ByteArrayInputStream, I-199
        in class FileInputStream, I-238
        in class InputStream, I-255
        in class PipedInputStream, I-266
        in class RandomAccessFile, I-285
        in class SequenceInputStream, I-300
    int read(byte[])
        in class DataInputStream, I-206
    int read(byte[], int, int)
        in class BufferedInputStream, I-193
        in class DataInputStream, I-207
        in class FileInputStream, I-237
        in class FilterInputStream, I-246,
            I-247, I-248
        in class InputStream, I-256
        in class LineNumberInputStream,
            I-259, I-260
        in class PushbackInputStream, I-279,
            I-280
        in class RandomAccessFile, I-284
        in class StringBufferInputStream,
            I-310, I-311
    LineNumberInputStream, I-259
    PipedInputStream, I-266
    PushbackInputStream, I-279
    RandomAccessFile, I-284

SequenceInputStream, I-300
StringBufferInputStream, I-310
readBoolean
    boolean readBoolean()
        in class DataInputStream, I-207
        in class RandomAccessFile, I-286
        in interface DataInput, I-312
    DataInput, I-312
    DataInputStream, I-207
    RandomAccessFile, I-286
readByte
    byte readByte()
        in class DataInputStream, I-208
        in class RandomAccessFile, I-286
        in interface DataInput, I-313
    DataInput, I-313
    DataInputStream, I-208
    RandomAccessFile, I-286
readChar
    char readChar()
        in class DataInputStream, I-208
        in class RandomAccessFile, I-287
        in interface DataInput, I-313
    DataInput, I-313
    DataInputStream, I-208
    RandomAccessFile, I-287
readDouble
    DataInput, I-313
    DataInputStream, I-209
    double readDouble()
        in class DataInputStream, I-209
        in class RandomAccessFile, I-287
        in interface DataInput, I-313
    RandomAccessFile, I-287
readFloat
    DataInput, I-314
    DataInputStream, I-209
    float readFloat()
        in class DataInputStream, I-209
        in class RandomAccessFile, I-288
        in interface DataInput, I-314
    RandomAccessFile, I-288
readFully
    DataInput, I-314
    DataInputStream, I-210
    in interface DataInput, I-314

RandomAccessFile, I-288
void readFully(byte[])
    in class DataInputStream, I-210
    in class RandomAccessFile, I-288,
        I-289
    in interface DataInput, I-314
void readFully(byte[], int, int)
    in class DataInputStream, I-210
readInt
    DataInput, I-315
    DataInputStream, I-211
    int readInt()
        in class DataInputStream, I-211
        in class RandomAccessFile, I-289
        in interface DataInput, I-315
    RandomAccessFile, I-289
readLine
    DataInput, I-315
    DataInputStream, I-211
    RandomAccessFile, I-290
    String readLine()
        in class DataInputStream, I-211
        in class RandomAccessFile, I-290
        in interface DataInput, I-315
readLong
    DataInput, I-315
    DataInputStream, I-212
    long readLong()
        in class DataInputStream, I-212
        in class RandomAccessFile, I-290
        in interface DataInput, I-315
    RandomAccessFile, I-290
readShort
    DataInput, I-316
    DataInputStream, I-212
    RandomAccessFile, I-291
    short readShort()
        in class DataInputStream, I-212
        in class RandomAccessFile, I-291
        in interface DataInput, I-316
readUnsignedByte, I-316
    DataInputStream, I-213
    int readUnsignedByte()
        in class DataInputStream, I-213
        in class RandomAccessFile, I-291
        in interface DataInput, I-316

RandomAccessFile, I-291
readUnsignedShort
    DataInputStream, I-213
    int readUnsignedShort()
        in class DataInputStream, I-213
        in class RandomAccessFile, I-292
        in interface DataInput, I-316
    RandomAccessFile, I-292
ReadUTF, I-317
readUTF
    RandomAccessFile, I-293
    static String readUTF(DataInput)
        in class DataInputStream, I-215
    String readUTF()
        in class DataInputStream, I-214
        in class RandomAccessFile, I-293
        in interface DataInput, I-317
readUTPF
    DataInputStream, I-214
receive, I-380
Rectangle
    Class in package java.awt, II-194
    constructors, II-194
    fields, II-194
    methods, II-194
    Rectangle() in class Rectangle, II-195
    Rectangle(Dimension) in class Rectangle,
        II-195
    Rectangle(int, int) in class Rectangle,
        II-195
    Rectangle(int, int, int, int) in class
        Rectangle, II-196
    Rectangle(Point) in class Rectangle,
        II-196
    Rectangle(Point, Dimension) in class
        Rectangle, II-196
    role of, II-194
red, II-29
    static Color red in class Color, II-29
regionMatches
    boolean regionMatches(boolean, int,
        String, int, int) in class String, I-105
    boolean regionMatches(int, String, int,
        int) in class String, I-106
rehash, I-348
RELATIVE, II-136

REMAINDER, II-136
remove
    Container, II-69
    Dictionary, I-343
    Frame, II-109
    Hashtable, I-348
    in class MenuBar, II-182
    interface, II-235
    Menu, II-179
    MenuBar, II-182
    Object remove(Object)
        in class Dictionary, I-343
        in class Hashtable, I-348
        in class Menu, II-180
        in class MenuBar, II-182
        in interface MenuContainer, II-235
    void remove(Component)
        in class Container, II-69
    void remove(int)
        in class Menu, II-180
    void remove(MenuComponent)
        in class Frame, II-110
remove Consumer
    MemoryImageSource, II-268
removeAll, II-70
removeAllElements, I-367
removeConsumer
    FilteredImageSource, II-250
    interface, II-295
    void removeConsumer(ImageConsumer)
        in class FilteredImageSource, II-251
        in class MemoryImageSource, II-268
removeElement, I-368
removeElementAt, I-368
removeLayoutComponent
    BorderLayout, II-6
    CardLayout, II-14
    FlowLayout, II-94
    GridBagLayout, II-142
    GridLayout, II-147
    interface, II-234
    void removeLayoutComponent
        (Component)
        in class BorderLayout, II-6
        in class CardLayout, II-14
        in class FlowLayout, II-94

in class GridBagLayout, II-142
in class GridLayout, II-147
in interface LayoutManager, II-234
removeNotify
  Component, II-58
  Container, II-70
  List, II-165
  Menu, II-180
  MenuComponent, II-184
  TextComponent, II-214
  void removeNotify()
    in class Component, II-58
    in class Container, II-70
    in class List, II-165
    in class Menu, II-180
    in class MenuBar, II-183
    in class MenuComponent, II-185
    in class TextComponent, II-214
renameTo, I-232
repaint
  Component, II-58
  ComponentPeer, II-306
  void repaint() in class Component, II-58
  void repaint(int, int, int, int) in class
    Component, II-58
  void repaint(long)
    in class Component, II-58
    in interface ComponentPeer, II-306
  void repaint(long, int, int, int, int) in class
    Component, II-59
replace, I-106
replaceItem, II-165
replaceText, II-212
  void replaceText(String, int, int) in class
    TextArea, II-212
  void replaceText(String, int, int)
    in interface TextAreaPeer, II-320
requestFocus
  Component, II-59
  ComponentPeer, II-306
  void requestFocus()
    in class Component, II-59
    in interface ComponentPeer, II-306
requestTopDownLeftRightResend, II-268
  FilteredImageSource, II-250
  interface, II-295

void requestTopDownLeftRight-
    Resend(ImageConsumer)
  in class FilteredImageSource, II-251
  in class MemoryImageSource, II-269
  in interface ImageProducer, II-295
resendTopDownLeftRight, II-254
reset
  BufferedInputStream, I-193
  ByteArrayInputStream, I-199
  ByteArrayOutputStream, I-201
  FilterInputStream, I-248
  InputStream, I-256
  LineNumberInputStream, I-260
  StringBufferInputStream, I-311
  void reset()
    in class BufferedInputStream, I-193
    in class ByteArrayInputStream, I-199
    in class ByteArrayOutputStream,
      I-201
    in class FilterInputStream, I-248
    in class InputStream, I-256
    in class LineNumberInputStream,
      I-260
    in class StringBufferInputStream,
      I-311
resetSyntax, I-307
reshape
  Component, II-59
  ComponentPeer, II-306
  Rectangle, II-198
  void reshape(int, int, int, int)
    in class Component, II-59
    in class Rectangle, II-199
    in interface ComponentPeer, II-306
resize
  Applet, II-332
  Component, II-60
  in class Component, II-60
  Rectangle, II-198
  void resize(Dimension) in class Applet,
    II-332
  void resize(int, int)
    in class Applet, II-332
    in class Component, II-60
    in class Rectangle, II-199
resolveClass, I-22

resume
    Thread, I-142
    ThreadGroup, I-152
    void resume()
        in class Thread, I-142
        in class ThreadGroup, I-152
reverse
    StringBuffer reverse() in class String-
        Buffer, I-124
reverses, I-124
RGBImageFilter
    Class in package java.awt.image, II-277
    constructors, II-277
    fields, II-277
    methods, II-277
    RGBImageFilter() in class RGBImage-
        Filter, II-279
    role of, II-277
RGBtoHSB, II-34
RIGHT
    Event, II-83
    FlowLayout, II-92
    Label, II-154
    static int RIGHT
        in class Event, II-83
        in class FlowLayout, II-92
        in class Label, II-154
right, II-151
rint, I-64
round, I-65
    static int round(float) in class Math, I-65
    static long round(double) in class Math,
        I-65
run
    interface, I-157
    Thread, I-143
    void run()
        in class Thread, I-143
        in interface Runnable, I-157
runFinalization
    Runtime, I-82
    static void runFinalization() in class
        System, I-132
    System, I-132
    void runFinalization() in class Runtime,
        I-82

Runnable
    Interface in package java.lang, I-156
Runtime
    Class in package java.lang, I-76
    methods, I-77
    role of, I-76
RuntimeException, I-170
    Class in package java.lang, I-170
    RuntimeException() in class Runtime-
        Exception, I-171
    RuntimeException(String) in class
        RuntimeException, I-171

S
S_RESIZE_CURSOR, II-107
sameFile, I-405
SAVE, II-87
save, I-354
SAVE_FILE, II-80
SCROLL_ABSOLUTE, II-80
SCROLL_LINE_DOWN, II-81
SCROLL_LINE_UP, II-81
SCROLL_PAGE_DOWN, II-81
SCROLL_PAGE_UP, II-81
Scrollbar
    Class in package java.awt, II-200
    constructors, II-200
    fields, II-200
    methods, II-200
    role of, II-200
    Scrollbar() in class Scrollbar, II-202
    Scrollbar(int) in class Scrollbar, II-203
    Scrollbar(int, int, int, int, int) in class
        Scrollbar, II-203
ScrollbarPeer, II-317
SE_RESIZE_CURSOR, II-107
search, I-357
SecurityException, I-171
    Class in package java.lang, I-171
    SecurityException() in class Security-
        Exception, I-171
    SecurityException(String) in class
        SecurityException, I-171
SecurityManager, I-84
    Class in package java.lang, I-83
    constructors, I-85

methods, I-85
role of, I-84
SecurityManager() in class Security-
    Manager, I-85
seek, I-293
select
    Choice, II-26
    ChoicePeer, II-300
    List, II-165
    ListPeer, II-314
    TextComponent, II-214
    void select(int)
        in class Choice, II-26
        in class List, II-166
        in interface ChoicePeer, II-300
        in interface TextComponentPeer,
            II-321
    void select(int) in interface ListPeer,
        II-314
    void select(int, int) in class Text-
        Component, II-214
    void select(String) in class Choice, II-26
selectAll, II-214
send, I-380
separator, I-225
separatorChar, I-225
SequenceInputStream
    Class in package java.io, I-299
    constructors, I-299
    methods, I-300
    role of, I-299
    SequenceInputStream(Enumeration) in
        class SequenceInputStream, I-299
    SequenceInputStream(InputStream,
        InputStream) in class Sequence-
        InputStream, I-299
ServerSocket
    Class in package java.net, I-384
    constructors, I-385
    methods, I-386
    role of, I-384
    ServerSocket(int) in class ServerSocket,
        I-385
    ServerSocket(int, int) in class Server-
        Socket, I-385
set

BitSet, I-330
    void set(int) in class BitSet, I-330
setAlignment
    Label, II-156
    LabelPeer, II-311
    void setAlignment(int)
        in class Label, II-156
        in interface LabelPeer, II-311
setAllowUserInteraction, I-418
setBackground
    Component, II-60
    ComponentPeer, II-306
    void setBackground(Color)
        in class Component, II-60
        in interface ComponentPeer, II-306
setChanged, I-351
setCharAt, I-124
setCheckboxGroup
    Checkbox, II-18
    CheckboxPeer, II-299
    void setCheckboxGroup(Checkbox-
        Group)
        in class Checkbox, II-18
        in interface CheckboxPeer, II-299
setColor, II-128
    void setColor(Color) in class Graphics,
        II-129
setColorModel
    ImageFilter, II-254
    interface, II-287
    PixelGrabber, II-274
    RGBImageFilter, II-281
    void setColorModel(ColorModel)
        in class ImageFilter, II-254
        in class PixelGrabber, II-274
        in class RGBImageFilter, II-281
        in interface ImageConsumer, II-287
setConstraints, II-142
setContentHandlerFactory, I-419
setCurrent, II-20
setCursor
    Frame, II-109
    FramePeer, II-310
    void setCursor(int)
        in class Frame, II-110
        in interface FramePeer, II-310

setDaemon
  Thread, I-143
  ThreadGroup, I-152
  void setDaemon(boolean)
    in class Thread, I-143
    in class ThreadGroup, I-152
setDate, I-339
setDefaultAllowUserInteraction, I-419
setDefaultRequestProperty, I-419
setDefaultUseCaches, I-419
setDimensions
  CropImageFilter, II-242
  ImageFilter, II-255
  interface, II-287
  PixelGrabber, II-275
  void setDimensions(int, int)
    in class CropImageFilter, II-242
    in class ImageFilter, II-255
    in class PixelGrabber, II-275
    in interface ImageConsumer, II-287
setDirectory
  FileDialog, II-89
  FileDialogPeer, II-309
  void setDirectory(String)
    in class FileDialog, II-89
    in interface FileDialogPeer, II-309
setDoInput, I-420
setDoOutput, I-420
setEchoCharacter, II-220
  void setEchoCharacter(char)
    in class TextField, II-220
    in interface TextFieldPeer, II-322
setEditable, II-214
  void setEditable(boolean)
    in class TextComponent, II-215
    in interface TextComponentPeer,
      II-321
setElementAt, I-368
setFile
  FileDialog, II-90
  FileDialogPeer, II-309
  void setEditable(boolean)
    in interface FileDialogPeer, II-309
  void setFile(String)
    in class FileDialog, II-90
setFilenameFilter

FileDialog, II-90
FileDialogPeer, II-309
  void setFilenameFilter(FilenameFilter)
    in class FileDialog, II-90
    in interface FileDialogPeer, II-309
setFont
  Component, II-61
  ComponentPeer, II-307
  Graphics, II-129
  MenuComponent, II-185
  void setFont(Font)
    in class Component, II-61
    in class Graphics, II-129
    in class MenuComponent, II-185
    in interface ComponentPeer, II-307
setForegroud
  Component, II-61
setForeground
  ComponentPeer, II-307
  void setForeground(Color)
    in class Component, II-61
    in interface ComponentPeer, II-307
setHelpMenu, II-183
setHints
  ImageFiltersetPixels
    ImageFilter, II-255
  interface, II-288
  PixelGrabber, II-275
  void setHints(int)
    in class ImageFilter, II-255
    in class PixelGrabber, II-275
    in interface ImageConsumer, II-288
setHours, I-339
setIconImage
  Frame, II-110
  FramePeer, II-310
  void setIconImage(Image)
    in class Frame, II-110
    in interface FramePeer, II-310
setIfModifiedSince, I-420
setLabel
  Button, II-9
  ButtonPeer, II-298
  Checkbox, II-18
  CheckboxPeer, II-299
  MenuItem, II-187

MenuItemPeer, II-316
void setLabel(String)
  in class Button, II-9
  in class Checkbox, II-18
  in class MenuItem, II-187
  in interface ButtonPeer, II-298
  in interface CheckboxPeer, II-299
  in interface MenuItemPeer, II-316
setLayout, II-70
setLength, I-124
setLineIncrement
  Scrollbar, II-206
  ScrollbarPeer, II-317
  void setLineIncrement(int)
    in class Scrollbar, II-206
    in interface ScrollbarPeer, II-318
setLineNumber, I-260
setMaxPriority, I-152
setMenuBar
  Frame, II-110
  FramePeer, II-310
  void setMenuBar(MenuBar)
    in class Frame, II-110
    in interface FramePeer, II-310
setMinute, I-339
setMonth, I-339
setMultipleSelections
  List, II-166
  ListPeer, II-314
  void setMultipleSelections(boolean)
    in class List, II-166
    in interface ListPeer, II-314
setName, I-143
setPageIncrement
  Scrollbar, II-206
  ScrollbarPeer, II-317
  void setPageIncrement(int)
    in class Scrollbar, II-206
    in interface ScrollbarPeer, II-318
setPaintMode, II-129
setPixels
  CropImageFilter, II-242
  in interface ImageConsumer, II-289
  interface, II-289
  PixelGrabber, II-275
  RGBImageFilter, II-282

void setPixels(int, int, int, int, Color-
    Model, byte[], int, int)
  in class CropImageFilter, II-243,
    II-244
  in class ImageFilter, II-255, II-256
  in class PixelGrabber, II-275, II-276
  in class RGBImageFilter, II-282,
    II-283
  in interface ImageConsumer, II-289
setPriority, I-144
setProperties
  CropImageFilter, II-244
  ImageFilter, II-256
  interface, II-290
  PixelGrabber, II-276
  static void setProperties(Properties) in
    class System, I-132
  System, I-132
  void setProperties(Hashtable)
    in class CropImageFilter, II-244
    in class ImageFilter, II-256
    in class PixelGrabber, II-276
    in interface ImageConsumer, II-290
setRequestProperty, I-420
setResizable
  Dialog, II-72
  DialogPeer, II-308
  Frame, II-110
  FramePeer, II-310
  in class Frame, II-111
  void setResizable(boolean)
    in class Dialog, II-73
    in interface DialogPeer, II-308
    in interface FramePeer, II-310
setSeconds, I-339
setSecurityManager, I-133
setSeed, I-356
setSize, I-369
setSocketFactory, I-387
setSocketImplFactory, I-392
setState
  Checkbox, II-19
  CheckboxMenuItem, II-22
  CheckboxMenuItemPeer, II-298
  CheckboxPeer, II-299
  void setState(boolean)

in class Checkbox, II-19
in class CheckboxMenuItem, II-22
in interface CheckboxMenuItemPeer,
II-298
in interface CheckboxPeer, II-299
setStub
Applet, II-332
void setStub(AppletStub) in class Applet,
II-332
setText
Label, II-156
LabelPeer, II-311
TextComponent, II-214
void setText(String)
in class Label, II-156
in class TextComponent, II-215
in interface LabelPeer, II-311
in interface TextComponentPeer,
II-321
setTime, I-339
setTitle
Dialog, II-73
DialogPeer, II-308
Frame, II-110
FramePeer, II-310
void setTitle(String)
in class Dialog, II-73
in class Frame, II-111
in interface DialogPeer, II-308
in interface FramePeer, II-310
setURL, I-424
setURLStreamHandlerFactory, I-405
setUseCaches, I-420
setValue
Scrollbar, II-206
ScrollbarPeer, II-317
void setValue(int)
in class Scrollbar, II-206
in interface ScrollbarPeer, II-318
setValues, II-206
ScrollbarPeer, II-318
void setValues(int, int, int, int)
in class Scrollbar, II-206
in interface ScrollbarPeer, II-318
setXORMode, II-129
setYear, I-340

SHIFT_MASK, II-83
shiftDown, II-86
show
CardLayout, II-15
Component, II-61
ComponentPeer, II-307
void show()
in class Component, II-61
in class Window, II-232
in interface ComponentPeer, II-307
void show() in class Component, II-61
void show(Container, String) in class
CardLayout, II-15
showDocument
AppletContext, II-335
void showDocument(URL) in interface
AppletContext, II-335
void showDocument(URL, String) in
interface AppletContext, II-336
showStatus
Applet, II-332
AppletContext, II-336
void showStatus(String)
in class Applet, II-332
in interface AppletContext, II-336
sin, I-65
SINGLEFRAME, II-286
SINGLEFRAMEDONE, II-285
SINGLEPASS, II-286
size, I-201, I-369, II-95
BitSet, I-330
Component, II-62
DataOutputStream, I-218
Dictionary, I-343
Dimension size()
in class ByteArrayOutputStream,
I-201
in class Component, II-62
in class DataOutputStream, I-218
in class Dictionary, I-343
in class Hashtable, I-349
in class Vector, I-369
Hashtable, I-349
int size in class Font, II-95
int size() in class BitSet, I-330
skip

BufferedInputStream, I-194
ByteArrayInputStream, I-200
FileInputStream, I-239
FilterInputStream, I-249
InputStream, I-257
LineNumberInputStream, I-261
long skip(long)
   in class BufferedInputStream, I-194
   in class ByteArrayInputStream, I-200
   in class FileInputStream, I-239
   in class FilterInputStream, I-249
   in class InputStream, I-257
   in class LineNumberInputStream,
      I-261
   in class StringBufferInputStream,
      I-311
StringBufferInputStream, I-311
skipBytes
   DataInput, I-317
   DataInputStream, I-216
   int skipBytes(int)
      in class DataInputStream, I-216
      in class RandomAccessFile, I-294
      in interface DataInput, I-317
   RandomAccessFile, I-294
slashSlashComments, I-308
slashStarComments, I-308
sleep, I-144
   static void sleep(long) in class Thread,
      I-144
   static void sleep(long, int) in class Thread,
      I-144
Socket
   Class in package java.net, I-388
   constructors, I-389
   methods, I-391
   role of, I-388
   Socket(InetAddress, int) in class Socket,
      I-389
   Socket(InetAddress, int, boolean) in class
      Socket, I-389
   Socket(String, int) in class Socket, I-390
   Socket(String, int, boolean) in class
      Socket, I-390
SocketException, I-427
   Class in package java.net, I-427

SocketException, I-427
SocketException() in class Socket-
      Exception, I-428
SocketException(String) in class
      SocketException, I-428
SocketImpl
   Class in package java.net, I-393
   field, I-393
   methods, I-394
   role of, I-393
   SocketImpl, I-394
   SocketImpl() in class SocketImpl, I-394
SocketImplFactory, I-425
   Interface in package java.net, I-425
   SocketImplFactory, I-425
SOMEBITS, II-292
SOUTH, II-135
SOUTHEAST, II-135
SOUTHWEST, II-135
sqrt, I-66
Stack
   Class in package java.util, I-356
   constructors, I-356
   methods, I-356
   role of, I-356
   Stack() in class Stack, I-356
StackOverflowError
   Class in package java.lang, I-182
   Error, I-182
   StackOverflowError() in class Stack-
      OverflowError, I-182
   StackOverflowError(String) in class
      StackOverflowError, I-182
start, I-145
   Applet, II-333
   void start()
      in class Applet, II-333
      in class Thread, I-145
startProduction, II-269
   FilteredImageSource, II-251
   interface, II-295
   void startProduction(ImageConsumer)
      in class FilteredImageSource, II-251
      in class MemoryImageSource, II-269
      in interface ImageProducer, II-295
startsWith, I-106

boolean startsWith(String) in class String, I-106

boolean startsWith(String, int) in class String, I-107

STATICIMAGEDONE, II-285

status, II-276

statusAll, II-174

    int statusAll(boolean) in class MediaTracker, II-174, II-175

statusID, II-174

stop

    Applet, II-333

    AudioClip, II-338

    Thread, I-145

    ThreadGroup, I-153

    void stop()

        in class Applet, II-333

    void stop(Throwable)

        in class Thread, I-145, I-146

        in class ThreadGroup, I-153

        in interface AudioClip, II-339

Stream concatenation, I-188

Stream marks, I-188

StreamTokenizer

    Class in package java.io, I-302

    constructors, I-304

    fields, I-303

    methods, I-305

    role of, I-302

    StreamTokenizer(InputStream) in class StreamTokenizer, I-304

String

    Class in package java.lang, I-96

    constructors, I-97

    methods, I-99

    role of, I-97

    String() in class String, I-97

    String(byte[], int) in class String, I-97

    String(byte[], int, int, int) in class String, I-98

    String(char[]) in class String, I-98

    String(char[], int, int) in class String, I-98

    String(String) in class String, I-99

    String(StringBuffer) in class String, I-99

StringBuffer

    Class in package java.lang, I-112

constructors, I-113

methods, I-114

role of, I-112

StringBuffer() in class StringBuffer, I-113

StringBuffer(int) in class StringBuffer, I-113

StringBuffer(String) in class String-Buffer, I-114

StringBufferInputStream

    Class in package java.io, I-309

    constructors, I-310

    fields, I-309

    methods, I-310

    role of, I-309

    StringBufferInputStream(String) in class StringBufferInputStream, I-310

StringIndexOutOfBoundsException

    Class in package java.lang, I-172

    Exception, I-172

    StringIndexOutOfBoundsException() in class StringIndexOutOfBounds-Exception, I-172

    StringIndexOutOfBoundsException(int) in class StringIndexOutOf-BoundsException, I-172

    StringIndexOutOfBounds Exception(String) in class String-IndexOutOfBoundsException, I-172

StringTokenizer

    Class in package java.util, I-358

    constructors, I-359

    methods, I-359

    role of, I-358

    StringTokenizer(String) in class String-Tokenizer, I-359

    StringTokenizer(String, String) in class StringTokenizer, I-359

    StringTokenizer(String, String, boolean) in class StringTokenizer, I-359

stringWidth, II-105

style, II-96

substituteColorModel, II-283

substring, I-107

    String substring(int) in class String, I-107

String substring(int, int) in class String, I-107
suspend
    Thread, I-146
    ThreadGroup, I-153
    void suspend()
        in class Thread, I-146
        in class ThreadGroup, I-153
sval, I-303
SW_RESIZE_CURSOR, II-107
    static int SW_RESIZE_CURSOR in class Frame, II-108
sync, II-229
System
    Class in package java.lang, I-125
    fields, I-126
    methods, I-127
    role of, I-125

T
tan, I-66
target, II-78
TCP, I-373
TEXT_CURSOR, II-107
    static int TEXT_CURSOR in class Frame, II-108
TextArea
    Class in package java.awt, II-207
    constructors, II-207
    methods, II-207
    role of, II-207
    TextArea() in class TextArea, II-208
    TextArea(int, int) in class TextArea, II-208
    TextArea(String) in class TextArea, II-209
    TextArea(String, int, int) in class Text-Area, II-209
TextAreaPeer, II-319
    Interface in package java.awt.peer, II-319
TextComponent
    Class in package java.awt, II-213
TextComponentPeer
    Interface in package java.awt.peer, II-320
TextField
    Class in package java.awt, II-215

constructors, II-215
methods, II-215
role of, II-215
TextField() in class TextField, II-217
TextField(int) in class TextField, II-217
TextField(String) in class TextField, II-217
TextField(String, int) in class TextField, II-217
TextFieldPeer
    Interface in package java.awt.peer, II-321
Thread
    Class in package java.lang, I-134
    constructors, I-137
    fields, I-136
    methods, I-139
    role of, I-134
    Thread() in class Thread, I-137
    Thread(Runnable) in class Thread, I-137
    Thread(Runnable, String) in class Thread, I-137
    Thread(String) in class Thread, I-137
    Thread(ThreadGroup, Runnable) in class Thread, I-138
    Thread(ThreadGroup, Runnable, String) in class Thread, I-138
    Thread(ThreadGroup, String) in class Thread, I-139
ThreadDeath
    Class in package java.lang, I-182
    Error, I-182
    ThreadDeath() in class ThreadDeath, I-183
ThreadGroup
    Class in package java.lang, I-147
    constructors, I-148
    methods, I-148
    role of, I-147
    ThreadGroup(String) in class Thread-Group, I-148
    ThreadGroup(ThreadGroup, String) in class ThreadGroup, I-148
Throwable
    Class in package java.lang, I-154
    constructors, I-155
    methods, I-155

role of, I-154
Throwable() in class Throwable, I-155
Throwable(String) in class Throwable,
          I-155
toBack
     void toBack() in class Window, II-232
     void toBack() in interface WindowPeer,
          II-323
toBinaryString
     Integer, I-44
     Long, I-54
     static String toBinaryString(int) in class
          Integer, I-44
     static String toBinaryString(long) in class
          Long, I-54
toByteArray, I-201
toCharArray, I-107
toExternalForm
     String toExternalForm() in class URL,
          I-406
     String toExternalForm(URL) in class
          URLStreamHandler, I-424
     URL, I-406
     URLStreamHandler, I-424
toFront
     void toFront()
          in class Window, II-232
          in interface WindowPeer, II-323
toGMTString, I-340
toHexString
     Integer, I-45
     Long, I-54
     static String toHexString(int) in class
          Integer, I-45
     static String toHexString(long) in class
          Long, I-54
Tokenization, I-188
toLocaleString
     String toLocaleString() in class Date,
          I-340
toLocalString, I-340
toLowerCase
     Character, I-14
     static char toLowerCase(char) in class
          Character, I-14, I-15
     String, I-108

String toLowerCase() in class String,
          I-108
toOctalString
     Integer, I-45
     Long, I-55
     static String toOctalString(int) in class
          Integer, I-45
     static String toOctalString(long) in class
          Long, I-55
Toolkit
     Class in package java.awt, II-221
     constructors, II-221
     methods, II-221
     role of, II-221
     Toolkit() in class Toolkit, II-222
top, II-152
TOPDOWNLEFTRIGHT
     static int TOPDOWNLEFTRIGHT
          in interface ImageConsumer, II-286
TOPDOWNLEFTRIGHT = 2, II-286
toString
     BitSet, I-330
     Boolean, I-4
     BorderLayout, II-7
     ByteArrayOutputStream, I-202
     CardLayout, II-15
     Character, I-14
     CheckboxGroup, II-20
     Class, I-18
     Color, II-34
     Component, II-62
     Date, I-340
     Dimension, II-75
     Double, I-30
     Event, II-86
     File, I-233
     Float, I-37
     FlowLayout, II-94
     Font, II-99
     FontMetrics, II-105
     Graphics, II-129
     GridBagLayout, II-142
     GridLayout, II-147
     Hashtable, I-349
     InetAddress, I-383
     Insets, II-152

Integer, I-45
Long, I-55
MenuComponent, II-185
Object, I-71
Point, II-190
Rectangle, II-198
ServerSocket, I-387
Socket, I-392
SocketImpl, I-397
static String toString(double) in class
    Double, I-31
static String toString(int) in class Integer,
    I-46
static String toString(int, int) in class
    Integer, I-46
static String toString(long) in class Long,
    I-55
static String toString(long, int) in class
    Long, I-55
StreamTokenizer, I-308
String, I-108
String toString()
    in class BitSet, I-330
    in class Boolean, I-4
    in class BorderLayout, II-7
    in class ByteArrayOutputStream,
        I-202
    in class CardLayout, II-15
    in class Character, I-14
    in class CheckboxGroup, II-20
    in class Class, I-18
    in class Color, II-34
    in class Component, II-62
    in class Date, I-340
    in class Dimension, II-75
    in class Double, I-30
    in class Event, II-86
    in class File, I-233
    in class Float, I-37, I-38
    in class FlowLayout, II-94
    in class Font, II-99
    in class FontMetrics, II-105
    in class Graphics, II-130
    in class GridBagLayout, II-142
    in class GridLayout, II-147
    in class Hashtable, I-349

    in class InetAddress, I-383
    in class Insets, II-152
    in class Integer, I-45
    in class Long, I-55
    in class MenuComponent, II-185
    in class Object, I-71
    in class Point, II-190
    in class Rectangle, II-199
    in class ServerSocket, I-387
    in class Socket, I-392
    in class SocketImpl, I-397
    in class StreamTokenizer, I-308
    in class String, I-108
    in class StringBuffer, I-125
    in class Thread, I-146
    in class ThreadGroup, I-153
    in class Throwable, I-156
    in class URL, I-406
    in class URLConnection, I-420
    in class Vector, I-369
String toString(int) in class ByteArray-
    OutputStream, I-202
StringBuffer, I-125
Thread, I-146
ThreadGroup, I-153
Throwable, I-156
URL, I-406
URLConnection, I-420
Vector, I-369
totalMemory, I-82
toTitleCase, I-15
toUpperCase
    Character, I-15
    static char toUpperCase(char) in class
        Character, I-15
    String, I-108
    String toUpperCase() in class String,
        I-108
traceInstruction, I-82
traceInstructions
    void traceInstructions(boolean) in class
        Runtime, I-82
traceMethodCalls, I-82
translate
    Event, II-86
    Graphics, II-130

Point, II-191
Rectangle, II-199
void translate(int, int)
    in class Event, II-86
    in class Graphics, II-130
    in class Point, II-191
    in class Rectangle, II-199
trim, I-108
trimToSize, I-369
TRUE, I-2
TT_EOF
    static int TT_EOF in class Stream-
        Tokenizer, I-304
TT_EOL, I-304
TT_NUMBER, I-303, I-304
TT_WORD, I-303, I-304
ttype, I-303

U
UDP, I-374
uncaughtException, I-153
UndefinedProperty, II-148
Unicode attribute table, I-6
union
    Rectangle, II-199
    Rectangle union(Rectangle) in class
        Rectangle, II-200
UnknownError
    Class in package java.lang, I-183
    Error, I-183
    UnknownError() in class UnknownError,
        I-183
    UnknownError(String) in class Unknown-
        Error, I-183
UnknownHostException, I-428
    Class in package java.net, I-428
    UnknownHostException, I-428
    UnknownHostException() in class
        UnknownHostException, I-428
    UnknownHostException(String) in class
        UnknownHostException, I-428
UnknownServiceException, I-429
    Class in package java.net, I-429
    UnknownServiceException, I-429
    UnknownServiceException() in class
        UnknownServiceException, I-429

UnknownServiceException(String) in
    class UnknownServiceException,
    I-429
unread, I-280
UnsatisfiedLinkError
    Class in package java.lang, I-184
    Error, I-184
    UnsatisfiedLinkError() in class
        UnsatisfiedLinkError, I-184
    UnsatisfiedLinkError(String) in class
        UnsatisfiedLinkError, I-184
UP, II-83
update, I-371
    Component, II-62
    void update(Graphics) in class
        Component, II-62
    void update(Observable, Object) in
        interface Observer, I-371
URL, I-411
    Class in package java.net, I-398
    constructors, I-400
    description of, I-373
    methods, I-403
    role of, I-398
    URL(String) in class URL, I-400
    URL(String, String, int, String) in class
        URL, I-400
    URL(String, String, String) in class URL,
        I-401
    URL(URL, String) in class URL, I-402
URLConnection
    Class in package java.net, I-407
    constructors, I-411
    fields, I-410
    methods, I-412
    role of, I-407
    URLConnection(URL) in class URL-
        Connection, I-411
URLEncoder
    Class in package java.net, I-421
URLStreamHandler
    Class in package java.net, I-422
    constructors, I-422
    methods, I-423
    role of, I-422

URLStreamHandler() in class URL-
StreamHandler, I-422
URLStreamHandlerFactory, I-425
Interface in package java.net, I-425
URLStreamHandlerFactory, I-425
useCaches, I-411
user.dir, I-130
user.home, I-130
user.name, I-130
UT Universal Time, I-333
UTC
Date, I-341
static long UTC(int, int, int, int, int, int) in
class Date, I-341
UTC(Coordinated Universal Time), I-333
UTFDataFormatException
Class in package java.io, I-326
Exception, I-326
UTFDataFormatException() in class
UTFDataFormatException, I-326
UTFDataFormatException(String) in
class UTFDataFormatException,
I-326

V
valid, I-234
validate
Component, II-62
Container, II-70
void validate()
in class Component, II-62
in class Container, II-70
valueOf
Boolean, I-4
Double, I-31
Float, I-38
Integer, I-46
Long, I-56
static Boolean valueOf(String) in class
Boolean, I-4
static Double valueOf(String) in class
Double, I-31
static Float valueOf(String) in class Float,
I-38
static Integer valueOf(String) in class
Integer, I-46

static Integer valueOf(String, int) in class
Integer, I-47
static Long valueOf(String) in class Long,
I-56
static Long valueOf(String, int) in class
Long, I-56
static String valueOf(boolean) in class
String, I-109
static String valueOf(char) in class String,
I-109
static String valueOf(char[]) in class
String, I-109
static String valueOf(char[], int, int) in
class String, I-110
static String valueOf(double) in class
String, I-110
static String valueOf(float) in class String,
I-110
static String valueOf(int) in class String,
I-111
static String valueOf(long) in class String,
I-111
static String valueOf(Object) in class
String, I-111
String, I-109
Vector
Class in package java.util, I-362
constructors, I-363
fields, I-363
methods, I-364
role of, I-362
Vector() in class Vector, I-363
Vector(int) in class Vector, I-363
Vector(int, int) in class Vector, I-364
VerifyError
Class in package java.lang, I-184
Error, I-184
VerifyError() in class VerifyError, I-185
VerifyError(String) in class VerifyError,
I-185
VERTICAL
GridBagConstraints, II-136
Scrollbar, II-202
static int VERTICAL
in class GridBagConstraints, II-136
in class Scrollbar, II-202

VirtualMachineError
    Class in package java.lang, I-185
    Error, I-185
    VirtualMachineError() in class Virtual-
        MachineError, I-185
    VirtualMachineError(String) in class
        VirtualMachineError, I-185

W

W_RESIZE_CURSOR, II-107
    static int W_RESIZE_CURSOR in class
        Frame, II-108
wait, I-72
    void wait() in class Object, I-72
    void wait(long) in class Object, I-72
    void wait(long, int) in class Object, I-73
WAIT_CURSOR, II-107
    static int WAIT_CURSOR in class
        Frame, II-108
waitFor, I-76
waitForAll, II-175
    boolean waitForAll(long) in class
        MediaTracker, II-176
    void waitForAll() in class MediaTracker,
        II-175
waitForID, II-176
    boolean waitForID(int, long) in class
        MediaTracker, II-177
    void waitForID(int) in class Media-
        Tracker, II-176
weightx, II-134
weighty, II-134
WEST, II-135
when, II-78
white, II-29
whitespaceChars, I-308
WIDTH, II-292
width, II-195
    Dimension, II-74
    int width
        in class Dimension, II-74
        in class Rectangle, II-195
Window
    Class in package java.awt, II-230
    constructors, II-230
    methods, II-230

role of, II-230
    Window(Frame) in class Window, II-230
WINDOW_DEICONIFY, II-81
WINDOW_DESTROY, II-81
WINDOW_EXPOSE, II-81
WINDOW_ICONIFY, II-81
WINDOW_MOVED, II-81
WindowPeer
    Interface in package java.awt.peer, II-323
wordChars, I-309
World Wide Web
    network library, I-58
write
    BufferedInputStream, I-196
    ByteArrayOutputStream, I-202, I-203
    DataOutput, I-318
    DataOutputStream, I-219
    FileOutputStream, I-242
    FilterOutputStream, I-251
    in class FilterOutputStream, I-252
    in class RandomAccessFile, I-294
    in interface DataOutput, I-319
    OutputStream, I-263
    PipedOutputStream, I-268
    PrintStream, I-276
    RandomAccessFile, I-294
    void write(byte[])
        in class ByteArrayOutputStream,
            I-202
        in class DataOutputStream, I-219
        in class FileOutputStream, I-242,
            I-243
        in class FilterOutputStream, I-251,
            I-252
        in class OutputStream, I-263, I-264
        in class PipedOutputStream, I-268,
            I-269
        in class PrintStream, I-276, I-277
        in class RandomAccessFile, I-294,
            I-295
        in interface DataOutput, I-318, I-319
    void write(byte[]) in class OutputStream,
        I-263
    void write(byte[], int, int) in class
        BufferedOutputStream, I-196

void write(int) in class BufferedOutput-
Stream, I-196
writeBoolean, I-319
DataOutput, I-319
DataOutputStream, I-219
RandomAccessFile, I-295
void writeBoolean(boolean)
in class DataOutputStream, I-219
in class RandomAccessFile, I-295
in interface DataOutput, I-319
writeByte, I-320
DataOutput, I-320
DataOutputStream, I-220
RandomAccessFile, I-295
void writeByte(int)
in class DataOutputStream, I-220
in class RandomAccessFile, I-295
in interface DataOutput, I-320
writeBytes, I-320
DataOutput, I-320
DataOutputStream, I-220
RandomAccessFile, I-296
void writeBytes(String)
in class DataOutputStream, I-220
in class RandomAccessFile, I-296
in interface DataOutput, I-320
writeChar, I-320
DataOutput, I-320
DataOutputStream, I-220
RandomAccessFile, I-296
void writeChar(int)
in class DataOutputStream, I-220
in class RandomAccessFile, I-296
in interface DataOutput, I-320
writeChars, I-320
DataOutput, I-320
DataOutputStream, I-221
RandomAccessFile, I-296
void writeChars(String)
in class DataOutputStream, I-221
in class RandomAccessFile, I-296
in interface DataOutput, I-320
writeDouble, I-321
DataOutput, I-321
DataOutputStream, I-221
RandomAccessFile, I-297

void writeDouble(double)
in class DataOutputStream, I-221
in class RandomAccessFile, I-297
in interface DataOutput, I-321
writeFloat, I-321
DataOutput, I-321
DataOutputStream, I-221
RandomAccessFile, I-297
void writeFloat(float)
in class DataOutputStream, I-221
in class RandomAccessFile, I-297
in interface DataOutput, I-321
writeInt, I-321
DataOutput, I-321
DataOutputStream, I-222
RandomAccessFile, I-297
void writeInt(int)
in class DataOutputStream, I-222
in class RandomAccessFile, I-297
in interface DataOutput, I-321
writeLong, I-321
DataOutput, I-321
DataOutputStream, I-222
RandomAccessFile, I-298
void writeLong(long)
in class DataOutputStream, I-222
in class RandomAccessFile, I-298
in interface DataOutput, I-321
writeShort, I-322
DataOutput, I-322
DataOutputStream, I-222
RandomAccessFile, I-298
void writeShort(int)
in class DataOutputStream, I-222
in class RandomAccessFile, I-298
in interface DataOutput, I-322
writeTo, I-203
writeUTF, I-322
DataOutput, I-322
DataOutputStream, I-223
RandomAccessFile, I-298
void writeUTF(String)
in class DataOutputStream, I-223
in class RandomAccessFile, I-298
in interface DataOutput, I-322
written, I-217

X

x, II-189, II-195
    Event, II-78
    int x
        in class Event, II-78
        in class Point, II-189
        in class Rectangle, II-195
xor, I-331
xpoints, II-191

Y

y, II-189, II-195
    Event, II-79
    int y
        in class Event, II-79
        in class Point, II-189
        in class Rectangle, II-195
yellow, II-29
yield, I-147
ypoints, II-192